Where Are They Now?

Huddersfield Town

Lee Morris

www.where-are-they-now.co.uk/huddersfield-town

First published in 2019 by
Media House Books

© Media House Books 2019

ISBN 978-1-912027-60-6

Original cover design by Marten Sealby
Book edited by Leonie Grantham-Davis

Foreword

By Julian Winter

Lee has put an enormous amount of time and effort into creating a book that catalogues every player to play professionally for Huddersfield Town FC, amazingly I am one of them, and he's kindly asked me to provide the foreword for the book.

As a locally born boy, spending my pre-school years in Kirkheaton and the remaining years to the age of 23, in Linthwaite, Colne Valley, I have had an attachment to Huddersfield Town FC in many ways. I have been a fan of the club from the age of about 10 or 11, being taken to my first games with my older brother Stephen and our neighbour Ian Martindale, who convinced our mum that he would look after us when taking us to our first game at Leeds Road – what an experience that was!

I signed schoolboy forms at the age of 14 and moved on to be an apprentice at the age of 16, joining the club with Liam Robinson, Peter Butler and Andy Baker – I am to this day best friends with Liam and Peter, but sadly lost communication with Andy.

I was offered professional terms at 18, having made my debut at home against Oxford United a few weeks before. My playing career took me to Sheffield United FC in 1989, but sadly 10 knee operations later, I was forced to retire from playing the game at 27 years of age. I went back to University and secured a First-Class Honours degree in Leisure & Recreation Management at Sheffield Hallam University, vowing never to step foot inside a football club until I had created a new career for myself. As fate would dictate, I came back into football, working in community development for Grimsby Town, FFE & VTS, Sheffield Wednesday and Watford. At Watford, I progressed to Deputy Chief Executive Officer (CEO) and ultimately took over as CEO.

Since that time, I have been the CEO at Sheffield United and had a brief stint at Notts County before the role of CEO came up at HTFC in early 2016. After a rigorous recruitment process, I decided, 27 years after leaving Town, to come back to work for the club that had engaged me as a fan, embraced me as a player and ultimately placed me in leadership role in a period that has proved to be a historic in many ways. I feel proud to have played my part over the last two and half years, where we have achieved promotion to the top tier of English football, widely accepted to be the best in the world, and achieved survival in that same league.

Overall, I feel privileged to have had the opportunities to play the game of football, particularly for my hometown club. The players listed in this book, some who I know and many that I don't, will have had varied and interesting careers - I'm certain that most, if not all will have enjoyed their time with Huddersfield Town FC – a truly grounded, honest but forward-thinking club that has embraced periods of challenge, failure and success with equal commitment from all involved – particularly the fans.

Enjoy the book and UTT!!

Julian Winter

Introduction

It's quite difficult to explain to non-football fans why you are interested in the sport but football fans, no matter who you support, totally "get" exactly why you are interested and support a team. I have seen my team, Huddersfield Town, gain promotion from the fourth tier (Division Three) to the first tier (Premier League) in 13 short years.

From being stood on the terrace at Moss Rose when Macclesfield Town battered us 4-0 in 2003 to being in the stands at the John Smith's Stadium when we triumphed 2-1 over Manchester United in 2017, I have seen a lot of changes (good and bad) at Huddersfield Town A.F.C. I have also seen a lot of players (good and bad!) play during that time and each and every one of them are documented in this book. In fact, every player to play a professional game for the club is included in the book and I have tried to document what each and every player did after they left the club.

When I was a kid, I could count the number of Town fans at my school on one hand, playing teams like Bury, Macclesfield Town, York City, Boston United and Kidderminster Harriers when all my mates at school supported Liverpool, Manchester United, Arsenal and Chelsea. So it's good to see so many kids in Town shirt these days, no doubt school classes are brimming with young fans, although my apprenticeship in watching Town was much more tougher than theirs will be!

I have enjoyed putting this book together and have made many discoveries about players past and present. During the research for this book I managed to track down the oldest living Town player. Albert Bateman played for Town between 1943 and 1950 and is still alive and well at the age of 94! I had the pleasure of meeting him at his home in Lancashire and this book is dedicated to him and every other player that has played for us from 1908 onwards. Some honourable mentions go out to Albert, Jimmy Nicholson, Alec Smith, Paul Walker, Alan Sweeney, Bob Mountain, Wayne Goldthorpe, Martin Fowler, Kevin Johnson, Graham Cooper, Chris Hay and also Julian Winter for providing the foreword and being a great help.

Big thanks also go out to Andy Pringle, for making this happen and also my parents, Steve and Jane. But the biggest thanks goes out to all the Town players past and present and if it wasn't for them, this book wouldn't need to be written!

Enjoy the book.

Up the Town!

Lee Morris

ABBOTT, Pawel

Forward
Town Years: 2004 (loan), 2004-2007
Born: *1982 York, North Yorkshire*
Playing career: *ŁKS Łodź, Preston North End, Bury (loan), Huddersfield Town (loan), Huddersfield Town, Swansea City, Darlington, Oldham Athletic, Charlton Athletic, Ruch Chorzow, Zawisza Bydgoszcz, Arka Gdynia, Stomil Olsztyn (1999-Still Playing)*

'Pav' originally signed on loan from Preston North End during the latter half of the 2003-04 season. Three goals in his first three games persuaded Peter Jackson to sign him permanently for £125,000. Abbott's goals helped the promotion push and he was part of the side that won the 2004 Division Three Play-off Final against Mansfield Town. He also scored 26 goals the following season, which saw Town miss out on the playoffs by just one point. He was sold to Swansea City in 2007 having fallen out of favour with 'Jacko' but lasted less than a year at the Welsh club before being sold to Darlington. Spells at Oldham Athletic and Charlton Athletic followed before moving to Poland to play for a number of clubs. Although born in York, Pawel's mother was Polish and he did play one match for their Under 21 side. Stomil Olsztyn were his most recent employers but he left the club in 2018 and is currently a free agent.

ADAMS, Daniel 'Danny'

Left-back
Town Years: 2005 (loan), 2005-2007
Born: *1976 Manchester, Greater Manchester*
Playing career: *Altrincham, Macclesfield Town, Stockport County, Huddersfield Town, Morecambe, Stalybridge Celtic, Witton Albion (1997-2010)*

The former Macclesfield Town left-back was known for his tough tackling and committed performances on the pitch, always being relied upon to give 100%. After a falling out with Peter Jackson in the 2006-07 season, his contract was cancelled. The manager had told him and two other players that they were to be sold but to keep quiet about it, which prompted him to call in to Radio Leeds to vent his frustrations. He soon signed for Morecambe and later had spells at non-league Stalybridge Celtic and Witton Albion before hanging up his boots and retiring from football. Since his playing days came to an end, Adams has been working as a taxi driver in Altrincham.

AFOBE, Benik

Forward
Town Years: 2010-2011 (loan)
Born: *1993 Leyton, London*
Playing career: *Arsenal, Huddersfield Town (loan), Reading (loan), Bolton Wanderers (loan), Millwall (loan), Sheffield Wednesday (loan), Milton Keynes Dons (loan), Wolverhampton Wanderers, Bournemouth, Wolverhampton Wanderers (loan), Wolverhampton Wanderers, Stoke City (loan) (2010-Still Playing)*

Afobe arrived on loan from Arsenal in 2010 and played a huge part in that season's promotion push. Having made his debut against Sheffield Wednesday in November 2010, he played up front for the rest of that campaign, including the 2011 Playoff Final, which Town lost. At the end of the 2010-11 season, Afobe returned to his parent club and later enjoyed loan spells at Reading, Bolton Wanderers, Millwall, Sheffield Wednesday and Milton Keynes Dons before he signed for Wolverhampton Wanderers on a permanent transfer in 2015. He left for Bournemouth in 2016 and spent two years at the club before rejoining Wolves after an initial loan spell in 2018. He was immediately loaned out to Stoke City at the beginning of the 2018-19 season with the intention of making the transfer permanent at the end of the season. Despite being born in London, Afobe has played for the DR Congo national side since 2017, winning 5 caps and scoring 1 goal.

Benik Afobe

AHMED, Adnan

Midfielder
Town Years: 2003-2007
Born: *1984 Burnley, Lancashire*
Playing career: *Huddersfield Town, Tranmere Rovers, Mansfield Town (loan), Port Vale (loan), Ferencvaros, Aboomoslem, Bradford Park Avenue, Nelson, Droylsden (2003-2014)*

Ahmed came through the youth ranks at Town and turned professional at the beginning of the 2003-04 season. When he made his debut during that season, Ahmed became the first Town player of Pakistani heritage to play a professional match for the club, coming on as a substitute against Rochdale in a 1-1 draw at Spotland. He never really cemented a place in the first team, although he did play a number of games during the 2005-06 and 2006-07 seasons. After his release at the end of 2006-07, Ahmed went on to play for Tranmere Rovers, Ferencvaros (Turkey), Bradford Park Avenue, Nelson and Droylsden before hanging up his boots. Burnley born Ahmed has also won 27 caps for the Pakistan national team and is now the operating director of the family bedroom furniture company, Sweet Dreams in Burnley. He also runs his own company, Rubix Sports Management.

AIMSON, Paul

Forward
Town Years: 1968-1969
Born: *1943 Prestbury, Cheshire*
Died: *2008 Christchurch, Dorset*
Playing career: *Manchester City, York City, Bury, Bradford City, Huddersfield Town, Bournemouth, Colchester United (1960-1974)*

Aimson signed from Bradford City in March 1968 and spent just one season at Town. He never managed to cement a place in Ian Greaves' side, before heading back to his old club York City in August 1969. Famed for scoring a memorable hat-trick in 1965 which included one goal with his left foot, another with his right and a third with his head. Spells at Bournemouth and Colchester followed before his retirement in 1974. Aimson then became a physical recreation officer for Dorset Probation Service before suffering a fatal heart attack in Christchurch in 2008 following a short illness. A York City 'legend', he was described as "the perfect centre forward and a perfect gentleman".

AINSWORTH, Lionel

Winger
Town Years: 2009-2010
Born: *1987 Nottingham, Nottinghamshire*
Playing career: *Derby County, Bournemouth (loan), Halifax Town (loan), Wycombe Wanderers (loan), Hereford United, Watford (loan), Watford, Hereford United (loan), Huddersfield Town, Brentford (loan), Shrewsbury Town, Burton Albion (loan), Rotherham United, Aldershot Town (loan), Motherwell (loan), Motherwell, Plymouth Argyle (2006-Still Playing)*

One of Lee Clark's first signings, Ainsworth arrived at the club in January 2009 from Watford, having played against Town the previous month whilst on loan at Hereford United. He had impressed manager Lee Clark in that fixture but ultimately only lasted a year at the club before he was sold to Shrewsbury Town in 2010. Ainsworth later played for Rotherham United and Motherwell but is now playing for Plymouth Argyle having been at the club since 2017.

Lionel Ainsworth

8

AKINS, Lucas
Forward
Town Years: 2006-2008
Born: *1989 Huddersfield, West Yorkshire*
Playing career: *Huddersfield Town, Tranmere Rovers, Stevenage, Burton Albion (2006-Still Playing)*
Akins was an academy graduate who played five games for the club during the 2007-08 season. Akins later played for Tranmere Rovers and Stevenage, but is now at Burton Albion where he has played over 150 games since arriving at the club in 2014.

ALLARDYCE, Samuel 'Sam'
Centre-half
Town Years: 1984-1985
Born: *1954 Dudley, Worcstershire*
Playing career: *Bolton W, Sunderland, Millwall, Coventry C, Huddersfield T, Bolton W, Preston NE, West Bromwich Albion (player-coach), Limerick (player-manager), Preston North End (1968-1992)*
'Big' Sam arrived at the club in time for the 1984-85 season from Coventry City but only played one season for the club before leaving for Bolton Wanderers. He is perhaps best remembered at Town for an incident that occurred in a match against Crystal Palace at Leeds Road which saw David Burke suffer a horrific leg break after a foul by David Hopkin. Allardyce was sent from the pitch after attacking Hopkin and punching him numerous times. He is also said to have attempted to kick the away dressing room door in an attempt to carry on the attack! Allardyce later became the player-manager of Limerick in 1991 before he returned to England as a coach and manager at Preston North End, Blackpool and Notts County. Allardyce resigned from his post in 1999 to take over as the manager of former club Bolton Wanderers. His managerial merry-go-round continued with stops at Newcastle United, Blackburn Rovers, West Ham United and Sunderland before being appointed manager of the England national team in 2016. This turned out to be an ill-fated spell as he was sacked after just one game when allegations of corruption were printed in a newspaper. He then took the Crystal Palace job in 2017 and kept them in the Premier League at the end of the 2016-17 season and performed a similar feat at Everton in 2017 before being sacked at the end of the 2017-18 season.

Sam Allardyce

ALLEN, James 'Jimmy'
Right-half
Town Years: 1934-1935
Born: *1913 Amble, Northumberland*
Died: *1979 Hammersmith, Greater London*
Playing career: *Huddersfield Town, Queens Park Rangers, Clapton Orient (1933-1938)*
Allen signed from Stakeford Albion in March 1934 but his debut wasn't a successful one as he struggled to cope with J.G Bell, the Preston North End inside-left and it turned out to be Allen's only game for the club. After his retirement from football in 1938, he went to work on the railways as a labourer for Perway Maintenanc. He died in 1979,

ALLINSON, Lloyd
Goalkeeper
Town Years: 2010-2016
Born: *1993 Rothwell, West Yorkshire*
Playing career: *Huddersfield Town, Ilkeston (loan), Chesterfield (loan), FC United of Manchester (2010-Still Playing)*
Allinson was an academy graduate who turned professional in 2010 and spent six years in the first team squad without making a single appearance. By twist of fate, he was called into action during the final game of the 2015-16 season, replacing the injured Jed Steer. He was released at the end of that season and had a short spell at Chesterfield during the 2016-17 season and signed for non-league F.C. United of Manchester.

Dr Wayne Allison

ALLISON, Wayne

Forward
Town Years: 1997-1999
Born: *1968 Huddersfield, West Riding of Yorkshire*
Playing career: *Halifax Town, Watford, Bristol City, Swindon Town, Huddersfield Town, Tranmere Rovers, Sheffield United, Chesterfield, Chester City (player-assistant manager) (1987-2008)*

Allison was a Huddersfield lad that signed for Town from Swindon Town in 1997, going on to play a huge part in the 1997-98 Great Escape season. He fell out of favour after Peter Jackson was sacked in favour of Steve Bruce in 1999 and left for Tranmere Rovers during the 1999-2000 season. 'The Chief' later played for Sheffield United and Chesterfield before he became player-assistant manager at Chester City, later taking caretaker charge for a short time in 2008. Spells at Bury and Tranmere Rovers followed before he retired from the game and became a lecturer in sport at Kirklees College. He also had a short spell at Bradford City as development coach before becoming Coaching Research Manager at the FA, later progressing to Coach Inclusion and Diversity Manager. Allison also had a short time as manager of Cardiff Metropolitan University FC in 2017 but he left later on in the same year due to work commitments and is now working as Technical Director at the League Managers Association. In 2010, Dr. Allison completed a PhD in the effects of high-intensity exercise on decision-making in soccer.

ANDERSON, George

Inside-right
Town Years: 1934-1936
Born: *1904 Saltcoats, Scotland*
Died: *1974 Cambridge, Cambridgeshire*
Playing career: *Dalry Thistle, Airdrieonians, Brentford, Chelsea, Norwich City, Carlisle United, Gillingham, Cowdenbeath, Yeovil & Petters United, Bury, Huddersfield Town, Mansfield Town, Newark, Ayr United, Saltcoats Victoria (1925-1937)*

Anderson signed from Bury in December 1934 and played in the first team for just over a year before joining Mansfield Town in January 1936. Later played for Newark, Ayr United and Saltcoats Victoria before retiring from football during World War Two. Anderson later worked as a roof slater in Mansfield before he passed away in Cambridge in December 1974.

ARCHER, John

Inside-left
Town Years: 1968-1969
Born: *1941 Biddulph, Staffordshire*
Playing career: *Port Vale, Bournemouth & Boscombe Athletic, Crewe Alexandra, Huddersfield Town (loan), Chesterfield, Sandbach Ramblers (player-manager) (1958-1972)*

Archer signed from Crewe Alexandra in 1968 and played nine games for the first team during the 1968-69 season. He later played for Chesterfield and had a spell as the player-manager of Sandbach Ramblers, but is now living in retirement in Congleton.

ARFIELD, Scott

Midfielder
Town Years: 2010-2013
Born: *1988 Dechmont, Scotland*
Playing career: *Falkirk, Huddersfield Town, Burnley, Rangers (2007-Still Playing)*

Arfield arrived at the club in 2010 after he was signed from Falkirk by then-manager Lee Clark. After three uneventful years, he left for Burnley in 2013. He was well received at Turf Moor and won two promotions at the club before leaving in 2018 to play for Rangers. Despite being born in Scotland and representing their international sides at under-19, 21 and 'B' levels, in 2016 Arfield decided to switch allegiance and has since played 13 times and captained Canada's national side, qualifying due to his Canadian father who was born in Toronto.

ARISMENDI, Diego
Midfielder
Town Years: 2012 (loan)
Born: *1988 Montevideo, Uruguay*
Playing career: *Nacional, Stoke City, Brighton & Hove Albion (loan), Barnsley (loan), Huddersfield Town (loan), Nacional, Al-Shabab, Nacional (2006-Still Playing)*

Arismendi was Simon Grayson's first signing, coming in on loan from Stoke City during the 2011-12 season. He returned to his parent club later on during that season and is now playing for Nacional in his native Uruguay, his third spell at the club. In addition, Arismendi made four appearances for the Uruquay national side.

ARMOUR, Andrew 'Andy'
Outside-right
Town Years: 1911-1914
Born: *1883 Irvine, North Ayrshire, Scotland*
Died: *1955 Kilmarnock, Scotland*
Playing career: *Queen's Park, Kilmarnock, Huddersfield Town, Kilmarnock (c1905-1914)*

Signing from Kilmarnock in 1911, Armour went straight into the first team at Leeds Road and played most of the rest of the 1911-12 season. He was almost an ever-present during the 1912-13 season, missing just 2 matches. Armour was then ever-present for the 1913-14 season before he left Leeds Road at the end of it. Armour returned home to Scotland to play for Kilmarnock before working as a general practioner. Passed away in 1955.

ARMSTRONG, Alun
Forward
Town Years: 2000 (loan)
Born: *1975 Gateshead, Tyne and Wear*
Playing career: *Newcastle United, Stockport County, Middlesbrough, Huddersfield Town (loan), Ipswich Town, Darlington (1993-2007)*

Armstrong signed on loan from Middlesbrough in 2000 and played four games for Steve Bruce's side before returning to Teeside. Spells were enjoyed at at Ipswich Town, Darlington and Rushden & Diamonds before he retired in 2007. Set up a series of soccer schools and since 2016 has been Blyth Spartans manager whilst also running his own sports centre in Shildon.

ARMSTRONG, Craig
Defender
Town Years: 1999-2002
Born: *1975 South Shields, Tyne and Wear*
Playing career: *Nottingham F, Huddersfield T, Sheffield W, Bradford C, Cheltenham T, Gillingham, Kidderminster H, Mansfield T, (1992-2012)*

Armstrong signed from Nottingham Forest in 1999 and is best remembered for being part of the 2001-02 promotion push under Lou Macari. Moved on to Sheffield Wednesday after Town had lost to Brentford in the playoffs. Went on to manage in non-league with Eastwood Town and Quorn and also worked as Elite Development Coach at his first club, Nottingham Forest. He is now working as a Regional co-ordinator for Arsenal.

ARMSTRONG, Terence 'Terry'
Midfielder
Town Years: 1976-1980
Born: *1958 Barnsley, West Riding of Yorkshire*
Playing career: *Huddersfield Town, Port Vale, Nuneaton Borough, Northwich Victoria (1976-1985)*
After beginning his career at the club as an apprentice, Armstrong played a number of games in the first team before falling out of favour by the time Mick Buxton became the manager in 1978. Joined the Prison Service when he hung up his boots and became a prison warden. Armstrong has been a wagon driver since the early 2000s.

ASHCROFT, Lee
Forward
Town Years: 2002 (loan)
Born: *1972 Preston, Lancashire*
Playing career: *Preston North End, West Bromwich Albion, Notts County (loan), Preston North End (loan), Preston North End, Grimsby Town, Wigan Athletic, Port Vale (loan), Huddersfield Town (loan), Southport, Chorley (loan), Kendal Town (player-manager) (1987-2010)*
Ashcroft was signed on loan from Wigan Athletic by Mick Wadsworth after a wealthy Town fan offered to pay his wages. Later played for Southport and managed Kendal Town, Northwich Victoria but was removed from this post in December 2013 after he was involved in a confrontation with an opposition coach. Took the manager's job at Longridge Town in 2014, where he remains.

ATKINS, Denis
Right-back
Town Years: 1953-1955 (amateur), 1955-1968
Born: *1938 Bradford, West Riding of Yorkshire*
Died: *2016 Bradford, West Yorkshire*
Playing career: *Huddersfield Town, Bradford City (1955-1971)*
Atkins began his career at Leeds Road in 1953 and during the next sixteen years, played over 200 games for Town under managers Andy Beattie, Bill Shankly, Eddie Boot and Tom Johnston. Ended his career at Bradford City, where he played from 1968 to 1971. Atkins then pursued a career in teaching and in 1984 and made a brief return to Bradford City to work as their liaison officer, aiding relationships between the club, schools and junior organisations. The Yorkshireman passed away, aged 77, in 2016 whilst living in Bradford.

ATKINSON, Christopher 'Chris'
Midfielder
Town Years: 2010-2014
Born: *1992 Halifax, West Yorkshire*
Playing career: *Huddersfield Town, Darlington (loan), Chesterfield (loan), Tranmere Rovers (loan), Bradford City (loan), Crewe Alexandra, Crawley Town (loan), Salford City, Farsley Celtic (2010-Still Playing)*
Academy graduate who is best remembered for scoring against Leeds United in 2012, but never managed to cement a place in the first team and left the club in 2014 to join Crewe Alexandra. Atkinson then spent one season at Salford City before signing for his current club Farsley Celtic.

AUSTIN, Terence 'Terry'
Forward
Town Years: 1980-1983
Born: *1954 Isleworth, Middlesex*
Playing career: *Crystal Palace, Ipswich Town, Plymouth Argyle, Walsall, Mansfield Town, Huddersfield Town, Doncaster Rovers (1972-1984)*
Austin signed from Mansfield Town for a record transfer fee of £100,000. Sadly, he didn't live up to expectations at Town and wasn't the most popular player during his spell at the club. After three years and only 42 games at Leeds Road, Austin was sold by Mick Buxton in 1983 to Doncaster Rovers and he later played for Northampton Town before retiring in 1984. He is now a financial advisor in Mansfield with his own company, TLAPC Limited, but is semi-retired, spending much of his time at his second home in Gran Canaria.

BAILEY, Thomas 'Graham'
Right-back
Town Years: 1936-1946 (amateur), 1946-1948
Born: *1920 Dawley, Shropshire*
Playing career: *Donnington Wood, Huddersfield Town, Sheffield United (1936-1949)*
Hailing from Dawley, Shropshire, Bailey signed as an amateur in 1936 from Donnington Wood. After ten years at the club, he finally turned professional in 1946 and went on to play over 30 matches for David Steele's side. Left the club in March 1948 to join Sheffield United in a part exchange deal involving Albert Nightingale which also saw George Hutchinson leave the club. Bailey spent a year at Bramall Lane before retiring from professional football in 1949.

BAIN, Alexander 'Alex'

Centre-forward
Town Years: *1957-1960*
Born: *1936 Edinburgh, Scotland*
Died: *2014 unknown*
Playing career: *Motherwell, Huddersfield Town, Chesterfield, Falkirk, Bournemouth(1954-1963)*

Bain was a forward who signed from Motherwell in August 1957 and spent three years at the club, scoring 11 goals in his 30 games. Most of these had come under manager Bill Shankly. His successor, Eddie Boot, sold the Scotsman to Chesterfield in 1960. Bain announced his retirement in 1963. He ran a painting and decorating business in Bournemouth before passing away in 2014.

BAINES, Stephen 'Steve'

Centre-half
Town Years: *1975-1978*
Born: *1954 Newark, Nottinghamshire*
Playing career: *Nottingham Forest, Huddersfield Town, Bradford City, Walsall, Bury (loan), Scunthorpe United, Chesterfield (1972-1987)*

Baines signed from Nottingham Forest in 1975 and was a mainstay in the Town defence throughout his time at the club. In total 114 league games were notched up before he transferred to Bradford City in 1978. Baines worked in insurance before becoming a Football League linesman in 1994. He was promoted to referee just a year later in 1995 and served for eight years before retiring in 2003 due to the rules in place at the time. Baines later worked as a property broker and was last known to be working in commodities dealing with people in different parts of the world and is living in Chesterfield.

BAIRD, Harry

Inside-forward
Town Years: *1938-1946*
Born: *1913 Belfast, Northern Ireland*
Died: *1973 Belfast, Northern Ireland*
Playing career: *Dunmurry, Bangor, Linfield, Windsor Park Swifts, Manchester United, Huddersfield Town, Ipswich Town (1932-1953)*

Baird joined Town from Manchester United in 1938 and spent a couple of years with Town in the Wartime League. He remained on the books at Leeds Road throughout the Second World War and during this time he also guested for a number of other clubs. After the hostilities had ended, Baird joined Ipswich in 1946 and remained at Portman Road until 1952 when he retired as a player and began work as a coach at the club. He passed away in 1973 back in his hometown of Belfast.

BAKER, James 'Jim'

Half-back
Town Years: *1914-1920*
Born: *1891 Ilkeston, Derbyshire*
Died: *1966 Leeds, West Riding of Yorkshire*
Playing career: *Derby County, Portsmouth, Hartlepool United, Huddersfield Town, Leeds United, Nelson, Colne Valley (1910-1927)*

Baker joined from Hartlepools United in 1914 and he played for four years in the Wartime League at Leeds Road, whilst also serving in the First World War. He remained at the club until 1920, when he joined Leeds United, the club that Town had almost merged with just a year earlier. Baker spent six years at Elland Road, becoming their first ever captain and remained so until his departure in 1926. The latter stages of his playing career were spent at non-league Nelson and Colne Valley before becoming a director at Elland Road, as well as a scout at the club. Baker later worked as the landlord of the Smythes Arms Hotel in Leeds and also the Mexborough Arms in Chapeltown before he passed away in 1966.

BAKER, Steven 'Steve'

Defender
Town Years: *1999 (loan)*
Born: *1978 Pontefract, West Yorkshire*
Playing career: *Middlesbrough, Huddersfield Town (loan), Darlington (loan), Hartlepool United (loan), Scarborough (loan), Scarborough, Gateshead, Newcastle Blue Star (1997-c2009)*

Baker was signed by Steve Bruce on loan in the 1999-2000 season and played four games for the club before returning to his parent club Middlesbrough. Loan spells at Darlington, Hartlepool and Scarborough followed before he joined the Seasiders permanently in 2002. Baker spent four years at the McCain Stadium before rounding off his career with spells at non-league Gateshead and Newcastle Blue Star. After his retirement, Baker worked at Burdon Engineering as a production supervisor and worked at SSI Steel in Redcar as a materials controller. Now works for Marshalls PLC in Eaglescliffe as an engineering planner.

BALDERSTONE, Christopher 'Chris'

Inside-forward
Town Years: 1956-1958 (amateur), 1958-1965
Born: *1940 Longwood, Huddersfield, West Riding of Yorkshire*
Died: *2000 Carlisle, Cumbria*
Playing career: *Shrewsbury Town, Huddersfield Town, Carlisle United, Doncaster Rovers, Queen of the South (1956-1978)*

Hailing from Huddersfield, Balderstone joined his home-town club in 1956 on the groundstaff, before turning professional in 1958. After five years as a professional, he left in 1965 to enjoy a ten year spell at Carlisle United, where he made 376 league appearances. Balderstone played for Doncaster Rovers and Queen of the South before retiring from professional football in 1978. The inside-forward had combined his football career with a cricket career, first playing for Yorkshire in 1961 before moving to Leicestershire in 1971 with whom he won the Benson and Hedges Cup in 1972. Continued to play cricket until 1986 before retiring and becoming an umpire including two Test matches in the 1990s. Balderstone passed away in 2000 in Carlisle having suffered from prostate cancer.

BALDRY, Simon

Winger
Town Years: 1993-2003
Born: *1976 Huddersfield, West Yorkshire*
Playing career: *Huddersfield Town, Bury (loan), Notts County, Ossett Town, Bradford Park Avenue, Guiseley AFC, Bradford Park Avenue, Workington, Ossett Town, Frickley Athletic (1993-2014)*

Baldry began his career at his hometown club and managed to break into the first team towards the end of the 1993-94 season, also managing to play in the Autoglass Final at Wembley and going on to score in the final match at the old Leeds Road ground. Baldry also scored the goal that saved Town from relegation in the 1997-98 season. He suffered from injury problems but managed to stay on the books until 2003, when he was eventually released for economy measures, after the club were put into administration. Baldry later played for Notts County, Bradford Park Avenue, Guiseley, Ossett Town, Workington and Frickley Athletic but is now living in Australia where he works with disadvantaged children.

BALL, John 'Jack'

Forward
Town Years: 1934
Born: *1907 Banks, Lancashire*
Died: *1976 Luton, Bedfordshire*
Playing career: *Banks Juniors, Southport, Darwen, Chorley, Manchester United, Sheffield Wednesday, Manchester United, Huddersfield Town, Luton Town, Excelsior Roubaix, Luton Town, Vauxhall Motors, St. Albans City, Biggleswade Town (1923-1940)*

Ball signed from Manchester United in September 1934 but only played 5 games at Leeds Road before joining Luton Town the following month. The Lancastrian remained at Kenilworth Road until 1935, when he transferred to French club Excelsior Roubaix. This spell was a short one and he returned to Luton in the same year and helped them to the Third Division (South) championship in 1937, chipping in with 8 goals during that season. Ball joined Vauxhall Motors in 1937 and also played for St. Albans City and Biggleswade Town before he announced his retirement in 1940. After football, Ball had 20 years service at Vauxhall Motors before working for a wholesale manufacturing chemist and he was also a trained masseur and once he retired he helped out in his son's pub. Ball later passed away in Luton at the age of 69 in February 1976.

BANKS, Ian
Midfielder
Town Years: 1986-1988
Born: *1961 Mexborough, West Riding of Yorkshire*
Playing career: *Barnsley, Leicester City, Huddersfield Town, Bradford City, WBA, Barnsley, Rotherham United, Darlington, Emley (1978-1999)*
'Banger' was signed from Leicester City in 1986 by Mick Buxton during some difficult times and was the captain during Town's record 10-1 defeat to Manchester City in November 1987. He left at the end of the 1987-88 season after the club had endured relegated as the bottom team and signed for neighbours Bradford City before returning to his first club Barnsley before rounding off his professional career with spells at Rotherham United and Darlington. He was then part of the famous Emley team that played West Ham United in a 1997 FA Cup 3rd Round tie. Became assistant manager to Nicky Law at Chesterfield between 2000 and 2001 and at former club Bradford City and had a short spell as Wakefield and Emley manager. Worked in Huddersfield as a financial advisor as well as managing former club Emley between 2008 and 2010. Banks has since re-trained as an electrician and now lives in Rotherham.

BARCLAY, Robert 'Bobby'
Inside-right
Town Years: 1937-1946
Born: *1906 Scotswood, Northumberland*
Died: *1969 Huddersfield, West Riding of Yorkshire*
Playing career: *Derby County, Sheffield United, Huddersfield Town, Hurst (1923-c1946)*
Bobby Barclay had enjoyed a decent career in football before joining Town in March 1937, having previously played for Derby County and Sheffield United. He was a regular at Leeds Road and was a member of the the 1938 FA Cup Final side which lost to Preston North End at Wembley. The outbreak of World War Two saw the Football League suspended and many players guested for other teams in the Wartime League. Town retained his registration throughout the War but Barclay was released in 1946. The Scotswood-born inside-right later had a spell at Hurst in the Cheshire League before returning to Leeds Road as assistant trainer. He passed away in 1969 and was still living in Huddersfield at the time of his death.

BARHAM, Mark
Midfielder
Town Years: 1987-1988
Born: *1962 Folkestone, Kent*
Playing career: *Norwich City, Huddersfield Town, Middlesbrough, Hythe Town, WBA, Brighton & Hove Albion, Shrewsbury Town (1980-1998)*
Barham had spent seven years at Norwich City and had won 2 caps for England but he joined a Town side that had been struggling against relegation for a couple of years. He is one of the eleven players that featured in Town's 10-1 defeat at Maine Road. Barham now works for the MITIE Group in Norwich as Business Development Manager.

BARKAS, Edward 'Ned'
Full-back
Town Years: 1921-1928
Born: *1901 Gateshead, Durham*
Died: *1962 Birmingham, Warwickshire*
Playing career: *Huddersfield Town, Birmingham, Chelsea, Solihull Town (player-manager) (1919-1943)*
Arriving at Leeds Road from Norwich City in January 1921, Ned Barkas eventually became first choice right-back and is one of the few players to have won all three of Town's domestic titles. He left for Birmingham in December 1928 for a fee of £4,000 and spent nine years there before a two-year spell at Chelsea. Later worked as player-manager of Solihull Town and as a police reserve in Birmingham during the Second World War. Barkas passed away in Birmingham in 1962, at the age of 60.

SOUTH TERRACE SEAT (Uncovered)
ENTER AT TURNSTILES (See Plan on back) **A**
ENTRANCE **26**
Row Seat
22 16
EMPIRE STADIUM, WEMBLEY
THE FOOTBALL ASSOCIATION CUP COMPETITION
FINAL TIE
SATURDAY, APRIL 30th, 1938
Kick-off 3 p.m.
Price 5/- (Including Tax)
MANAGING DIRECTOR, Wembley Stadium Limited.
THIS PORTION TO BE RETAINED (See Conditions on back)

BARKER, Jeffrey 'Jeff'

Wing-half
Town Years: 1945-1948
Born: 1915 Scunthorpe, Lincolnshire
Died: 1985 Scunthorpe, Lincolnshire
Playing career: *Goole Town, Scunthorpe and Lindsey United, Aston Villa, Huddersfield Town, Scunthorpe United, Goole Town, Ashby Institute (1935-1956)*

Barker arrived at the club after World War Two, signing from Aston Villa. He played for three years before heading back to his hometown club Scunthorpe United. Barker later worked as chief scout for Scunthorpe (once scouting a young player called Kevin Keegan) and acted as their caretaker manager in 1974 for a three game spell. He passed away in Scunthorpe in 1985 seventy years after his birth in the same town.

BARLOW, Patrick 'Pat'

Outside-right
Town Years: 1938-1939
Born: 1914 Athlone, Ireland
Died: 1986 Dublin, Ireland
Playing career: *Newry Town, Huddersfield Town, Sligo Rovers, Dundalk, Limerick, Chelmsford City, Wisbech Town (1935-1950)*

Barlow's career at Town was cruelly interrupted by the outbreak of World War Two. He returned to his native Ireland, turning out for Sligo Rovers and then Dundalk, where he is still considered to be one of their best ever right-wingers. Barlow came back to England to sign for Chelmsford City in 1946. Two decades after he left the club, Barlow returned to Dundalk in 1966 as acting manager whilst a replacement was found. Barlow passed away in Dublin in 1986.

BARNES, Paul

Forward
Town Years: 1998-1999
Born: 1967 Leicester, Leicestershire
Playing career: *Notts County, Stoke City, Chesterfield (loan), York City, Birmingham City, Burnley, Huddersfield Town, Bury (1985-2005)*

After arriving at Town from Burnley in a swap deal for Andy Payton, Barnes played a small part in the 1997-98 'Great Escape' season. He left the club in 1999 to sign for Bury.Barnes has been running his own business, PLB Asset Finance Limited since 2006 and is now living in his hometown of Leicester.

BARNETT, Gary

Midfielder
Town Years: 1990-1993
Born: 1963 Stratford-upon-Avon, Warwickshire
Playing career: *Coventry City, Oxford United, Wimbledon (loan), Fulham (loan), Fulham, Huddersfield Town, Leyton Orient, Barry Town (player-manager), Kidderminster Harriers (player-assistant manager) (1981-2001)*

Eoin Hand brought Barnett to the club in 1990, signing him from Fulham and he was a regular fixture in the first team until Neil Warnock's arrival at the start of the 1993-94 season. He was soon transferred to Leyton Orient and remained at Brisbane Road until 1995, before he became the player-manager of Barry Town. Barnett spent four years at Barry, leading them to the UEFA Cup in 1996 before joining Jan Molby as player-assistant manager at Kidderminster Harriers in 1999. The pair had a brief rather unsuccessful stint at Hull City in 2002 before returning to Kidderminster the following year. Their second spell also only lasted a year at Aggborough before they were both sacked in 2004. Barnett later managed Moreton Rangers (and is still the director of football there) but now works as a personal trainer from his base in Chipping Campden, Gloucestershire.

BARRY, Michael 'Mike'

Wing-half
Town Years: 1968-1973
Born: 1953 Hull, East Riding of Yorkshire
Playing career: *Hull City (amateur), Huddersfield Town, Carlisle United, Washington Diplomats (loan), Bristol Rovers, Columbus Magic, Pittsburgh Spirit (indoor), Cleveland Force (indoor), Cleveland Cobras, New Jersey Rockets (indoor), Columbus Capitals (indoor) (1968-1985)*

Barry caught the eye of the club's scouts while playing for Hull City as an amateur and prompted the management team at Leeds Road to offer him a professional contract. This led to five years of steady service before a move to Carlisle United in 1973. He later emigrated to the United States many years ago to initially play for Columbus Magic. Barry went on to play for Cleveland Cobras before his retirement and coached a number of clubs in Columbus, Ohio. The Yorkshireman is now the Technical Director and Professional Coach at Locomotive Soccer Club in Columbus.

BARTLETT, William 'Billy'

Left-half
Town Years: 1910-1912
Born: *1878 Newcastle-upon-Tyne, Northumberland*
Died: *1939 Belfast, Northern Ireland*
Playing career: *Brandon, Gateshead NER, Sheffield Wednesday, Huddersfield Town, Linfield (1903-1918)*
Bartlett signed from Sheffield Wednesday in 1910 and played at Leeds Road for two years before heading over to play for Linfield in Ireland, where he eventually became assistant trainer. Bartlett later worked as a distillery trainer and then as a scout at Blackburn Rovers before he worked in the Belfast Corporation Surveyor's Department. The former left-half later passed away after a short illness in 1939, at the age of 61.

BARTRAM, Vincent 'Vince'

Goalkeeper
Town Years: 1997 (loan)
Born: *1968 Birmingham, Warwickshire*
Playing career: *Wolves, Blackpool (loan), Cheltenham Town (loan), WBA, Bournemouth, Arsenal, Huddersfield Town (loan), Gillingham (1985-2005)*
Bartram was brought in on loan from Arsenal during the 1997-98 season to replace the out of favour, Steve Francis. After a number of other temporary stops, he eventually found a semi-permenant home at Gillingham but his was brought to a sudden end when he was involved in an unusual on-field accident. His wrist was injured when clattered by the opposing goalie who had ventured up front in the dying stages of the game in an attempt to snatch a last minute goal. Bartram then joined William Hill as deputy manager and worked as a sales executive for Seward Cars in Bournemouth before becoming the goalkeeping coach at AFC Bournemouth. A spell coaching at Portsmouth's academy followed before he made the short move up the M27 to take up a similar role with their arch rivals Southampton. He has been there ever since.

Vince Bartram

Albert Bateman

BATEMAN, Albert

Outside-right
Town Years: 1943-1950
Born: *1924 Stocksbridge, West Riding of Yorkshire*
Playing career: *Yorkshire Iron & Steelworks, Huddersfield Town (1943-1950)*
Albert Bateman had previously been playing for the illustrious Yorkshire Iron & Steelworks before signing on the dotted line in September 1943. He turned professional in 1946 and played in the first team for three years before injury problems forced him to retire from the professional game. A career in retail followed and this included the running his own newsagents and grocery stores. Once retired, he played tennis and badminton well into his 70s and also worked as a caretaker until 80 years of age. This only came to an end because he couldn't be insured to work at his age. Bateman is still alive and well, living in Thornton-Cleveleys, is in his mid 90s and he still looks out for Town's results every weekend.

BATTYE, John

Half-back
Town Years: 1943-1949 (amateur), 1949-1959
Born: *1926 Scissett, Huddersfield*
Died: *2016 Clayton West, Huddersfield,*
Playing career: *Huddersfield Town, York City (1943-1960)*

Battye signed for his hometown club in 1943 and stayed for the next sixteen years. Strangely, he had been on the transfer list when he made his debut in 1949 but then remained in the side until Bill McGarry was signed in 1951. Battye remained at the club for another eight years, finally leaving for York City in 1959. He only lasted a year at Bootham Crescent before retiring from professional football in 1960. Whilst still a professional at the club, the tenacious half-back set up North Star Tyre Remoulds in 1953 with Eddie Boot and this was based in Scissett. Battye still lived in Huddersfield until his death in June 2016, he was 90.

BEASLEY, Albert 'Pat'

Outside-left
Town Years: 1936-1945
Born: *1913 Stourbridge, Worcestershire*
Died: *1986 Taunton, Somerset*
Playing career: *Cookley, Stourbridge, Arsenal, Huddersfield Town, Fulham, Bristol City (1931-1952)*

After a spell at Arsenal, Beasley arrived at Leeds Road in 1936 and went straight into the side at outside-left, taking the place of Reg Chester. He remained first choice inside-left until the Second World War interrupted the Football League in 1939. Beasley didn't feature for the club in the Wartime League until 1945, appearing just once and when the Football League resumed later in 1945, he transferred to Fulham. Whilst at Town, he appeared in the FA Cup Final in 1938 and also won his only England cap in 1939, when England faced Scotland. After leaving Fulham in 1950, Beasley was appointed player-manager of Bristol City that same year, continuing to play for another two years before becoming the sole manager in 1952. He remained at Ashton Gate until 1958 before being sacked and a year later, Beasley had a spell as Birmingham City boss but only remained there until 1960. Beasley later had a spell as manager of Dover and was also a scout for Fulham before retiring to Chard, Somerset and later passed away in Taunton at the age of 72 in 1986.

COPE'S "CLIPS" CIGARETTES

432. — BEATON
Huddersfield Town
Noted Footballers

BEATON, Simon

Right-half
Town Years: 1910-1919
Born: *1888 Inverness, Scotland*
Died: *1959 Middlesbrough*
Playing career: *Newcastle United, Huddersfield Town (1910-1919)*

After playing for Newcastle United, Beaton signed for Town during the club's first ever professional season in 1910-11 and was a regular in the side, playing at right-half, until the First World War broke out in 1914. The Football League was suspended shortly afterwards but Beaton did remain on Town's books. However he did leave the club when things resumed in 1919. Later worked as an electrical fitter in Redcar before passing away in 1959, in Middlesbrough.

"DID YOU KNOW?"

"Town's first professional season was 1910-11."

BEATTIE, Andrew 'Andy'

Manager
Town Years: 1952-1956
Born: *1913 Kintore, Scotland*
Died: *1983 Nottingham, Nottinghamshire*
Management career: *Barrow, Stockport County, Huddersfield Town, Scotland, Carlisle United, Scotland, Nottingham Forest, Plymouth Argyle, Wolverhampton Wanderers, Notts County (1947-1967)*

Beattie was approached to become the manager at Leeds Road after George Stephenson was sacked in 1952 and was tasked with saving the club from relegation to the Second Division but was unable to do so. An immediate return to the First Division was achieved during the 1952-53 season, games which included beatings handed out to Everton (8-2), Barnsley (6-0), Lincoln City (5-0) and Southampton (5-0). Under Beattie's management, Town managed a third place finish in the first season back in the big time but a decline in Town's fortunes followed in the following years. Town were eventually relegated in 1956 and Beattie was replaced by his assistant manager, Bill Shankly.
He later worked as a sub-postmaster in Preston before returning to the game to manage Carlisle United, Nottingham Forest, Plymouth Argyle, Wolves and Notts County. Whilst at Town, Beattie was appointed manager of the Scotland national team, taking charge of their 1954 World Cup campaign. His resignation was tendered at the end of the tournament with amid claims that being expected to play four games with a squad of only 13 players was asking too much of him. Despite this he did return to the role between 1959 and 1960 before resigning again due to his commitments with Nottingham Forest. He passed away in September 1983 at the age of 70.

SCOTLAND 1954

BEATTIE, John 'Jack'

Inside-forward
Town Years: 1938
Born: *1912 Newhills, Aberdeen, Scotland*
Died: *1992 Wolverhampton, West Midlands*
Playing career: *Wolves, Blackburn R, Birmingham, Huddersfield Town, Grimsby Town (1931-1946)*

After a spell at Birmingham, Beattie joined Town in 1938 but only made 3 appearances for the first team before leaving for Grimsby Town in the same year. Beattie lived in Wolverhampton for the rest of his life, later working in tyre manufacturing. He passed away in 1992 at the age of 79.

BEAUMONT, Leonard 'Len'

Outside-left
Town Years: 1931-1936
Born: *1915 Huddersfield, West Riding of Yorkshire*
Died: *2002 Nottingham, Nottinghamshire*
Playing career: *Huddersfield Town, Portsmouth, Peterborough United (1931-1949)*

Beaumont played for his hometown club between 1931 and 1936 but only managed 3 full first team games. He had short spells at Portsmouth and Nottingham Forest. By 1939, he was living in Sheffield and working as a furnaceman in the steel trade there. After World War Two, the former winger later worked as a government contracts officer for Ericsson. Later in life, he joined Nottinghamshire Cricket in 1981 and acted as their first team scorer between 1987 and 1993. Beaumont passed away in 2002.

BECKETT, Luke

Forward
Town Years: 2005 (loan), 2006-2008
Born: *1976 Sheffield, South Yorkshire*
Playing career: *Barnsley, Chester City, Chesterfield, Stockport County, Sheffield United, Huddersfield Town, (1991-2012)*

Signed by Peter Jackson on loan from Sheffield United, he made an instant impression by scoring 6 goals in 7 games at the end of the 2004-05 season. His permanent £85,000 transfer did eventually take place but not for over a year, during which time, he had also spent time on loan at Oldham. 23 goals were then bagged in 78 league games before he fell out of favour. This was in 2008 when Stan Ternent became the manager. He is now working as a personal trainer, running his own company Luke Beckett Fitness in Doncaster.

BECKFORD, Jermaine
Forward
Town Years: 2012-2013 (loan)
Born: *1983 Ealing, Greater London*
Playing career: *Leeds United, Carlisle United (loan), Scunthorpe United (loan), Everton, Leicester City, Huddersfield Town (loan), Bolton Wanderers, Preston North End, Bury (2003-Still Playing)*
The Galpharm Stadium became one of Beckford's many stops around the country when he was borrowed from Leicester City for the 2012-13 season. Unfortunately a series of niggling injuries marred his stay and finally forced him to return to his parent club. He later played for Bolton and Preston before signing for Bury in 2017. Beckford has played six international games for Jamaica, all of those appearances coming in 2013.

BEECH, Albert
Wing-half
Town Years: 1934-1937
Born: *1912 Fenton, Staffordshire*
Died: *1985 Stoke-on-Trent, Staffordshire*
Playing career: *Port Vale, Altrincham, Huddersfield Town, Notts County, Northwich Victoria (1930-1938)*
Beech signed from Altrincham in May 1934 and played at Leeds Road for three years before his departure in June 1937, when he signed for Notts County. He remained at Meadow Lane for a year and later had a short spell at non-league Northwich Victoria before hanging up his boots and retiring from football. Beech passed away in Fenton, Stoke-on-Trent in 1985.

BEECH, Christopher 'Chris'
Midfielder
Town Years: 1998-2002
Born: *1974 Blackpool, Lancashire*
Playing career: *Blackpool, Hartlepool United, Huddersfield Town, Rochdale, Doncaster Rovers, Carlisle United (1993-2005)*
Signed from Hartlepool United in 1998, Beech spent four years at Town before joining Rochdale in 2002. After stops at Doncaster Rovers and Carlisle United he retired from the professional game in 2005. Beech worked as youth team manager at Rochdale and he took the job of caretaker manager in 2011 following the sacking of Steve Eyre. He returned to his previous role following the appointment of John Coleman. Following Keith Hill's appointment in 2013, Beech became assistant manager at Spotland.

ROD BELFITT
Ipswich

BELFITT, Roderick 'Rod'
Forward
Town Years: 1975-1976
Born: *1945 Bournemouth, Hampshire*
Playing career: *Leeds United, Ipswich Town, Everton, Sunderland, Huddersfield Town, Town (1964-1976)*
Rod Belfitt had made his name as part of the great Leeds United squad of the late 60's and early 70's. He only spent a year at Town, playing under Tom Johnston, before heading for Worksop in 1976. Belfitt returned to his original career as a draughtsman and later worked for the Inland Revenue and also as a financial advisor before retiring in 2001. He was last known to be living in Pontefract.

BELL, Graham
Right-half
Town Years: 1981 (loan)
Born: *1955 Middleton, Lancashire*
Playing career: *Oldham Athletic, Preston North End, Huddersfield Town (loan), Carlisle United, Bolton Wanderers, Tranmere Rovers (1974-1992)*
Bell arrived on loan from Preston North End in 1981 and played a couple of games for Mick Buxton's side before returning to Deepdale. He spent the latter part of his career in non-league football, eventually becoming assistant manager at Mossley. Became a newsagent when he finally left the game.

BENNETT, Ian
Goalkeeper
Town Years: 2010-2014
Born: *1971 Worksop, Nottinghamshire*
Playing career: *QPR, Newcastle United, Peterborough United, Birmingham City, Sheffield United (loan), Coventry City (loan), Leeds United, Sheffield United, Huddersfield Town (1988-2014)*

'Benno' joined from Sheffield United in 2010 as cover for the young and upcoming Alex Smithies. However, due to injuries to the young keeper, Bennett was drafted in and impressed manager Lee Clark, despite his advancing years. He played much of the 2010-11 season after cementing his place as Town's No.1, including the playoff semi-finals and the playoff final. Bennett also played most of the 2011-12 promotion season but unfortunately picked up in an injury in the second leg of the play-off semi-finals. Smithies came in and ended up scoring the winning penalty. Bennett stayed on at Town, again as cover for Smithies and in 2014 became the goalkeeping coach for Town's Academy. He is now the goalkeeping coach for Nottingham Forest's academy side having taken on the role at the beginning of the 2015-16 season.

BENT, Junior
Winger
Town Years: 1985-1990
Born: *1970 Huddersfield, West Riding of Yorkshire*
Playing career: *Huddersfield Town, Burnley (loan), Bristol City, Stoke City (loan), Shrewsbury Town (loan), Blackpool, (1985-2003)*

Bent began his Town career in the youth team and although he broke into the side during the 1987-88 season, but never really became a regular fixture in the first team. Transferred to Bristol City in 1990 and played over 200 games at Ashton Gate. A four year spell at Blackpool followed before Bent joined Kettering Town in 2001, later enjoying a short spell at Lancaster City. He later entered the banking world as a mortgage advisor in Preston and worked as the branch manager of Barclays Bank in Lancaster. Bent then worked as Business Relationship Manager at NatWest until 2014 when he joined Lombard as Relationship Manager before becoming Senior Relationship Manager in 2017. The former winger has also coached the youth teams at Preston North End for a number of years.

BERESFORD, David
Midfielder
Town Years: 1997-2001
Born: *1976 Manchester, Greater Manchester*
Playing career: *Oldham Athletic, Swansea City (loan), Huddersfield Town, Preston North End (loan), Hull City, Plymouth Argyle, (1994-2006)*

Beresford arrived at the McAlpine in 1997. He spent spent four uneventful years at Town before leaving for Hull City in 2001. Later played for Plymouth Argyle, Tranmere Rovers and Macclesfield Town before hanging up his boots. Beresford obtained a sports science degree at Manchester Metropolitan University and is now teaching at Wardle Academy in Rochdale.

BERRETT, James
Midfielder
Town Years: 2006-2010
Born: *1989 Halifax, West Yorkshire*
Playing career: *Huddersfield Town, Carlisle United, Yeovil Town, York City, Grimsby Town, F.C. Halifax Town (2006-Still Playing)*

Berrett was an academy graduate who spent four years in the first team squad before leaving in 2010 for Carlisle United. He spent four years at Brunton Park before enjoying short spells at Yeovil Town and York City, later heading to Grimsby Town in 2016 and spending two years at the club. After being released by the Mariners, Berrett is currently playing for non-league F.C. Halifax Town in the National Conference.

James Berrett

BETTANY, John
Wing-half
Town Years: 1959-1960 (amateur), 1960-1965
Born: *1937 Laughton Common*
Playing career: *Thurcroft, Huddersfield Town, Barnsley, Rotherham United, Goole Town (1959-1971)*

Having begun his career with non-league Thurcroft, Bettany arrived at Leeds Road in 1959 as an amateur from Wolverhampton Wanderers. He played for the club until 1965 before he moved to Barnsley, playing over 200 matches for the Tykes before leaving in 1970 to join Rotherham United. Bettany is currently living in Rotherham and is retired but unfortunately suffers from Alzheimer's.

BEVAN, Scott
Goalkeeper
Town Years: 2002-2003 (loan)
Born: *1979 Southampton, Hampshire*
Playing career: *Southampton, Huddersfield Town (loan), Woking (loan), Wycombe Wanderers (loan), Milton Keynes Dons, Tamworth (loan), Kidderminster Harriers, Shrewsbury Town, Torquay United, Bristol Rovers, Havant & Waterlooville (1997-2014)*

Bevan was signed on loan from Southampton at the beginning of the 2002-03 season and managed 30 league appearances before he picked up an injury and was replaced by the young keeper Phil Senior. He returned to his parent club in early 2003 and eventually left St. Mary's in 2004 to join Milton Keynes Dons. Bevan hung up his gloves, after a spell at non-league Havant & Waterlooville in 2014. Having previously worked as the goalkeeping coach for Portsmouth, Bevan is now the Under 23s goalkeeping coach at Birmingham City and also coaches goalkeepers, with Darryl Flahavan, for the Premier One Goalkeeping Academy, which is based in Southampton.

Paul Bielby

BIELBY, Paul
Left-winger
Town Years: 1978-1980
Born: *1956 Darlington, County Durham*
Playing career: *Manchester United, Hartlepool United, Huddersfield Town (1973-1980)*

Bielby signed from Hartlepool United in 1978 in a swap deal for Wayne Goldthorpe and played a handful of games during the 1978-79 season. He later damaged his ankle ligaments in a game and never played again, leaving the club and retiring from the game in 1980. Bielby worked as a director for a Blue Chip Food Company for fourteen years before setting up the Masterskills Football Academy in 1997. He has also been a player's agent since 1999 and is licenced by the Football Association. During the same year, Bielby formed the Darlington Primary Schools Football Association and is now running Paul Bielby's Football Academy. This tireless dedication was recognised in 2008 when he was awarded with an M.B.E. for his work in sport with young people.

BILLY, Christopher 'Chris'
Right-back, Right-winger
Town Years: 1991-1995
Born: *1973 Huddersfield, West Riding of Yorkshire*
Playing career: *Huddersfield Town, Plymouth Argyle, Notts County, Bury, Carlisle United, Halifax Town, Farsley Celtic, Ossett Town (loan) (1991-2008)*

Chris began his career at Leeds Road, breaking into the side during in 1991-92.

He played both at right-back and right-wing during his time at the club and scored the winning goal in the 1995 play-off final. It turned out to be his last game for the club as he joined Neil Warnock at Plymouth Argyle early on in the 1995-96 season. Billy later played for Bury, Notts County, Carlisle United and Halifax Town before eventually hanging up his boots in 2008. After his professional career ended, Billy began working for GE in Morley in customer retention. He went on to work as an Internal Key Account Manager for Pause... Thoughtful Refreshment in Wakefield and as a Business Development Manager at Reactiv Media in Halifax. He then spent nearly six years as an Internal Account Manager for PFF Packaging Group before taking his current role at eSales Hub in Doncaster where he works in Business Development. Billy has also had coaching spells at Bradford Park Avenue and Kirkburton and is now living in Elland.

COPE'S "CLIPS" CIGARETTES

No. 435.—BLACKBURN
Huddersfield Town
Noted Footballers

BINKS, Sidney 'Sid'

Centre-forward
Town Years: 1924-1925
Born: *1899 Bishop Auckland, County Durham*
Died: *1978 Sheffield, South Yorkshire*
Playing career: *Sheffield Wednesday, Huddersfield Town, Blackpool, Portsmouth, Southend United, Fulham, Chesterfield, Sheffield Wednesday (1919-1933)*
Binks arrived at Leeds Road in 1924 after signing from Sheffield Wednesday. He played four league games for Herbert Chapman's side before leaving the club and signing for Blackpool a year later. He remained at Bloomfield Road until 1927, and went on to play for Portsmouth, Southend United, Fulham, Chesterfield, had a further spell at Sheffield Wednesday and also played for non-league Ashington before he retired from the game in the mid 1930s. Binks later worked in Sheffield as a confectioner and baker, before he passed away in 1978.

BIRD, Kevin

Right-back
Town Years: 1983
Born: *1952 Doncaster, West Riding of Yorkshire*
Playing career: *Doncaster Rovers, Mansfield Town, Huddersfield Town (1972-1983)*
Bird arrived at Leeds Road prior to the 1983-84 season on non-contract forms.

He only played one solitary match for the club before leaving and later retiring from the game. Having played for Mansfield Town prior to his Town days, Bird returned to the area following his retirement and worked for supermarket chain, Tesco. He is currently suffering from Alzheimer's disease and a number of charity events have been organised at Mansfield Town in his honour.

BLACKBURN, George

Outside-right
Town Years: 1910-1912
Born: *1888 Worksop, Nottinghamshire*
Died: *1954 Worksop, Nottinghamshire*
Playing career: *Bradford Park Avenue, Huddersfield Town (1910-1912)*
Signing from Bradford Park Avenue in 1910, Blackburn played for Town during their first two years as a professional club and left Leeds Road in 1912. His playing career came to an end and Blackburn later returned to his native Worksop and worked as a coal hewer. The former outside-right was later incapacitated whilst working down the pit and subsequently passed away in 1954.

BLACKMAN, Frederick 'Fred'
Right-back
Town Years: 1911-1914
Born: *1884 Kennington, London*
Died: *1942 Gillingham, Kent*
Playing career: *Woolwich Arsenal, Hastings & St Leonards United, Brighton & Hove Albion, Huddersfield Town, Leeds City, Queens Park Rangers (1907-1922)*

Dick Pudan brought Blackman to Leeds Road in 1911, signing him from Brighton & Hove Albion. He spent three years at the club before his departure in 1914, when he signed for Leeds City. Blackman later played for Queens Park Rangers and ran a hotel in Gravesend before he passed away in 1942. Blackman had been a carpenter, cabinet-maker and keen piano player before he began his professional career.

BLACKWELL, Jack
Inside-forward
Town Years: 1931-1932
Born: *1909 Ecclesall, West Riding of Yorkshire*
Died: *2001 Sheffield, South Yorkshire*
Playing career: *Chapel-en-le-Frith, Huddersfield Town, Charlton Athletic, Port Vale, Boston United, Ipswich Town, Bridlington Town (1931-1937)*

Blackwell joined in 1931 and spent a year at the club without ever managing to cement a place in Clem Stephenson's side. He later played for Charlton Athletic, Port Vale, Boston United and Ipswich Town before heading into non-league to play for Bridlington Town. Blackwell later became the licensee of the Wentworth House Hotel in Sheffield at the before he passed away in 2001 at the age of 91.

BLACKWELL, Kevin
Goalkeeper, Reserve Manager, Youth Coach
Town Years: 1993-1995
Born: *1958 Luton, Bedfordshire*
Playing career: *Cambridge United, Barnet, Boston United, Scarborough, Notts County, Torquay United, Huddersfield Town, Plymouth Argyle, Sheffield United (1979-2000)*

'Blackie' arrived with Neil Warnock and combined his playing duties at Town with managing the reserves and youth teams (the latter with Gerry Murphy). After achieving promotion in 1995, Neil Warnock left for Plymouth Argyle and Kevin Blackwell followed him, along with assistant manager Mick Jones. Following Warnock's sacking in 1997, Mick Jones became manager and employed Blackwell as his assistant. He was reunited with Warnock at Bury in 1998, and then Sheffield United. After four years at the club, Blackwell left to join Leeds United as Peter Reid's assistant manager in 2003. He became the first team manager in 2004, lasting two years at Elland Road before getting the axe. He went on to manage Luton Town and Sheffield United and former club Bury. After previously falling out with Neil Warnock, they patched things up and he became Warnock's assistant manager at Crystal Palace in August 2014, but they only lasted until December before being relieved of their duties. After a short spell coaching at Barnet in 2015, Blackwell was reunited with Warnock at Queens Park Rangers as his assistant. He had a short spell as Warnock's assistant at Rotherham United in 2016 and is now his assistant manager at Cardiff City, having taken the job in October 2016.

BOJAJ, Florent 'Flo'
Forward
Town Years: 2014-2017
Born: *1996 London*
Playing career: *Boreham Wood, Huddersfield Town, Kilmarnock (loan), Newport County (loan), Welling United, Walton & Hersham, Pirin Blagoevgrad, Etar (2013-Still Playing)*

An academy graduate who made a handful of appearances in the first team before his departure in 2017. Since leaving the club, Bojaj has had short spells at Welling United and Walton & Hersham before signing for Pirin Blagoevgrad in Bulgaria, although he is now playing for Etar in the same country.

BOOT, Edmund 'Eddie'

Left-half, Reserve Team Coach, Caretaker Manager, Manager
Town Years: 1937-1952, 1952-1960 (reserve team coach), 1959-1960 (caretaker manager), 1960-1964 (manager)
Born: *1915 Laughton Common*
Died: *1999 Dewsbury, West Yorkshire*
Playing career: *Aughton, Denaby United, Sheffield United, Huddersfield Town (1934-1952)*
Management career: *Huddersfield T (1959-1964)*

Eddie Boot signed from Sheffield United in 1937 and this turned out to be the start of a twenty plus year association with Huddersfield Town. He played 325 games for the club and this included the 1938 FA Cup Final. After fifteen years as a player, Boot retired from professional football in 1952 and joined the coaching staff at Leeds Road, becoming the Reserve Coach. He remained in this post until 1960 when he took the manager's job following Bill Shankly's resignation. Boot resigned in 1964 and left football altogether, he had started his own business (with teammate John Battye), North Star Tyre Remoulds in 1953. He passed away in a Dewsbury care home in 1999.

BOOT, Leonard

Goalkeeper
Town Years: 1923-1925
Born: *1899 West Bromwich, Staffordshire*
Died: *1937 West Bromwich, Staffordshire*
Playing career: *York City, Huddersfield Town, Fulham, Bradford City, Nottingham Forest, Caernarfon Town, Worcester City (1923-1927)*

Boot was a goalkeeper that signed for Town in 1923 from York City. He managed ten appearances for the first team before he joined Fulham in 1925. A year at Craven Cottage was followed by spells at Nottingham Forest, non-league Caernarfon Town and Worcester City. Tragically died at the age of 38 after a motorcycle accident in West Bromwich in 1937.

"DID YOU KNOW?"

"Huddersfield Town became the first English club to win three successive league titles in 1924, 1925, and 1926 - a record which has been matched, but never overtaken."

Andy Booth

BOOTH, Andrew 'Andy'

Forward
Town Years: 1992-1996, 2001-2009
Born: *1973 Huddersfield, West Riding of Yorkshire*
Playing career: *Huddersfield Town, Scarborough, Sheffield Wednesday, Tottenham H (loan) (1992-2009)*

'Boothy', a club legend and a cult hero, played his first professional game for Town under Ian Ross in 1992 against Fulham. However, it was the arrival of Neil Warnock at Leeds Road that saw Booth become a lynchpin in the side. Boothy's best season was 1994-95, an exciting time for Town as the club moved to the new Alfred McAlpine Stadium and he and his strike partner Ronnie Jepson scored over 50 goals. Out of that 50 goals, Booth scored 30 and earned 3 England U21 caps, scoring 2 goals. Town were promoted in the Playoffs at Wembley at the end of the season with Booth scoring one of the goals. After Town failed to make the playoffs in the 1995-96 season, Boothy was sold to Sheffield Wednesday for a record fee of £2.7 million. He later had a 4 game spell on loan at Spurs and then returned to Town in a blaze of glory in 2001 but couldn't help Town from being relegated on the final day of the season. He decided to retire at the end of the 2008-09 season due to ongoing injury problems and after that announcement he managed 5 goals in the last 4 games of the season. He scored his 150th HTFC goal in his final game against Leyton Orient, leaving him 9 short of the record number set by George Brown in the 1920s. After turning down a coaching position in Lee Clark's backroom team, Boothy became Town's Club Ambassador.

Aidy Boothroyd

BOOTHROYD, Adrian 'Aidy'
Full-back
Town Years: 1987-1990
Born: *1971 Eccleshill, West Riding of Yorkshire*
Playing career: *Huddersfield Town, Bristol Rovers, Heart of Midlothian, Mansfield Town, Peterborough United (1987-1998)*

Boothroyd signed apprenticeship forms in 1987 and became a professional at Leeds Road in 1989. He only played 10 league games for the club before he signed for Bristol Rovers in 1990. Boothroyd had a short spell at Heart of Midlothian before joining Mansfield Town in 1993, he played 102 league games at Field Mill before ending his career at Peterborough United in 1998. After his retirement, Boothroyd coached the youth teams at London Road before joining Norwich City in 2001 as Youth Team Coach. Two years later he became the Youth Development Officer at West Bromwich Albion in 2003 but this was short-lived as he joined Leeds United as first team coach in 2004. Watford came calling in March 2005 and Boothroyd accepted the manager's job at the age of 34. Premier League status was obtained in Boothroyd's first full season in charge but the Hornets were relegated the season after. Boothroyd was sacked at Vicarage Road in 2008 after a poor run of results and he later had short spells as manager at Colchester United (2009-10), Coventry City (2010-11) and Northampton Town (2011-13). Boothroyd was appointed England U20 manager in 2014, later taking charge of the U19 team the year after and moving back to U20 side in 2016. Following Gareth Southgate's appointment as England manager in late 2016, Boothroyd became the manager of the England U21 side, where he remains.

BOOTY, Martyn
Full-back, Coach
Town Years: 2003-2004, 2004-2008 (coach)
Born: *1971 Kirby Muxloe, Leicestershire*
Playing career: *Coventry City, Crewe Alexandra, Reading, Southend United (loan), Southend United, Chesterfield, Huddersfield Town (1989-2009)*

Booty was snapped up from Chesterfield by Peter Jackson at the beginning of the 2003-04 season. He only managed four games in the first team before retiring and becoming a coach in Jackson's backroom staff. Booty remained as coach after Jackson's sacking in 2007 and worked under Andy Ritchie. When Stan Ternent became manager, Booty left the club along with John Dungworth at the end of the 2007-08 season. Booty later worked on the roads and as assistant manager at Hyde United. His son Regan has since played for Town's academy side.

BOTT, Wilfred 'Wilf'
Left-winger
Town Years: 1931-1934
Born: *1907 Featherstone, West Riding of Yorkshire*
Died: *1992 Hastings, East Sussex*
Playing career: *Edlington Colliery Welfare, Doncaster Rovers, Huddersfield Town, Newcastle United, Queens Park Rangers, Colchester United, Guilford City, Lancaster Town (1927-1946)*

Bott signed from Doncaster Rovers in 1931 and spent three years at Leeds Road, playing over a hundred games for the club before he signed for Newcastle United in 1934. After his retirement, Wilf became a bus conductor in Wembley but did come out of retirement to play two games for Colchester United in 1946. He passed away aged 85 in 1992.

BOTTRILL, Walter 'Billy'
Forward
Town Years: 1933-1934
Born: *1903 Eston, North Riding of Yorkshire*
Died: *1986 Eston, North Yorkshire*
Playing career: *Southbank, Middlesbrough, Nelson, Rotherham United, York City, Wolverhampton Wanderers, Huddersfield Town, Chesterfield (1922-1934)*

Bottrill signed from Wolverhampton Wanderers in 1933 and spent a year at Leeds Road before leaving for Chesterfield in 1934 for a fee of £400. He later lived in Eston, North Yorkshire where he worked as a fish and chips dealer before he passed away in 1986 at the age of 83.

BOYLE, William 'Will'
Defender
Town Years: 2015-2017
Born: *1995 Garforth, West Yorkshire*
Playing career: *Huddersfield Town, Kidderminster Harriers (loan), Macclesfield Town (loan), York City (loan), Kilmarnock (loan), Cheltenham Town (2015-Still Playing)*

Boyle began his career in the youth team in 2010, turning professional in 2015. He made 2 substitute appearances for the club and also had loan spells at Kidderminster Harriers, Macclesfield Town, York City and Kilmarnock before heading to Cheltenham Town on a permanent transfer in 2017. He is currently contracted at Whaddon Road until 2020.

BRANAGAN, James 'Jim'
Full-back
Town Years: 1977-1979
Born: *1955 Urmston, Lancashire*
Playing career: *Oldham Athletic, Cape Town City, Huddersfield Town, Blackburn Rovers, Preston North End, York City, Chorley (1974-1989)*

Branagan spent two years at Leeds Road before he left the club in 1979 to join Blackburn Rovers. He became a legend at Ewood Park and spent ten years there before rounding off his career with spells at Preston North End, York City and non-league Chorley, eventually hanging up his boots in 1989. After his retirement, Branagan worked in insurance for over 20 years before being made redundant. He now works for supermarket chain Tesco in East Lancashire.

BRANDON, Chris
Winger
Town Years: 2004-2008
Born: *1976 Bradford, West Yorkshire*
Playing career: *Bradford Park Avenue, Torquay United, Chesterfield, Huddersfield Town, Blackpool (loan), Bradford City (1995-2012)*

Peter Jackson brought Brandon in from Chesterfield for the 2004-05 season and he was immediately installed on the right-wing. He rarely missed a game during his four years at Town and he left the club in 2008, initially joining Bradford City, but then moved to Thailand in 2011 and joined BEC Tero Sasana. Brandon is back living in Bradford and owns a number of properties which he rents out and is also a registered FA Intermediary.

BREBNER, Ronald 'Ron'
Goalkeeper
Town Years: 1911-1912
Born: *1881 Darlington, County Durham*
Died: *1914 Chiswick, Middlesex*
Playing career: *Elgin City, Sunderland, Chelsea, Darlington, Leicester Fosse (1897-1914)*

Before his Town career began, Ron Brebner had competed in the 1908 London Olympics, keeping goal for the England team. He played for a year at Town, as an amateur, before signing for Leicester Fosse in 1912. He competed in the 1912 Stockholm Olympics, winning a gold medal. Brebner, who had worked as a dental surgeon, passed away in 1914 due to head injuries that he had sustained in a game.

1908 London Olympic Squad

BRENNAN, James 'Jim'
Defender
Town Years: 2001 (loan)
Born: *1977 East York, Ontario, Canada*
Playing career: *Bristol City, Nottingham Forest, Huddersfield Town (loan), Norwich City, Southampton, Toronto FC (1994-2010)*
Brennan spent a very short spell on loan at Town in 2001 from his parent club Nottingham Forest. He left the City Ground in 2003 for Norwich City, spending three years at Carrow Road before joining Southampton in 2006. Brennan's spell there was short lived and he moved back to Canada to play for Toronto FC in 2006. He later became their assistant general manager, head coach of their Academy U17 team, and then assistant coach of the first team until 2015. He took over as executive director of Aurora FC in 2015 and in 2017 become executive vice-president of York Sports & Entertainment. Jim is also Director of Soccer at York 9 F in Vaughan, Ontario.

BRIGGS, Thomas 'Tom'
Full-back
Town Years: 1946-1949
Born: *1919 Rotherham, West Riding of Yorkshire*
Died: *1999 Crewe, Cheshire*
Playing career: *Huddersfield T, Crewe (1946-1957)*
Briggs began his career at Leeds Road in 1946 after playing for the Army and managed just short of 50 appearances in the first team before his departure in 1949. He then went on to spend seven years at Crewe Alexandra, playing over 200 games at Gresty Road before his retirement in 1957. Briggs remained in Crewe after his retirement and passed away in 1999 at the age of 80.

BROADBENT, Daniel
Forward
Town Years: 2007-2009
Born: *1990 Leeds, West Yorkshire*
Playing career: *Howden Clough, Clifton, Huddersfield Town, Huddersfield Town, Rushden & Diamonds (loan), Gateshead (loan), Harrogate Town (loan), Harrogate Town, Frickley Athletic (loan), Frickley Athletic, Curzon Ashton, Hyde, Mossley (loan), Mossley (2007-2013)*
Broadbent began his career at Town and was well thought of as a young player. However, he only made a couple of substitute appearances before leaving the club in 2009 to sign for Harrogate Town.

He has since played for a number of non-league clubs including Frickley Athletic, Curzon Ashton, Hyde United and Mossley. Broadbent now makes his living by selling perfume online.

BROCK, Frederick 'Fred'
Left-back
Town Years: 1920-1921
Born: *1891 Bradford, West Riding of Yorkshire*
Died: *1947 Bradford, West Riding of Yorkshire*
Playing career: *Huddersfield Town (1920-1921)*
Brock had a very short spell at Leeds Road between 1920 and 1921 where he played one match for the first team before leaving at the end of the 1920-21 season. He later lived in Bradford and worked as a textile warehouseman in the city before passing away in 1947.

BROOK, Daryl
Forward
Town Years: 1977-1980
Born: *1960 Holmfirth, West Riding of Yorkshire*
Playing career: *Huddersfield Town (1977-1999)*
Brook signed as an apprentice in 1977 and made one solitary appearance. He went to play for non-league Emley and apart from one season in Germany, he served them for the best part of two decades. He now runs his own building company, Daryl Brook Builders in Shepley and has been a Town season ticket holder for many years.

BROOK, Lewis
Forward
Town Years: 1936-1937 (amateur), 1937-1948
Born: *1918 Halifax, West Riding of Yorkshire*
Died: *1996 Halifax, West Yorkshire*
Playing career: *Northowram, Halifax Town, Huddersfield Town, Oldham Athletic (1934-1957)*
Brook signed for the club in 1936 as an amateur, after previously having a spell at Halifax Town, and went on to spend twelve years at Leeds Road. However, the outbreak of World War Two interrupted his playing career and this limited him to only about 20 appearances in those twelve years before he headed to Oldham Athletic. He spent ten years at Boundary Park, playing over 200 games before his retirement in 1957 to take a position out of the game in his native Halifax. Brook was still living in Halifax when he passed away in 1996.

BROUGH, Henry 'Harry'

Wing-half
Town Years: 1913-1923
Born: *1896 Gainsborough, Lincolnshire*
Died: *1975 Longton, Staffordshire*
Playing career: *Kilnhurst, Huddersfield Town, Manchester United, Stoke City (1912-1925)*

Brough arrived at Leeds Road in 1913 from Kilnhurst but just a year later his career at Town was interrupted by the outbreak of war. Once the hostilities had ended he helped Town gain promotion to the First Division in 1920 under manager Ambrose Langley. He joined Manchester United in February 1923 but didn't last long at Old Trafford, later signing for Stoke City. Brough spent two years at the club and retired there in October 1925. Gainsborough-born Brough remained in Stoke-on-Trent and worked as a potter's dipper and passed away in 1975 at the age of 79.

BROWN, Alan

Centre-half
Town Years: 1933-1936, 1937-1946
Born: *1914 Corbridge, Northumberland*
Died: *1996 Bideford, Devon*
Playing career: *Corbridge United, Spen Black & White, Huddersfield Town, Burnley, Notts County (1930-1949)*

Brown began his career at Corbridge United in 1930 and played for Spen Black & White before his cousin, Austen Campbell, persuaded to him to come to Leeds Road in 1933 and join the club as a trainee. Brown had hoped that Town would sponsor his further education but this didn't happen and he left to join the police force in 1936. However, he still had the urge to be a professional footballer and returned to the game within a couple of years. Due to rules at the time, players were unable to change clubs so he rejoined Town and broke into the first team, but this coincided with the Second World War. He opened a restaurant in Burnley after his retirement and later worked as a coach at Sheffield Wednesday in 1951. Brown managed Burnley and Sunderland. During a second spell with Wednesday, he led them to the 1966 FA Cup Final where they lost to Everton. Suffering from ill health in his retirement, Alan Brown passed away in 1996 while he was living in Bideford, Devon.

BROWN, George 'Bomber'

Forward
Town Years: 1921-1929
Born: *1903 Mickley, Northumberland*
Died: *1948 Birmingham, Warwickshire*
Playing career: *Mickley Colliery, Huddersfield Town, Aston Villa, Burnley, Leeds United, Darlington (1921-1938)*

'Bomber' Brown, signed in 1921 from Mickley Colliery and spent eight years at the club during which time he scored 159 goals, a record that still stands today. During his time at the club, Brown won the 1922 FA Cup and Charity Shield and the 1924, 1925 and 1926 First Division titles. In 2018, those three medals were auctioned off for £20,000, although the club were not interested in bringing them back to their natural home. Brown left Town in 1929 to sign for Aston Villa, spending five years there before rounding his career off with short spells at Burnley, Leeds United and Darlington before retiring from the game in 1938. He later ran the Star Public House in Birmingham before passing away in 1948 at the age of 44.

BROWN, Isaiah 'Izzy'

Midfielder
Town Years: 2017 (loan)
Born: *1997 Peterborough, Cambridgeshire*
Playing career: *Leicester City, WBA, Chelsea, Vitesse (loan), Rotherham United (loan), Huddersfield Town (loan), Brighton & Hove Albion (loan), Leeds United (loan) (2013-Still Playing)*

One of Chelsea's up and coming youngsters, Brown arrived in early 2017 on loan from Stamford Bridge, having previously had a spell at Rotherham United. He scored in the 2-1 win over Leeds United in February and also scored the goal that sealed Town's play-off place in April against Wolves. Brown also played in the play-off final against Reading but returned to Chelsea shortly after that. He was loaned out to Brighton for the 2017-18 season but suffered an injury in his first game. Brown spent the 2018-19 season on loan at Leeds United.

"DID YOU KNOW?"

"Peter Hart is the youngest player to ever play for Town at 16 years and 229 days."

BROWN, Kenneth 'Kenny'

Defender
Town Years: 1995 (loan)
Born: *1967 Barking, Essex*
Playing career: *Norwich City, Plymouth Argyle, West Ham United, Huddersfield Town (loan), Reading (loan), Southend United (loan), Crystal Palace (loan), Reading (loan), Birmingham City (loan), Birmingham City, Millwall, Gillingham, Kingstonian, Portadown, Barry Town, Tilbury, CD Torrevieja (1986-2003)*

Brian Horton brought Kenny Brown to the club during the 1995-96 season on loan from West Ham United. He played 5 matches for the first team before returning to Upton Park. He left the club the following year after spending time on loan at Reading, Southend United, Crystal Palace, Reading and Birmingham City. Brown later played for Millwall and Gillingham before heading into non-league in 1999, playing for Kingstonian, Portadown, Barry Town (as player-manager) and Tilbury before becoming the manager of Spanish club CD Javea in 2006. A return to the UK saw him become assistant manager to Julian Dicks at Grays Athletic, and then take on manager's job at Tooting & Mitcham United. He later worked as assistant manager at Chelmsford City in 2013, and acted as caretaker manager after Dean Holdsworth was sacked. Brown is currently the Head of Academy Coaching at Millwall's academy.

BROWN, Malcolm 'Mally'

Right-back
Town Years: 1977-1983, 1985-1989
Born: *1956 Salford, Lancashire*
Playing career: *Bury, Huddersfield Town, Newcastle United, Rochdale, Stockport County (1973-1992)*

Brown originally signed from Bury in 1977 by Tom Johnston and became a cult hero at Town. He forced his way into the first team at the expense of Alan Sweeney and made the place his own. It wasn't until Mick Buxton became manager that his talents were utilised fully. Brown was part of the 1979-80 Fourth Division winning side and also the 1982-83 promotion winning side. He played 259 consecutive matches for Town before getting a big money move to First Division Newcastle United. However, a bad leg break there meant that he hardly got any game time there and he returned to Leeds Road in 1985 and featured in the infamous 10-1 defeat at Manchester City in 1987.

Brown later left the club in 1989 after falling out of favour and stating that he didn't want to stay in the reserve side. Brown played for Rochdale twice and Stockport County before retiring from professional football in 1992. He is now a driving instructor in Droylsden, running his own business, MBM Driving School.

BROWN, Nathaniel 'Nat'

Defender, Winger, Forward
Town Years: 1998-2005
Born: *1981 Sheffield, South Yorkshire*
Playing career: *Huddersfield Town, Lincoln City, Wrexham, Macclesfield Town (loan), Macclesfield Town, Lincoln City (loan), FC Halifax Town (loan), Harrogate Town (loan), Boston United, Brighouse Town (player-assistant manager) (1998-Still Playing)*

Brown played in every outfield position for Town, originally a forward, he was later converted to centre half. Making his debut under Mick Wadsworth in the 2002-03 season, the Yorkshireman spent six years at Town before being released in 2005. Brown joined Lincoln City, spending three years at Sincil Bank before leaving the club in 2008 and later went on to have spells at Wrexham, Macclesfield Town and Boston United but is now player-assistant manager at Brighouse Town and also works as a bus driver for Stagecoach in his native Sheffield.

BROWN, William 'Buster'

Wing-half
Town Years: 1935-1937
Born: *1909 Silvertown, London*
Died: *1993 Ealing, Greater London*
Playing career: *Luton Town, Huddersfield Town, Leyton Orient, Chingford Town (1930-1948)*

Brown spent two years at Leeds Road but only managed a handful of appearances at the club before he transferred to Brentford in March 1937. He spent ten years at Griffin Park but a huge chunk of his career there was interrupted by the outbreak of the Second World War. After the hostilities had ended, Brown signed for Leyton Orient in 1947 but only remained at the club for a year before his departure in 1948. After a spell at Chingford Town, Brown hung up his boots and retired from professional football, later working as a coach at Wycombe Wanderers. Brown remained down South and was living in Ealing when he passed away in 1993 at the age of 82.

BROWNING, Marcus
Midfielder
Town Years: 1997-1999
Born: *1971 Bristol, Gloucestershire*
Playing career: *Bristol Rovers, Gloucester City (loan), Weymouth (loan), Gloucester City (loan), Hereford United (loan), Huddersfield Town, Gillingham (loan), Gillingham, Bournemouth, Weymouth, Bath City, Poole Town (1989-2010)*

Browning signed from Bristol Rovers in 1997, spent two years at Town but only played a handful of games before he left for Gillingham. He played there for three years before ending his career at AFC Bournemouth in 2007. When his Football League career ended and he began to turn out for non-league Weymouth. Browning later had spells at Bath City and Poole Town and also coached at former club Bournemouth but is now working as a window-cleaner, running his own business Superclean in Verwood, Dorset.

Steve Bruce

BRUCE, Alex
Centre-half
Town Years: 2011 (loan)
Born: *1984 Norwich, Norfolk*
Playing career: *Blackburn Rovers, Blackburn Rovers, Oldham Athletic (loan), Birmingham City, Oldham Athletic (loan), Sheffield Wednesday (loan), Tranmere Rovers (loan), Ipswich Town, Leicester City (loan), Leeds United, Huddersfield Town (loan), Hull City, Wigan Athletic (loan), Bury, Wigan Athletic (2004-Still Playing)*

Bruce joined the club on a loan deal in the 2011-12 season after falling out with Leeds United manager Simon Grayson in late 2011. He only managed to play 3 matches for Town before heading back to Leeds early on in 2012. The son of Steve Bruce, he has since spent timel at Hull City with his father and that was followed by short spells at Bury and Wigan Athletic but is now plying his trade for Kilmarnock.

BRUCE, Stephen 'Steve'
Manager
Town Years: 1999-2000
Born: *1960 Corbridge, Northumberland*
Management career: *Sheffield United, Huddersfield Town, Wigan Athletic, Crystal Palace, Birmingham City, Wigan Athletic, Sunderland, Hull City, Aston Villa (1998-present)*

After a spell as manager of Sheffield United, Town moved to appoint Bruce as manager at the end of the 1998-99 season.

His first season is fondly remembered by Town fans and the football that was played by Bruce is often described as some of the best ever seen at the club. Town led Division One for a spell during the season and promotion to the Premier League seemed likely. However, in February 2000 Bruce sold Marcus Stewart to Ipswich Town and the season was derailed, Town ended up finishing 8th, thus missing out on a playoff place. Bruce only won one match the following season before getting sacked in October 2000 after the disastrous start to the season, Town were rooted to the bottom of the table. He later had short spells at Wigan Athletic and Crystal Palace in 2001 before he joined Birmingham City, spending six years at the club, achieving promotion to the Premier League. He was appointed manager of former club Wigan in 2007 and spent two years at the JJB Stadium before he was offered the Sunderland job in 2009. Bruce spent two years at the Stadium of Light before he was sacked in 2011. He also managed Hull City between 2012 and 2016 before becoming the manager of Aston Villa in October 2016. Bruce was sacked from his job at Villa Park in October 2018 after a poor run of results but didn't have to wait long before being offered the hotseat at Sheffield Wednesday.

BULLOCK, Darren

Central-midfielder
Town Years: 1993-1997
Born: 1969 Worcester, Worcestershire
Playing career: Nuneaton Borough, Huddersfield Town, Swindon Town, Bury, Rushden & Diamonds (loan), Sheffield United (loan), Worcester City (1992-2002)

'Bully' was a window cleaner and was playing part-time for Nuneaton Borough before Neil Warnock plucked him from obscurity during the 1993-94 season. He instantly became a cult hero at Town for his no-nonsense and committed style of play and managed to break into the side near the end of the 1993-94 season and played in the Autoglass Final at Wembley. Bullock was a major player in the 1994-95 promotion season and scored the winning penalty in the playoff semi-final penalty shootout against Brentford and also played in the Playoff Final, again at Wembley Stadium. Known for his hot head and fiery temper, Bullock was made captain by Brian Horton during the 1995-96 season, a role that he revelled in. He eventually left Town for Swindon Town in 1997 and later had spells at Bury, Rushden and Diamonds (loan) and Sheffield United (loan) before heading back to his hometown to sign for non-league Worcester City. He later played in the district league in Worcester and works a window cleaner there. 'Bully' is still well received when he returns to Huddersfield, receiving a hero's welcome on each occasion.

BULLOCK, Frederick 'Fred'

Left-back
Town Years: 1910-1922
Born: 1886 Whitton, London
Died: 1922 Huddersfield, West Riding of Yorkshire
Playing career: Hounslow Town, Custom House, Ilford, Huddersfield Town (1909-1922)

Bullock joined Town in 1910 and quickly became the captain of the side. The outbreak of World War One in 1914 saw Bullock serving with the 1st Football Battalion, the 17th Middlesex. He saw action at Delville Wood and Guillemont on the Somme and was wounded in both the shoulder and knee in 1918. Following the end of the hostilities, Bullock returned to Leeds Road and even supported the fundraising which saved the club from merging with Leeds United in 1919.

He was the captain of the side that won promotion to the First Division and finished runners-up in the FA Cup, both in 1920. Bullock retired from the game in 1922 and became the landlord of the Slubbers Arms in Huddersfield. However, tragedy struck later that year as Bullock was found by his wife next to a beer bottle that had contained ammonia. Although it wasn't established whether Bullock had meant to take the ammonia, the coroner believed that he had done. His funeral was attended by Herbert Chapman and the entire Town squad.

BUNGAY, Frank

Centre-forward
Town Years: 1931-1933
Born: 1909 Ecclesfield, West Riding of Yorkshire
Died: 1990 Sheffield, South Yorkshire
Playing career: Ecclesfield, Ecclesfield Red Rose, Norton Woodseats, Bolton Wanderers, Mexborough Athletic, Huddersfield Town, Southend United, Boston Town, Gresley Rovers, Grantham Town (1931-1936)

Bungay signed from Mexborough Athletic in 1931 but only managed 1 solitary appearance in the 1931-32 season, he made the rest of his appearances in the 1932-33 season and was sold to Southend United at the end of that season. He went on to have a successful spell at Boston Town and later played for Grantham Town and Gresley Rovers before he hung up his boots. Bungay later worked as a fitter in Wortley and passed away in Sheffield in April 1990.

BUNN, Harry

Forward
Town Years: 2014-2017
Born: 1992 Oldham, Lancashire
Playing career: Manchester City, Crewe Alexandra (loan), Sheffield United (loan), Huddersfield Town (loan), Huddersfield Town, Bury (2011-Still Playing)

After beginning his career at Manchester City, Bunn arrived at the club on a short term deal towards the end of the 2013-14 season. His performances impressed Mark Robins and he was given a new contract for the 2014-15 season and remained at the club until 2017, even playing a couple of games in Town's first Premier League season before David Wagner allowed him to sign for Lee Clark's Bury. During the 2018-19 season, Bunn spent time on loan at Southend United.

BURKE, David

Left-back
Town Years: 1981-1987
Born: *1960 Liverpool, Lancashire*
Playing career: *Bolton Wanderers, Huddersfield Town, Crystal Palace, Bolton Wanderers, Blackpool (1977-1996)*

'Burkey' enjoyed a six year spell at Leeds Road, impressing with his classy performances at left-back, replacing the popular Fred Robinson, who had suffered from injuries and had been forced to retire. Burke played in the 1982-83 promotion season and was a mainstay in the side before he suffered a horrific leg break in 1985, inflicted by Jeff Hopkin. He only managed 35 appearances in the next three seasons before departing for Crystal Palace in 1987. Burke remained at Selhurst Park until 1990, when he rejoined his first club Bolton Wanderers and was later signed by his former Bolton and Town team-mate, Sam Allardyce at Blackpool in 1994, remaining at Bloomfield Road until his retirement from the game in 1996. He is now thought to be working for Nationwide Bank and living in Warrington.

BURKE, Ronald 'Ronnie'

Centre-forward
Town Years: 1949-1953
Born: *1921 Dormanstown, Redcar, North Riding of Yorkshire*
Died: *2004 Watford, Hertfordshire*
Playing career: *St Albans City, Luton Town, Manchester United, Manchester United, Huddersfield Town, Rotherham United, Exeter City, Tunbridge Wells United, Biggleswade Town (1941-1961)*

Burke signed from Manchester United in 1949 and spent four years at Leeds Road. Although Burke did manage to break into the side, he never really managed to hold down a permanent place in the line-up and after spending the 1952-53 season out of action he was sold to Rotherham United by Andy Beattie. He had a very successful spell at Millmoor, managing 56 goals in just 73 league appearances before heading to Exeter City in 1955. Burke spent two years playing for the Grecians before he headed into non-league, playing for both Tunbridge Wells United and Biggleswade Town before hanging up his boots. After working for Rolls Royce as a progress section leader, Burke passed away in 2004 at the age of 82.

BURNETT, Wayne

Midfielder
Town Years: 1996 (loan), 1996-1998
Born: *1971 Lambeth, Greater London*
Playing career: *Leyton Orient, Blackburn Rovers, Plymouth Argyle, Bolton Wanderers, Huddersfield Town (loan), Huddersfield Town, Grimsby Town (loan), Grimsby Town, Peterborough U (1989-2004)*

Burnett was brought to the McAlpine by Brian Horton in 1996, originally on a loan deal from Bolton Wanderers. Dropped into non-league football and spells as manager at Fisher Athletic (twice), Dulwich Hamlet and Grays Athletic. Burnett joined Dagenham & Redbridge in 2009 as John Still's assistant manager, later becoming caretaker manager and then permanent manager in 2013. He was lacked in 2015 and has been the head coach of Tottenham Hotspur's Under 23 side ince 2017, replacing Ugo Ehiogu who had sadly died shortly beforehand.

BURNISTON, Gordon

Forward
Town Years: 1910-1912
Born: *1888 Knaresborough, West Riding of Yorkshire*
Died: *1934 Wharfedale, West Riding of Yorkshire*
Playing career: *Darlington, Huddersfield Town, Merthyr Town (1910-1912)*

Burniston arrived at Leeds Road in August 1910 after signing from Darlington. He spent two years at the club before he signed for Merthyr Town in July 1912. Burniston passed away in Wharfedale in 1934 after suffering from dementia paralytica. He had been working as a motor driver before his diagnosis and subsequent death.

BURRELL, Gerald 'Gerry'

Outside-right
Town Years: 1953-1956
Born: *1924 Belfast, Northern Ireland*
Died: *2014 Belfast, Northern Ireland*
Playing career: *Dundee, Huddersfield Town, Chesterfield, Portadown (1947-c1958)*

After spells in Scotland at St Mirren and Dundee, Gerry Burrell arrived at Leeds Road in December 1953. He spent three years at the club, playing at outside-right, before he moved on to Chesterfield where he remained until moving back to his native Northern Ireland to play for Portadown and several more local sides. For over fifty years, Burrell scouted for Linfield before he passed away at the age of 90 in 2014.

BUTLER, Andrew 'Andy'

Centre-half
Town Years: 2008-2010
Born: *1983 Doncaster, South Yorkshire*
Playing career: *Scunthorpe United, Grimsby Town (loan), Huddersfield Town, Blackpool (loan), Walsall, Sheffield United, Walsall (loan), Doncaster Rovers (loan), Doncaster Rovers (2002-Still Playing)*

One of Stan Ternent's signings at the beginning of the 2008-09 season, Butler signed from Scunthorpe United and went straight into the first team at centre-half, but eventually fell out of favour with new manager, Lee Clark. He spent a time on loan at Blackpool before eventually leaving the club in 2010, for Walsall wherre he became their club captain . He had a short spell at Sheffield United before joining Doncaster Rovers in 2015, where he remains. Butler has expressed an interest in becoming a referee, once his playing days come to an end.

BUTLER, Michael 'Mick'

Forward
Town Years: 1976-1978
Born: *1951 Barnsley, West Riding of Yorkshire*
Playing career: *Worsbrough Bridge MW, Barnsley, Huddersfield Town, Bournemouth, Bury (1972-1982)*

Butler signed from Barnsley in 1976 and lasted two years at Leeds Road. He won the Player of the Year award at the end of the 1977-78 season after finishing top scorer with 19 goals in all competitions. He left for Bournemouth shortly after and spent two years down South before heading back to the North to play for Bury. Butler left Bury in 1982 and retired from professional football. The Yorkshireman was originally a colliery electrician at Dodworth Colliery and returned to his roots once his playing career ended. He later worked at Selby Coalfield and is now living in Barnsley in retirement and he plays a lot of golf, including with former Town player, Bob Mountain.

BUTLER, Peter

Midfielder
Town Years: 1982-1986, 1992 (loan)
Born: *1966 Halifax, West Riding of Yorkshire*
Playing career: *Huddersfield Town, Cambridge United (loan), Bury, Cambridge United, Southend United, Huddersfield Town (loan), West Ham United, Notts County, Grimsby Town (loan), West Bromwich Albion (loan), West Bromwich Albion, Halifax Town, Sorrento FC (1984-2002)*

Butler began his career in the youth team at Leeds Road in 1982 but was sold to Bury in 1986, making only five league appearances. He had a successful career in league football, turning out Cambridge United and Southend United in the late 1980s to early 1990s. Butler returned to Leeds Road towards the end of the 1991-92 promotion chasing season and was a crucial part in Town's upturn of fortunes but was refused permission to play in the play-offs by his parent club Southend. He signed for West Ham United the same year, and spent two years there before heading to Notts County. Butler had a short spell as caretaker manager at Halifax Town in 2000 before heading abroad to be player-manager of Sorrento FC in Australia. Since then he has had a long career in management taking in Sabah FA in Borneo, the Singapore Armed Forces team, Persida in Indonesia, the Kelentan FA side, technical director of Yangoon United in Burma, BEC Tero Sasana in Thailand, Terengganu in Malaysia, the Botswana national side, Platinum Stars in South Africa and was last working as the manager of Persipura Jayapura in Indonesia.

BUTT, Leonard 'Len'

Inside-forward
Town Years: 1935-1937
Born: *1910 Wilmslow, Cheshire*
Died: *1994 Macclesfield, Cheshire*
Playing career: *Morley Rovers, Ashton National, Stockport County, Macclesfield Town, Huddersfield Town, Blackburn Rovers, York City, Mansfield Town, Mossley (1925-1948)*

Clem Stephenson signed Butt from Macclesfield Town in 1935 and he spent two years at the club, playing over 70 games at Leeds Road. Butt was ever-present during the 1935-36 season, when the club finished third in Division One but he left for Blackburn Rovers in January 1937 and spent ten years at Ewood Park before moving onto York City in 1947. Butt only lasted a year at Bootham Crescent before he signed for Mansfield Town in 1948. He retired from professional football later in the same year and went on to work as a stonemason and also managed Mossley and Macclesfield Town on a part-time basis. Butt passed away in 1994 aged 83 in Macclesfield after suffering from a series of strokes.

BUTTERFIELD, Jacob
Midfielder
Town Years: 2014-2015
Born: *1990 Bradford, West Yorkshire*
Playing career: *Barnsley, Norwich City, Bolton Wanderers (loan), Crystal Palace (loan), Middlesbrough, Huddersfield Town, Derby County, Sheffield Wednesday (loan) (2007-Still Playing)*

Signed from Middlesbrough in 2014 in exchange for Adam Clayton, Butterfield was well liked by Town fans and was highly rated. However, before a crucial away game during the 2014-15 season, he refused to board the team coach when he found out that Derby County were interested in buying him. He was later sold to Derby County for £5 million and remains at Pride Park, but spent a spell on loan at Sheffield Wednesday during the 2017-18 season.

Mick Buxton

BUXTON, Michael 'Mick'
First Team Coach, Physiotherapist, Caretaker Manager, Manager
Town Years: 1977-1978 (first team coach and physiotherapist), 1978 (caretaker manager), 1978-1986 (manager), 1993 (first team coach)
Born: *1943 Corbridge, Northumberland*
Management career: *Huddersfield Town, Scunthorpe United, Sunderland, Scunthorpe United (1978-1997)*

Buxton joined Town in 1977 as physiotherapist and also took training under Tom Johnston. Johnston resigned early on in the 1978-79 season and the board of directors asked Buxton to take caretaker charge of the club. After 12 games, Buxton was given the manager's job on a full time basis and he set about putting his mark on the club. He steered the club to the Fourth Division title in the 1979-80 season and the team scored 101 goals as they fired towards promotion. The 1979-80 team are legends at the club and are still warmly received whenever they return to the club, reunions have been organised in 2000, 2010, 2016 and 2017. He also managed Town to a second promotion in the 1982-83 season. After that, the club were battling relegation in the Second Division and although they survived a number of successive seasons, Town were in the the relegation zone when he was sacked in December 1986. Buxton had a spell as manager at Scunthorpe United between 1987 and 1991 and later returned to Town in 1993, where they were bottom of the league, as First Team Coach under

Ian Ross and oversaw 'The Great Escape' with Town surviving relegation. He left to join Sunderland as Terry Butcher's assistant manager later that year and took over as manager of the first team when Butcher was sacked. He left Roker Park in 1995 and between 1996 and 1997 managed Scunthorpe for a second time. Buxton later worked for the Premier League as a technical monitor but is now living in retirement in Doncaster with Maureen and receives a hero's welcome each and every time he returns to Huddersfield and also has a life season ticket which was given to him, John Haselden, Jimmy Robson, Steve Smith and the whole of the 1979-80 promotion winning side.

BYERS, John 'Jack'
Winger
Town Years: 1921-1923
Born: *1897 Selby, North Riding of Yorkshire*
Died: *1931 Worcester, Worcestershire*
Playing career: *Huddersfield Town, Blackburn Rovers, West Bromwich Albion, Worcester City, Torquay United, Kidderminster Harriers (1920-1931)*

Byers arrived from Selby Town in 1921 but didn't make his debut until 1922 against Tottenham Hotspur. He made a handful of appearances at Leeds Road before he left the club to sign for Blackburn Rovers in April 1923. Spells at West Brom, Worcester City, Torquay United and Kidderminster Harriers followed. He passed away in 1931 whilst living in Worcester.

Mick Byrne (centre)

BYRNE, Michael 'Mick'

Forward

Town Years: 1988-1990
Born: *1960 Dublin, Ireland*
Playing career: *ADO Den Haag, Huddersfield Town, Shelbourne (loan), Sligo Rovers, Dundalk, Monaghan United, Dundalk (loan), Dundalk, St James's Gate (player-manager), Athlone Town, Shamrock Rovers (player-manager) (1978-1999)*

Byrne signed from Shamrock Rovers in 1988 and he spent two years at Leeds Road, remembered for his skillful performances, Byrne headed back to Shamrock Rovers in 1990. He later had spells at Sligo Rovers, Dundalk, Shelbourne and Monaghan United before becoming player-manager of St. James Gate in 1996. Byrne left for Shamrock Rovers in 1997 to become their player-manager, remaining until 1999. He is a legend at Shamrock Rovers and is the manager of their legends team, manager of the Republic of Ireland Master's side and also runs his own business, MB Kitchens and Floors in his native Dublin. Byrne returned to Huddersfield in 2017, nearly thirty years after his departure, to attend the Manchester United game at the John Smith's Stadium, which saw Town win 2-1 in the Premier League fixture.

CADAMARTERI, Daniel 'Danny'

Winger, Forward

Town Years: 2007-2009, 2011-2012
Born: *1979 Cleckheaton, West Yorkshire*
Playing career: *Everton, Fulham (loan), Bradford City, Leeds United, Sheffield United, Grays Athletic, Leicester City, Doncaster Rovers (loan), Huddersfield Town, Dundee United, Carlisle United (1996-2014)*

After a short spell at Leicester City, 'Cads' was signed by Andy Ritchie for the 2007-08 season.

However, he was blighted by injuries in his first season and missed most of it either through suspension or injury. Despite this, he made a massive impact the season after, mostly under new manager Lee Clark and was instrumental in a late play-off push which saw Town miss out by just one point. He left at the end of the 2008-09 season as he was unhappy with the contract that was on the table. He signed for Dundee United and spent a season and a half there before he returned to Town in the January 2011 transfer window. Cadamarteri was employed as an impact sub for the next two seasons before being released by Simon Grayson at the end of 2011-12. He had a two year spell at Carlisle United before being forced to retire due to a knee injury. After a short period spent coaching Leeds Ladies, 'Cads' began coaching at the Sheffield Wednesday academy and in 2017. He moved to Burnley to work as the U18s Professional Development Phase Coach but left the role in October 2018 to pursue other opportunities. Cadamarteri also runs his own football academy and is helped by former Town players Phil Wilson and Dave Nichols, amongst other coaches.

Danny Cadamarteri

Terry Caldwell

He only played 4 league games before moving to neighbours Leeds United in 1959. After two years at Elland Road, he joined Carlisle United in 1961 and remained at Brunton Park until 1970, playing over 350 games for the club. Short spells at Barrow and Wakefield followed before Caldwell called time on his career in the early 1970s. He now resides in Royston, Barnsley in retirement.

CALLAGHAN, Nigel

Right-winger
Town Years: 1992 (loan)
Born: *1962 Singapore*
Playing career: *Watford, Derby County, Aston Villa, Derby County (loan), Watford (loan), Huddersfield Town (loan), Stafford Rangers, Hellenic (1980-1994)*
Callaghan joined Eoin Hand's side on loan from Aston Villa in 1991 and played 8 games before he returned to Villa Park. Callaghan left Villa the year after, later playing for Stafford Rangers and Hellenic before he hung up his boots in 1994. Callaghan was diagnosed with bowel cancer in 2009 but has now thankfully recovered. He now works as a DJ, performing all over the world, while residing in Stafford.

CALDWELL, Terence 'Terry'

Right-back
Town Years: 1956-1957 (amateur), 1957-1959
Born: *1938 Wakefield, West Riding of Yorkshire*
Playing career: *Huddersfield Town, Leeds United, Carlisle United, Barrow, Wakefield (1956-1972)*
Caldwell joined the club as an amateur player in 1956 before turning professional a year later in 1957.

Nigel Callaghan

CAMERON, Jack

Centre-forward
Town Years: 1911
Born: *Dornoch, Scotland*
Died: *1916 (Killed in Action)*
Playing career: *Huddersfield Town (1911)*

Cameron arrived at the club in August 1911 after playing for Dornoch in his native Scotland. He spent two months at the club, playing 2 matches in the first team before he was released in October of the same year. Private Cameron was later killed in World War One in early 1916.

CAMPBELL, Austen 'Aussie'

Left-half
Town Years: 1929-1935
Born: *1901 Hamsterley, County Durham*
Died: *1981 Blackburn, Lancashire*
Playing career: *Spen Black & White, Leadgate Park, Coventry City, Leadgate Park, Blackburn Rovers, Huddersfield Town, Hull City, Darwen (1917-1938)*

Campbell transferred to Leeds Road in 1929 from Blackburn Rovers, where he had played on the team responsible for defeating Town in the 1928 FA Cup Final. He spent six years at Town, playing over 200 games at left-half before he left the club to sign for Hull City in 1935. However, he only managed 11 games during the 1935-36 season and left to join Darwen in 1936. After his retirement, Campbell returned to Blackburn and worked in a brewery, later running a public house in the area, before he passed away at the age of 80 in 1981.

CAMPBELL, Robert 'Bobby'

Forward
Town Years: 1975-1977, 1978
Born: *1956 Belfast, Northern Ireland*
Died: *2016 Huddersfield, West Yorkshire*
Playing career: *Aston Villa, Halifax Town (loan), Huddersfield Town, Sheffield United, Vancouver Whitecaps, Halifax Town, Brisbane City, Bradford City, Derby County, Bradford City, Wigan Athletic (1972-1988)*

Campbell arrived at Leeds Road from Aston Villa in 1975, and spent two years at Town before he left for Sheffield United in 1977. He left Bramall Lane the following year and played for Vancouver Whitecaps before Town's board of directors brought him back to the club during the 1978-79 season. Mick Buxton had, by then, become manager and was not a fan of Campbell, showing him the door after only seven matches.

He spent time at Halifax Town and Brisbane City before he joined Bradford City in 1979. Campbell is Bradford's record goal scorer, he played for them between 1979 and 1983 and again between 1983 and 1986. He finished his career at Wigan Athletic in 1988 and became the steward of Lindley WMC, serving there for 25 years before he and his wife were arrested for fraud in 2013. The case was dropped in 2014 and Campbell sued for unfair dismissal, receiving an out of court settlement later that year as he was proved to be an innocent man. He later passed away in 2016 aged 60.

CAMPBELL, David 'Dave'

Defender
Town Years: 1990-1992
Born: *1969 Dublin, Ireland*
Playing career: *Stella Maris, Bohemians, Huddersfield Town, Shamrock Rovers, St Patrick's Athletic, Shelbourne, Newry Town (loan), Bray Wanderers, Dublin City, Bray Wanderers (1989-2003)*

After a spell at Irish club Bohemians, Campbell was brought to the club by Eoin Hand, arriving at Leeds Road in 1990. He only managed a couple of appearances before his departure in 1992 and after a very short spell at Shamrock Rovers he signed for St. Patrick's Athletic in the same year. Campbell played for the club for four years before signing for Shelbourne in 1996, remaining at the club until the year 2000. He had short spells at Bray Wanderers and Dublin City before calling time on his footballing career in 2003. Campbell is currently working as Opposition Analyst & Head of Recruitment at Sligo Rovers having previously been Chief Scout at St. Patrick's Athletic.

CAMPBELL, James

Goalkeeper
Town Years: 1911
Born: *London*
Died: *unknown*
Playing career: *Custom House FC, Huddersfield Town, Custom House FC (1911)*

Campbell was a goalkeeper who arrived at Leeds Road in April 1911 on a trial basis. He played 1 match for the club before he returned to Custom House FC later that same month.

CAMPBELL, James 'Jimmy'

Left-half
Town Years: 1920-1921
Born: *1886 Newhaven, Scotland*
Died: *1925 Newhaven, Scotland*
Playing career: *Leith Athletic, The Wednesday, Huddersfield Town, St Bernard's (1908-1925)*

After a number of years at The Wednesday, Campbell arrived at Leeds Road in 1920, however, he only managed a single appearance in the first team before he left in 1921 to sign for St. Bernards. He had served in the First World War and suffered ill health before he retired from football in 1925, later passing away shortly after in May of the same year.

CAMPBELL, William 'Willie'

Right-half
Town Years: 1928-1929
Born: *1900 Dunfermline, Scotland*
Died: *unknown*
Playing career: *Cowdenbeath, Alloa Athletic, Huddersfield Town, Manchester City, Raith Rovers (1927-1929)*

After a spell at Alloa Athletic in his native Scotland, Campbell arrived at Leeds Road in January 1928 after being signed by Jack Chaplin. He spent just over a year at the club before he signed for Manchester City in March 1929, later signing for Raith Rovers.

CARAYOL, Mustapha

Winger
Town Years: 2015-2016 (loan)
Born: *1988 Banjul, Gambia*
Playing career: *Swindon Town, Macclesfield Town, Milton Keynes Dons, Crawley Town (loan), Torquay United, Kettering Town (loan), Lincoln City, Bristol Rovers, Middlesbrough, Brighton & Hove Albion (loan), Huddersfield Town (loan), Leeds United (loan), Nottingham Forest, Ipswich Town, Apollon Limassol (2007-Still Playing)*

One of Chris Powell's signings for the 2015-16 season, Carayol arrived from his parent club Middlesbrough. Originally a season long loan deal, new manager David Wagner cancelled it and Carayol was sent back in January 2016. He had a spell at Leeds United on loan and returned to his parent club at the end of that season before being released. Carayol spent two years at Nottingham Forest before signing for Ipswich Town in 2018. He left at the end of the 2017-18 season and signed for Apollon Limassol in Cyprus.

CAREY, Graham

Midfielder
Town Years: 2010-2011 (loan)
Born: *1989 Blanchardstown, Ireland*
Playing career: *Shelbourne, Celtic, Bohemians (loan), St Mirren (loan), Huddersfield Town (loan), St Mirren, Ross County, Plymouth Argyle (2005-Still Playing)*

Carey arrived on loan from Celtic at the start of the 2010-11 season and broke straight into the first team. However, his loan spell expired in January 2011 and Lee Clark was unsuccessful in securing his return. He signed for St. Mirren in 2011, remaining until 2013 when he signed for Ross County. Carey has played for Plymouth Argyle since leaving Ross County in 2015.

CARMODY, Michael 'Mick'

Left-back
Town Years: 1985
Born: *1966 Huddersfield, West Riding of Yorkshire*
Playing career: *Emley, Huddersfield Town, Emley, Tranmere Rovers, Altrincham, Ashton United (Loan), Ashton United (1984-2007)*

Carmody was signed on non-contract forms towards the end of the 1984-85 season. He played a couple of matches for the club in an unfamiliar position of left-back before returning to non-league Emley. Carmody later had a spell at Tranmere Rovers and also played in the 1988 FA Vase Final for Emley and later played for Altrincham for many years. Carmody is considered a legend at 'Alty' and has since worked as a scaffolder, still living in Huddersfield.

CARR, William 'Billy'

Half-back
Town Years: 1926-1934
Born: *1905 Framwellgate Moor, County Durham*
Died: *1989 Conisbrough, South Yorkshire*
Playing career: *Horden Athletic, Huddersfield Town, Southend United, Blackwell Colliery Welfare (1926-1939)*

Carr arrived at Leeds Road from Horden Athletic in 1926 and remained at the club for eight years, playing exactly 100 games for the first team. After he left the club in 1934, Carr later played for Southend United and after his retirement as a professional, worked as a general labourer in Conisbrough before he passed away in 1989.

CARR, Daniel
Forward
Town Years: 2013-2015
Born: *1994 Lambeth, Greater London*
Playing career: *Eastbourne Borough, Dulwich Hamlet, Huddersfield Town, Fleetwood Town (loan), Mansfield Town (loan), Dagenham & Redbridge (loan), Cambridge United, Aldershot Town (loan), Woking (loan), Dulwich Hamlet, Leatherhead (loan), Karlstad BK, Shamrock Rovers (2012-Still Playing)*
Carr was signed from Dulwich Hamlet in 2013 by Mark Robins, spending two years at the club before being released in 2015. He only made 2 appearances for the first team and spent time on loan at Fleetwood Town, Mansfield Town and Dagenham & Redbridge. After spells at Cambridge United and his former club Dulwich Hamlet, Carr is now playing for Shamrock Rovers.

CARR, Edward 'Eddie'
Forward
Town Years: 1945-1946
Born: *1917 Wheatley Hill, County Durham*
Died: *1998 Hartlepool, County Durham*
Playing career: *Arsenal, Margate (loan), Huddersfield Town, Newport County, Bradford City, Darlington (1935-1954)*
After working down the pit during the Second World War, Carr joined Town in 1945 and remained at the club for just one year before leaving for Newport County. Carr retired in 1954 and became chief trainer at Darlington before being promoted to become their first team manager in 1960. Carr remained as the boss until 1964 and later had a five year spell at the helm of Tow Law Town and as scout at Newcastle United. Carr was living in Hartlepool when he passed away in 1998.

CARR, John 'Jackie'
Outside-left
Town Years: 1950-1952
Born: *1926 Durban, South Africa*
Died: *1996 South Africa*
Playing career: *Huddersfield Town (1950-1952)*
Hailing from Durban in South Africa, Carr arrived at Leeds Road in 1950, but left the club in 1952 after making just a single appearance for the first team. He later returned to his native South Africa, passing away in 1996 at the age of 70.

CARROLL, Jake
Left-back
Town Years: 2013-2015
Born: *1991 Dublin, Ireland*
Playing career: *Home Farm, Belvedere, St Patrick's Athletic, St Patrick's Athletic, Huddersfield Town, Bury (loan), Partick Thistle (loan), Hartlepool United, Cambridge United (2011-Still Playing)*
Originally from Dublin, Carroll arrived in 2013 after Mark Robins brought him to the club from St. Patrick's Athletic. He played a couple of games at left-back before spending time on loan at both Bury and Partick Thistle. Later left for Hartlepool United in 2015 but is now plying his trade for Cambridge United.

CARSS, Anthony 'Tony'
Midfielder
Town Years: 2003-2006
Born: *1976 Alnwick, Northumberland*
Playing career: *Bradford City, Blackburn Rovers, Darlington, Cardiff City, Chesterfield, Carlisle United, Oldham Athletic, Huddersfield Town (1994-2006)*
Peter Jackson brought Tony Carss to the club at the beginning of the 2003-04 season from Oldham Athletic. He was a big part of the promotion winning side, converting a penalty in the playoff final shootout and then scoring perhaps the greatest goal ever seen at the McAlpine Stadium, However, injury ended his career in 2006 and Carss became a coach at the Academy whilst studying for a sports writing degree at Staffordshire University. He became the Professional Development Coach in 2012 later being promoted to Lead Professional Development Coach in 2014. Carss became Head of Academy Coaching in 2016 before leaving the club in August 2017 on the eve of Town's first ever Premier League campaign. He is now working as the Head of Academy Coaching at former club Blackburn Rovers.

CATTLIN, Christopher 'Chris'

Left-back
Town Years: 1964-1968
Born: *1946 Milnrow, Lancashire*
Playing career: *Huddersfield Town, Coventry City, Brighton & Hove Albion (1964-1979)*

Cattlin began his career at Leeds Road in 1964 and spent four years at the club before he signed for Coventry City in 1968. He spent six years at Highfield Road before rounding off his career with a three year spell at Brighton & Hove Albion, retiring from professional football in 1979 and settling in the city. After he finished playing, Cattlin bought a rock shop on the seafront in Brighton, and later becoming the Brighton manager in 1983, enjoying a three year spell before getting the sack in 1986. Cattlin carried on running the rock shop before his retirement and is still living in Hove.

CAVANAGH, Thomas 'Tommy'

Inside-forward
Town Years: 1952-1956
Born: *1928 Liverpool, Lancashire*
Died: *2007 Driffield, East Yorkshire*
Playing career: *Preston North End, Stockport County, Huddersfield Town, Doncaster Rovers, Bristol City, Carlisle United (1948-1961)*

Cavanagh arrived at Leeds Road in 1952 from Stockport County and spent four years at the club before he left for Doncaster Rovers in 1956. He took his first job in management in 1961 at Cheltenham Town but didn't last long, losing his job after two supporters' club members complained about him swearing during matches. He later took the Brentford manager's job in 1965, leaving the following year to become coach at Nottingham Forest. Cavanagh spent six years at the City Ground before he accepted a job offer from Manchester United's Tommy Docherty in 1972, to coach the first team at Old Trafford. In 1977, he became the assistant manager to Dave Sexton but left the club once Ron Atkinson was appointed manager in 1981. He had worked as Danny Blanchflower's assistant between 1976 and 1979 for the Northern Ireland national team. After a spell as Newcastle United's coach, Cavanagh became the manager of Norwegian side Rosenborg in 1983. He worked at the FA School of Excellence until he retired. Died in 2007 having suffered from Alzheimer's disease in his later days.

CAWTHORNE, Harold 'Harry'

Right-half
Town Years: 1919-1927
Born: *1900 Darnall, Sheffield, West Riding of Yorkshire*
Died: *1966 Sheffield, West Riding of Yorkshire*
Playing career: *Darnall Old Boys, Handsworth Army Football, Dronfield Woodhouse, Huddersfield Town, Sheffield United, Connah's Quay, Manchester Central, Middlewich, Kettering Town (player-coach), Denaby United, Woodhouse Alliance, Altofts (1919-1936)*

Cawthorne was signed from Dronfield Woodhouse in October 1919 and went on to spend eight years at Leeds Road. He played in each of three First Division title winning teams of 1924, 1925 and 1926 and although he was a defender, he also played in midfield and up front for Town. Cawthorne's last game for the club was during the 1926-27 season and he left the club in February 1927. He left to sign for Sheffield United and he spent two years at Bramall Lane, after which he hung up his boots in 1929 and retired from professional football. After his career ended, Cawthorne left football completely and worked as a coal miner and in the pub trade before he passed away in 1966 in his native Sheffield.

"DID YOU KNOW?"

"Lloyd Maitland was the first black player to play for the club in 1975."

CECERE, Michele 'Mike'

Forward
Town Years: 1988-1990
Born: *1968 Chester, Cheshire*
Playing career: *Oldham Athletic, Huddersfield Town, Walsall, Exeter City, Rochdale (1986-1997)*

Cecere began his career at Oldham Athletic and had been at the club for two years before Eoin Hand brought him to the club in 1988. Although he spent two years at Leeds Road, Cecere is perhaps more famous at Town for his girlfriend at the time, actress Sally Ann Matthews, Jenny Bradley from Coronation Street. He moved to Walsall and played there for four years until 1994 when he moved to Exeter City. This was followed by a short spell at Rochdale between 1996 and 1997 before he retired from professional football. Cecere is now back living in his native Chester and works in a bank.

CHAPLIN, John 'Jack'

Trainer, Manager
Town Years: 1921-1926, 1929-1939 (trainer), 1926-1929 (manager)
Born: *1882 Dundee, Scotland*
Died: *1952 Doncaster, West Riding of Yorkshire*
Management career: *Huddersfield Town (1926-1929)*

Chaplin arrived at Leeds Road in 1921 and was employed as the trainer of the team. He spent five years in this role before he was asked to take over from Cecil Potter as manager in 1926, shortly after the team had won their third First Division title on the bounce. Chaplin led the team to 2nd place in both the 1926-27 and 1927-28 seasons and also reached the 1928 FA Cup Final, which Town lost to Blackburn Rovers, before being replaced by Clem Stephenson in the same year and reverting back to his old role of trainer. He remained at the club until the outbreak of the Second World War, leaving his role in 1939 and seemingly retiring from the professional game. Chaplin died in suspicious circumstances in 1952, the death certificate states "hypostatic consolidation of the lungs following barbiturate poisoning there being insufficient evidence to show how the poison was administered".

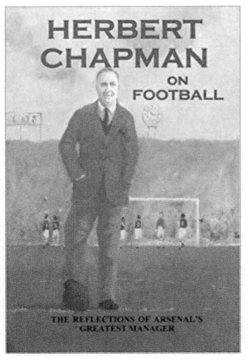

HERBERT CHAPMAN

ON FOOTBALL

THE REFLECTIONS OF ARSENAL'S GREATEST MANAGER

CHAPMAN, Herbert

Assistant Secretary, Assistant Manager, Secretary-manager
Town Years: 1920-1921 (assistant manager), 1921-1925 (secretary-manager)
Born: *1878 Kiveton Park, West Riding of Yorkshire*
Died: *1934 Hendon, Middlesex*
Management career: *Northampton Town, Leeds City, Huddersfield Town, Arsenal (1907-1934)*

Probably the greatest manager in the club's history, Herbert Chapman arrived at Leeds Road under a cloud in September 1920 as assistant secretary. He had been banned for life from football for corruption but had successfully appealed the ban before his arrival at Leeds Road. Within five months of his arrival, Chapman had replaced Ambrose Langley as secretary-manager and he guided Town to their only FA Cup win in 1922, beating Preston North End 1-0 at Stamford Bridge. He then won two successive First Division titles in 1924 and 1925 before leaving the club for Arsenal at the end of the 1924-25 season, but not before securing the services of Alec Jackson, his last act before his departure from the club. Cecil Potter clinched the third successive title and Town became the first club to win the top division three times in succession, a record that has never been beaten and only equalled three times. Chapman was that well thought of at Leeds Road, his staff donated a gold pencil to him upon his exit from the club. He won the 1930 FA Cup with Arsenal and then won two successive First Division titles in 1932 and 1933. Arsenal equalled Town's record in 1934 but Chapman unfortunately died in the January of that year after contracting pneumonia.

CHAPMAN, Leslie 'Les'

Outside-left, Youth Coach
Town Years: 1969-1974, 1997 (youth coach)
Born: *1948 Oldham, Lancashire*
Playing career: *Oldham Athletic, Huddersfield Town, Oldham Athletic, San Jose Earthquakes, Stockport County, Bradford City, Rochdale, Stockport County (player-manager), Preston North End (player-coach) (1966-1987)*

'Chappy' signed from Oldham Athletic in 1969 and quickly established himself in the first team. He was a part of the 1969-70 Second Division winning side and stayed with Town during their slide down the Football League.

He was eserve team coach at Manchester City between 1993 an 1996. Chapman later joined Town as youth coach but didn't last long due to Brian Horton's sacking in 1997. He returned to Maine Road to become the kitman and remained there for seventeen years before moving into semi-retirement. Chapman has since been producing video content for the club's website but suffered from a heart attack in March 2017, although it appears that he has recovered.

CHAPMAN, Vincent 'Vince'

Defender
Town Years: 1988-1989
Born: *1967 Newcastle upon Tyne, Northumberland*
Playing career: *Wallsend Boys Club, Tow Law Town, Huddersfield Town, Rochdale (1985-1991)*
Malcolm Macdonald brought Chapman to the club in January 1988 from Tow Law Town, the fee being paid by the Patron's Association, and he managed a couple of first team matches but suffered from injury problems during his stay at the club. Eoin Hand later released Chapman in 1989 and he played for Rochdale before retiring due to persistent knee problems. He has since run his own company, Chap Stitch & Print and is also coaching Tingley Athletic Ladies.

CHARLES, Jake

Forward
Town Years: 2015-2016
Born: *1996 Mirfield, West Yorkshire*
Playing career: *Huddersfield Town, Barnsley, Stafford Rangers (2015-Still Playing)*
Charles began his career at Town in the youth team and made a couple of appearances in the first team before he was sold to Barnsley in 2016. Charles is now playing for non-league Stafford Rangers.

CHARLTON, Simon

Left-back
Town Years: 1989-1993
Born: *1971 Huddersfield, West Riding of Yorkshire*
Playing career: *Huddersfield Town, Southampton, Birmingham City , Bolton Wanderers, Norwich City, Oldham Athletic, (1989-2010)*
Simon Charlton began his career at Leeds Road in 1988 as an apprentice before signing professional forms in 1989. He eventually became Town's first choice left-back and impressed with his performances. Charlton soon attracted interest from Premier League clubs and was signed by Southampton in 1993. He has since spent a time coaching with Global Soccer Network, worked as match summariser for Bolton games for BBC Radio Manchester and is now living and working in Dubai.

1922 squad with Herbert Chapman on left.

Trevor Cherry

CHERRY, Trevor
Left-half, Associate Director
Town Years: 1962-1972, 1991-2001 (director)
Born: 1948 Huddersfield, West Riding of Yorkshire
Playing career: Huddersfield Town, Leeds United, Bradford City (player-manager) (1962-1985)
A Huddersfield boy, Trevor Cherry signed professional forms in 1965 and was quickly established as a solid defender and was a mainstay in the defence of the 1969-70 Second Division winning team. After two seasons in the top flight Town were relegated and Cherry left for Leeds United in 1972. He became a Leeds United legend and was also capped by England, eventually leaving Elland Road in 1982 to join Bradford City as player-manager. Cherry won the 3rd Division Championship in 1985 and was the manager during the Bradford Fire Disaster. He remained until 1987 before he was sacked and later ran a successful hospitality business and also a waste paper company. Cherry became a director at Town in the early 1990s and rose up to the title of Associate Director, he was also a director during the late 1990s and early 2000s when Town almost went out of business, resigning in 2001. He has also been the director of Soccer City, his own consultancy firm and is currently the director of Ramsden and Colne Developments. Cherry now resides in Fenay Bridge, Huddersfield.

CHESTER, Reginald 'Reg'
Outside-left
Town Years: 1935-1937
Born: 1904 Long Eaton, Derbyshire
Died: 1977 Long Eaton, Derbyshire
Playing career: Long Eaton Rangers, Peterborough & Fletton United, Stamford Town, Aston Villa, Manchester United, Huddersfield Town, Darlington, Arnold, Woodborough United, Grantham (1919-1939)
After spells at Aston Villa and Manchester United, Chester arrived at Leeds Road in December 1935 and went straight into the side, playing the rest of the season at outside-left. Chester later retired from professional football and returned to his native Long Eaton, where he worked as an insurance agent before he passed away in April 1977.

CHILWELL, Benjamin 'Ben'
Left-back
Town Years: 2015-2016 (loan)
Born: 1996 Milton Keynes, Buckinghamshire
Playing career: Leicester City, Huddersfield Town (loan) (2015-Still Playing)
One of the first things that new manager David Wagner did in November 2015 was to highlight the left-back position as an area for improvement. He brought in Ben Chilwell to replace the lacklustre Jason Davidson and he spent a three month loan spell at the club during the 2015-16 season where he impressed with his classy performances. He is now Leicester City's first choice left back and was called up to the England national team in 2018, after spending a number of years playing for the U20s and U21s.

CHIPPENDALE, Aidan
Winger
Town Years: 2009-2012
Born: 1992 Bradford, West Yorkshire
Playing career: Bradford City, Huddersfield Town, York City (loan), Inverness Caledonian Thistle (loan), Accrington Stanley, Bury, Chester (loan), AFC Fylde, Ashton United, Stalybridge Celtic, Bradford Park Avenue, Ossett United (2009-Still Playing)
Chippendale progressed through the youth ranks at Town, signing professional in 2009. He only managed to make a couple of appearances in his three years as a professional before leaving in 2012 to sign for Accrington Stanley. Now playing for Ossett United.

Ben Chilwell

CHIVERS, Francis 'Frank'
Centre-forward
Town Years: 1936-1938
Born: *1909 Drybrook, Gloucestershire*
Died: *1942 Don Valley, West Riding of Yorkshire*
Playing career: *Goldthorpe United, Barnsley, Huddersfield Town, Blackburn Rovers (1929-1938)*

Chivers signed for Town from Barnsley in January 1936 and went straight into the first team, playing at centre-forward. He played a number of matches in the first team but never really cemented a regular place in the side before he left the club towards the end of the 1937-38 season. Chivers later went on to play for Blackburn Rovers and after his retirement as a player, worked as a miner before being killed in War service in a mining accident at Barnborough Main Colliery in 1942.

CHRISTIE, Gilbert
Forward
Town Years: 1913-1914
Born: *1892 Dundee, Scotland*
Died: *1973 Wakefield, West Riding of Yorkshire*
Playing career: *Dundee Fairfield FC, Huddersfield Town, Halifax Town (1913-1914)*

Christie had been playing for Dundee Fairfield FC before he arrived at Leeds Road in June 1913. He played just 2 matches during the 1913-14 season before he signed for Halifax Town. After his retirement as a professional, Christie remained in the area and became a Police Constable in the West Yorkshire Police and during the Second World War volunteered as a War reserve constable, while he resided in Rothwell. He later passed away in Wakefield in 1973.

CHRISTIE, Norman
Centre-half
Town Years: 1931-1934
Born: *1909 Jarrow, County Durham*
Died: *1989 Malton, North Yorkshire*
Playing career: *Bishop Auckland, Huddersfield Town, Blackburn Rovers. Macclefield Town (1931-1940)*

Christie joined from non-league Bishop Auckland in July 1931 and spent three years at Leeds Road playing at centre-half. He managed over 40 appearances for the club before he moved to Blackburn Rovers in December 1934, later hanging up his boots in 1940 at Macclesfield Town. Christie later passed in 1989 whilst living in North Yorkshire.

CHURCH, Simon
Forward
Town Years: 2012 (loan)
Born: *1988 Amersham, Buckinghamshire*
Playing career: *Reading, Crewe Alexandra (loan), Yeovil Town (loan), Wycombe Wanderers (loan), Leyton Orient (loan), Huddersfield Town (loan), Charlton Athletic, Milton Keynes Dons, Aberdeen (loan), Roda JC Kerkrade, Scunthorpe United, Plymouth Argyle (2007-2018)*

Church signed on loan from Reading in November 2012 and scored 1 goal in 7 appearances before returning to his parent club in late December. He later had spells at Charlton Athletic, Milton Keynes Dons, Roda JC Kerkrade, Scunthorpe United and Plymouth Argyle before announcing his retirement in 2018 due to a recurring hip injury. Since his retirement, Church has set-up an investment advisory firm for footballers. Although he was born in Buckinghamshire, Church played for the Wales national side between 2009 and 2016, winning 38 caps, scoring 2 goals and playing during Euro 2016 when Wales reached the semi-finals of the competition.

CLARK, Brian
Forward
Town Years: 1966-1968
Born: *1943 Bristol, Gloucestershire*
Died: *2010 Cardiff, Wales*
Playing career: *Bristol City, Huddersfield T, Cardiff C, Bournemouth, Millwall, Newport C (1960-1979)*

Clark arrived at Leeds Road in 1966 from Bristol City where he cost £2,500, with Johnny Quigley going the other way. He only lasted 16 months at Leeds Road before being sold to Cardiff City in 1968 for £8,000. Clark was popular at Ninian Park, scoring against Real Madrid in the quarter final of the European Cup-Winners' Cup. He was sold to Bournemouth in 1972 for £70,000 and then spent two years at Millwall before heading back to Cardiff in 1975, helping them to promotion from the Third Division. He left again the year later and spent three years playing part-time for Newport County before retiring in 1979. Clark worked as a sales representative for a firm that sold industrial safety equipment and he later had spells with non-league Maesteg, AFC Cardiff and Bridgend Town all as player-manager. Brian Clark passed away in 2010 from Lewy body dementia aged 67.

BLACK OR WHITE NO GREY AREAS

Lee Clark with Will Scott

CLARK, Lee

Manager
Town Years: 2008-2012
Born: *1972 Wallsend, Northumberland*
Management career: *Huddersfield Town, Birmingham City, Blackpool, Kilmarnock, Bury (2008-2017)*

After working as Glenn Roeder's assistant manager at Norwich City, Clark was brought in to replace Stan Ternent in December 2008. During his time at the club, Clark reached the 2010 playoff semi-finals and the 2011 playoff final. Town lost to Peterborough in the 2011 final and Clark was sacked in February 2012 after a loss to Sheffield United, ironically it had been only his third loss in around 50 league matches. He became the Birmingham City manager later that year and remained at St. Andrews until his sacking in 2014. Clark later took the Blackpool manager's job in 2015 but were relegated to League Two at the end of the season with the club in financial turmoil and resigned at the end of the season, later becoming the Kilmarnock manager in 2016, resigning his post just a year later to take the Bury manager's job. Clark lasted less than a year at Gigg Lane before being sacked in October 2017 with the club in the relegation zone.

CLARKE, Dennis

Right-back
Town Years: 1968-1973
Born: *1948 Stockton-on-Tees, County Durham*
Playing career: *West Bromwich Albion, Huddersfield Town, Birmingham City (1963-1975)*

Clarke signed from West Bromwich Albion in 1968 and was soon established in the first team, playing at right-back during the 1969-70 Second Division winning season and was one of seven ever-present players in the side. He remained at Leeds Road until 1973, transferring to Birmingham City to see out his career before annuncing his retirement in 1975. Clarke later ran a pub in Honley after retiring and was believed to be living and working in Spain at some point but he is now known to be running a decorating business in West Bromwich.

CLARKE, Nathan

Centre-half
Town Years: 2001-2012
Born: *1984 Halifax, West Yorkshire*
Playing career: *Huddersfield Town, Colchester United (loan), Oldham Athletic (loan), Bury (loan), Leyton Orient, Bradford City, Coventry City, Grimsby Town, FC Halifax Town (2001-Still Playing)*

A product of the club's academy system, Clarke began his career at Town against Stoke City under then manager Lou Macari. Although only 18 years old, he was quick to cement his place in the side with his consistent performances. During this time, Clarke was linked with moves to both Liverpool and Aston Villa, much to Macari's annoyance. He also played during the 2003-04 promotion season but was injured in the second half of the season. Clark was one of Town's first choice centre backs up until Lee Clark's arrival in 2008. He only played a few more games before he left in 2012 to sign for Leyton Orient and was at one point the captain of the side. Clarke also had spells at Bradford City and Coventry City but is now playing for his hometown club FC Halifax Town in the National Conference.

"DID YOU KNOW?"

"George Brown is the club's record goalscorer with 159 goals in all competitions."

CLARKE, Peter
Centre-half
Town Years: 2009-2014
Born: *1982 Southport, Merseyside*
Playing career: *Everton, Blackpool (loan), Port Vale (loan), Coventry City (loan), Blackpool, Southend United, Huddersfield Town, Bury, Oldham Athletic, Bury (loan) (1999-Still Playing)*

Signed from Southend United in 2009, Clarke went straight into the first team for the 2009-10 season and was immediately installed as captain. Well liked for his committed performances in a Town shirt, despite his advancing years, he always gave his all and captained Town to promotion in 2012. He left in 2014 but is still regarded as a club legend. He joined Blackpool and was reunited with former Town boss Lee Clark. He left in 2015 to join Bury, but only remained for one year when he joined Oldham Athletic. He remains at Oldham but had a loan spell back at Bury during the 2017-18 season.

CLARKE, Timothy 'Tim'
Goalkeeper
Town Years: 1991-1993
Born: *1964 Stourbridge, Worcestershire*
Playing career: *Halesowen Town, Coventry City, Huddersfield Town, Rochdale (loan), Altrincham, Shrewsbury Town, York City, Scunthorpe United (loan), Scunthorpe United, Kidderminster Harriers (loan), Kidderminster Harriers(1989-2008)*

Renowned for his errors during games, Clarke was nicknamed 'Coco' and signed from Coventry City in 1991. He remained for two years before being told he could leave Leeds Road by Neil Warnock and he ended up at Shrewsbury Town, playing at Gay Meadow until 1996 when he joined York City for a season. Clarke then joined Scunthorpe United in 1997, remaining at the club until 1999. After a two year spell at Kidderminster Harriers, he was signed by former Town team-mate Gary Barnett in 2001 for Barry Town and Clarke has the distinction of playing for the first Welsh side to ever reach the Champions League. He later had spells with non-league Halesowen Town, Willenhall Town, Evesham United and Bromsgrove Rovers and has also been goalkeeping coach at Halesowen, Willenhall and Hinckley. Clarke currently works for ITL Heating in Willenhall and is a qualified plumber.

CLARKE, Thomas 'Tom'
Defender/Midfielder
Town Years: 2005-2013
Born: *1987 Halifax, West Yorkshire*
Playing career: *Huddersfield Town, Halifax Town (loan), Bradford City (loan), Leyton Orient (loan), Preston North End (2005-Still Playing)*

Brother of Nathan, Tom Clarke came through Gerry Murphy's academy system and made his debut for the first team in 2005. He spent a lot of time either out on loan or on the fringes of the first team until the 2009-10 season, he cemented a place in the team but was unlucky with injuries, injuring his cruciate ligaments. He did make a recovery but couldn't cement a regular place in the team so moved on to Preston in 2013, where he remains and is club captain.

CLAYTON, Adam
Midfielder
Town Years: 2012-2014
Born: *1989 Manchester, Greater Manchester*
Playing career: *Manchester City, Carlisle United (loan), Leeds United (loan), Leeds United, Peterborough United (loan), Milton Keynes Dons (loan), Huddersfield Town, Middlesbrough (2008-Still Playing)*

Clayton signed from Leeds United for £350,000 in 2012 and spent two years in the centre of midfield before leaving for Middlesbrough in a part exchange deal with Jacob Butterfield. Manchester-born Clayton remains at the Riverside Stadium as of 2019.

CLAYTON, Gary
Midfielder
Town Years: 1994-1995
Born: *1963 Sheffield, West Riding of Yorkshire*
Playing career: *Rotherham United, Gainsborough Trinity, Burton Albion, Doncaster Rovers, Cambridge United, Peterborough United (loan), Huddersfield Town, Plymouth Argyle, Torquay United (1985-1999)*

Neil Warnock signed Clayton from Cambridge United in 1994 and played a handful of games at the tail-end of the 1993-94 season and played in the final ever match at Leeds Road. He made a couple of appearances the season after before signing for Neil Warnock's Plymouth Argyle at the beginning of the 1995-96 season, spending two years there and another two years at Torquay United before retiring from the game in 1999. Clayton is now a self employed plasterer in his native Sheffield.

CLEGG, Donald 'Don'

Goalkeeper
Town Years: 1940-1943 (amateur) 1943-1948
Born: *1921 Huddersfield, West Riding of Yorkshire*
Died: *2005 Lancaster, Lancashire*
Playing career: *Huddersfield Town, Bury, Stoke City, Yeovil Town (1940-1951)*

Clegg was playing for the local ICI team before signing for his hometown club in 1940 as an amateur player. He signed on as a professional and managed to play three games in goal before his departure in July 1948, being released by George Stephenson. Clegg later turned out for Bury, Stoke City and Yeovil Town before retiring from the game in the early 1950s. He later lived in Lancaster before he passed away at the age of 84 in 2005.

COADY, Conor

Central-midfielder
Town Years: 2014-2015
Born: *1993 Liverpool, Merseyside*
Playing career: *Liverpool, Sheffield United (loan), Huddersfield Town, Wolverhampton Wanderers (2012-Still Playing)*

Signing from hometown club Liverpool, Coady only spent the 2014-15 season at the club before signing for Wolverhampton Wanderers for £2 million and remains there as the club captain, having converted to centre-half.

COCK, John 'Jack'

Centre-forward
Town Years: 1914-1919
Born: *1893 Hayle, Cornwall*
Died: *1966 Kensington, London*
Playing career: *Brentford, Huddersfield Town, Brentford (guest), Chelsea, Everton, Plymouth Argyle, Millwall, (1908-1932)*

After a short spell at Brentford, Jack Cock signed for the club in 1914 but didn't have chance to make much of an impact as the Football League was soon suspended as World War One commenced. Cock served in the British Army during the hostilities and rose to the rank of Acting Sergeant-Major, earning the Military Medal for "Bravery in the Field" and a Mentioned in Despatches for "gallantry". At one point during the War, Cock was reported as "missing, presumed dead" but he returned to Leeds Road in 1919 after the end of the War but was quickly sold to Chelsea for a then-record £2,500 as

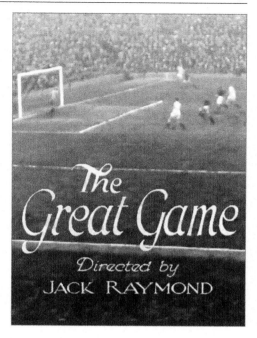

Town were in dire financial state. He spent four years at Stamford Bridge before joining Everton in 1923. After spending two years at Goodison Park, Cock had spells at Plymouth Argyle and Millwall before moving into non-league football in 1930. He turned out for Folkestone and Walton & Hersham before finally retiring in 1932. An England international, Jack Cock was also known for his singing abilities and had appeared in music halls on many occasions and had also appeared in several films, including The Great Game in 1930. Cock was running The White Hart in Deptford by 1939 and later had a spell as Millwall manager. He also ran a pub in New Cross before passing away in 1966, at the age of 72.

COCKERILL, Ronald 'Ron'

Centre-half
Town Years: 1951-1952 (amateur), 1952-1958
Born: *1935 Sheffield, West Riding of Yorkshire*
Died: *2010 Grimsby, Lincolnshire*
Playing career: *High Green Villa, Huddersfield Town, Grimsby Town (1951-1968)*

Cockerill arrived at the club after signing from High Green Villa in 1951 as an amateur before turning professional at Leeds Road in 1952. He spent six years as a professional at the club before being sold to Grimsby Town in 1958.

He remained there for ten years until his departure in 1968, playing 323 games in the process. Cockerill retired after leaving Grimsby and later worked as a car salesman. He also worked for Prudential Insurance and then worked as a HGV Instructor and driver at Anglo Danish and finally spent two years working at LES Engineering before his retirement. Cockerill passed away in Grimsby in 2010.

CODDINGTON, John
Centre-half
Town Years: 1953-1958 (amateur), 1958-1967
Born: *1937 Worksop, Nottinghamshire*
Playing career: *Huddersfield Town, Blackburn Rovers, Stockport County, Great Harwood Town, Drogheda United (1953-1973)*

Coddington arrived at the club as a part timer in 1953, becoming a full time professional in 1958 after completing his National Service. He spent fourteen years at Leeds Road and by the time he left in 1967, he was club captain. The centre-half left for Blackburn Rovers, remaining at Ewood Park until 1971 when moved into non-league football with Great Harwood. Coddington also had a spell in Ireland, playing for Drogheda United, who were managed by his former Town teammate Kenneth Turner. He later worked as a coach at Bradford City before becoming chief coach at Middlesbrough in 1974 under Jack Charlton. He later became the manager of the Ship Inn in Eston but was persuaded to rejoin Middlesbrough in 1985, before he was sacked just five months later in January 1986 to be replaced by Bruce Rioch. Coddington now lives in retirement in Middlesbrough. To add, his grandson Luke Coddington was on Town's books during the 2016-17 season but is now playing for Northampton Town.

COLGAN, Nicholas 'Nick'
Goalkeeper, Academy Goalkeeping Coach, First Team Goalkeeping Coach
Town Years: 2010 (loan), 2011-2013, 2012-2014 (academy goalkeeping coach), 2014-2017 (first team goalkeeping coach)
Born: *1973 Drogheda, Ireland*
Playing career: *Drogheda United, Chelsea, Bournemouth, Hibernian, Stockport County (loan), Barnsley, Dundee United (loan), Ipswich Town, Sunderland, Grimsby Town, Huddersfield Town (loan), Huddersfield Town (1991-2013)*

Colgan originally signed on loan from Grimsby Town in 2010 as goalkeeping cover, later signing on permanently in 2011. He became the Academy goalkeeping coach at Town in 2012, combining his playing duties with his new role. Colgan announced his retirement in 2013 but began as the goalkeeping coach for the first team in 2014. Once Town were promoted to the Premier League in 2017 he was released in favour of Paul Clements and is now working as the goalkeeping coach at Wigan Athletic.

COLLINS, Robert 'Bobby'
Manager
Town Years: 1974-1975
Born: *1931 Govanhill, Scotland*
Died: *2014 Leeds, West Yorkshire*
Management career: *Huddersfield Town, Hull City, Barnsley (1974-1985)*

After a long career in football with clubs such as Leeds United, Everton and Celtic, Collins became the manager at Leeds Road following the resignation of the long-serving Ian Greaves. He took charge of the club in the Third Division in 1974, subsequently taking the club down into the Fourth Division and resigned in December 1975, citing interference from the newly appointed General Manager, Tom Johnston. Collins then worked as a youth coach at Leeds United from 1976 to 1977 before he gained the Hull City manager's position. He only lasted around four months at The Tigers, his spell coming between October 1977 and February 1978, following this, between March 1978 and May 1978, Collins worked as a coach at Blackpool. He was given the job of youth coach at Barnsley in 1980 and later became their manager between 1984 and 1985 after a period working as assistant manager. He also assisted former teammate Peter Lorimer at Guiseley between 1987 and 1988. After his time in football ended, Collins worked in the wholesale fashion business and then as a chauffeur for two years at the Leeds University Garage, after which he retired. In his retirement Collins played a lot of golf and was involved in charity football matches before suffering from ill health in his later years, suffering from Alzheimer's. He passed away in 2014 after a long battle with the disease.

Michael Collins

COLLINS, Michael

Central-midfielder
Town Years: 2004-2010
Born: *1986 Halifax, West Yorkshire*
Playing career: *Huddersfield Town, Scunthorpe United, AFC Wimbledon (loan), Oxford United, York City (loan) (2004-2018)*

Part of Gerry Murphy's influx of Academy players, Collins made his debut for Town in the 2004-05 season and went on to become a permanent fixture in the first team under Peter Jackson. Collins remained a regular until the end of the 2009-10 season and was placed on the transfer list by Lee Clark at the end of that season and he was sold to Scunthorpe United. He remained at Glanford Park until 2014 when he joined Oxford United and played most of his first season at the Kassam Stadium but failed to make any appearances in his second season and was released in January 2016.

Collins joined Indian side Bengaluru soon after and played in the I-League for five months. He returned to England and had a short spell at Leyton Orient but left after they were relegated from the Football League. He was the under 18s lead coach at Bradford City, while also playing part-time for F.C. Halifax Town, but was given the manager's job at Bradford City at the start of the 2018-19 season. Collins lasted just 6 league games before being axed in favour of David Hopkin. Collins has since played for non-league Alfreton Town.

COLLINS, Samuel 'Sam'

Centre-half
Town Years: 1997-1999
Born: *1977 Pontefract, West Yorkshire*
Playing career: *Huddersfield Town, Bury, Port Vale, Hull City (loan), Hull City, Swindon Town (loan), Hartlepool United (1994-2015)*

Originally a trainee at Town, Collins signed pro forms in 1997 and made sporadic appearances before being sold to Neil Warnock's Bury in 1999 for £75,000. He spent three years at Gigg Lane before heading to Port Vale in 2002. Four years later, Collins joined Hull City for two seasons before moving to Hartlepool United in 2008. Collins was club captain at Victoria Park where he is considered a legend, having had two spells as player-caretaker manager in 2014 following the exits of Colin Cooper and Paul Murray respectively. Ronnie Moore made Collins his assistant manager following those two spells and Collins another spell as caretaker manager in 2017 when Craig Hignett was sacked. After a time as the Professional Development Coach at Bradford City, Collins is now the manager at York City and having had a spell as caretaker manager of the side, previously working as the youth team manager.

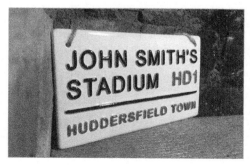

COLLINS, Simon
Utility
Town Years: 1992-1997
Born: *1973 Pontefract, West Riding of Yorkshire*
Playing career: *Huddersfield Town, Halifax Town (loan), Plymouth Argyle, Macclesfield Town, Shrewsbury Town (loan), Frickley Athletic, Belper Town, Bradford Park Avenue, Belper Town, Frickley Athletic, Grantham Town, Ossett Town, Stocksbridge Park Steels (1992-2007)*

Brother of Sam Collins, Simon came through the youth ranks and signed professional in 1992. He spent five years at Town, making intermittent appearances over those years and playing in a number of different positions. Collins left to join Plymouth Argyle in 1997, signed by former Town assistant manager Mick Jones. He later played for Macclesfield Town and a host of non-league clubs in the North of England, balancing this with his job as PE Coordinator at Felkirk School in Wakefield. Collins later worked as UK Sports Development Manager for Total Soccer International Limited and became the Ossett Town manager. Collins later spent a short while at Bradford Park Avenue in 2010 (employing Chris Billy and Simon Baldry as coaches). He now lives in America and from 2014 to 2018 was the Director of Coaching at St. Cloud Soccer Club, however, he now works in New Jersey as Technical Director for EDP Soccer.

COMRIE, George
Left-half
Town Years: 1912-1913
Born: *1885 Denny, Stirlingshire, Scotland*
Died: *1958 Falkirk, Scotland*
Playing career: *Dundee, Huddersfield Town, Forfar Athletic (1903-1913)*

After a spell at Dundee, Comrie arrived at Leeds Road in June 1912 and made 15 league appearances before leaving in June 1913, after just one season at the club. Comrie later played for Forthar Athletic and served in the First World War, where he was posted to France in May 1915 and was discharged in December 1918. He was a corporal in the Royal Engineers before becoming a sergeant (No. S/2863) and was awarded three medals; The Allied Victory Medal, The British War Medal and The 1914-15 Star. Comrie returned to his native Scotland after the War and later passed away in 1958 whilst he was residing in Falkirk.

CONMY, Oliver 'Ollie'
Winger
Town Years: 1957-1964
Born: *1939 Mulrany, County Mayo, Ireland*
Died: *2014 Southport, Merseyside*
Playing career: *Huddersfield Town, Peterborough United, Cambridge City (1957-1974)*

Ollie Conmy was first picked up by Town after being seen playing for a junior side in Ireland. He made his debut for the first team in 1960 but as he was the understudy to the club legend Kevin McHale, Conmy couldn't get into the side and was sold to Peterborough United in 1964. He was very popular at London Road and remained there until 1972, making a total of 304 appearances. Conmy ended his career at non-league Cambridge City and later took the job of youth coach at former club Peterborough. He later worked as a civil servant before retiring to Southport in 2001, where he lived until his death in 2014.

CONNOR, John 'Jack'
Winger
Town Years: 1952-1960
Born: *1934 Maryport, Cumberland*
Died: *2010 Formby, Merseyside*
Playing career: *Huddersfield Town, Bristol City, Formby (1952-1976)*

Connor signed for Town in 1952 at 18 years old after he was seen playing junior football in his native Cumbria. He soon went off to do National Service from which he returned from in 1954. Connor spent a total of eight years at Leeds Road and was awarded a benefit by the board of directors in 1958. He moved to Bristol City in 1960 and spent a total of eleven years at Ashton Gate until his departure in 1971. Connor later coached at Everton. Died in Formby in 2010, aged 75.

CONNOR, John 'Jack'
Outside-right
Town Years: 1914-1915
Born: *1893 Durham*
Died: *unknown*
Playing career: *Houghton Rovers, Huddersfield Town (1914-1915)*

After a spell at Houghton Rovers, Connor arrived at the club in May 1914 and spent a year at Leeds Road between 1914 and 1915, making three appearances for the first team before leaving the club at the end of the 1914-15 season.

CONWELL, Anthony 'Tony'

Right-back
Town Years: 1955-1959
Born: *1932 Bradford, West Riding of Yorkshire*
Died: *2017 Bradford, West Yorkshire*
Playing career: *Sheffield Wednesday, Huddersfield Town, Derby County, Doncaster Rovers (1953-1964)*
After a couple of years at Sheffield Wednesday, Conwell arrived at Leeds Road in 1955 where he would play over 100 games in four years at right-back. Conwell wnt on to work as a milkman and a bricklayer before he retired. Passed away in May 2017 at the age of 85.

COOK, George 'Billy'

Inside-forward
Town Years: 1923-1927
Born: *1895 Evenwood, County Durham*
Died: *1980 Colwyn Bay, Wales*
Playing career: *Evenwood Juniors, Trindle Juniors, Bishop Auckland, Rotherham County, Huddersfield Town, Aston Villa, Tottenham Hotspur, Brentford, Colwyn Bay United (1914-1932)*
Cook played in each of the three First Division winning seasons before signing for Aston Villa in 1927. Cook later played for non-league Colwyn Bay and worked in the civil service in Durham. Died in 1980.

COOPER, Graham

Forward
Town Years: 1984-1988
Born: *1962 Huddersfield, West Riding of Yorkshire*
Playing career: *Emley, Huddersfield Town, Wrexham, York City (loan), Northwich Victoria, Halifax Town (1984-1992)*
Cooper was signed from non-league Emley in 1984 and remained at his hometown club for four years. He played 86 games for the club during that time, most of his games coming under manager Mick Buxton. He later became a legend at Wrexham and is still welcomed at the club as part of their Former Player's Association. After leaving Wrexham, Cooper headed back to Yorkshire to play a season and a half for Halifax Town before retiring from professional football due to injury. He later lived in Torquay, Devon for a number of years but he is now back living in his home town of Huddersfield. Cooper has worked in care for many years and has season tickets at the John Smith's Stadium and Wrexham's Racecourse Ground.

COOPER, Liam

Centre-half
Town Years: 2011 (loan)
Born: *1991 Hull, Humberside*
Playing career: *Hull City, Carlisle United (loan), Huddersfield Town (loan), Chesterfield (loan), Chesterfield, Leeds United (2008-Still Playing)*
Lee Clark brought Cooper to the Galpharm Stadium on a short term loan deal from Hull City at the beginning of 2011-12 season but only managed a couple of appearances before he was sent back to his parent club. He left the Tigers for Chesterfield in 2013, only lasting a year at the club before signing for Leeds United in 2014. He has now played over 100 games at Elland Road and is captain of the side.

DID YOU KNOW?"

"Former youth product Mark Lillis has been the caretaker manager of Town on four separate occasions in 2012, 2013, 2014 and 2015."

COOPER, Mark

Midfielder
Town Years: 1993
Born: *1968 Wakefield, West Riding of Yorkshire*
Playing career: *Bristol City, Exeter, Birmingham City, Fulham, Huddersfield Town (loan), Wycombe W, Exeter C, Hartlepool U, Leyton Orient (1987-2009)*
Ian Ross brought Cooper to Leeds Road on a short loan in 1993 from Fulham. He later played for Wycombe Wanderers, Exeter City, Hartlepool United, Leyton Orient, Rushden & Diamonds before becoming player-manager of Tamworth in 2004. Cooper remained at the club until 2007 before he joined Kettering Town. He was poached by Peterborough United in 2009 but was sacked shortly after his appointment, in 2010. Cooper joined Darlington that same year, however he only remained at the club for a year before he had a one game spell back at Kettering in 2012 and a 5 game spell at AFC Telford United before being appointed assistant manager at Swindon Town in 2013. He later got the manager's job, remaining for two years before being fired in 2015. Cooper had a short spell at Notts County in 2016 before taking the Forest Green job, which is where he remains.

COOPER, Paul

Right-back
Town Years: 1973-1977
Born: *1957 Birmingham, Warwickshire*
Playing career: *Huddersfield Town, Grimsby Town, Nuneaton Borough (1973-1978)*

Cooper signed for the club as an apprentice in 1973 and played for the team that reached the FA Youth Cup Final in 1974, progressing into the first team in 1975. He only played 2 matches for the club before leaving Leeds Road in 1977. Cooper later played for Grimsby Town and Nuneaton Borough before returning to Birmingham, where he now lives and works.

COOPER, Sedley

Forward
Town Years: 1936-1937
Born: *1911 Garforth, West Riding of Yorkshire*
Died: *1981 Garforth, West Yorkshire*
Playing career: *Carlton Athletic, Halifax Town, Sheffield Wednesday, Huddersfield Town, Notts County (1928-1939)*

After five years at Sheffield Wednesday, Cooper arrived at Town in July 1936, but only made 5 appearances in the first team before moving on in March 1937 to sign for Notts County. After his retirement as a professional, Cooper returned to his home of Garforth and worked as a colliery worker before he passed away in 1981.

CORK, David

Forward
Town Years: 1985-1989
Born: *1962 Doncaster, West Riding of Yorkshire*
Playing career: *Arsenal, GAIS (loan), Huddersfield Town, West Bromwich Albion (loan), Scunthorpe United, Darlington, Boston United (1978-1992)*

David Cork was signed from Arsenal in 1985 by Mick Buxton and was quickly established in the first team. He remained in the side under Buxton, Steve Smith and Malcolm Macdonald before he left the club in 1989 after refusing to sign a new contract. He was one of the 11 players to play in the club's 10-1 record defeat against Manchester City in 1987. Cork signed for Mick Buxton's Scunthorpe United in 1989 and also spent time at Darlington and Boston United before retiring from the game in 1992. He now resides in Doncaster and works for Norking Aluminium.

COULSON, William 'Willie'

Outside-left
Town Years: 1975 (loan)
Born: *1951 Benwell, Newcastle upon Tyne*
Playing career: *Chelsea, Newcastle United, Southend United, Aldershot (loan), Huddersfield Town (loan), Darlington (loan), Hong Kong Rangers, Frankston City (1969-1980)*

Coulson signed on a short loan from Southend United in 1975 and played a couple of games before returning to Roots Hall. He left his parent club in 1976 to play in Hong Kong for four years before moving on to Melbourne, Australia where he has coached for a number of years.

Tom Cowan

COWAN, Thomas 'Tom'

Left-back
Town Years: 1994 (loan), 1994-1999
Born: *1969 Bellshill, Scotland*
Playing career: *Clyde, Rangers, Sheffield United, Stoke City (loan), Huddersfield Town (loan), Huddersfield Town, Burnley, Cambridge United (loan), Cambridge United, Peterborough United (loan), York City, Dundee, Carlisle United, (1988-2007)*

Tom Cowan is a Town legend. He signed permanently from Sheffield United at the beginning of the 1994-95 season.

He was the first choice left-back for the promotion that year. Well liked for his consistent performances and his victory salute to the Town faithful, Cowan was a regular in the side until his suffered a cruciate ligament injury just before the 1997-98 season. Moved on to Burnley in 1999 and then Cambridge United after an initial loan in 2000. After two years there, Cowan joined York City for a year before teaming up with ex Town teammate, Chris Billy at Carlisle. Short spells at non-league clubs followed before he finally retired in 2007. Cowan is now a fireman in Sheffield and occasionally attends Town games as a guest, he is always greeted with a warm reception and has been known to recreate his famous salute on request!

COWELL, William 'Billy'

Goalkeeper
Town Years: 1921-1924
Born: *1902 Acomb, Hexham, Northumberland*
Died: *1999 Newcastle, Tyne and Wear*
Playing career: *Newburn Athletic, Mickley, Newburn Athletic, Huddersfield Town, Hartlepools United, Derby County, Grimsby Town, Millwall, Carlsile United (1921-1926)*
Cowell arrived at the club in 1921 after signing from Newburn FC but only managed 9 appearances in the league before he left the club three years later in 1924. He later turned out for Hartlepools United, Derby County and Grimsby Town and after his retirement, Cowell worked as a greyhound trainer in Middlesex and also as an engineer before his death on Tyneside in 1999, at the age of 86.

COWLEY, Arthur

Outside-right
Town Years: 1911-1912
Born: *1887 Hendon, Middlesex*
Died: *1956 Tolworth, London*
Playing career: *Brentford, Nunhead, Huddersfield Town, Aberdare Athletic (1909-1912)*
Signing in 1911 from Nunhead, Cowley only managed a handful of appearances for Dick Pudan's side before leaving the club in 1912. He later played for Aberdare Athletic and worked as a labourer, loading munitions whilst living in Reading, Berkshire. Cowley passed away in Tolworth in 1956.

COWLING, David 'Dave'

Left-winger
Town Years: 1977-1988
Born: *1958 Doncaster, West Riding of Yorkshire*
Playing career: *Mansfield Town, Huddersfield Town, Reading, Scunthorpe United (1976-1991)*
Cowling joined Town in 1977 from Mansfield Town and this began an eleven year association with Huddersfield Town. He played crucial parts in both the 1979-80 and 1982-83 promotion winning sides and scored the goal that clinched promotion in 1983 against Newport County. Cowling also scored a famous goal against Leeds United in the Milk Cup in 1982. Described by teammate Steve Kindon as a "team-mates delight", Cowling was never the bravest but could cross the ball with ease. He played at Leeds Road until 1988, by which time he had fallen out of favour, when he left for Reading. He later played at Scunthorpe United, with Mick Buxton, before calling time on his playing career in 1991. Cowling started as coach at Scunthorpe United before becoming youth coach at Doncaster Rovers, later spending 10 days as first team manager at Belle Vue before resigning due to interference from chairman Peter Richardson. He had a short spell as Goole's manager before becoming the Director of Youth at Bury. Cowling then moved to Darlington as youth development officer and Darlington College as the director of the football development centre there. Since 2011, he has run his own football academy Esprit which is based at Doncaster's Keepmoat Stadium.

COX, Brian

Goalkeeper
Town Years: 1981-1988
Born: *1961 Sheffield, West Riding of Yorkshire*
Playing career: *Sheffield Wednesday, Huddersfield Town, Mansfield Town, Hartlepool United, Buxton (1978-1991)*
Cox signed from Sheffield Wednesday in March 1982 due to injuries to both Dick Taylor and Andy Rankin. He kept goal during the 1982-83 promotion season but was also involved in a number of relegation battles towards the end of Mick Buxton's time. Cox is perhaps unfortunately best remembered for playing in the 10-1 defeat to Manchester City in 1987 and never really recovered from that game. Cox has since worked in the health industry, in a betting shop and is still thought to be living in his native Sheffield.

COX, Maurice

Inside-right
Town Years: 1982
Born: *1959 Torquay, Devon*
Playing career: *Torquay United, Huddersfield Town, Falmouth Town (1979-1983)*
Mick Buxton brought Cox to Leeds Road on a short term deal from Torquay United in 1982 but only made a handful of appearances before being released later on in the 1982-83 season. He later played for non-league Falmouth Town before leaving football altogether. Cox has lived and worked in Italy for many years.

CRAIG, Benjamin 'Benny'

Right-back
Town Years: 1934-1938
Born: *1915 Leadgate, Consett, County Durham*
Died: *1982 Newcastle upon Tyne, Tyne and Wear*
Playing career: *Eden Colliery Welfare, Huddersfield Town, Newcastle United (1933-1949)*
Craig arrived at Leeds Road as an amateur in January 1934 from Eden Colliery Welfare and he spent four years at the club. After four years at Town, Craig returned to the North East to sign for Newcastle United. He played at St. James Park until 1949, when he hung up his boots and began training as a chiropodist and trainer, later becoming the trainer at Newcastle. He spent a number of years at the club on the backroom staff before he passed away in 1982 at the age of 66.

CRANEY, Ian

Midfielder
Town Years: 2008-2010
Born: *1982 Liverpool, Merseyside*
Playing career: *Everton, Altrincham, Accrington Stanley, Swansea City (loan), Swansea City, Accrington Stanley (loan), Accrington Stanley, Huddersfield Town, Morecambe (loan), Fleetwood Town, Accrington Stanley, (1995-2014)*
Stan Ternent brought Craney to the club during the 2008-09 season from Accrington Stanley. He was a regular during the 2008-09 season but fell out of favour with new manager Lee Clark. Craney spent the 2009-10 season on loan at Morecambe before eventually leaving Town in 2010 to sign for Fleetwood Town. He later played for Stanley again as well as Rochdale, AFC Telford United, Stockport County and Conwy Borough before his retirement from the game in 2014. Craney is now working for a Merseyside based bread distribution company owned by his parents and has a season ticket at Anfield.

CRANIE, Martin

Right-back
Town Years: 2015-2018
Born: *1986 Yeovil, Somerset*
Playing career: *Southampton, Bournemouth (loan), Yeovil Town (loan), Portsmouth, Queens Park Rangers (loan), Charlton Athletic (loan), Coventry City, Barnsley, Huddersfield Town, Middlesbrough (2003-Still Playing)*
Chris Powell brought Cranie to the club and he played a number of games during the 2016-17 promotion season. He left the club in early 2018 to join Middlesbrough but was released at the end of the season 2017-18 season. Cranie joined Sheffield United in September 2018 on a short term deal.

CRINSON, William 'Bill'

Goalkeeper
Town Years: 1908-1909
Born: *1883 Sunderland, County Durham*
Died: *1949 Sunderland, County Durham*
Crinson was part of Town's first ever starting XI and played in goal for Fred Walker's side in 1908-09. He left the club at the end of the season to sign for Brighton & Hove Albion and later returned to his birthplace of Sunderland and worked as a plater in the local shipyards before his death in 1949 at the age of 77.

CROFT, Lee
Winger
Town Years: 2010-2011 (loan)
Born: *1985 Billinge Higher End, Greater Manchester*
Playing career: *Manchester City, Oldham Athletic (loan), Norwich City, Derby County, Huddersfield Town (loan), St Johnstone (loan), Oldham Athletic (loan), Oldham Athletic, St Johnstone, Oldham Athletic, Southport (2004-Still Playing)*

Croft arrived on loan for the start of the 2010-11 season but failed to impress and Lee Clark sent him back to Derby after playing a couple of games. He wasn't in Nigel Clough's plans at the time and in 2012 he was loaned out to St. Johnstone but suffered from injury problems. After his short time on loan, Croft re-signed for Oldham Athletic in 2013 but left at the end of the season after rejecting a new contract. Croft returned to St. Johnstone and remained until 2015 when he again returned to Oldham. He left Boundary Park in 2017 to join non-league Southport.

CROOKS, Matthew 'Matt'
Centre-half
Town Years: 2010-2015
Born: *1994 Leeds, West Yorkshire*
Playing career: *Huddersfield Town, FC Halifax Town (loan), Radcliffe Borough (loan), Hartlepool United (loan), Accrington Stanley (loan), Accrington Stanley, Rangers, Scunthorpe United (loan), Northampton Town (2010-Still Playing)*

Crooks came through the youth ranks at Town and played just one game in 2014, the first game of the 2014-15 season which saw Town battered 4-0 by AFC Bournemouth and Mark Robins' resignation. After spells at Accrington Stanley and Rangers, he now plays for Northampton Town.

CROSBY, Gary
Midfielder
Town Years: 1994-1997
Born: *1964 Sleaford, Lincolnshire*
Playing career: *Lincoln United, Lincoln City, Grantham Town, Nottingham Forest, Grimsby Town (loan), Huddersfield Town, Rushden & Diamonds, Burton Albion (1982-2005)*

Brought to the club by Neil Warnock in 1994, Crosby spent three years at Town, playing in the 1995 Playoff Final against Bristol Rovers. He left in 1997 to join Rushden & Diamonds and after a brief period at his first club Lincoln United, he joined Burton Albion as Nigel Clough's player-assistant manager.

He left in 2005 but returned in 2006, remaining until Nigel Clough took the Derby County job and his whole coaching staff with him in 2009. Following Clough's sacking in 2013, Crosby followed him to his new job at Sheffield United. Crosby is now assistant manager at Burton Albion and has been since Clough's return in 2015.

CROWNSHAW, George
Inside-left
Town Years: 1929-1934
Born: *1908 Sheffield, West Riding of Yorkshire*
Died: *1992 Weybridge, Surrey*
Playing career: *Huddersfield T, Luton T (1929-1934)*

Crownshaw arrived at Leeds Road in 1929 and spent five years at the club playing at inside-left. He only managed 27 appearances for Clem Stephenson's side before joining Luton Town in 1934. Crownshaw later worked as an LCC hospital instructor in Watford before he passed away in 1992 whilst he was living in Weybridge.

"DID YOU KNOW?"

"Only five players have played in all four divisions for Town. They are; Terry Poole, Geoff Hutt, Jim Lawson, Steve Smith and Terry Dolan."

CROWTHER, George
Centre-forward
Town Years: 1912-1913
Born: *1892 Bishop Middleham, County Durham*
Died: *1957 Halifax, West Riding of Yorkshire*
Playing career: *Manchester United, Huddersfield Town, Rotherham Town, Halifax Town, Bradford PA, West Ham, Hartlepools U, Tranmere R (1911-1923)*

Before his footballing career began, Crowther worked as an apprentice engineer for the Marines and he joined Town in 1912 and played 2 games for Arthur Fairclough's side before his departure in 1913. Crowther later played for Rotherham Town, Halifax Town, Hurst, Bradford Park Avenue, West Ham United, Hartlepools United and he finished his professional career at Tranmere Rovers in 1923. Crowther later worked as a steel erector in Halifax before he passed away in 1957. He had served as a private in the 17th (Service) Battalion of the Middlesex Regiment during World War One.

CUMMING, Laurence 'Laurie'

Inside-left
Town Years: 1927-1929
Born: *1905 Derry, Ireland*
Died: *1980 Renfrew, Scotland*
Playing career: *Alloa Athletic, Huddersfield Town, Oldham Athletic, Southampton, Alloa Athletic, Queen of the South, St Mirren (1927-1938)*

Cumming arrived at Leeds Road in 1927 and was the equal fourth top goal scorer in the 1928-29 season. Those 6 goals that he scored that season were the only ones he managed to score in his 19 appearances for the club. He moved on to Oldham Athletic in 1929 and then to Southampton in 1930 for a fee of £500. Cumming again only lasted a year there and moved on to Alloa Athletic and then Queen of the South before moving to St. Mirren in 1938. Following his retirement as a professional, Cumming worked as a reporter and worked for the Scottish Daily Express for many years while also helping to found the Scottish Football Writers' Association. Cumming died in 1980 at the age of 75.

CURRAN, Edward 'Terry'

Forward
Town Years: 1985-1986
Born: *1955 Kinsley, West Riding of Yorkshire*
Playing career: *Kinsley Boys, Doncaster Rovers, Doncaster Rovers, Nottingham Forest, Bury (loan), Derby County, Southampton, Sheffield Wednesday, Atvidaberg (loan), Sheffield United, Everton (loan), Everton, Huddersfield Town, Panionios, Hull City, Sunderland, Grantham Town, Grimsby Town, Chesterfield (1973-1987)*

After a long career in the Football League, Curran arrived in 1985 after his time at Everton. He didn't play many games for the club but is probably best remembered for scoring against Leeds United and for promptly bowing to the Leeds fans. He left in 1986 and rounded off his career with periods at Hull City, Sunderland, Grantham Town, Grimsby Town and Chesterfield. Curran later managed Goole Town and Mossley as well as running a transport cafe before selling the land to property developers in the early 1990s. He has since coached at Doncaster Rovers academy and ran a hotel in West Yorkshire. Now retired and watches his son, Jock, who plays for Grimsby Town. His autobiography 'Regrets of a Football Maverick' was published in October 2012

CURRIE, David

Forward
Town Years: 1994 (loan)
Born: *1962 Stockton, County Durham*
Playing career: *Middlesbrough, Darlington, Barnsley, Nottingham Forest, Oldham Athletic, Barnsley, Rotherham United (loan), Huddersfield Town (loan), Carlisle United, Scarborough (1982-1998)*

Neil Warnock brought Currie to the club in the 1993-94 season on loan where he played 7 games, scoring 1 goal. He was released by Barnsley at the end of that season and joined Carlisle United before moving to Scarborough in 1997 where he spent one year at the McCain Stadium before retiring. Currie is living in Thornaby and was last known to be working as a lorry driver.

DALEY, Thomas 'Tom'

Goalkeeper
Town Years: 1957-1958
Born: *1933 Grimsby, Lincolnshire*
Playing career: *Grimsby Town, Huddersfield Town, Peterborough United (1951-1960)*

Daley arrived at Leeds Road in 1957 from Grimsby Town but only played one first team match in Bill Shankly's side. He later played for Peterborough United, Boston United and Gainsborough Trinity. Daley is now living in retirement in Cleethorpes.

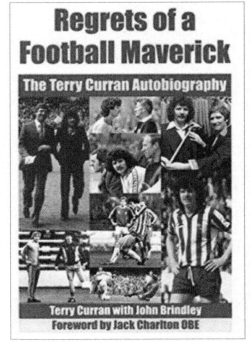

Regrets of a Football Maverick
The Terry Curran Autobiography
Terry Curran with John Brindley
Foreword by Jack Charlton OBE

DALTON, Paul
Winger
Town Years: 1995-2000
Born: *1967 Middlesbrough, North Riding of Yorkshire*
Playing career: *Brandon United, Manchester United, Hartlepool United, Plymouth Argyle, Huddersfield Town, Carlisle United (loan), Gateshead (1986-2001)*
Brian Horton signed 'Dolly' in 1995 but he struggled to settle into the side. However, following Horton's sacking in 1997, Peter Jackson gave him more of a "free role". His performances improved and became a major player in the 1997-98 Great Escape season. He was eventually released in the year 2000 after falling out of favour with Steve Bruce. Dalton returned to his home in the North East to play for Gateshead. Later coached the youngsters at Middlesbrough and also had a spell working at Darlington College. Dalton left England in the early 2010's and headed to America and is now Director of Coaching at Chicago Fire Juniors West.

DANNS, Neil
Midfielder
Town Years: 2013 (loan)
Born: *1982 Liverpool, Merseyside*
Playing career: *Blackburn Rovers , Blackpool (loan), Hartlepool United (loan), Colchester United (loan), Colchester United, Birmingham City, Crystal Palace, Leicester City, Bristol City (loan), Huddersfield Town (loan), Bolton Wanderers (loan), Bolton Wanderers, Bury, Blackpool (loan) (2000-Still Playing)*
Danns arrived in 2013 on loan from Leicester City but returned to his parent club at the end of the 2012-13 season. He later had a spell on loan at Bolton Wanderers before signing for them permanently in 2014. Danns remained there until 2016 when he signed for Bury.

Jason Davidson

DAVIDSON, Jason
Left-back
Town Years: 2015-2017
Born: *1991 Melbourne, Victoria, Australia*
Playing career: *WBA, Huddersfield Town, Rijeka, Olimpija Ljubljana (loan), Perth Glory (2009-date)*
Davidson was signed by Chris Powell at the beginning of the 2015-16 season but lost his place in the side once new manager David Wagner had taken charge. He never played for Wagner again after speaking to the newspapers and criticising the new manager's rotation policy. The Australian was promptly loaned out to Gronigen in Holland and when he returned to training prior to the 2017-18 season, was told to find a new club. He later joined Rijeka in Croatia and is currently playing for Perth Glory in his native Australia.

DAVIE, William 'Willie'
Inside-left
Town Years: 1951-1957
Born: *1925 Paisley, Scotland*
Died: *1996 Huddersfield, West Yorkshire*
Playing career: *St Mirren, Luton Town, Huddersfield Town, Walsall (1947-1958)*
Signing from Luton in 1951, Davie spent almost seven years at Leeds Road. He played over 100 games for the club before ending his career at Walsall in 1958. Davie later worked as an ambulance driver but died in 1996 in Huddersfield.

DAVIES, Harry
Inside-forward
Town Years: 1929-1932
Born: *1904 Gainsborough, Lincolnshire*
Died: *1975 Blurton, Staffordshire*
Playing career: *Bamfords Athletic, Stoke City, Huddersfield Town, Stoke City, Port Vale (1922-1939)*
After seven years at Stoke City, Davies arrived at Leeds Road in 1929. During World War Two, he earned a military medal while serving with the Royal Army Service Corps. After the War ended he became the owner of the Priory Hotel in Abbey Hulton and later became the owner of the Plume of Feathers in Barlaston. He also wrote a newspaper column during his playing days where he was paid sixpence a word, after writing 200 words per column he was earning £5 a week which was the same as his footballing wage. Davies passed away in 1975 at the age of 71.

DAVIES, Simon
Midfielder
Town Years: 1996 (loan)
Born: *1974 Winsford, Cheshire*
Playing career: *Manchester United, Exeter City (loan), Huddersfield Town (loan), Luton Town, Macclesfield Town, Rochdale, Bangor City, Total Network Solutions, Bangor City, Rhyl, Chester City, Airbus UK (1992-2007)*

Davies began his career as a youngster at Manchester United and arrived on loan in 1996, playing 3 matches for Brian Horton's side, before he returned to Old Trafford. He left United a year later and joined Luton Town. After spells at Macclesfield and Rochdale, Davies played for a number of non-league teams including Bangor City, Rhyl, Airbus UK and Total Network Solutions before joining the coaching staff at Chester City in 2006. He originally worked in the club's youth setup before becoming caretaker manager in 2007. Davies returned to his role of Youth Team manager following the appointment of Bobby Williamson, later taking over as caretaker manager once again in 2008 after Williamson was sacked. He later took on the job full time but was sacked himself in November 2008. He worked as assistant manager of Manchester City reserves between 2013 and 2015 before becoming the manager in 2016. Davies has been the Head of Academy Coaching at the club since 2018.

Bobby Davison

DAVIS, Edwin 'Ted'
Goalkeeper
Town Years: 1913-1922
Born: *1892 Bedminster, Bristol, Gloucestershire*
Died: *1954 Bristol, Gloucestershire*
Playing career: *Clapton Orient, Huddersfield Town, Blackburn Rovers (1913-192?)*

After playing for non-league Clapton Orient, goalkeeper Davis signed in 1913 and played over 50 games for Arthur Fairclough's side. He also played a number of matches in the following season before League football was suspended. He returned to the first team after the end of World War One and played until the 1921-22 season, where he appeared in every round of the FA Cup until the semi-final. Town later won the FA Cup by beating Preston North End in the final. Davis left at the end of that season to join Blackburn Rovers and signed for Bath City in 1926 firstly as a player and then as manager. He spent eleven years at the club, whilst also working in the insurance industry. During the Second World War, Davis worked as a progress fitter for aeroplanes. He passed away in 1954 whilst living in Bristol. It is interesting to note that his nephew Sid Bird played for Town after Davis sold him to the club in 1929 from Bath City.

DAVISON, Robert 'Bobby'
Forward
Town Years: 1980-1981
Born: *1959 South Shields, County Durham*
Playing career: *Leeds United, Huddersfield Town, Halifax Town, Derby County, Leeds United, Derby County (loan), Sheffield United (loan), Leicester City, Sheffield United, Rotherham United, Hull City (loan), Guiseley (player-manager) (1980-2000)*

Davison played just twice for Mick Buxton's side before leaving in 1981 to sign for Halifax Town. He played just over a year at The Shay but is probably best remembered for his 200+ games for Derby County and five years at Leeds United. Towards the end of his playing career he turned out for Leicester City, Sheffield United and Rotherham United before retiring in 1996. Davison became the player-manager of Guiseley in 1998, before working as as Colin Todd's assistant manager at Bradford City. Davison has since coached at Sheffield United, Ferencvaros in Hungary and the Leeds United academy but is now living in Shipley and coaches locally.

DEARDEN, Kevin
Goalkeeper
Town Years: 1999 (loan)
Born: *1970 Luton, Bedfordshire*
Playing career: *Luton Town, Tottenham Hotspur, Rochdale, Huddersfield Town (loan), Wrexham, Torquay United (1988-2005)*

Dearden arrived on loan from Brentford in 1999 but only played in the reserves. After a playing career which took in more than a dozen League clubs, he coached the goalkeepers at Brentford, Millwall, Luton Town and Stevenage before taking on the combined role of goalkeeping coach and chief scout at Leyton Orient in 2008. He left the club in 2014 and later joined Luton Town as goalkeeping coach.

DELANEY, Damien
Centre-half
Town Years: 2002 (loan)
Born: *1981 Cork, Ireland*
Playing career: *Cork City, Leicester City, Huddersfield Town (loan), Hull City, QPR, Ipswich Town, Crystal Palace, Cork City (1998-Still Playing)*

Delaney had a short loan at the club in 2002 making two appearances for Lou Macari's side before returning to Leicester City. He left Filbert Street later in 2002 to join Hull City. Delaney then played for QPR, Ipswich Town, Crystal Palace, before signing for his home-town club Cork City in 2018. Twitter followers were baffled in May of the same year when Italian giants AS Roma mysteriously tweeted a photo of him with the hashtag #GracieDamien. Nobody ever appears to have come up with an explanation and the club themselves were quoted as saying that "the fans theories were far better than anything that they could have come up with".

DEMPSEY, Kyle
Right-back, Central-midfielder
Town Years: 2015-2017
Born: *1995 Whitehaven, Cumbria*
Playing career: *Carlisle United, Huddersfield Town, Fleetwood Town (2014-Still Playing)*

Dempsey arrived at the club in time for the 2015-16 season and played a number of matches for both Chris Powell and David Wagner before being loaned out to Fleetwood Town. At the end of 2016-17 season he made the move to Fleetwood a permanent one and is still at Highbury.

DENNIS, Harold 'Harry'
Outside-right
Town Years: 1924-1926
Born: *1901 Ancaster, Lincolnshire*
Died: *1989 Lincoln, Lincolnshire*
Playing career: *Newark Town, Grantham Town, Huddersfield Town, Southend United (1924-1926)*

Dennis joined the club after signing from Newark Town in 1924 and managed a single appearance for Cecil Potter's side during the 1925-26 First Division winning season. He remained at the club until the end of that season and signed for Southend United. After his retirement as a player, Dennis returned to his native Lincolnshire, and lived and worked in Lincoln before he passed away in 1989.

DENT, John 'Johnny'
Forward
Town Years: 1926-1929
Born: *1903 Spennymoor, County Durham*
Died: *1979 Nottingham, Nottinghamshire*
Playing career: *Spennymoor Rangers, Tudhoe United, Durham City, Tow Law Town, Durham City, Huddersfield Town, Nottingham Forest, Kidderminster Harriers (c1923-1939)*

Dent signed from non-league Durham City in 1926 and played over 50 games up front for the club before his departure to Nottingham Forest. He served in the RAF during the Second World War and after the end of the hostilities, worked as a carpenter in West Bridgford until his death in 1979.

DID YOU KNOW?"

"Steve Smith is the only manager in the club's history to come from Huddersfield."

DEVLIN, William

Forward
Town Years: 1926-1927
Born: *1899 Bellshill, North Lanarkshire, Scotland*
Died: *1972 Glasgow, Scotland*
Playing career: *Cowdenbeath, Huddersfield Town, Liverpool, Heart of Midlothian, Macclesfield Town, Cowdenbeath, Mansfield Town, Burton, Shelbourne, Olympic Marseille, Bangor, Boston, Ashton National, Olympic Marseille, FC Zurich (1921-1936)*

Devlin arrived at Leeds Road in 1926 after signing from Cowdenbeath and he played the majority of the 1926-27 season at Town before leaving for Liverpool in 1927. Whilst at Anfield, Devlin managed 15 league goals in 19 league matches before heading back to Scotland to play for Heart of Midlothian. His career then yo-yoed between England and Scotland but also included stops in France, Ireland and Switzerland. Devlin passed away in Glasgow in July 1972.

DEWHURST, Robert 'Rob'

Defender
Town Years: 1992 (loan)
Born: *1971 Keighley, West Riding of Yorkshire*
Playing career: *Blackburn Rovers, Darlington (loan), Huddersfield Town (loan), Hull City, Exeter City, Scunthorpe United (1990-2000)*

Dewhurst arrived on loan from Blackburn Rovers in 1992 and played seven games for Ian Ross' side before returning to Ewood Park. He left Blackburn in 1993 to sign for Hull City and went on to spend six years at Boothferry Park, playing over 140 matches for the first team. He later played for Exeter and Scunthorpe before retiring from football. Dewhurst has since worked as a postman in East Yorkshire as well as running his own soccer coaching schools and out of school clubs in North Ferriby.

Andy Dibble

DIBBLE, Andrew 'Andy'

Goalkeeper
Town Years: 1987 (loan)
Born: *1965 Cwmbran, Wales*
Playing career: *Cardiff City, Luton Town, Sunderland (loan), Huddersfield Town (loan), Manchester City, Aberdeen (loan), Middlesbrough (loan), Bolton Wanderers (loan), West Bromwich Albion (loan), Sheffield United (loan), Rangers, Sheffield United, Luton Town, Middlesbrough, Altrincham, Barry Town, Hartlepool United, Carlisle United (loan), Stockport County, Wrexham, Accrington Stanley (1982-2006)*

Dibble joined Town on a short term loan deal in 1987 from parent club Luton Town. He returned to Kenilworth Road later that same year and remained at Luton until 1988. Dibble then had a nine year spell at Manchester City before heading over the border to play for Rangers in 1997. He later played for Sheffield United, Luton (again), Middlesbrough, Altrincham, Hartlepool United, Stockport County, Wrexham and Accrington Stanley before hanging up his boots in 2006. He was also the goalkeeping coach at Accrington before moving to Coventry City in 2006, Peterborough United in 2007 and Rotherham United in 2009. Dibble remained at Rotherham until 2017 when Neil Warnock's Cardiff City offered him the role of goalkeeping coach.

DICKINSON, Liam

Forward
Town Years: 2008 (loan)
Born: *1985 Salford, Greater Manchester*
Playing career: *Blackpool, Bolton Wanderers, Blackburn Rovers, Stockport County, Derby County, Huddersfield Town (loan), Brighton & Hove Albion, Plymouth Argyle, Southend United, Stockport County, SGuiseley, Bradford Park Avenue, Stalybridge Celtic, FC United of Manchester (2002-Still Playing)*

Dickinson was signed on loan from Derby County by Stan Ternent at the start of the 2008-09 season. He flattered to deceive at Town, although his statistics do look quite impressive. Dickinson returned to Derby and was loaned back out to Blackpool and Leeds United during the same season. He is something of a journeyman player and has turned out for a number of clubs, including Brighton , Barnsley, Plymouth Argyle, Southend, Stockport County. He is currently playing up front for F.C. United of Manchester. Now working for Hobs Repro in Manchester.

DINNIE, Charles

Defender
Town Years: 1910-1913
Born: *1887 Arbroath, Scotland*
Died: *1965 Springfield, United States*
Playing career: *Dundee, Huddersfield Town (1909-1913)*

After a stint at Dundee, Dinnie arrived at Leeds Road in May 1910, signing for Dick Pudan's side. Dinnie played at right-back, left-back and centre-half for the club and stayed for three years before being released by Arthur Fairclough in April 1913. After hanging up his boots, Dinnie emigrated to the United States of America in 1924 and lived and worked there until he died in 1965 in Springfield, Massachusetts.

DINSDALE, Peter

Wing-half
Town Years: 1956-1959 (amateur), 1959-1967
Born: *1938 Bradford, West Riding of Yorkshire*
Died: *2004 Port Moody, Canada*
Playing career: *Yorkshire Amateurs, Huddersfield Town, Vancouver Royals, Bradford Park Avenue (loan) (1956-1968)*

Dinsdale signed as an amateur from Yorkshire Amateurs in 1956. He turned professional in 1959 and played for the first team for eight years, making over 200 appearances for the club, including being ever-present during the 1962-63 and 1963-64 seasons. Dinsdale emigrated to Canada in 1967, where he played for Vancouver Royals and later given the national team manager's job in 1968 with the aim of qualifying for the World Cup in 1970. Having failed in the attempt, he had a two year spell as Brighton & Hove Albion assistant manager between 1970 and 1972 before he returning back to Canada. He lived in Vancouver and worked as a real estate agent. Dinsdale passed away in 2004 after a three year battle with cancer.

DIXON, Ernest 'Ernie'

Forward
Town Years: 1929
Born: *1901 Pudsey, West Riding of Yorkshire*
Died: *1941 Bradford, West Riding of Yorkshire*
Playing career: *Bradford City, Halifax Town, Burnley, Huddersfield Town, Nelson, Tranmere Rovers, Gresley Rovers, Mossley (1921-1933)*

Dixon had been playing for Burnley and had also been Halifax Town's record goalscorer when he joined the club in September 1929.

He spent just a month at the club and played 5 games for Clem Stephenson's side before he signed for Nelson. He later worked as a fish frier in Pudsey before passing away in 1941 in Bradford.

DIXON, Paul

Left-back
Town Years: 2012-2015
Born: *1986 Aberdeen, Scotland*
Playing career: *Monifieth Athletic, Dundee, Dundee United, Huddersfield Town, Grimsby Town (1994-Still Playing)*

Having moved from Dundee United in 2012, Dixon's career at Town lasted three years where he was respected for his consistent performances at left-back. Dixon then returned to Dundee United in 2015, ventured back 'south of the border' to play for Grimsby Town, but is now back in Scotland with Falkirk.

DOBSON, Colin

Forward
Town Years: 1966-1972
Born: *1940 Eston, North Riding of Yorkshire*
Playing career: *Sheffield Wednesday, Huddersfield Town, Brighton & Hove Albion (loan), Bristol Rovers (1961-1976)*

After five years at Sheffield Wednesday, Dobson arrived at Leeds Road in 1966 and part of the 1969-70 promotion team. He played in each of the two seasons that Town were in the First Division before leaving in 1972 to sign for Bristol Rovers. He won promotion to the Second Division with Bristol in 1974 before announcing his retirement in 1976. Dobson became the youth coach at Coventry City shortly after leaving the Gas and later worked as a coach at Port Vale on a voluntary basis. After this he began coaching Al Rayyan in Qatar and West Riffa in Bahrain before returning to England to become the youth coach at Aston Villa. He has since worked as youth coach at Sporting Lisbon and Gillingham. Dobson later worked as first team coach of Kuwaitee Al Arabi before once again returning home to Port Vale during the 1995-96 season. He coached Oman Under 17s in 1997 ahead of becoming chief scout at Stoke City in 2000. Dobson left that post in 2005 and scouted for Watford before returning to Stoke as a scout in 2008, finally retiring in 2013.

DODGIN, William 'Bill'

Left-half
Town Years: 1929-1933
Born: *1909 Gateshead, County Durham*
Died: *1999 Godalming, Surrey*
Playing career: *Huddersfield Town, Lincoln City, Charlton Athletic, Bristol Rovers, Clapton Orient, Southampton (1928-1946)*

Dodgin began his professional career at Leeds Road in 1929, having previously worked as a miner, but only managed a handful of appearances until his departure to Lincoln City in 1933. After two years at Sincil Bank, Dodgin moved on to Bristol Rovers in 1936, spending just one year there before transferring to Clapton Orient in 1937, remaining until 1939. He signed for Southampton but World War Two interrupted his playing days. During the War, he worked at the Hamble-le-Rice aircraft factory just outside Southampton. This meant that he was perfectly placed to take on the managerial vacancy at the Dell in 1946. This was the start of a new career which included four years at Fulham, a year in Italy, and a number of roles with Bristol Rovers. At one time, he also ran a tobacconists and sweet shop in Byfleet. Dodgin later worked at Eastville as their chief scout and passed away in 1999 at the age of 90.

DOGGART, Arthur

Goalkeeper
Town Years: 1909
Born: *1882 Workington, Cumberland*
Died: *1957 Workington, Cumberland*
Playing career: *Huddersfield Town (1908-1909)*

Doggart arrived in time for the 1909-10 season from his hometown club Workington and played four matches in the FA Cup for Fred Walker's side before being released in November 1909. Doggart returned to Workington and worked as a steelworker in the local foundry. He remained in his hometown for the rest of his life before he died in October 1957.

"DID YOU KNOW?"

"David Wagner became the club's first foreign manager (excluding Ireland) when he was appointed Head Coach in 2015."

DOHERTY, Peter

Inside-left
Town Years: 1946-1949
Born: *1913 Magherafelt, County Londonderry, Ireland*
Died: *1990 Fleetwood, Lancashire*
Playing career: *Station United, Coleraine, Glentoran, Blackpool, Manchester City, Derby County, Huddersfield Town, Doncaster Rovers (1931-1953)*

Doherty signed for David Steele's side in 1946 after a spell at Derby County and is considered to be one of Town's best ever players. He played at the club for three years before his departure in 1949 to become the player-manager of Doncaster Rovers. After nine years in the post, Doherty left in 1958 to become the manager of Bristol City. He had taken the Northern Ireland manager's job in 1952, balancing this with his jobs at Doncaster Rovers and Bristol City. Doherty took his national team to the 1958 World Cup where they reached the quarter-finals. Another interesting snippet is that, while working as a scout for Liverpool, he encouraged the club to sign a young striker who he had spotted playing for Scunthorpe United – one Kevin Keegan. Doherty was living in Fleetwood when he passed away in April 1990 at the age of 76.

DOLAN, Terence 'Terry'
Midfielder
Town Years: 1970-1976
Born: *1950 Bradford, West Riding of Yorkshire*
Playing career: *Bradford Park Avenue, Huddersfield Town, Bradford City, Rochdale (1967-1981)*

Terry Dolan joined Town from Bradford Park Avenue in 1970 and is one of very few players that have played for Town in all four divisions. He later took the Youth Coach job at Bradford in 1985, progressing to first team coach in 1986, under his former Town team-mate Trevor Cherry. Cherry's sacking in 1987 led to Dolan becoming the new manager at Valley Parade and he remained in the post until he himself was sacked in 1989. Dolan moved to Rochdale to become their manager and he lasted until 1991, when he controversially left the club for Hull City. He spent six years with the Tigers and suffered two relegations during that time. Dolan re-joined Town in 1997 as Peter Jackson's reserve team coach and Steve Bruce kept him on following Jacko's sacking in 1999, later leaving the McAlpine Stadium in 2000. Dolan has since worked for the League Managers Association as a mentor, Head of Recruitment at Notts County and was last involved in football as a director at Bradford Park Avenue before his departure at the end of the 2017-18 season. He is currently living in North Ferriby.

DONIS, Giorgos 'George'
Midfielder
Town Years: 1999-2000
Born: *1969 Frankfurt, West Germany*
Playing career: *Blackburn Rovers, AEK Athens, Sheffield United, Huddersfield Town (1986-2000)*

After a short stint at Sheffield United, Donis signed for Town for a £1 million fee, re-joining his former boss Steve Bruce. Donis was a spectacular flop and he was quickly offloaded in 2000 after he failed to return for pre-season training claiming he had been forced to do national service in his native Greece, just a year after his transfer. Sadly, Town fans did not see the goalscoring prowess that earned him the nickname "The Train" earlier in his career. He has since embarked on an extensive managerial career, beginning with Ilisiakos in 2002. Donis has been the manager of Panathinaikos since 2018.

DONOVAN, Kevin
Midfielder
Town Years: 1988-1992
Born: *1971 Halifax, West Riding of Yorkshire*
Playing career: *Huddersfield Town, Halifax Town (loan), West Bromwich Albion, Grimsby Town, Barnsley, Rochdale, York City (1988-2007)*

Donovan turned professional at Leeds Road. He played for the club until 1992, when he was sold to West Brom after a number of impressive performances for Ian Ross' side. He later turned out for Grimsby Town, Barnsley, Rochdale, York City and Alfreton Town before hanging up his boots in 2007. Donovan now coaches local football in West Yorkshire and runs his own coaching business KD Coaching, runs soccer schools in Brighouse and has also worked as Head of Football at Kirklees College.

DOW, James
Left-half
Town Years: 1912-1915
Born: *1889 Sunderland, County Durham*
Died: *1972 Sunderland, County Durham*
Playing career: *Sunderland Southwick, Huddersfield Town, Carlisle United (1912-1915)*

Dow played 49 games for Arthur Fairclough's side at left-half before leaving in May 1915 to sign for Carlisle United. He later returned to his native Sunderland and worked as a platers helper in his hometown before passing away in 1972.

DOYLE, Stephen 'Steve'
Midfielder
Town Years: 1982-1987
Born: *1958 Neath, Wales*
Playing career: *Preston North End, Huddersfield Town, Sunderland, Hull City, Rochdale (1974-1994)*

Doyle signed from Preston North End in 1982 and went straight into Mick Buxton's side at Leeds Road, playing a huge part in the 1982-83 promotion winning side. He remained at Town until 1987 before signing for Sunderland and then Hull City in 1989. He spent two years at Boothferry Park before joining his former Town team-mate Dave Sutton at Rochdale in 1991. Doyle remained at Spotland until 1994 before he ended his career, retiring from professional football. He is now working as a systemic psychotherapist in his hometown of Swansea.

DRAKE, Alonzo

Inside-forward
Town Years: 1909-1910
Born: 1884 Parkgate, Rotherham
Died: 1919 Huddersfield, West Riding of Yorkshire
Playing career: Parkgate, Doncaster Rovers, Sheffield United, Birmingham, Queens Park Rangers, Huddersfield Town, Rotherham Town (1902-1915)

Drake signed for the club in 1909 from Queens Park Rangers and played for Fred Walker's side for a year before club turned professional in 1910. He also played 157 cricket matches for Yorkshire between 1909 and 1914. Drake twice tried to enlist during WW1, only to be refused because of health issues which had been caused by heavy smoking. He died aged 34 in February 1919.

DRING, Raymond 'Ray'

Goalkeeper
Town Years: 1944-1948
Born: 1924 Lincoln, Lincolnshire
Died: 2003 Lincoln, Lincolnshire
Playing career: Huddersfield Town, Colchester United (1944-1948)

Dring signed for the club as an amateur in 1944 but only played four matches before his departure four years later. He had served in the forces and became a school teacher after WW2. Dring later refused pro terms at Colchester United due to his school teaching career. It is thought that he continued in that profession whilst he kept goal for Town. Dring had been living in a Lincoln care home at the time of his death in 2003.

DRINKWATER, Daniel 'Danny'

Central-midfielder
Town Years: 2009-2010 (loan)
Born: 1990 Manchester, Greater Manchester
Playing career: Man United, Huddersfield Town (loan), Cardiff City (loan), Watford (loan), Barnsley (loan), Leicester City, Chelsea (2008-Still Playing)

Drinkwater came to Town on loan from Manchester United in the 2009-10 season and settled into the midfield pretty quickly. He impressed with his performances but Lee Clark was unable to bring him back for the following season. He was loaned out to Cardiff City, and Barnsley before signing for Leicester City in 2012. Drinkwater played a huge part in Leicester's Premier League triumph in the 2015-16 season and his impressive performances encouraged Chelsea to sign him for £35 million in 2017.

DUGGAN, Andrew 'Andy'

Defender
Town Years: 1988-1991
Born: 1967 Bradford, West Riding of Yorkshire
Playing career: Barnsley, Rochdale (loan), Huddersfield Town, Hartlepool United (loan), Rochdale (1986-1991)

Duggan moved from Barnsley in 1988 in a swap deal with Malcolm Shotton and spent two years in Eoin Hand's side before heading for the exit door and signing for Rochdale. After his retirement, Duggan became Lead IT Project Manager for Abbey National in 1992. Duggan has worked for Lloyds Banking Group in Leeds since 2005 in the same role and lives in Bingley.

DUNGWORTH, John

Forward, Academy Coach, Reserve Team Coach, First Team Coach
Town Years: 1970-1975, 2002-2003 (academy coach), 2003-2006 (reserve team coach), 2006-2008 (first team coach)
Born: 1955 Rotherham, West Riding of Yorkshire
Playing career: Huddersfield Town, Barnsley (loan), Oldham Athletic, Rochdale (loan), Aldershot, Shrewsbury Town, Hereford United (loan), Mansfield Town, Rotherham United (1969-1988)

Dungworth began his career at Leeds Road in 1970 and signed professional forms in 1972. He only managed a handful of appearances in his three years at the club before he headed to Oldham Athletic in 1975. Long spells at Alderdhot, Shrewsbury Town, Mansfield Town and Rotherham United followed before he ended his career in 1988. Dungworth has worked for many years in youth football, including roles at Sheffield United and Leeds United's academy. He rejoined Town to work as a youth coach in the Academy and later took on the reserve team under Peter Jackson in 2003 before being appointed as First Team Coach to replace the ill Terry Yorath in 2006. Dungworth remained on the staff under the following manager Andy Ritchie. However, he was fired in 2008 along with Ritchie and Martyn Booty. He later worked with the reserves at Sheffield Wednesday but left the club in 2009 after the sacking of manager, Brian Laws. Dungworth is now working for Sheffield United as the Under-21's coach and has been there since 2013.

Danny Drinkwater

DUNN, Iain

Forward
Town Years: 1992-1997
Born: *1970 Goole, East Riding of Yorkshire*
Playing career: *York City, Chesterfield, Scarborough, Peterborough United, Scarborough, Goole Town, Huddersfield Town (1988-1999)*

'Dunny' started his career at York City in 1988 and played at Bootham Crescent for three years before short periods at Chesterfield, Scarborough and Peterborough followed. Dunn was snapped up by Town from Goole Town and scored on his debut against Bradford City in the FA Cup. He became known as Town's 'super sub' and was utilised many times from the bench, including in the 1995 play-off final when he supplied the cross for Chris Billy's winning goal. Dunn also became the first player in English football to score a golden goal, coming against Lincoln City in the Auto Windscreens Shield in 1994. By 1996, Dunn had fallen out of favour with manager Brian Horton and was loaned to Mick Buxton's Scunthorpe United. 'Dunny' left Town in 1997 and joined Chesterfield for a two year stint before retiring from league football in 1999. He was voted Town's Ultimate Cult Hero in 2004 and is now working for York Council as a street environment officer and has been for many years. 'Dunny' still receives a hero's welcome whenever he returns to Huddersfield.

DUTHIE, Ian

Outside-right
Town Years: 1949-1954
Born: *1930 Trumperton, Forfar, Scotland*
Died: *2010 Huddersfield, West Yorkshire*
Playing career: *Forfar Celtic, Huddersfield Town, Bradford City, Witton Albion, Northwich Victoria (1949-1956)*

After spending some time at Forfar Celtic, Ian Duthie headed South in 1949 and completed his National Service in the RAF whilst at Town. He left for Bradford City in 1954, before announcing his retirement in 1956, when he returned to his original trade as a painter and decorator. Duthie remained in Huddersfield and trained as a teacher, becoming a lecturer in interior decorating at the Northwich School of Art. He then worked at Manchester College of Art and then Holly Bank College (part of Huddersfield Polytechnic).

Duthie later became a senior lecturer and had a degree in education from Leeds University and also a Master's degree from Sheffield University. Since his arrival in Huddersfield in 1949, Duthie had set up home in Salendine Nook and later moved to Honley before his death in Huddersfield at the age of 80 in 2010.

DUXBURY, Lee

Midfielder
Town Years: 1994-1995
Born: *1969 Keighley, West Riding of Yorkshire*
Playing career: *Bradford City, Rochdale, Huddersfield Town, Bradford City, Oldham Athletic, Bury, Harrogate Town, Farsley Celtic, Glenavon (1985-2006)*

Neil Warnock brought Duxbury to the club from local rivals Bradford City in 1994. He played throughout the 1994-95 promotion season but returned to Bradford the following year. He later had periods at Oldham Athletic, Bury, Harrogate Town, Farsley Celtic and Glenavon before retiring in 2006. After spells coaching at Oldham Athletic and managing both Eccleshill United and Thackley, Duxbury joined Holy Family Catholic School in Keighley as a student mentor.

DUXBURY, Robert

Right-back
Town Years: 1910-1912
Born: *1890 Haslingden, Lancashire*
Died: *1962 Darwen, Lancashire*
Playing career: *Huddersfield Town (1910-1912)*

Duxbury arrived at the club in January 1910, unannounced by the media, but he became of the one of few players that were retained by the club after the election to the Football League. The Lancastrain spent two years at the club before his release in 1912, having played just 6 FA Cup games at Leeds Road. Duxbury later lived in Darwen and worked as a motor driver and bread salesman before he died in 1962.

DYER, Alexander 'Alex'

Defender, Assistant Manager
Town Years: 1997-1998, 2014-2015 (asst manager)
Born: *1965 Forest Gate, Greater London*
Playing career: *Watford, Blackpool, Hull City, Crystal Palace, Charlton Athletic, Oxford United, Lincoln City, Barnet, F.C. Maia, Huddersfield Town, Notts County, Kingstonian, Hayes (1982-2001)*

Dyer arrived at the McAlpine Stadium in 1997 after playing for Maia in Portugal and although predominantly a defender, the Londoner also spent time playing up front for Brian Horton's side. He left Town towards the end of the 1997-98 season after Peter Jackson let him join Notts County. Dyer remained at Meadow Lane until 2000 when he joined Kingstonian but this only lasted a year and he retired following a short spell at non-league Hayes. Dyer worked as assistant manager to Chris Powell at Charlton Athletic before they both joined Town early in the 2014-15 season. Both were sacked in November 2015 to make way for David Wagner and Christoph Buehler. For a short period, he was also manager of Welling United in 2017 but is now working as assistant manager to Steve Clarke at Kilmarnock.

Peter Eastoe

DYSON, Jonathan 'Jon'
Utility Player
Town Years: 1990-2002, 2002-2003
Born: *1971 Mirfield, West Riding of Yorkshire*
Playing career: *Huddersfield Town, Nuneaton Borough (loan), Farsley Celtic (1990-2003)*

Jon Dyson signed for Town in 1990 on a part time basis, whilst he studied his Business degree at the University of Huddersfield. After playing for the reserves for a couple of years, Dyson broke into the first team during the 1992-93 season under Ian Ross. Neil Warnock certainly rated him as he played him for half of the 1993-94 and 1994-95 seasons. Played his part in the 1995 promotion by appearing in the team at Wembley in the Play-off Final. Dyson often filled in as a utility player and during his time at the club, played at right-back, centre-half, left-back, in midfield and even up front. Dyson was known for his consistent performances when called upon and always gave 100% effort. In 2002 (his testimonial year) Dyson was released by the club as part of a series of cost cutting measures but was later re-signed on a short term contract by new manager Mick Wadsworth. Dyson was loaned out to Nuneaton Borough during that season and left the club along with most of the squad at the end of the 2002-03 season as Town fell into administration. He now works as a financial advisor at Ebor in Bradford and lives in Honley.

EASTOE, Peter
Forward
Town Years: 1984 (loan)
Born: *1953 Dordon, Tamworth, Staffordshire*
Playing career: *Wolves, Swindon Town,QPR, Everton, West Bromwich Albion, Leicester City (loan), Huddersfield Town (loan), Walsall (loan), Leicester City (loan), Wolverhampton Wanderers (loan), Farense, Louletano, Atherstone United (1971-1987)*

Eastoe signed on loan from West Bromwich Albion in 1983. Having failed to get on the scoresheet during his time at the club it was no surprise when he returned to the Hawthorns in the same year. He later had spells in Portugal with Faranse and Louletano before ending his career at Atherstone United. Eastoe now works at Solus Garden in Droitwich as a picker and regularly watches former club Everton.

EASTWOOD, Simon
Goalkeeper
Town Years: 2006-2010
Born: *1989 Luton, Bedfordshire*
Playing career: *Huddersfield Town, Oxford United, Portsmouth, Blackburn Rovers (2006-Still Playing)*

Eastwood began his career in Town's Academy and was tipped for big things. Was unfortunate to suffer an injury which seemed to stall his progress. Eastwood only managed one first team appearance for the club. Since leaving in 2010, he has played for Oxford United, Halifax Town, Portsmouth, Blackburn Rovers. In 2016 Eastwood returned to Oxford United.

ECCLES, Terence 'Terry'
Forward
Town Years: 1977-1978
Born: *1952 Leeds, West Riding of Yorkshire*
Playing career: *Blackburn Rovers, Mansfield Town, Huddersfield Town, Ethnikos Piraeus, York City, Scarborough (1969-1982)*

Eccles arrived in 1977 from Mansfield Town and he spent just over a year at Leeds Road before heading to Greece to play for Ethnikos Piraeus. He returned to the UK in 1979 and had stints at York City and Scarborough before his retirement. Eccles became a publican and was the landlord of the White Horse in Poppleton, York. Now lives in retirement in Spain and is a practicing Buddhist.

ECCLESTON, Nathan
Forward
Town Years: 2010 (loan)
Born: *1990 Newton Heath, Manchester, Greater Manchester*
Playing career: *Bury, Liverpool, Huddersfield Town (loan), Charlton Athletic (loan), Rochdale (loan), Blackpool, Tranmere Rovers (loan), Carlisle United (loan), Coventry City (loan), Partick Thistle, Kilmarnock, Bekescsaba, Előre (2005-2016)*

Eccleston came on loan from Liverpool towards the end of the 2009-10 season but made very little impact in Lee Clark's side and he returned to Anfield. He later had spells on loan at Charlton Athletic and Rochdale before being offloaded to Blackpool in 2012. Eccleston only made a small amount of appearances in two years at Bloomfield Road and spent time on loan at Tranmere Rovers, Carlisle United and Coventry City before signing for Partick Thistle in 2014. Eccleston has been without a club since 2016 and now runs his own women's clothing range, Peaches Sportswear.

EDGAR, David
Defender
Town Years: 2015 (loan)
Born: *1987 Kitchener, Ontario, Canada*
Playing career: *London City, Newcastle United, Burnley, Swansea City (loan), Birmingham City, Huddersfield Town (loan), Sheffield United (loan), Vancouver Whitecaps FC, Whitecaps FC 2 (loan), Nashville SC, Ottawa Fury (2005-Still Playing)*

Ontario born Edgar was signed by Chris Powell on loan from Birmingham City in 2015 but his performances failed to impress and he quickly returned to his parent club. He had a one year spell at MLS club Vancouver Whitecaps before leaving in 2017. Edgar last played for Ottowa Fury in the United Soccer League but departed in 2018.

EDMONDSON, Darren
Defender
Town Years: 1997-2000
Born: *1971 Coniston, Cumberland*
Playing career: *Carlisle United, Huddersfield Town, Plymouth Argyle (loan), York City, Chester City, Barrow, Workington (1990-2013)*

Before he joined Town in 1997, Edmondson had spent seven years at Carlisle United as a professional, making over 250 appearances for the first team. However, in the three years he spent at Town, Edmondson would struggle to make 50 appearances for the first team. He was sold to York City in 2000 and spent four years at Bootham Crescent, he was part of the team that were relegated from the Football League in 2004. He later had a spell at non-league Barrow and became player-manager of Workington in 2007, remaining at the club until 2013 when he left to take over at Barrow. He was later sacked in 2015. Edmondson also had a short spell as caretaker manager of Bradford Park Avenue in early 2016 before becoming Head of Academy at Carlisle United. He had previously worked as a sports tutor at Lakes College in Cumbria for five years before leaving in 2014.

EDWARDS, Keith
Forward
Town Years: 1990 (loan), 1990-1991
Born: *1957 Stockton-on-Tees, County Durham*
Playing career: *Wolves, Sheffield United, Hull City, Leeds United, Aberdeen, Stockport County, Huddersfield Town (1974-1990)*

Edwards originally joined on loan from Stockport County in 1990 and signed for Eoin Hand's side permanently that same year. Although he didn't play many games, he did manage to bag the last hat-trick of his professional career during his stay. After retiring from the game, Edwards has worked for a national charity, as a lorry driver and commentates on Sheffield United games for BBC Radio Sheffield.

EDWARDS, Robert 'Robbie'

Left-back/Midfielder
Town Years: 1996-2000, 2003-2005
Born: *1970 Manchester, Lancashire*
Playing career: *Crewe Alexandra, Huddersfield Town, Chesterfield, Huddersfield Town (1988-2006)*

Rob Edwards is a Town legend. He arrived at the McAlpine in 1996 from Crewe as a winger but was converted to left-back by Peter Jackson. Later scored a famous goal against Manchester City which had come at the end of a 16 pass move. Edwards fell out of favour under Steve Bruce and was moved on to Chesterfield in 2000. When Peter Jackson returned to the club in 2003 he re-signed Edwards and instantly made him club captain. Edwards eventually lost his place to youngster Anthony Lloyd but this was not the end of the story though - he cemented his place in Town history by coming on as a substitute during the second leg of the play-off semi-final against Lincoln City and firing in the winning goal. He also came off the bench in the final and converted the first penalty in the shoot-out which saw Town promoted to Division Two. He was released in 2005. Edwards was later involved with Holmfirth Town, is currently Shelley F.C.'s coach and also works as a joiner from his home in Huddersfield.

ELLAM, Roy

Centre-half
Town Years: 1966-1972, 1974-1975
Born: *1943 Hemsworth, West Riding of Yorkshire*
Playing career: *Bradford City, Huddersfield Town, Leeds United, Philadelphia Atoms, Mossley, Washington Diplomats (1961-1980)*

Ellam had two stints at Leeds Road, first joining Town in 1966 from Bradford City. He was an ever-present at centre-half during the 1969-70 promotion campaign but left in controversy due to himself, Frank Worthington, Trevor Cherry and Jimmy Lawson demanding a cash incentive to help Town, who were rooted at the bottom of the First Division, stay up. Ellam left Town to join Leeds United at the end of the 1971-72 season but only managed a few games before returning to Town in 1974. Ellam later had a spell playing in America for Philadelphia Atoms and Washington Diamonds before rounding off his career at non-league Mossley and Gainsborough Trinity, the latter as player-manager. He later worked as a compost salesman before becoming the landlord of the Nelson Inn in Thornhill Lees, Dewsbury. In recent years, he can be found helping out in his daughter's gym in Mirfield. Ellam also watches Town regularly with his grandson.

ELLIOTT, Thomas 'Tom'
Forward
Town Years: 1912-1919
Born: *1890 Annfield Plain, County Durham*
Died: *1955 Ryton-on-Tyne, County Durham*
Playing career: *Annfield Plain, West Stanley, Gainsborough Trinity, West Stanley, Huddersfield Town, Grimsby Town, Nottingham Forest, Brentford, Durham City, Crewe Alexandra, Annfield Plain, Crawcrook Albion, Newcastle Tramways (1910-1924)*
Elliott signed from non-league Gainsborough Trinity in 1912 but four years of his career were interrupted by World War One. Although after the War had ended, Elliott remained on the books until his departure in 1919 when he joined Grimsby Town for a short time. Elliott was deaf and is thought to have passed away in May 1955.

ELLIOTT, Anthony 'Tony'
Goalkeeper
Town Years: 1992-1993
Born: *1969 Nuneaton, Warwickshire*
Playing career: *Birmingham City, Hereford United, Huddersfield Town, Carlisle United, Cardiff City, Scarborough (1986-1999)*
Elliott signed from Hereford United in 1992 but only managed a modicum of appearances during the 1992-93 season before being offloaded to Carlisle United. He lasted three years in Cumbria before rounding off his career with time at Cardiff City and Scarborough, retiring in 1999. Elliott then worked as the assistant manager at Workington Reds between 1999 and 2000 before becoming a goalkeeping coach for Lancashire Football Association. Elliott later worked for Speedmark UK as a fundraising events coordinator as well as working as assistant at Newcastle Blue Star and goalkeeping coach at Gretna for a short spell in 2008. Elliott has also had spells as a scout at Manchester City and assistant manager at Workington but has worked for the FA since 2007 in a number of roles. He was the goalkeeping coach for England's Futsal Squad (2007-2016), the head of women's international youth goalkeeping (2016-2017), goalkeeping coach of the England Cerebal Palsy Squad (2013-2018) and now combines his roles as goalkeeping coach of England's Blind Squad, head coach of England Women's Deaf Futsal Squad and goalkeeping coach of Birmingham City Ladies.

ENDEAN, Barry
Forward
Town Years: 1975-1976
Born: *1946 Chester-le-Street, County Durham*
Playing career: *Everton, Watford, Charlton Athletic, Blackburn Rovers, Huddersfield Town, Workington (loan), Hartlepool United (1968-1977)*
Endean joined in 1975 after signing from Blackburn Rovers but only made a few appearances for Tom Johnston's side before heading to Hartlepool United the following year. After retiring as a player in 1977, Endean became a builder in his native Chester-le-Street and still resides there.

EVANS, David 'Dai'
Half-back
Town Years: 1928-1929
Born: *1902 Abercanaid, Merthyr Tydfil, Wales*
Died: *1951 Glamorgan, Wales*
Playing career: *Bolton W, Reading, Huddersfield Town, Bury, Burton Town, Bangor City (1920-1935)*
After four years at Reading, Welsh international Evans signed for Town. He played 18 games during the 1928-29 season for Jack Chaplin's side. Evans then lasted a year at Bury before joining Burton Town in 1930. Later died in 1951 in Glamorgan.

EVANS, Gareth
Left-back
Town Years: 2001-2003
Born: *1981 Leeds, West Yorkshire*
Playing career: *Leeds United, Huddersfield Town, Blackpool (1998-2006)*
Signing from Leeds United in 2001, Evans spent two injury plagued years at the club before he was released whilst the club were in administration at the end of the 2002-03 season. He spent three years at Blackpool before he announced his retirement in 2006. After his playing days ended, Evans soon landed a job at nPower as a Data Correction Data Administrator, later becoming a Volume Allocation Data Analyst and also a Business Analyst. He left for Farnell Element14 in 2009 and worked as European CRM Executive, combining that role with that of Marketing and Media Director at his local rugby league club, Hunslet Hawks. Since 2015, Evans has been the Senior CRM Manager for Premier Farnell in Leeds and cMarketing and Media Director at Hunslet RLFC, his second spell there, being heavily involved with the rebrand of that club.

EVES, Melvyn 'Mel'

Forward
Town Years: 1984 (loan)
Born: *1956 Darlaston, Staffordshire*
Playing career: *Wolverhampton Wanderers, Huddersfield Town (loan), Sheffield United, Gillingham, Mansfield Town (loan), Walsall, King's Lynn (loan), Cheltenham Town (loan), Willenhall Town, Telford United (1975-1990)*

Eves arrived at the club in 1984 on loan from Wolverhampton Wanderers and scored 4 goals in 7 matches before returning to his parent club. Eves rounded off his career at Telford United, retiring from football in 1990. After his career had come to an end, Eves became an independent financial advisor and also a licensed FA agent. He is now currently a Performance Master Coach and does radio commentary on Wolves matches for BBC Radio WM.

EWING, David

Left-back
Town Years: 1909-1910
Born: *1881 Elsecar, West Riding of Yorkshire*
Died: *1926 Axminster, Devon*
Playing career: *Firth Park Wesleyans, Worksop Town, Meadowhall, Tinsley, Ranmoor Wesleyans, Workington, Brunswick Mission, Chesterfield Town, Brentford, Huddersfield Town, Castleford Town, Machen, Queens Park Rangers, Newport County (1907-1913)*

Ewing signed from Brentford in 1909 and played just one season for Fred Walker's side before he left the club in 1910, once the club turned professional. He signed for Castleford Town in July 1910 and later played for Queens Park Rangers and Newport County before he left football in 1913. Ewing later worked as an engineer before he died in June 1926.

FACEY, Delroy

Forward
Town Years: 1997-2002, 2005 (loan)
Born: *1981 Huddersfield, West Yorkshire*
Playing career: *Huddersfield Town, Bolton Wanderers, WBA, Hull City, Huddersfield Town (loan), Oldham Athletic, Tranmere Rovers, Rotherham United, Gillingham, Notts County, Lincoln City, Hereford United, (1996-2015)*

Facey made his debut for Town in 1997 and by the start of the next century he was highly thought of at Town, attracting interest from bigger clubs, eventually being sold to Premier League Bolton Wanderers in 2002. He was arrested in 2013 for allegations of match fixing before being jailed in 2015 for two and a half years. Facey is now a free man and works in care back in his hometown.

FAIRCLOUGH, Arthur

Manager
Town Years: 1912-1919
Born: *1873 Barnsley, West Riding of Yorkshire*
Died: *1947 Sheffield, West Riding of Yorkshire*
Management career: *Barnsley, Huddersfield Town, Leeds United (1898-1930)*

Fairclough arrived at Town from Barnsley in 1912 and was said to have laid down the platform for Herbert Chapman's later successes at Town. He was part of the proposed merger with Leeds City, which was foiled by the Town faithful who bought £1 shares to prevent the merger. In 1919, Fairclough became the first manager of the new Leeds United and he remained at the club for eight years until his departure in 1927. He became manager at Barnsley for a short time until 1930 when he returned in 1935 as Director of Football and later died in a Sheffield nursing home in 1947.

FAIRCLOUGH, Michael 'Mick'
Midfield / Forward
Town Years: 1971-1975
Born: *1952 Drogheda, Ireland*
Playing career: *Drogheda, Huddersfield Town, CIE/Transport, Dundalk, Drogheda United, Sligo Rovers, Newry Town (1970-1986)*

Irishman Fairclough arrived in 1971 from Drogheda and spent four years at the club. Unfortunately, he suffered an injury and retired from the professional game in 1975. He made a comeback in 1979 when he played for Irish club CIE/Transport and signed for Dundalk in 1980, spending three years at the club and playing over 100 matches and scoring over 50 goals for the club. Fairclough helped the club to qualify for the 1981 UEFA Cup and also scored in the FAI Cup Final against Sligo Rovers in the 1980-81 season. It was during his time at Dundalk when Fairclough was capped by the Republic of Ireland twice in 1982. Fairclough went on to play for former club Drogheda, Sligo Rovers and Newry Town before announcing his retirement in 1986. He now works for IBM as Europe Software Group IT Manager in Ireland.

FAYERS, Frederick 'Fred'
Centre-half
Town Years: 1910-1915
Born: *1890 King's Lynn, Norfolk*
Died: *1954 Huddersfield, West Riding of Yorkshire*
Playing career: *Watford, Huddersfield Town, Manchester City (1907-1923)*

Originally a Watford player, 'Tiny' Fayers arrived at Leeds Road towards the end of the 1909-1910 season to sign for Fred Walker's side. The club turned professional in 1910 and Dick Pudan took over from Walker in time for the new season, Fayers was part of the first ever professional side at Leeds Road and played up until the suspension of League football in 1915, after the outbreak of World War One. Fayers remained on Town's books throughout the War, and made 1 appearance during the 1916-17 season and 2 further appearances during the following season. He later left the club in 1919 to join Manchester City, where he played until he moved to Halifax Town in 1923. Fayers retired from professional football in 1924 after a full season at Halifax, later coaching the team at some point. Following this, he worked as a bricklayer. Died in 1954.

FEARNLEY, Harold 'Harry'
Goalkeeper
Town Years: 1951-1963
Born: *1935 Penistone, Barnsley,*
Died: *2013 Poole, Dorset*
Playing career: *Penistone Church, Huddersfield Town, Oxford United, Doncaster Rovers (1951-1967)*

Fearnley signed from Penistone Church in 1951, turning professional a year later and keeping goal in the reserves. After his National Service, Fearnley broke into the first team in 1955 and was a regular in the first team whilst the club were in the Second Division. He was given a benefit in 1958 and left for Oxford United in 1963 for a fee of £3,500. Fearnley moved to Doncaster Rovers in 1966 and later became the manager of non-league Emley in 1968. His time at Emley coincided with their rise up the leagues and after leaving in 1971 he returned in 1972 with Kevin McHale as his assistant manager. Fearnley left Emley in 1975, moving to Poole where he died in 2013.

FELSTEAD, Thomas
Goalkeeper
Town Years: 1909-1911
Born: *1887 Bolsover, Derbyshire*
Died: *1956 Market Warsop, Nottinghamshire*
Playing career: *Bradford City, Huddersfield Town, Mirfield United (1909-1911)*

Felstead came to Leeds Road in 1909 from nearby Bradford City and kept goal for Fred Walker's side during the 1909-10 season. After the club turned professional in 1910, Felstead played just 2 professional games for Dick Pudan's side during the 1910-11 season before he was released. Felstead lived the rest of his days in Warsop, where he worked as a miner before he was injured in an acident. He later passed away in 1956.

FIRTH, Francis 'Franny'
Winger
Town Years: 1973-1978
Born: *1956 Dewsbury, West Riding of Yorkshire*
Died: *2018 Wakefield, West Yorkshire*
Playing career: *Huddersfield Town, Halifax Town, Bury, Witton Albion (1973-1983)*

Firth began his career at Town in the youth team and was part of the side that reached the Youth Cup Final in 1974. He eventually made his debut towards the end of the 1974-75 season, becoming a regular in the side mid-way through the 1975-76 season.

After a bad leg break early in the 1976-77 season, Firth didn't play another game at Leeds Road and he joined Halifax Town in 1978. He ended his career at Bury, after which he started a coffee company called Fran and Co., running this for a number of years before joining Royal Mail and working as a postman. Firth later worked in care before his death in May 2018 in Pinderfields Hospital, Wakefield.

FLETCHER, Peter

Forward
Town Years: 1978-1982
Born: *1953 Manchester, Lancashire*
Playing career: *Manchester United, Hull City, Stockport County, Huddersfield Town (1969-1982)*
Fletcher arrived from Stockport County in 1978. He was a regular in the side during 1978-79 season and played a big part in the 1979-80 promotion side, chipping in with 17 goals. Unfortunately, Fletcher spent the entire 1980-81 season out with a back injury but returned for the 1981-82 season. However, he had to retire due to the back injury that had kept him out the season before and was granted a testimonial along with Dick Taylor. He ended up working in security in Stockport for almost thirty years before retiring at the age of 60. Fletcher now lives in retirement in Stockport.

Michael Flynn

FLYNN, Michael

Midfielder
Town Years: 2008-2009
Born: *1980 Newport, Wales*
Playing career: *Newport County, Barry Town, Wigan Athletic, Blackpool (loan), Gillingham, Blackpool, Huddersfield Town, Darlington (loan), Bradford City, Newport County, Undy Athletic (1999-2017)*
Flynn was brought in by Stan Ternent at the start of the 2008-09 season and was a regular in the side until Ternent was sacked in November 2008. He was immediately loaned out to Darlington by caretaker manager Gerry Murphy and left the club at the end of the season, signing for Bradford City. Flynn played over 100 games at Valley Parade before joining hometown club Newport County in 2012. In 2014, Flynn became director of Newport's academy but was overlooked for the role of Academy Manager in 2015 and left to become Undy Athletic's player-manager, but returned to become Newport's first team coach in 2016. He was later appointed Football and Business Development Director before again joining the coaching staff. Following the removal of Graham Westley in 2017, Flynn became caretaker manager and saved them from relegation to the Conference. He was given the job permanently and remains the manager at Newport County.

FOGG, William 'Billy'

Right-half
Town Years: 1928-1933
Born: *1903 Birkenhead, Cheshire*
Died: *1991 Oxton, Hoylake, Cheshire*
Playing career: *Wirral Railways, Tranmere Rovers, Bangor City, Huddersfield Town, Clapton Orient, New Brighton (1924-1937)*
Fogg signed from Bangor City in May 1928 for a fee of £20 and played a couple of games for Jack Chaplin's side during the 1928-29 season. He became a regular in the side during the season after under new manager, Clem Stephenson. Fogg played throughout the 1930 FA Cup campaign but suffered an injury in the semi-final, he still received a runners-up medal despite missing the final game all together. Fogg left Leeds Road in 1933 to sign for Clapton Orient where he spent three years before joining New Brighton. After his retirement as a player, Fogg later worked as a shipbuilder in Birkenhead before he passed away in 1991.

FOSTER, Jack
Centre-forward
Town Years: 1909-1910
Born: *1878 Rawmarsh, West Riding of Yorkshire*
Died: *1944 Sheffield, West Riding of Yorkshire*
Playing career: *Rotherham Church Institute, Thornhill United, Blackpool, Rotherham Town, Watford, Sunderland, West Ham United, Southampton, Huddersfield Town, Castleford Town, Morley (1901-1911)*

Foster arrived from Southampton as an amateur in May 1909 and he played in Town's last season as an amateur side and once the club turned professional, he left the club in July 1910 to sign for Castleford Town. He returned to Leeds Road in 1912 as assistant trainer and later worked as assistant manager at Bradford City between 1926 and 1928 and also had a spell as caretaker manager at Valley Parade in 1928. Foster later worked as a scout at Portsmouth before his retirement in 1938 and later died in September 1944 while he was living in Sheffield.

FOWLER, Lee
Midfielder
Town Years: 2003-2004 (loan) 2004-2006
Born: *1983 Cardiff, Wales*
Playing career: *Coventry City, Huddersfield Town (loan), Huddersfield Town, Scarborough (loan), Burton Albion, Newport County (loan), Newport County, Forest Green Rovers, Kettering Town, Oxford United, Cirencester Town, Halesowen Town, Forest Green Rovers, Wrexham, Fleetwood Town, Doncaster Rovers, Forest Green Rovers (loan), Burton Albion (loan), Kidderminster Harriers, The New Saints, Cefn Druids, Nuneaton Town, Crawley Town (loan), Wrexham, Tamworth (loan), AFC Telford United, Holywell Town F.C. (1999-201?)*

After starting his career at Coventry City, Fowler arrived at the McAlpine at the start of the 2003-04 season on loan and played a number of matches during the season but received two red cards in the process. He came on as a substitute in the 2004 Playoff Final and ended up scoring the winning penalty in the shootout at the end of the game. Fowler signed permanently in 2004 but fell out of favour with Peter Jackson in 2005 and never played for the club again, being loaned out to Scarborough for the 2005-06 season. Since he left the club, Fowler has played for no fewer than twenty different clubs including Burton Albion, Newport County, Kettering Town, Forest

Green Rovers, Wrexham, Doncaster Rovers, Nuneaton Town and AFC Telford United. His last known club was Holywell Town in the Welsh League and he has worked as a football coach for North Wales Elite Soccer. After a spell as assistant manager at Nuneaton Borough, Fowler is now the manager of Ilkeston Town.

FOWLER, Martin
Midfielder
Town Years: 1974-1978
Born: *1957 York, North Riding of Yorkshire*
Playing career: *Huddersfield Town, Blackburn Rovers, Hartlepool United (loan), Stockport County, Scunthorpe United, Rowntree Mackintosh (1974-1983)*

Fowler came through the youth ranks at Town and was part of the 1974 youth team that reached the FA Youth Cup Final. He later turned professional, breaking into the first team and at one point, then Manchester United manager enquired about signing Fowler. The deal fell through when Tom Johnston demanded Docherty paid £100,000, Docherty refused and told Johnston he wouldn't pay that figure for a Fourth Division player. Fowler played for the side up until 1978, when he headed for Blackburn Rovers. He remained at Ewood Park until 1980 and moved to Stockport County. Two years at Stockport County saw him cement a regular first team place in the side and he later enjoyed a period at Scunthorpe United before retiring from the game in 1983. Fowler later worked for Royal Mail as a postman and is now working for a national bookmaker's chain.

FRANCE, Michael 'Paul'
Defender
Town Years: 1985-1989
Born: *1968 Huddersfield, West Riding of Yorkshire*
Playing career: *Huddersfield Town, Cobh Ramblers, Bristol City, Burnley, Altrincham, Stalybridge Celtic, Ashton United (1985-1999)*

After a very uneventful career which saw him make 19 league appearances in five years for Town, Bristol City and Burnley, France moved to Altrincham. He later worked as Football in the Community Officer at Town before moving to Burnley to become the Assistant Football in the Community Officer in 2015.

FRANCE, Anthony 'Tony'
Inside-forward
Town Years: 1956-1961
Born: *1939 Sheffield, West Riding of Yorkshire*
Playing career: *Huddersfield Town, Darlington, Stockport County (1956-1964)*

Signing from school, France only managed a handful of appearances for the first team in his five years at Leeds Road. All of France's appearances came during Bill Shankly's reign but Eddie Boot was in charge by the time he left the club in 1961 to sign for Darlington. He later signed for Stockport County in 1963 before ending his proffesional career in 1964. France now resides in Poole in retirement.

FRANCIS, Stephen 'Steve'
Goalkeeper
Town Years: 1993-1999
Born: *1964 Billericay, Essex*
Playing career: *Chelsea, Reading, Huddersfield Town, Northampton Town (1982-1999)*

Francis signed from Reading in 1993 and was immediately installed as the first choice goalkeeper in Neil Warnock's side. He remained as the primary goalkeeper at Town up until the 1997-98 season and played in both Wembley Finals (1994 and 1995) and only missed a few games during that four year strech. Town had a disastrous start to the 1997-98 season and didn't win until the 15th game of the season, Francis began the season as the first choice keeper but was dropped for Derek O'Connor in what turned out to be Brian Horton's last game. Former team-mate Peter Jackson came in as manager and decided straight away that Francis was not good enough and dropped him for the rest of the season. Left for Northampton Town in 1999. He was last known to be working as a postman in Henley-in-Arden and is living in Solihull.

FRASER, William 'Billy'
Outside-left
Town Years: 1963-1965
Born: *1945 Edinburgh, Scotland*
Playing career: *Huddersfield Town, Heart of Midlothian, Washington Whips, Boston Beacons, Washington Darts, Miami Gatos (1963-1972)*

Fraser signed for Town straight from school and played a number of matches on the wing during his time at the club but suffered from a broken hip.

He returned to his home country of Scotland and played for Heart of Midlothian and later moved to America to play for Washington Darts, also playing for Miami Gators in later years. Fraser worked in America on a building site and in a pub before he moved to Australia to play for Granville Soccer Club in Sydney. Whilst in Australia, Fraser had worked for a sporting goods company before he returned to the UK to work in marketing and is running his own business in Edinburgh.

FREAR, Bryan
Inside-forward
Town Years: 1949-1950 (amateur), 1950-1957
Born: *1933 Cleckheaton, West Riding of Yorkshire*
Died: *1997 Bradford, West Yorkshire*
Playing career: *Liversedge, Huddersfield Town, Chesterfield, Halifax Town (1949-1965)*

Hailing from Cleckheaton, Frear was contracted for a local side Liversedge FC as an amateur in 1949 and signed professional forms in 1950. He made sporadic appearances over the next seven years before leaving for Chesterfield in 1957. Frear remained at Saltergate for seven years before rounding off his career at Halifax Town, retiring in 1965 after one year at The Shay preceeding his death in 1997.

FREEMAN, Neil
Goalkeeper
Town Years: 1981 (loan) [two spells]
Born: *1955 Northampton, Northamptonshire*
Playing career: *Arsena, Grimsby Town, Southend United, Birmingham City, Walsall (loan), Huddersfield Town (loan), Peterborough United, Northampton Town (1971-1983)*

Neil Freeman had two spells at Leeds Road on loan during the 1980-81 season and was brought in after injuries to Andy Rankin and Dick Taylor. He came on loan from Birmingham City and at the conclusion of his loan deal wished to stay but Jim Smith, his manager at Birmingham, wouldn't hear of it. Freeman later had spells at Peterborough United and Northampton Town before retiring from professional football in 1983. He was offered a return to professional football with Hull City but turned it down in favour of becoming a policeman in the Northamptonshire area. Freeman retierd in the early 2010s and now lives in East Haddon.

GALLACHER, Kevin
Forward
Town Years: 2002
Born: *1966 Clydebank, Scotland*
Playing career: *Dundee United, Coventry City, Blackburn Rovers, Newcastle United, Preston North End, Sheffield Wed, Huddersfield Town (1983-2002)*
Gallacher signed on a short term deal under Mick Wadsworth in the 2002-03 season and played 7 games for the side before leaving the club and announcing his retirement from professional football. He now resides in Blackburn and runs his own soccer school, named 'G8 Soccer School' as well as working as a freelance co-commentator on Premier League and Football League fixtures.

GALLEN, Kevin
Forward
Town Years: 2000-2001
Born: *1975 Hammersmith, Greater London*
Playing career: *QPR, Huddersfield Town, Barnsley, Plymouth Argyle (loan), Milton Keynes Dons, Luton Town (loan), Luton Town, Barnet (loan) (1992-2013)*
After six years at Queens Park Rangers, Gallen signed for Town in 2000 but spent just one season at the McAlpine before he left for Barnsley in 2001. Despite this, he returned to QPR that same year. He spent another six years at his first club and later spent time at Milton Keynes Dons, Luton Town, Braintree Town, Leverstock Green and finally Aylesbury United, before finally retiring in 2013. Gallen is currently working for QPR's academy as a youth development coach.

GALLOGLY, Charlie 'Chas'
Right-back
Town Years: 1949-1952
Born: *1919 Gilford, County Down, Northern Ireland*
Died: *1993 New York, United States*
Playing career: *Shelbourne, Belfast Celtic, Waterford, Glenavon, Huddersfield Town, Watford, Bournemouth & Boscombe Athletic (1945-1955)*
Moving from Glenavon, Gallogly arrived at Leeds Road in 1949 and spent three years at the club before heading to Watford in 1952. He left Vicarage Road after two years at the club in 1954 and had a one year stint at Bournemouth before hanging up his boots in 1955. Gallogly emigrated to America in 1958 and later ran a public house in a New York suburb before he passed away in 1993.

GARNER, Joseph 'Joe'
Forward
Town Years: 2010-2011 (loan)
Born: *1988 Blackburn, Lancashire*
Playing career: *Blackburn Rovers, Carlisle United, Nottingham Forest, Huddersfield Town (loan), Watford, Preston North End, Rangers, Ipswich Town, Wigan Athletic (2005-Still Playing)*
Garner joined on loan in 2010 from Nottingham Forest but never managed to score a goal for Lee Clark's side before he returned to his parent club in 2011. He had a further loan period at Scunthorpe United before being sold to Watford the same year. He later spent time at Preston North End and Rangers before signing for Ipswich Town in 2017. Garner spent just a year at Portman Road before joining Paul Cook's Wigan Athletic in time for the 2018-19 season.

GARNER, Paul
Left-back
Town Years: 1972-1975
Born: *1955 Edlington, Doncaster, West Riding of Yorkshire*
Playing career: *Huddersfield Town, Sheffield United, Gillingham (loan), Mansfield Town (1972-1989)*
Garner began his career at Town in 1972 in the youth team and was part of the team that reached the FA Youth Cup Final in 1974. He also played in the first team during this time, making over 100 appearances before heading to Sheffield United in 1975. Garner spent nine years at Bramall Lane, making over 250 appearances before moving to Mansfield Town in 1984 and eventually retiring in 1989. He later worked as an insurance agent and a milkman before becoming a plumber. Garner is still living in his home of Sheffield and watches Sheffield United on occasion.

GARTLAND, Paul
Left-back
Town Years: 1976-1980
Born: *1959 Shipley, Bradford,*
Playing career: *Huddersfield Town (1976-c1990)*
Paul Gartland signed for Town in 1976 as an apprentice and later turned professional in 1977, playing a number of matches during the reign of Tom Johnston. Although he remained on the books after Mick Buxton took over in 1978, he left the club in 1980 to sign for non-league Guiseley.

Gartland went on to play for Emley for many years, including in the 1988 FA Vase Final at Wembley. He also graduated from Leeds University in 1985 and joined Horton Housing Association in Bradford in 1988, progressing to Services Manager in 1993 where has held the role of Chief Executive Officer there since 2014.

GARWOOD, Colin
Forward
Town Years: 1974-1976
Born: 1949 Heacham, Norfolk
Playing career: *Peterborough United, Oldham Athletic, Huddersfield Town, Colchester United, Portsmouth, Aldershot, Boston United (1967-1982)*
Garwood signed from Oldham Athletic in 1974 and spent two years at the club before his departure in 1976 to sign for Colchester United. After two years there, Garwood signed for Portsmouth in 1978 and is fondly remembered by the Pompey faithful and he still returns to Portsmouth often. He spent another two years at Aldershot where his professional career come to an end in 1982. Garwood has since worked for an engineering company in Wisbech, where he lives.

GAVIN, Jason
Centre-half
Town Years: 2003 (loan)
Born: 1980 Dublin, Ireland
Playing career: *Crumlin United, Middlesbrough, Hartlepool United (loan), Grimsby Town (loan), Huddersfield Town (loan), Bradford City, Shamrock Rovers, Drogheda United, St Patrick's Athletic, Stirling Lions (1996-2012)*
Gavin spent a short loan spell at Town during the 2002-03 season before he returned to his parent club, Middlesbrough. He was released at the end of that season and signed for Bradford City, playing at Valley Parade for two years before returning to his native Ireland. Gavin turned out for Shamrock Rovers, Drogheda United and St. Patrick's Athletic before he moved to Australia to sign for Stirling Lions in 2010.

DID YOU KNOW?"

"Chris Powell became the first black manager in Town's history when he became the manager in 2014."

GERRARD, Anthony
Centre-half
Town Years: 2012-2015
Born: 1986 Huyton
Playing career: *Everton, Walsall, Cardiff City, Huddersfield Town, Shrewsbury Town, Oldham Athletic, Carlisle United (2004-Still Playing)*
Gerrard was signed by Simon Grayson for the 2012-13 season and spent three years at the club before he fell out of favour and joined Shrewsbury Town in 2015. After the short time at Shrewsbury, Gerrard went on to play for Oldham Athletic but he was sacked in 2018. His former manager John Sheridan signed him for Carlisle United during the 2018-19 season.

GIBSON, Brian
Full-back
Town Years: 1951-1962
Born: 1928 Huddersfield, West Riding of Yorkshire
Died: 2010 Mirfield, West Yorkshire
Playing career: *Huddersfield Town (1951-1962)*
Gibson arrived at Leeds Road in 1951 after playing for his local side, Paddock Athletic and made 171 appearances for his hometown club before ending his career in 1962. Gibson remained at Leeds Road to run the pools scheme with former team-mate Eddie Brennan until 1970 when he eventually left the club. From 1970 until his retirement in 2006, Gibson ran Taylor Hill dripping refiners AW Chambers. He passed away, four years later, in 2010 aged 82.

GILBOY, Bertram
Inside-forward
Town Years: 1912-1913
Born: 1894 Islington, London
Died: 1974 Southampton, Hampshire
Playing career: *Southend United, Huddersfield Town, Preston North End, Swansea Town, Brentford, Gillingham, Treherbert (1911-1922)*
After a stint at Southend United, Gilboy arrived at Leeds Road in 1912, signing for Arthur Fairclough's side and spent just one year at the club before his exit in 1913. Following his departure from Town, Gilboy played for Preston North End and Swansea Town before the outbreak of World War One. Gilboy served as a gunner in the Royal Garrison Artillery and the Labour Corps during the War. He later worked as a civil servant in Southampton prior to his death in March 1974 at the age of 79.

GILLIGAN, John
Forward
Town Years: 1976 (loan)
Born: *1957 Abingdon, Oxfordshire*
Playing career: *Swindon Town, Huddersfield Town (loan), Northampton Town (loan), Sligo Rovers (1975-1977)*

Gilligan was loaned to Town in 1976 from Swindon Town, making a solitary appearance for Tom Johnston's side before he returned to his parent club. He was later loaned out to Northampton Town and also had a short spell at Sligo Rovers before his career came to an end. Gilligan is now living in his home town of Abingdon and was last thought to be working as a coach driver for Stagecoach.

GILLIVER, Allan
Forward
Town Years: 1961-1966
Born: *1944 Swallownest, Rotherham, West Riding of Yorkshire*
Playing career: *Huddersfield Town, Blackburn Rovers, Rotherham United, Brighton & Hove Albion, Lincoln City, Bradford City, Stockport County, Baltimore Comets, Boston United, Gainsborough Trinity, Bradford City (1961-1979)*

Gilliver began his career at Town in 1961 and remained on the books for five years. Although he scored 22 league goals in 45 league games, he was rarely a first team regular over those years. He left in 1966 to join Blackburn Rovers where he played for two years before he signed for Rotherham United for a year between 1968 and 1969. Towards the end of that year he signed for Brighton & Hove Albion. After some time at Lincoln City, Gilliver signed for Bradford City in 1972, scoring over 30 goals in 70 games before leaving to spend a year at Stockport County. He drifted into non-league towards the end of the 1970s but played 2 matches as a non-contract player for Bradford between 1978 and 1979. After his retirement as a player, Gilliver held many roles at Valley Parade including groundsman, safety officer and commercial manager, because of this, he was granted a testimonial in 1998 and finally retired in 2007. In the early 2010s, Gilliver was diagnosed with dementia causing he and his wife to become very involved with charity work to raise awareness of the disease.

GLAZZARD, Jim
Forward
Town Years: 1943-1956
Born: *1923 Normanton, West Riding of Yorkshire*
Died: *1996 Huddersfield, West Yorkshire*
Playing career: *Altofts Colliery, Huddersfield Town, Everton, Mansfield Town (1942-1957)*

Indigenous to Normanton, Glazzard signed for the club in 1943, whilst working as a miner, and played in the Wartime League for the club until the Football League resumed in 1946. He was a regular in the team from 1946 onwards and was part of the 1952-53 promotion winning side. Glazzard played centre forward and was very good with his head, scoring many goals from crosses by his good friend Vic Metcalfe. He left for Everton in 1956, having scored 142 goals for Town. Following his retirement in 1957, Glazzard returned to Huddersfield and ran a greengrocer's shop for many years in Sheepridge before suffering from dementia in the last years of his life. He was still best friends with former teammate Vic Metcalfe, who helped him with his shopping and other things when Glazzard was ill. "Gentleman Jim" passed away in 1996.

GLENNON, Matthew 'Matt'
Goalkeeper
Town Years: 2006-2010
Born: *1978 Stockport, Cheshire*
Playing career: *Bolton Wanderers, Hull City, Carlisle United, Falkirk, St Johnstone, Huddersfield Town, Bradford City, Stockport County (1997-2017)*

Glennon signed from Carlisle United in 2006 and quickly became the No.1 choice between the sticks and had two solid seasons. Caretaker manager Gerry Murphy later dropped Glennon in favour of 18 year old Alex Smithies. Glennon never regained his place in the team and was loaned out to Bradford City before he left the Galpharm in 2010. He headed to his hometown club Stockport County and spent two years at Edgeley Park, followed by a short time spent at non-league Chester. Glennon then joined F.C. Halifax Town in 2012 and spent four years at The Shay, reaching the Conference North playoffs in 2013 and also winning the West Riding County Cup in the same year. He is now the goalkeeping coach at A.F.C. Emley, match summariser for Town games on BBC Radio Leeds and also runs his own hairdressers G27 in Emley.

GLOVER, Lee
Forward
Town Years: 1997 (loan)
Born: *1970 Kettering, Northamptonshire*
Playing career: *Nottingham Forest, Leicester City (loan), Barnsley (loan), Luton Town (loan), Port Vale, Rotherham United, Huddersfield Town (loan), Macclesfield Town, Mansfield Town, Burton Albion, Corby Town, Grantham Town (1987-2006)*

Glover came on loan at Town during the 1996-97 season after arriving from Rotherham United and after a few appearances in Brian Horton's side, he returned to his parent club later in the season. He remained at Millmoor until 2000 before he transferred to Macclesfield Town, remaining at Moss Rose until 2002. Glover played for both Mansfield Town and Burton Albion before becoming the player-manager of Corby Town in 2002, leaving the club two years later in 2004 to become the Grantham Town player-manager. He later worked as assistant manager at King's Lynn (before resigning in 2010) and as Senior Professional Development Coach at Derby County. Glover became the assistant manager at Peterborough United in 2016 but was removed from the position by Director of Football Barry Fry in 2017. He is now working as Opposition Analyst at Doncaster Rovers, having been given the job in July 2018.

GOBERN, Oscar
Midfielder
Town Years: 2011-2015
Born: *1991 Birmingham, West Midlands*
Playing career: *Aston Villa, Southampton, Milton Keynes Dons (loan), Huddersfield Town, Chesterfield (loan), Queens Park Rangers, Doncaster Rovers (loan), Mansfield Town, Ross County, Yeovil Town, Eastleigh (2008-Still Playing)*

Gobern signed from Southampton in 2011 with great promise but didn't live up to the hype. He was released in 2015 after Dean Hoyle over-ruled Chris Powell's decision to award him a new contract. Queens Park Rangers signed him soon after but loaned him out to Doncaster Rovers, later releasing him at the end of the 2015-16 season. The Brummie midfielder has since had short spells at Mansfield Town, Ross County and Yeovil Town before joining non-league Eastleigh in 2018.

GOLDTHORPE, Wayne
Forward
Town Years: 1971-1978
Born: *1957 Staincross, Barnsley,*
Playing career: *Huddersfield Town, Hartlepool United, Crewe Alexandra (1971-1980)*

Wayne Goldthorpe signed schoolboy forms at Town in 1971 and was part of the youth team squad that got to the final and then semi-finals of the FA Youth Cup in 1974 and 1975 respectively. He later made his debut for the first team in 1975 but didn't make many appearances due to injuries. Goldthorpe almost signed for Arsenal in 1977 but Tom Johnston refused to let him go without receiving a big fee so he returned to Town after his trial at Highbury had come to an end. He remained in the first team squad but left in 1978, joining Hartlepool United in a swap deal with Paul Bielby. At Hartlepool, he played with former Town teammates Bob Newton, Kevin Johnson, John Watson and Alan Sweeney and later played for Crewe before. After his playing days, Goldthorpe ran a number of pubs, in Kendal, Ulverston and Broughton. He also ran a greetings card shop in Grange-over-Sands but now lives in retirement in Morecambe.

GOODALL, Frederick 'Roy'

Right-back, Trainer
Town Years: 1921-1937, 1949-1965 (trainer)
Born: *1902 Dronfield, Derbyshire*
Died: *1982 Huddersfield, West Yorkshire*
Playing career: *Huddersfield Town (1921-1937)*
Goodall was the club's captain during their most decorative part of their history. He won the FA Cup and Charity Shield in 1922, the three First Division titles in 1924, 1925 and 1926 and also played in the 1928 and 1930 FA Cup Finals. After a total of sixteen years at Leeds Road, Goodall retired, joining Nottingham Forest in 1937 as a coach where he remained at the City Ground until 1944. He was appointed secretary/manager of Mansfield Town in 1945, and spent four years at Field Mill before his departure in 1949 which saw him return to Leeds Road as trainer. Goodall spent another sixteen years at the club in this capacity until he finally retired from the professional game in 1965. He saw out his days in Huddersfield and lived in Oakes before he passed away in 1982. Goodall was buried by one of the players that he used to coach at Leeds Road, Ray Wilson, who was then working as an undertaker.

GOODWIN, James 'Jim'

Right-back/Midfielder
Town Years: 2008-2010
Born: *1981 Waterford, Ireland*
Playing career: *Celtic, Stockport County, Scunthorpe United, Huddersfield Town, Oldham Athletic (loan), Hamilton Academical, St Mirren, Alloa Athletic (2000-Still Playing)*
Stan Ternent brought Goodwin to the club at the beginning of the 2008-09 season and he was immediately installed in central-midfield. He also filled in at right-back during that season and remained in the season after Ternent's sacking and Lee Clark's appointment. However, by the 2009-10 season, Goodwin had lost his place in the side and signed for Hamilton Academical in 2010. He later spent five years at St. Mirren before he became the Alloa Athletic player-manager, a role he is still in today. Goodwin also worked for Hudson in Glasgow as a Recruitment Consultant and stayed there, eventually working as Field Sales Executive at Mondelez International, a position he still holds.

GORDON, Robert

Right-half
Town Years: 1936-1940
Born: *1917 Shankhouse, Northumberland*
Died: *1940 Ely, Cambridgeshire*
Playing career: *Huddersfield Town (1935-1940)*
Robert Gordon arrived at Town in 1936 and played as a right-half, unfortunately, his career was interrupted in 1939 by the outbreak of the Second World War. He volunteered for the RAF, becoming a Leading Aircraftmen in the IX Squadron. Gordon was killed in action in September 1940 and at the time of his death, was still on Town's books.

GORRE, Dean

Midfielder
Town Years: 1999-2001
Born: *1970 Paramaribo, Suriname*
Playing career: *SV Hoogvliet, SVV, SVV/ Dordrecht'90, Feyenoord, Groningen, Ajax, Huddersfield Town, Barnsley, Blackpool, (1987-2005)*
Steve Bruce brought Gorre to the club from Ajax in 1999 and he managed two years at Town before moving on to Barnsley in 2001. He is still remembered by the Town faithful for his classy performances, performances of a calibre that had not been witnessed at the club for many a year. He remained at Oakwell until 2004 when he spent a very short time at Blackpool before retiring as a professional footballer. Gorre has since had spells as a coach at both Stoke City and Southampton before being appointed manager of RBC Roosendaal in 2011. He later began as a youth coach at old club Ajax before becoming the Scotland under 17 coach in 2012. Gorre became the manager of his home country Suriname in 2014. Now scouts for Reading and is the Manager of Business Development for TruSox while combining this with his duties as manager of Suriname. When he isn't coaching the Suriname national side, Gorre resides in Little Bollington, Cheshire.

"DID YOU KNOW?"

"The final league match at Leeds Road was on 30 April 1994 and Huddersfield's oldest-surviving former player, Joe Walter, was guest of honour."

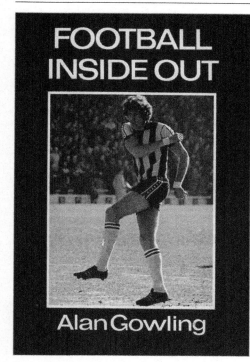

FOOTBALL INSIDE OUT

Alan Gowling

GOWLING, Alan

Forward
Town Years: 1972-1975
Born: *1949 Stockport, Cheshire*
Playing career: *Manchester United, Huddersfield Town, Newcastle United, Bolton Wanderers, Preston North End (1966-1983)*

Town were in the Second Division when they signed Alan Gowling from Manchester United for £65,000 in 1972 and he was ever present in his first season, scoring 17 goals in 42 appearances. However, this wasn't enough to stop Town sliding into the Third Division at the end of the 1972-73 season. He managed 24 goals the following season, which saw Town finish mid-table. However, the 1974-75 season saw Gowling's last season as a Town player, during which he managed 17 goals. Despite this, Town finished rock bottom of the Third Division and Gowling left for Newcastle United in 1975, remaining until 1978 when he signed for Bolton Wanderers. He spent four years at Bolton, partnering Frank Worthington and after just a year at Preston North End, Gowling retired from the game in 1983. He later worked as the general manager of a chemicals company in Derbyshire but is now retired.

GOY, Peter

Goalkeeper
Town Years: 1965-1967
Born: *1938 Beverley, East Riding of Yorkshire*
Playing career: *Arsenal, Southend United, Watford, Huddersfield Town (1954-1967)*

Goy only managed 4 appearances in the whole of his two years at Leeds Road before retiring from the game in 1967. He later moved to South Africa but is now back in England and was last known to be living in Southend-on-Sea in retirement.

GRAHAM, David

Forward
Town Years: 2006 (loan)
Born: *1978 Edinburgh, Scotland*
Playing career: *Rangers, Dunfermline Athletic, Torquay United, Wigan Athletic, Sheffield Wednesday, Huddersfield Town (loan), Gillingham, Lincoln City, (1995-2011)*

Graham signed on loan from Sheffield Wednesday during the 2005-06 season and he proved popular, scoring 7 goals in 16 league games. He also played in the Playoff semi-finals against Barnsley before returning to his parent club at the end of the season. Graham left Wednesday in 2007 and spent a year at Gillingham before leaving in 2008 to sign for Peter Jackson's Lincoln City. He later spent time at non-league Sheffield F.C., Ilkeston Town, Worksop Town and was last seen playing for Sheffield in his third spell at the club. Graham is still living in Sheffield, having remained in the area since his playing days.

GRAY, Ian

Goalkeeper
Town Years: 2003-2004
Born: *1975 Manchester, Lancashire*
Playing career: *Oldham Athletic, Rochdale (loan), Rochdale, Stockport County, Rotherham United, Huddersfield Town (1993-2004)*

One of Peter Jackson's first signings during his second time in charge, Gray was the first choice goalkeeper during the 2003-04 season until he injured his hand in an FA Cup tie with Accrington Stanley. This injury put him out for the rest of the season but he later returned to the first team at the beginning of the 2004-05 season. The recurring injury with his hand meant that Gray had to retire in 2004 and he now lives in his home of Altrincham and works as a printer.

GRAY, Kevin
Defender
Town Years: 1994-2002
Born: *1972 Sheffield, West Riding of Yorkshire*
Playing career: *Mansfield Town, Huddersfield Town, Stockport County (loan), Tranmere Rovers, Carlisle United, Chesterfield, Workington (1990-2009)*

Neil Warnock brought Kevin Gray to the club after signing him from Mansfield Town in time for the 1994-95 season as cover for centre halves Lee Sinnott and Pat Scully. Once those two eventually left the club a few years later Gray broke into the first team and went on to play a key part in the 1997-98 Great Escape and is remembered for his committed performances and ability to head the ball and defend for his life. He is also remembered for a foul on Bradford City's Gordon Watson, which broke his leg, and ended up costing £900,000. Gray later lost his place in the side under new manager Steve Bruce and was loaned out to Stockport County in 2000. He did return to the first team under new manager Lou Macari in 2001 but was sold to Tranmere Rovers in 2002. After a year at Prenton Park, Gray signed for Carlisle United where he was reunited with Chris Billy and Tom Cowan. He later played for Chesterfield and finished his career at Workington in 2009. Gray is now living in Staffordshire and works in construction.

GRAY, Terence 'Terry'
Winger
Town Years: 1972-1979
Born: *1954 Bradford, West Riding of Yorkshire*
Playing career: *Huddersfield Town, Southend United, Bradford City, Preston North End, (1972-1986)*

Gray began his career at Leeds Road as an apprentice and first broke into the team in 1973, firstly as a left-back but then went on to play on the wing. He was one of the better players in some very dark days in the club's history but was later sold to Southend United in 1979. After three years at Roots Hall, Gray transferred to Bradford City in 1982 and he spent two years at Valley Parade before he left for Preston in 1984. After two years at Deepdale, Gray retired from professional football and later had stints with non-league clubs and was Reserve Team Manager at Ossett United. Gray now runs his own financial advisors firm, Gray and Co Financial Solutions, in Liversedge.

Simon Grayson

GRAYSON, Simon
Manager
Town Years: 2012-2013
Born: *1969 Ripon, North Riding of Yorkshire*
Management career: *Blackpool, Leeds United, Huddersfield Town, Preston North End, Sunderland, Bradford City (2005-2018)*

After Lee Clark was sacked in February 2012, Grayson was brought in almost immediately to replace him and was tasked with getting the club promoted. He took Town to the Championship through the 2012 Playoffs and Town actually led the Championship table in August 2012. However, Grayson was sacked and became the manager of Preston North End in February 2013 and gained promotion to the Championship. He left the club in 2017 to become the manager of Sunderland but was dismissed early in the 2017-18 season. Later in the season, Grayson took the Bradford City job in 2018 but his contract was not renewed at the end of the 2017-18 season after Grayson decided it wasn't for him.

"DID YOU KNOW?"

"Town have won four Play Off Finals at three different grounds (Old Wembley, Millennium Stadium, New Wembley)."

GREAVES, Ian

Caretaker Manager, Senior Coach, Manager
Town Years: 1964 (caretaker manager), 1964-1968 (senior coach), 1968-1974 (manager)
Born: *1932 Crompton, Lancashire*
Died: *2009 Ainsworth, Greater Manchester*
Management career: *Huddersfield Town, Bolton Wanderers, Oxford United, Wolverhampton Wanderers, Mansfield Town (1964-1989)*

'Greavsie' worked as Youth Coach at Leeds Road and was given the manager's job in 1968 following the exit of Tom Johnston. Greaves had previously acted as caretaker manager for a short time in 1964 after Eddie Boot left the club. He led Town to the Second Division title in the 1969-70 season but after two seasons in the top tier, Town were relegated in 1972 and then again in 1973. Town had gone from the top of the First Division in the 1970-71 season to the Third Division by 1973. Greaves resigned in 1974 after six years as manager. He became the assistant manager to Jimmy Armfield at Bolton Wanderers and when Armfield left for Leeds United, Greaves was promoted to the top job. He managed to win promotion from the Second Division and also a League Cup semi-final appearance during his time at the club. Jobs at Oxford United and Wolverhampton Wanderers followed. His final job in football was as manager of Mansfield Town between 1983 and 1989 before retiring from football management. Greaves lived in Ainsworth in retirement before he passed away in 2009 at the age of 76 and Town observed a minute's silence in his honour in the game immediately following his death.

GREEN, Arthur

Left-back
Town Years: 1951-1952
Born: *1928 Liverpool, Lancashire*
Died: *1992 Liverpool, Merseyside*
Playing career: *Burscough, Huddersfield Town, Burton Albion (1951-1952)*

After spending some time at non-league Burscough, Green arrived at Leeds Road in 1951 and played 3 games for the first team at left-back before leaving for Burton Albion in October 1952. Green seemingly retired from the game after his spell at Burton Albion and he later died in 1992 back while living in his home of Liverpool.

GREEN, George

Right-half
Town Years: 1944-1947
Born: *1914 Northowram, Halifax*
Died: *1995 Halifax, West Yorkshire*
Playing career: *Bradford Park Avenue, Yeovil & Petters United, Huddersfield Town, Reading (1936-1949)*

Green had been playing at Bradford Park Avenue between 1936 and 1937 before he signed for Yeovil & Petters , remaining at the club until 1944, when he arrived at Leeds Road. He played only a few games for the club before he left for Reading in 1947. Green spent two years at Reading before hanging up his boots and retiring from professional football in 1949. He later passed away in his hometown Halifax in 1995.

GREENHALGH, Brian

Forward
Town Years: 1969-1971
Born: *1947 Chesterfield, Derbyshire*
Playing career: *Preston North End, Aston Villa, Leicester City, Huddersfield Town, Cambridge United, A.F.C. Bournemouth, Watford (1965-1976)*

Ian Greaves brought Greenhalgh to the club in July 1969, signing him from Leicester City. He played a few games in the 1969-70 promotion season but never cemented a regular place in the team and although he was a forward, he never scored a goal for the club. Greenhalgh left Leeds Road in 1971 and later played for Cambridge United, AFC Bournemouth and Watford before his retirement as a player in 1976. Following this, Greenhalgh was a partner in an optics company and later worked as Chief Scout at Everton. He has been been scouting for Watford ever since and is currently living in Southport.

GREENWOOD, Roy

Forward
Town Years: 1982-1984
Born: *1952 Leeds, West Riding of Yorkshire*
Playing career: *Hull City, Sunderland, Derby County, Swindon Town, Huddersfield Town, Tranmere Rovers (loan), Scarborough (1971-1984)*

Greenwood signed for Mick Buxton's side in 1982 from Swindon Town but he only managed 11 matches in his two years at the club before he left for Scarborough in 1984. Greenwood retired in 1984 and is now residing in Hull.

GROVES, Frederick

Inside-forward
Town Years: 1912-1914
Born: *1892 Lincoln, Lincolnshire*
Died: *1980 Lincoln, Lincolnshire*
Playing career: *South Bar, Lincoln City, Worksop Town, Sheffield United, Huddersfield Town, Worksop Town, Pontypridd, Tranmere Rovers, Stoke, Crystal Palace, Rhyl Athletic, Sutton Town, Hykeham (1908-1929)*

Groves signed from Sheffield United in 1912, and he spent two years at the club, making 4 appearances in two seasons for Arthur Fairclough's side. He left for Pontypridd in September 1914 and due to the First World War it appears that Groves didn't return to professional football until 1921 when he had a short stint at Tranmere Rovers. He left for Stoke City that same year and after two years at Stoke, he enjoyed one short year at Crystal Palace which ended in 1925. Groves played for Rhyl Athletic and Sutton Town before retiring from football in 1929, later passing away in 1980.

GRUNDY, William

Inside-left
Town Years: 1909-1910
Born: *1884 Bolton, Lancashire*
Died: *unknown*
Playing career: *Blackpool, Bolton Wanderers, Huddersfield Town, Northern Nomads (1906-1911)*

Grundy signed from Northern Nomads in 1909, playing one single game for Dick Pudan's side. He also guested for Port Vale in a Potteries derby with Stoke City Reserves in 1910, although the game was later abandoned due to a pitch invasion. Grundy returned to Town but left to return to Northern Nomads in October 1910. He later played for Blackpool and eventually worked as a cotton spinner in his home of Bolton.

GUDJONSSON, Joey

Midfielder
Town Years: 2010-2012
Born: *1980 Akranes, Iceland*
Playing career: *KA, IA, Racing Genk, MVV (loan), RKC Waalwijk, Betis, Aston Villa (loan), Wolverhampton Wanderers (loan), Leicester City, AZ, Burnley, Huddersfield Town, Fram Reykjavík, Fylkir, HK (1994-2016)*

Lee Clark brought Gudjonsson to the club in 2010 and immediately placed him in the first team.

However, he lost his place during the 2011-12 season as Clark refused to play him. After Clark was sacked in February 2012, Simon Grayson brought him back into the side but it didn't last and he left the club at the end of the season. He later signed for ÍA in his native Iceland where he remained for just a year. Gudjonsson had a spell at Fram Reykjavík in 2014 and one at Fylkir in 2015 before he was offered the manager's job at HK in 2016. He also played during his time as manager before leaving the club in 2017. Gudjonsson was appointed manager of former club ÍA in 2018 and also combined his playing days in Iceland with his role as a football agent.

GUNN, Alistair

Outside-right
Town Years: 1951-1954
Born: *1924 Broughty Ferry, Dundee, Scotland*
Died: *2010 Dundee, Scotland*
Playing career: *Dundee, Huddersfield Town, Bournemouth, Arbroath (1946-1957)*

After five years at Dundee, Gunn signed for Town in 1951 and went straight into George Stephenson's side, playing as a winger. He chipped in with a few goals in his two seasons at Leeds Road. He left for Bournemouth in 1953, spending two years there before heading back to Scotland to end his career at Arbroath, where he retired in 1957. Gunn returned to his hometown of Dundee and lived and worked as an accountant there until his passing in 2010 at the age of 85.

HAGUE, Neil

Left-half
Town Years: 1976-1977
Born: *1949 Thurcroft, Rotherham, West Riding of Yorkshire*
Playing career: *Rotherham United, Plymouth Argyle, Bournemouth, Huddersfield Town, Darlington (1967-1979)*

Hague joined Town from Bournemouth in 1976 and remained at Leeds Road for just one season, playing 30 games in all competitions for Tom Johnston's side. He left in 1977 to sign for Darlington before he retired from professional football in 1979. Hague returned to his native Yorkshire and set up a building firm before heading back to Plymouth in the 1980s to work in property development where he still lives.

HALL, Ellis

Centre-half
Town Years: 1910-1912
Born: *1889 Ecclesfield, Sheffield*
Died: *1947 Wortley, Sheffield*
Playing career: *Hull City, Millwall Athletic, Hastings & St. Leonards, Stoke, Huddersfield Town, South Shields, Hamilton Academical, Halifax Town, Rochdale, Consett (1905-1927)*

After signing from Stoke, Hall spent two seasons at Town, playing in Dick Pudan's side before he left the club for non-league South Shields in 1912. He spent seven years playing in their defence before heading further North to sign for Scottish club Hamilton Academical in 1919. Three years later, Hall joined Halifax Town and spent three years at The Shay before leaving in 1925 to sign for Rochdale. After a spell at non-league Consett, Hall retired in the late 1920s. He was living in Ilford by the late 1930s and died in 1947 whilst living in Wortley.

HALL, Harold 'Harry'

Outside-right
Town Years: 1910-1911
Born: *1883 Ecclesfield, Sheffield, West Riding of Yorkshire*
Died: *1972 Sheffield, West Riding of Yorkshire*
Playing career: *Hull City, Rotherham Town, Huddersfield Town, Grimsby Town (1906-1911)*

Dick Pudan brought Hall to Leeds Road from Rotherham Town in 1910 but he spent just one year at the club during the 1910-11 season before he left for Grimsby Town. His professional football career ended before the First World War, and Hall later worked as a cashier in Sheffield before he passed away in November 1972.

HAMILTON, Desmond 'Des'

Midfielder
Town Years: 1999 (loan)
Born: *1976 Bradford, West Yorkshire*
Playing career: *Bradford City, Newcastle United, Sheffield United (loan), Huddersfield Town (loan), Norwich City (loan), Tranmere Rovers (loan), Cardiff City, Grimsby Town, Barnet, Campion (1994-2010)*

Hamilton was on loan at Town for a short time during the 1998-99 season from his parent club Newcastle United. He went on to spend time on loan at Norwich City and Tranmere Rovers before he left Newcastle for Cardiff City in 2001. Hamilton packed up in 2010 and has since worked as a health mentor in Bradford schools and is currently assistant manager of Eccleshill United.

HAMILTON, Henry

Centre-forward
Town Years: 1910-1911
Born: *1887 South Shields, County Durham*
Died: *1937 South Shields, County Durham*
Playing career: *Craghead United, Sheffield Wednesday, Huddersfield Town, Southampton, Belfast Celtic, South Shields (1908-1914)*

Hamilton joined the club as an amateur before the club turned professional in 1910. He played 20 games and scored 13 goals for Dick Pudan's side before he left for Southampton in 1911, later playing for Belfast Celtic and South Shields before his career end coincided with the outbreak of the First World War. Hamilton died in 1937.

HAMMILL, Adam

Winger
Town Years: 2012-2013 (loan), 2013-2015
Born: *1988 Liverpool, Merseyside*
Playing career: *Liverpool, Barnsley, Wolves, Middlesbrough (loan), Huddersfield Town (loan), Huddersfield Town, Rotherham United (loan), Barnsley, St. Mirren (2006-Still Playing)*

Hammill originally arrived at Town on loan from Wolverhampton Wanderers during the 2012-13 season and the club stood by him when he was arrested for punching a female paramedic whilst drunk. He signed permanently in 2013 and remained until 2015 when he was released by Chris Powell. He returned to Barnsley in 2015 but left the club at the end of the 2017-18 season, going on to sign a short-term deal with St. Mirren during the 2018-19 season. Hammill then joined Scunthorpe United in January 2019.

Eoin Hand

HAND, Eoin

Assistant Manager, Caretaker Manager, Manager
Town Years: 1987-1988 (assistant manager), 1988 (caretaker manager), 1988-1992 (manager)
Born: *1946 Dublin, Republic of Ireland*
Management career: *Limerick United, St. Patrick's Athletic, Republic of Ireland, Al-Taawon, Huddersfield Town, AmaZulu, Shelbourne (1979-1994)*

After some time as manager of his country, Hand had been working in Saudi Arabia before he arrived at Leeds Road in November 1987 as assistant manager to Malcolm Macdonald. Following Supermac's sacking in May 1988, Hand was given the job as caretaker manager. As a result, he was given the job permanently the following month. Hand lost this poition in March 1992 in favour of his assistant manager, Ian Ross when the team had suffered some poor results. He later managed AmaZulu and Shelbourne before drifting out of football management. Hand nearly died in 1997 from pancreatitis but pulled through and gave up drinking and smoking, going on to work for the FAI as a career guidance officer. However, he now commentates for RTE and does charity work while living in Moyvane. Almost thirty years since he was pushed out, Hand returned to Huddersfield to attend the Crystal Palace match in September 2018 and was warmly welcomed.

HAND, James

Winger
Town Years: 2005-2007
Born: *1986 Drogheda, Ireland*
Playing career: *Huddersfield Town (2005-2007)*

Hand came through the academy system at Town and signed professional forms in time for the 2006-07 season. He made a couple of substitute appearances in Peter Jackson's side before being released in 2007 after the appointment of new manager, Andy Ritchie. Hand has played for a number of local clubs in his native Ireland and works on a farm.

"DID YOU KNOW?"

"Aaron Rowe became the first Town player to be born in the 2000s when he made his debut against AFC Bournemouth in March 2019."

HANSEN, Karl

Inside-right
Town Years: 1949
Born: *1921 Denmark*
Died: *1990 Denmark*
Playing career: *KFUM Boldklub, Akademisk Boldklub, Huddersfield Town, Atalanta, Juventus, Sampdoria, Catania (1940-1957)*

Originally from Denmark, Karl Hansen arrived in Huddersfield in 1948 after a stint at Akademisk Boldklub and lasted just one year at Leeds Road, helping Town avoid relegation in the 1948-49 season. He moved to Italy to sign for Atalanta Bergamo in 1949 before signing for Juventus in 1950. Following his retirement as a professional in 1957, Hansen returned to his home country of Denmark and later managed former club Akademisk Boldklub on two occasions in 1970 and then 1972 . Died in November 1990 at the age of 69.

HANVEY, Keith

Centre-half
Town Years: 1978-1984
Born: *1952 Manchester, Lancashire*
Playing career: *Manchester City, Swansea City, Rochdale, Grimsby Town, Huddersfield Town, Rochdale (1971-1985)*

Hanvey joined from Grimsby Town in 1978 and although he was a centre half, manager Tom Johnston played him on the left wing! Mick Buxton played him where he belonged once he got the job in late 1978 and Hanvey went on to play a massive part in both the 1979-80 and 1982-83 promotion seasons. He is fondly remembered for his centre-half partnership with Dave Sutton and for being a classy player in the centre of defence. After leaving the club, Hanvey spent one year at Rochdale before leaving his footballing career behind and beginning work as a sales executive at The Stamford Group in Stalybridge. However, he replaced Steve Kindon as the Commercial Manager at Leeds Road in 1986. He left that role in the late 1980s after his plans for a new stadium were refused and ironically, the plan did later go ahead after he had resigned. Hanvey also held similar roles at Bradford City and Leeds United and now runs his own hospitality company Keith Hanvey Associates from his base in South Crosland, Huddersfield and is also the compere on a match day at Elland Road.

Hoylandswaine Cricket Club

HARDWICK, Steven 'Steve'

Goalkeeper
Town Years: 1988-1991
Born: *1956 Mansfield, Nottinghamshire*
Playing career: *Chesterfield, Newcastle United, Detroit Express (loan), Oxford United, Crystal Palace (loan), Sunderland (loan), Huddersfield Town (1974-1991)*

Veteran goalkeeper, Hardwick signed for Eoin Hand's side in 1988 from Oxford United and spent three years at Leeds Road, playing over 100 games for the club before he retired from the game in 1991 and settled in Hoylandswaine. He has since been the groundsman for Hoylandswaine Cricket Club and also works as a technical sales representative.

HARDY, Aaron

Full-back
Town Years: 2005-2008
Born: *1986 South Elmsall, Wakefield, West Yorkshire*
Playing career: *Huddersfield Town, Harrogate Town, FC Halifax Town, Bradford Park Avenue, Farsley, Guiseley, Farsley, Tadcaster Albion (2005-Still Playing)*

Hardy began his career at Town, turning professional in 2005. He only managed a few games during his three year spell as a professional at the club before he was released at the end of the 2007-08 season by new manager, Stan Ternent. Hardy spent one year at Harrogate Town between 2008 and 2009 before he signed for F.C. Halifax Town at the beginning of the 2009-10 season. He went on to spent three years at The Shay, playing in two promotion winning teams before leaving in 2012 and after a short period at Farsley, he joined Guiseley in the same year. Hardy left Guiseley the following year to rejoin former club Farsley and after four years at Throstle Nest, he signed for Tadcaster Albion in 2017 as the ninth signing of the managers Michael Morton and Simon Collins.

HARKINS, Gary

Midfielder
Town Years: 2004 (loan)
Born: *1985 Greenock, Scotland*
Playing career: *Celtic, Blackburn Rovers, Huddersfield Town (loan), Bury (loan), Blackpool (loan), Grimsby Town, Partick Thistle, Dundee, Kilmarnock, Dundee, St Mirren, Oldham Athletic (loan), Dundee, Ayr United, Greenock Morton, Queen of the South (2001-Still Playing)*

Joined from Blackburn Rovers for a loan period at the tail-end of the 2003-04 season and made a couple of appearances in Peter Jackson's side before he returned to his parent club. Harkins left Blackburn in 2006 and after a short time at Grimsby Town he joined Partick Thistle in 2007. He has since had three separate spells at Dundee, Kilmarnock, St. Mirren, Oldham Athletic (loan), Ayr United, Greenock Morton, Queen of the South and is now playing his trade for Patrick Thistle.

HARKNESS, Steven 'Steve'

Left-back
Town Years: 1993 (loan)
Born: *1971 Carlisle, Cumberland*
Playing career: *Carlisle United, Liverpool, Huddersfield Town (loan), Southend United (loan), Benfica, Blackburn Rovers, Sheffield Wednesday, Chester City (1989-2002)*

Harkness arrived on loan from Liverpool in 1993 but only managed 5 league appearances in Neil Warnock's side before returning to his parent club. He spent a total of ten years at Anfield before being signed by former Liverpool boss Graeme Souness at Benfica in 1999. Harkness only lasted five months in Portugal before signing for Blackburn Rovers. After a year at the club, he left Ewood Park in 2000 and joined Sheffield Wednesday where he played for two years, and after a short time at Chester City in 2002, Harkness was forced to retire due to injury problems.

HARPER, Joseph 'Joe'

Forward
Town Years: 1966-1968
Born: *1948 Greenock, Scotland*
Playing career: *Morton, Huddersfield Town, Aberdeen, Everton, Hibernian, (1963-1984)*

After beginning his career at Morton, Harper arrived at Leeds Road in 1966, spending two uneventful years at the club.

Although, he later stated that this was a very unhappy spell in his career, even going as far as to slate the town of Huddersfield in a newspaper article in 2013, describing the town as "hell on Earth". Harper returned to Morton in 1968, leaving for Aberdeen the following year. He spent three years at Aberdeen, making over 100 appearances and knocking in over 70 goals. These impressive performances brought Harper to the attention of Everton who signed him in 1972. After two years at Everton, Harper left Goodison Park in 1974 for Hibernian where he spent two years before returning to Aberdeen in 1976. Another successful stint followed before he left for Peterhead in 1981 to become their player-manager. Harper later played for Keith before calling time on his career. Harper later managed Huntly before being replaced in 1990 and after his playing days ended, he worked as a rep for a whiskey company and has commentated on radio broadcasts in Scotland. Harper has also written newspaper columns for the Aberdeen Evening Express.

Steve Harper

HARPER, Stephen 'Steve'

Goalkeeper
Town Years: 1997-1998 (loan)
Born: *1975 Seaham, Tyne and Wear*
Playing career: *Newcastle United, Huddersfield Town (loan), Hull City, Sunderland (1992-2016)*
Regarded as one of Town's best ever goalkeepers, Harper played his part during the 1997-98 Great Escape season and impressed with his consistently impressive performances between the sticks. Peter Jackson was keen to sign him on a permanent transfer but Kenny Dalglish, then Newcastle manager, wanted too much money and Harper returned to St. James Park. He spent 20 years at Newcastle United before having a two year spell at Hull City and finishing his career as goalkeeping cover at Sunderland. Harper is now the academy goalkeeping coach at Newcastle.

HARRISON, Rennie

Right-back
Town Years: 1919-1920
Born: *1897 Burnley, Lancashire*
Died: *1951 Fylde, Lancashire*
Playing career: *Fulledge FC, Huddersfield Town, Rochdale (1919-1921)*
Harrison spent a year at Leeds Road between 1919 and 1920 after signing from his local football team. Harrison later played for Rochdale and worked as a bricklayer in Blackpool. He passed away in Fylde in 1951.

HART, Peter

Defender, Midfielder
Town Years: 1972-1980
Born: *1957 Mexborough, West Riding of Yorkshire*
Playing career: *Huddersfield T, Walsall (1974-1990)*
Peter Hart holds the record for being the youngest ever player to play for Huddersfield Town, he spent eight years at the club and captained Town to the Fourth Division Championship in 1980, which was his last act in a Town shirt. He joined Walsall at the end of that season, the team that Town had battled with for the title, and spent ten years there until retiring from professional football in 1990. Hart later became a vicar. After spending a number of years at St. Luke's Church in Cannock, he is now based at St. John the Baptist in Armitage and is also the Club Chaplain at Walsall.

HASELDEN, John

First Team Coach, Manager, Assistant Manager, Physiotherapist
Town Years: 1976-1977 (first team coach), 1977 (manager), 1977-1986 (first team coach, assistant manager, physiotherapist)
Born: *1943 Doncaster, West Riding of Yorkshire*
After a long career in football, Haselden joined the club as first team coach in 1976 and was voted in by the club's board to take over as manager from Tom Johnston in 1977. His spell only lasted 14 games and he was voted out again with Tom Johnston resuming his previous duties. When Mick Buxton was appointed manager in 1978, Haselden was his right hand man as well as taking on physiotherapy duties. The pair saved the club from relegation and achieved two promotions before Haselden was dismissed at the end of the 1985-86 season for economy measures. As well as running his own physiotherapy practice, Haselden later took over as the physio at Reading, Nottingham Forest, Aston Villa and Notts County before retiring in 2008. He now lives in Nottingham in retirement and is unfortunately suffering with Alzheimer's.

HASSALL, Harold

Forward
Town Years: 1946-1952
Born: *1929 Bolton, Lancashire*
Died: *2015 Bolton, Lancashire*
Playing career: *Huddersfield Town, Bolton Wanderers (1946-1955)*
Harold Hassall was playing local football in Bolton when Town snapped him up in 1946. He turned professional in 1948 and spent two years on the fringes of the team before becoming a regular in George Stephenson's side in 1950. After impressing in the Town first team he was picked by England in 1951 but left for Bolton Wanderers in 1952 where he played in the 1953 'Matthews Final'. Hassall had to retire from professional football in 1955 due to injuries and he later managed the England Youth Team. He also worked as a lecturer in physical education, managed the national team of Malaysia and worked as part of a study team that promoted football in emerging countries. Outside of football, Hassall also took the position of general secretary of the Amateur Swimming Association before he his death in Bolton in 2015.

HASTIE, Archibald

Inside-left
Town Years: 1936-1937
Born: *1915 Shotts, North Lanarkshire, Scotland*
Died: *1988 Bradford, West Yorkshire*
Playing career: *Huddersfield Town, Motherwell, Bradford City (1930-1945)*
Hastie was an inside-left who signed from Partick Thistle in 1936 and managed a handful of appearances in Clem Stephenson's side before heading back to Scotland to play for Motherwell. He returned to Yorkshire in 1938 when he signed for Bradford City but his career at Valley Parade was interrupted by the outbreak of World War Two. Hastie remained in Bradford after his playing days and worked as a brewery labourer before passing away in 1988.

HAWKSWORTH, Derek

Forward
Town Years: 1946-1948 (amateur), 1958-1960
Born: *1927 Bradford, West Riding of Yorkshire*
Playing career: *Bradford United, Bradford Park Avenue, Huddersfield Town, Bradford City, Sheffield United, Huddersfield Town, Lincoln City, Bradford City, Nelson (1942-1963)*
Hawksworth had a two year stint at Leeds Road between 1946 and 1948 as an amateur player before he moved to play for Bradford City and later for Sheffield United in 1950. He spent eight years at Bramall Lane and played over 250 games for the club before rejoining Town in 1958. Hawksworth still lives in Bradford and is in his 90s, having retired from his newsagents in the city.

HAY, Christopher 'Chris'

Forward
Town Years: 2000-2002
Born: *1974 Glasgow, Scotland*
Playing career: *Giffnock North, Celtic, Swindon Town, Huddersfield Town, St Johnstone, Stirling Albion (1992-2008)*
Steve Bruce signed Hay from Swindon Town in 2000 and he managed 49 league appearances and 5 goals in the first team before he left for St. Johnstone in 2002, where he remained until 2005. He then headed for Stirling Albion and finished his career at the club in 2008, announcing his retirement. Hay is now working as an office administrator for Preston Insurance Brokers in Sussex.

HAYES, William 'Bill'

Right-back
Town Years: 1932-1933 (amateur), 1933-1950
Born: 1915 Cork, Ireland
Died: 1987 Accrington, Lancashire
Playing career: *Huddersfield Town, Cork United, Huddersfield Town, Burnley (1932-1952)*

Hayes was playing local football when he was spotted by Town in 1932 and signed by Clem Stephenson. He played over 70 games for the first team before the outbreak of the Second World War in 1939. Hayes moved back to his native Ireland, where he turned out for Cork United. After the end of the War, Hayes returned to Leeds Road in 1946 and played over 100 times before he moved to Burnley in 1950. He spent two years at Turf Moor before calling time on his professional career a in 1952 and he passed away in 1987. To note, Hayes won all 6 of his international caps whilst at Leeds Road.

HAYES, Paul

Forward
Town Years: 2007 (loan)
Born: 1983 Dagenham, Greater London
Playing career: *Norwich City, Scunthorpe United, Barnsley, Huddersfield Town (loan), Scunthorpe United, Preston North End, Charlton Athletic, Brentford, Crawley Town (loan), Plymouth Argyle (loan), Wycombe Wanderers, Hemel Hempstead Town, Newport County, AFC Sudbury (2001-Still Playing)*

Hayes arrived at the Galpharm in 2007 on a short-term loan from parent club Barnsley and played 4 matches and managed a goal against local rivals Bradford City before returning to Oakwell. He left Barnsley at the end of the 2006-07 season and signed for Scunthorpe United, spending three years at Glanford Park before a one year spell at Preston North End followed. Hayes left for Charlton Athletic in 2011 before leaving the following year, he spent a year at Brentford followed between 2012 and 2013 and he returned to Scunthorpe in 2013. Hayes left the only a year later to join Wycombe Wanderers and spent three years at the club, playing over 100 games and scoring over 20 goals. After a short time at Hemel Hempstead Town in 2017, Hayes signed for Newport County before being released in 2018 by manager, Michael Flynn. He is now playing for AFC Sudbury in the Isthmian League North Division and also works as a coach at Charlton Athletic's academy.

HAYLOCK, Garry

Forward
Town Years: 1989-1992
Born: 1970 Bradford, West Riding of Yorkshire
Playing career: *Huddersfield Town, Shelbourne (loan) Shelbourne, Linfield, Portadown, Panionios, Shelbourne, Glentoran (loan), Dundalk, Ards (loan), Shamrock Rovers (loan), Basingstoke Town, Sutton United, Team Bath, Walton & Hersham, Cove, Yeading (1989-2007)*

Hailing from Bradford, Haylock signed for Town as an apprentice in the late 1980s and although he did make a few appearances in the first team, he spent most of Town career in the reserves and left for Shelbourne in 1992. He spent a long career in Ireland playing for clubs such as Linfield, Portadown, Dundalk and Glenavon before heading back to England in 2004 to play for Basingstoke Town. Stints at Sutton United, Team Bath, Walton & Hersham and Cove followed before Haylock became the manager of Yeading in 2006 and remained in charge of the club after it merged with Hayes. He remained at Hayes & Yeading United until 2011 before short spells at Farnborough and Bedfont Town followed. Haylock returned to Hayes & Yeading in 2015, leaving the following year. He has since had a spent a short time in charge of Bedfont & Feltham in 2017 but is now working as Head of Football at King Edward's School in Witley.

HEARY, Thomas

Defender
Town Years: 1996-2003
Born: 1979 Dublin, Republic of Ireland
Playing career: *Huddersfield Town, Bohemians, Dundalk, Galway United, Limerick (1996-2012)*

Heary was in the youth team at Town and signed professional forms in 1996, making his debut as a substitute in the 1996-97 season. He remained at the club until 2003, being released at the end of the 2002-03 season when the club were in financial meltdown. Heary returned to his native Ireland and signed for Bohemians, where he spent five years. He later played for Dundalk, Galway United and Limerick before his retirement in 2012. He spent a time working as a pallet truck driver for DHL in Dublin but is now working for Derrycourt Cleaning Specialists as a site manager.

HEFELE, Michael

Centre-half
Town Years: 2016-2018
Born: *1990 Pfaffenhofen (Ilm), West Germany*
Playing career: *Unterhaching II, Unterhaching, Greuther Furth II, Greuther Furth, Wacker Burghausen (loan), Dynamo Dresden, Huddersfield Town, Nottingham Forest (2009-Still Playing)*

'Heff' arrived at the club at the beginning of the 2016-17 season from Dynamo Dresden and enjoyed a centre-half partnership with Christopher Schindler and was well liked by the Town faithful. Hefele's popularity was helped when he scored the winning goal in a 2-1 win over local rivals Leeds United during the promotion season and described the goal as a "fxxxing dream" in the Sky Sports interview after the game. He also scored in the Playoff semi-final winning penalty shootout but also missed one in the Final shootout, although Town were still promoted at the end of the game. Heff left the club before the 2018-19 season to join Nottingham Forest for an undisclosed fee.

HEFFERNAN, Dean

Left-back
Town Years: 2010
Born: *1980 Sydney, New South Wales, Australia*
Playing career: *Wollongong Wolves, Sydney United, Sutherland Sharks, Central Coast Mariners, 1. FC Nurnberg (loan), Huddersfield Town, Melbourne Heart, Liaoning Whowin, Perth Glory, Western Sydney Wanderers (2002-2014)*

Famously signed by Lee Clark after seeing him on YouTube, Heffernan was signed towards the end of the 2009-10 season and was thrown in at left-back. He only lasted until the end of that season before being released from the club when his contract was not renewed. Heffernan later played for Melbourne Heart, Liaoning Whowin, Perth Glory and his last club was Western Sydney Wanderers where he left in 2014. He is now the Technical Director and Coach for Central Coast United.

HELLAWELL, Michael 'Mike'

Outside-right
Town Years: 1954-1955 (amateur), 1966-1968
Born: *1938 Keighley, West Riding of Yorkshire*
Playing career: *Huddersfield Town, Queens Park Rangers, Birmingham City, Sunderland, Huddersfield Town, Peterborough United, Bromsgrove Rovers (1954-1971)*

Hellawell only spent a year at the club as an amateur between 1954 and 1955 but he returned to the club in 1966. He later played for Peterborough and non-league Bromsgrove Rovers before hanging up his boots and retiring from professional football. He moved back to his hometown of Keighley to run a newsagents in the area and also worked for Damart in Bingley. Hellawell is now living in retirement.

HEPPLEWHITE, George

Centre-half
Town Years: 1939-1951
Born: *1919 Edmondsley, County Durham*
Died: *1989 Sunderland, Tyne and Wear*
Playing career: *Huddersfield Town, Preston North End, Bradford City (1939-1955)*

Hepplewhite arrived at Leeds Road in 1939 and signed for Clem Stephenson's side, just before the outbreak of World War Two. After the hostilities had ended and the Football League resumed in 1946, Hepplewhite found himself in the first team and he spent five years playing at centre-half. He left for Preston North End in 1951 and spent two years at Deepdale before his departure in 1953 after not making a single appearance. Hepplewhite rounded off his career with one year at Bradford City, retiring from the professional game in 1955 and returning to plumbing, his trade before becoming a footballer. Passed away in 1989.

HEPTON, Stanley 'Stan'

Forward
Town Years: 1957-1959
Born: *1932 Leeds, West Riding of Yorkshire*
Died: *2017 Leeds, West Yorkshire*
Playing career: *Ashley Road, Blackpool, Huddersfield Town, Bury, Rochdale, Southport, Northwich Victoria (1950-1966)*

Hepton signed from Blackpool in 1957 but only managed a couple of appearances at Leeds Road during his time at the club and he left to sign for Bury in 1959. He spent just one year at Gigg Lane before he signed for Rochdale in 1960. Hepton went on to spend four years at Spotland before he left in 1964 and had one year at Southport before his retirement in 1966 after a season with non-league Northwich Victoria. After his playing days had ended, Hepton returned to Leeds and later died in 2017 at the age of 84 after battling cancer.

HESFORD, Robert 'Bob'

Goalkeeper
Town Years: 1933-1934 (amateur), 1934-1950
Born: 1916 Bolton, Lancashire
Died: 1982 Blackpool, Lancashire
Playing career: *South Shore Weslayans, Blackpool (amateur), Huddersfield Town, Stalybridge Celtic (1933-1950)*

Hesford joined the club in 1933 as an amateur player and signed professionally in 1934, thus beginning a seventeen year association with Huddersfield Town. The goalkeeper played over 200 games at Leeds Road, including the 1938 FA Cup Final, which saw Town lose to Preston North End. During the Second World War, Hesford worked as a schoolteacher and returned to this profession after leaving Town in 1950. He also played for non-league Stalybridge Celtic before his retirement as a player. Hesford also worked as a teacher in Northern Rhodesia at some point, before he returned to England to live and work in Blackpool until his passing in 1982.

HESSEY, Sean

Defender
Town Years: 1998-1999
Born: 1978 Whiston, Merseyside
Playing career: *Leeds United, Wigan Athletic, Huddersfield Town, Kilmarnock, Blackpool, Chester City, Macclesfield Town (loan), Macclesfield Town, Accrington Stanley, Barrow, Prestatyn Town, Marine (loan) (1997-2015)*

Peter Jackson brought Hessey to the McAlpine during the 1997-98 season as defensive cover and spent a year at the club before he left in 1999 to sign for Kilmarnock. He spent five years at the club before leaving to sign for Blackpool. Hessey's time at Bloomfield Road was short-lived and he moved to Chester City in 2004, playing for four years at the Deva Stadium before his departure in 2008. He left to sign for Macclesfield Town and had two years at Moss Rose before he signed for Accrington Stanley in 2010. Hessey spent two years at the Crown Ground before he headed into non-league in 2012 and had stints at Barrow and Prestatyn Town before retiring as a player in 2015 and becoming the manager of Marine. He spent two years as manager of the club before he was sacked in 2017.

HICKS, Stuart

Defender
Town Years: 1993-1994
Born: 1967 Peterborough, Cambridgeshire
Playing career: *Peterborough United, Wisbech Town, Colchester United, Scunthorpe United, Doncaster R, Huddersfield Town, Preston NE, Scarborough, Leyton Orient, Chester City, Mansfield Town (1983-2003)*

After a spell at Doncaster Rovers, Hicks arrived at Leeds Road in 1993 and played a number of matches in Neil Warnock's side during the 1993-94 season. He left the club to join Preston North End at the end of that season but spent just a year at Deepdale before he left the club in 1995. Hicks joined Scarborough after departing Preston and went on to enjoy time at Leyton Orient, Chester City, Mansfield Town and Hucknall Town before announcing his retirement in 2003. Hicks has since founded the successful clothing company, Mainline Menswear and is living in North Yorkshire.

HICKSON, David 'Dave'

Centre-forward
Town Years: 1955-1957
Born: 1929 Salford, Lancashire
Died: 2013 Willaston, Cheshire
Playing career: *Ellesmere Port Town, Everton, Aston Villa, Huddersfield Town, Everton, Liverpool, Cambridge City, Bury, Tranmere Rovers (1948-1963)*

Hickson signed from Aston Villa in 1955 and spent two seasons at the club, playing for both Andy Beattie and Bill Shankly. He knocked in 28 league goals in 54 appearances before rejoining his first club Everton in 1957. In a rare move for an Everton player, Hickson joined rivals Liverpool in 1959. He later had spells at Cambridge City, Bury and Tranmere Rovers before leaving the sport in 1963. Hickson later managed Ballymena United and Bangor. He later worked as a bricklayer and then in a pub before settling in Ellesmere Port employed the local authority. Hickson also worked part time at Goodison Park as a tour guide until his death in 2013.

"DID YOU KNOW?"

"Every time Town have finished a season on 81 points, they have been promoted via the play offs (2004, 2012 and 2017)."

HIGGINBOTHAM, Kallum
Winger / Forward
Town Years: 2012-2013
Born: *1989 Salford, Greater Manchester*
Playing career: *Salford City, Oldham Athletic, Rochdale, Accrington Stanley (loan), Falkirk, Huddersfield Town, Barnsley (loan), Carlisle United (loan), Motherwell (loan), Partick Thistle, Kilmarnock, Dunfermline Athletic (2006-Still Playing)*

One of Lee Clark's last signings as Town manager, signing during the 2011-12 season, Higginbotham played 1 game under Clark, putting in a man-of-the-match performance before being immediately dropped. He was brought back into the side during the playoffs in that season by new manager Simon Grayson but he later left the club in 2013 after loan periods at Barnsley, Carlisle United and Motherwell during the 2012-13 season. Higginbotham has since played in Scotland for Partick Thistle and Kilmarnock but has been playing for Dunfermline Athletic since 2016.

HILL, Brian
Outside-left
Town Years: 1966-1969
Born: *1942 Mansfield, Nottinghamshire*
Playing career: *Ollerton Colliery, Grimsby Town, Huddersfield Town, Blackburn Rovers, Torquay United, Boston United (1960-1973)*

After a seven years at Grimsby Town, Hill arrived at Leeds Road in 1966 to sign for Tom Johnston's side and he spent three years at the club before leaving for Blackburn Rovers in 1969 . Hill rounded off his career with a spell at Boston United, which came to an end in 1973.

HINCHCLIFFE, Thomas 'Tom'
Inside-forward
Town Years: 1938
Born: *1913 Denaby Main, Doncaster*
Died: *1978 Rushcliffe, Nottinghamshire*
Playing career: *Grimsby Town, Huddersfield Town, Derby County, Nottingham Forest, Gainsborough Trinity, Denaby United (1930-1948)*

Hinchcliffe arrived at Leeds Road in 1938 after leaving Grimsby Town but spent less than a year at the club before he departed for Derby County. He was still at the club when the Second World War broke out and his football career was cruelly cut short. Tom Hinchcliffe died in 1978.

HINE, Ernest 'Ernie'
Inside-right
Town Years: 1932-1933
Born: *1901 Barnsley, West Riding of Yorkshire*
Died: *1974 Huddersfield, West Yorkshire*
Playing career: *Leicester City, Huddersfield Town, Manchester United (1921-1938)*

Signing from Leicester City in 1932, Ernie Hine spent just one season at Leeds Road and played 25 matches for Clem Stephenson's side before he moving on to Manchester United in February 1933. He again only spent one season at Old Trafford before transferring to Barnsley. Hine remained at Oakwell for four years before annoucing his retirement in 1938. He was retained as a coach at the club and also worked as a builder and labourer before his death in Huddersfield in 1974.

HIWULA, Jordy
Forward
Town Years:
Born: *1994 Manchester, Greater Manchester*
Playing career: *Manchester City, Yeovil Town (loan), Walsall (loan), Huddersfield Town, Coventry City (2012-Still Playing)*

Hiwula was brought to the club by Chris Powell in 2015 and he made his debut early in the 2015-16 season. However, he was loaned to Wigan Athletic soon after his debut but was recalled by new manager David Wagner in February 2016. He later joined Walsall for the remainder of the season before joining Bradford City on a season long loan in July 2016 and he spent the 2017-18 season on loan at Fleetwood Town. Hiwula was sold to Coventry City in August 2018 for an undisclosed fee.

HOBSON, Albert
Outside-right
Town Years: 1954-1956
Born: *1925 Glossop, Derbyshire*
Died: *2017*
Playing career: *Blackpool, Huddersfield Town, York City, Stalybridge Celtic (1945-1957)*

Hobson joined the club in 1954 after signing from Blackpool. He played just 14 matches at outside-right before leaving in 1956 to sign for York City. He ended his career less than a year later, announcing his retirement after a time at non-league Stalybridge Celtic. Hobson passed away in 2017 at the age of 92.

HOBSON, Robert 'George'

Right-half
Town Years: 1925-1927
Born: *1903 Leeds, West Riding of Yorkshire*
Died: *1993 Keighley, West Yorkshire*
Playing career: *Bishop Auckland, Huddersfield Town, Bradford City, Dulwich Hamlet, Yorkshire Amateur, Bradford City, Tunbridge Wells Rangers (1925-1937)*

Hobson joined Cecil Potter's side in 1925 after signing from Bishop Auckland on an amateur basis. He played 2 matches for the club before he left for Bradford City in 1927. Hobson spent two years at Valley Parade and later played for Dulwich Hamlet and Yorkshire Amateur and also gained 2 caps for England Amateur in 1931. He later worked as a second hand car dealer in his hometown of Leeds and later in life he moved to Keighley before he died in 1993 at the age of 90.

HODOUTO, Kwami

Defender
Town Years: 1999-2000
Born: *1974 Lomé, Togo*
Playing career: *AS Cannes, AJ Auxerre, Red Star Saint-Ouen (loan), Huddersfield Town (1995-2000)*

Steve Bruce signed Hodouto in 1999 after he had spent two years at AJ Auxerre but he only played 2 matches for the club and has the distinction of coming on as a substitute and being taken off in the same match. He left the club in 2000 and is considered one of the worst players to ever play in the blue and white stripes. Hodouto is now back living and working in France.

HOLDEN, James 'Stewart'

Half-back
Town Years: 1957-1965
Born: *1942 Grange Moor, Huddersfield, West Riding of Yorkshire*
Died: *2004 Royton, Oldham, Greater Manchester*
Playing career: *Huddersfield Town, Oldham Athletic, Rochdale, Wigan Athletic (1957-1968)*

Native of Clayton West, Holden signed for Town in 1957 and spent eight years at Leeds Road, playing 30 games for his hometown club. He moved on to Oldham Athletic in 1965 and later had a stint at Rochdale before retiring at Wigan Athletic in 1968. After his playing days had come to an end, Holden worked for ATS Tyres in Oldham for 30 years where he was the manager. He later died in 2004 after a short illness.

HOLDSWORTH, Andrew 'Andy'

Right-back/ Central-midfielder
Town Years: 2003-2009
Born: *1984 Pontefract, West Yorkshire*
Playing career: *Huddersfield Town, Huddersfield Town, Oldham Athletic, Morecambe, Alfreton Town, Guiseley (2003-2016)*

Holdsworth came through the youth ranks at Town and was drafted into the first team at the beginning of the 2003-04 season by Peter Jackson. Originally a midfielder, Holdsworth played right-wing-back in a 3-5-2 formation under 'Jacko' and was almost ever-present during the 2003-04 promotion season, once he'd broke into the side. He was a regular in the side under subsequent managers Andy Ritchie (mostly as a central midfielder), Stan Ternent and then Lee Clark. However, Clark told Holdsworth that he could leave at the end of the 2008-09 season and he did, joining Oldham Athletic on a free transfer. He had made a total of 300 appearances for Town. Holdsworth spent just over a year at Oldham before moving to Morecambe, again for just over a year before a brief time at Alfreton Town followed. Holdsworth then signed for Guiseley in 2011 and played at the club until 2016. After a spell as the Youth Development Phase Coach at Barnsley, Holdsworth became the Lead Professional Development Coach at Sheffield Wednesday in 2018.

HOLLAND, Christopher 'Chris'

Midfielder
Town Years: 2000-2004
Born: *1975 Whalley, Lancashire*
Playing career: *Preston North End, Newcastle United, Birmingham City (loan), Birmingham City, Huddersfield Town, Boston United, Southport, Leigh Genesis, Fleetwood Town (1993-2009)*

Steve Bruce brought Holland in to play for the club during the 1999-2000 season and he lasted four years at the McAlpine. By the time his departure came in 2004, Holland had fallen out of favour under manager Peter Jackson. He joined Boston United in time for the 2004-05 season and played there until 2007 when he headed to non-league Southport. Holland had periods playing at Leigh Genesis, Fleetwood Town, Burscough and Guiseley before finishing his career in 2009. He later worked as assistant manager at non-league Guiseley between 2010 and 2011.

HOLMES, Duane
Midfielder
Town Years: 2013-2016
Born: *1994 Columbus, Georgia, United States*
Playing career: *Huddersfield Town, Yeovil Town (loan), Bury (loan), Scunthorpe United, Derby County (2013-Still Playing)*

Holmes progressed through the youth ranks at Town and made his debut in 2013 and he initially showed great promise, yet he only played a handful of matches for the club before signing for Scunthorpe United in 2016. Holmes joined Frank Lampard's Derby County early on in the 2018-19 season, after spending two years at Glanford Park.

HOLMES, Ian
Midfielder
Town Years: 1977-1980
Born: *1950 Wath-upon-Dearne*
Playing career: *Sheffield United, York City, Huddersfield Town (1968-c1980)*

Joining from York City in 1977, 'Wally' Holmes had a couple of good seasons at Leeds Road before losing his place shortly into the 1979-80 promotion season. He left at the end of that season and played for non-league Gainsborough Trinity before he ended his playing days. Holmes worked in insurance as a salesman for a time but is now working as a taxi driver in Sheffield and resides in his hometown of Wath-upon-Dearne.

HOLMES, Michael 'Micky'
Midfielder
Town Years: 1988-1989
Born: *1965 Bradford, West Riding of Yorkshire*
Playing career: *Yeadon Celtic, Bradford City, Wolverhampton Wanderers, Huddersfield Town, Cambridge United, Rochdale, Torquay United, Carlisle United, Northampton Town, Wisbech Town (1984-1993)*

Holmes arrived at Leeds Road in 1988 but suffered injury problems and Eoin Hand allowed him to leave the club in 1989 to sign for Cambridge United. He later played for Rochdale, Torquay United, Carlisle United and Northampton Town before retiring as a professional in the early 1990s. Holmes went into the pub game with his wife Bernadette and ran a number of pubs before buying a sandwich shop, La Baguette, in Leicester. However, he is now selling stairlifts and lives in Nuneaton.

HOLMES, Norman
Right-back
Town Years: 1913-1914
Born: *1890 Darley Hillside, Matlock, Derbyshire*
Died: *1965 Liverpool, Lancashire*
Playing career: *Leeds City, Clapton Orient, Huddersfield Town, York City (1909-1914)*

After a stint at Clapton Orient, Holmes signed for Arthur Fairclough's side in 1913 but his career was interrupted by the outbreak of World War One. He served in the Middlesex Regiment, rising to the rank of lance corporal in the Football Battalion and he was later commissioned into the 21st (Service) Battalion in June 1918. He later played for York City and worked in Liverpool as a clerk before he passed away in 1965.

HOLMES-DENNIS, Tareiq
Left-back
Town Years: 2016-2018
Born: *1995 Farnborough, Greater London*
Playing career: *Charlton, Huddersfield Town, Portsmouth (loan), Bristol Rovers (2013-Still Playing)*

Holmes-Dennis arrived at the club from Charlton Athletic in 2016 and he played a number of games during the 2016-17 season but unfortunately suffered injury problems after he was loaned to Portsmouth. He left the club at the beginning of the 2018-19 season and signed for Shrewsbury Town.

HOLT, Grant
Forward
Town Years: 2014 (loan)
Born: *1981 Carlisle, Cumbria*
Playing career: *Carlisle United, Workington, Halifax Town, Sengkang Marine, Barrow, Sheffield Wed, Rochdale, Nottingham Forest, Shrewsbury Town, Norwich City, Wigan Athletic, Rochdale, Hibernian, King's Lynn Town, Barrow (1999-2018)*

Holt signed on loan from Wigan Athletic in 2014 and played 15 league games for Chris Powell's side before he went back to his parent club. He later returned to old club Rochdale in 2016 for a short spell before playing for Hibernian, King's Lynn Town and Barrow. In 2018, Holt signed a deal with the World Association of Wrestling to become a professional wrestler. He won his first fight when he was the last man standing in a 40-man Royal Rumble earning him the Crusher Mason Memorial Trophy.

HOLT, Raymond 'Ray'

Defender
Town Years: 1958-1965
Born: *1939 Thorne, Doncaster,*
Playing career: *Moor Ends Athletic, Huddersfield Town, Oldham Athletic, Halifax Town, Scunthorpe United (1958-1970)*

Originally from Thorne, Holt began his career at Town, turning professional in 1961. He only managed a small amount of games in the side before he left for Oldham Athletic in 1965. Holt left the following year to join Halifax Town. He retired as a professional at Scunthorpe in 1970 and later worked at Drax Power Station but is now back living in his home of Thorne in retirement.

HOOTON, William

Half-back
Town Years: 1908-1910
Born: *1879 Southport, Lancashire*
Died: *unknown*
Playing career: *Leeds City, Huddersfield (1908-1910)*

Hooton arrived at Leeds Road in 1908 having signed from Leeds City and played in each of Town's two seasons as an amateur side before he was released at the end of the 1909-10 season, once the club had turned professional. He remained in Huddersfield and later worked as a warehouseman in the town, living in Longwood.

HORNE, Barry

Midfielder
Town Years: 1997-2000
Born: *1962 St Asaph, Wales*
Playing career: *Wrexham, Portsmouth, Southampton, Everton, Birmingham City, Huddersfield Town, Sheffield Wednesday (1984-2002)*

Peter Jackson signed Barry Horne from Birmingham City in 1997 and he formed a partnership with his former Welsh international teammate David Phillips, where they were known as the "Old Gits". Horne was a crowd favourite at Town due to his reliable performances and key role in the 1997-98 Great Escape season. He was released by Steve Bruce in 2000. Horne has a degree in chemistry and is now teaching at The King's School Chester, where he also coaches the school football team. He was also a board member and Director of Football at Wrexham until his resignation in 2016 and he also acts as a co-commentator on Sky Sports.

HORTON, Brian

Manager
Town Years: 1995-1997
Born: *1949 Hednesford, Staffordshire*
Management career: *Hull City, Oxford United, Manchester City, Huddersfield Town, Brighton, Port Vale, Macclesfield Town (1984-2012)*

Horton arrived at the club in 1995 to replace outgoing manager, Neil Warnock and his first season in charge saw the club almost reach the First Division play-offs but his second season in charge saw the club narrowly avoid relegation. He began the 1997-98 season as manager but was sacked in October after failing to win a single match. Horton became the manager of Brighton & Hove Albion in 1998 but he left the following year to take charge of Port Vale. He remained at Vale Park for five years before his resignation at the end of the 2003-04 season. Horton quickly took the manager's job at Macclesfield Town in April 2004 and managed to prevent relegation to the Conference but was later dismissed in October 2006 after failing to win a match up to that point in the 2006-07 season. Horton had most recently been working as Phil Brown's assistant manager at Swindon Town but left the role at the conclusion of the 2017-18 season.

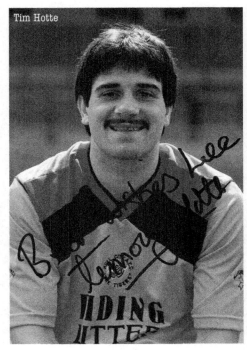

Tim Hotte

HOTTE, Timothy 'Tim'
Forward
Town Years: 1981-1983
Born: *1963 Bradford, West Riding of Yorkshire*
Playing career: *Huddersfield Town, Harrogate Town, Halifax Town, North Ferriby United, Hull City, York City (loan) (1981-1988)*

Hotte began his career at Arsenal before arriving at Leeds Road in 1981 and after making a handful of appearances at the club, he headed into non-league in 1983 when he signed for Harrogate Town. Hotte drifted back into non-league, where he played for many years. Hotte is now working for EYG in East Yorkshire as Trade Projects Manager and has done since 1990.

HOWARD, Stanley 'Stan'
Forward
Town Years: 1952-1960
Born: *1934 Chorley, Lancashire*
Died: *2004 Preston, Lancashire*
Playing career: *Chorley, Huddersfield Town, Bradford City, Barrow, Halifax Town, Chorley (1952-1965)*

Howard signed from his local club Chorley in 1952 as a youngster and eventually broke into the first team in 1957. He managed to play over 60 games for the first team, under managers Bill Shankly and Eddie Boot, before he transferred to local rivals Bradford City in 1960. Died in 2004.

HOWE, George
Full-back
Town Years: 1942-1954
Born: *1924 Wakefield, West Riding of Yorkshire*
Died: *1971 Lower Agbrigg, West Riding of Yorkshire*
Playing career: *Carlton United, Huddersfield Town, York City (1942-1962)*

After a stint at non-league Carlton United, Howe arrived at Leeds Road in 1942 as an amateur and played in the Wartime League until the Football League resumed in 1946. After the resumation of the Football League, Howe remained at the club for another eight years before signing for York City in 1954. He played over 300 games for York City, including an FA Cup semi-final in 1955, before retiring from professional football in 1962. The Yorkshireman later worked as a maintenance man in a Wakefield hospital before he died suddenly at the age of 47 in 1971.

HOWE, John 'Jack'
Full-back
Town Years: 1949-1951
Born: *1915 Hartlepool, County Durham*
Died: *1987 Hartlepool, County Durham*
Playing career: *Wingate United, Hartlepools United, Derby County, Huddersfield Town, King's Lynn (player-manager), Wisbech Town (1933-1955)*

After spells at Hartlepool United and Derby County, veteran Howe arrived at Leeds Road in 1950 at the age of 35, lasting one season, playing as a full-back. He left the club in 1951 and became the player-manager of King's Lynn. Howe later played for Wisbech Town before he ended his footballing career over the age of 40. The three-time England international passed away in 1987 and is the grandfather of former AFC Bournemouth legend Steve Fletcher.

HOWEY, Peter
Forward
Town Years: 1974-1979
Born: *1958 Kinsley, Pontefract, West Riding of Yorkshire*
Playing career: *Huddersfield Town, Leeds United, Newport County, Frickley Athletic, Scarborough, Ossett Town, Frickley Athletic (1974-1983)*

Howey signed for the club as an apprentice in 1974 and he played in Robin Wray's youth team until he made his professional debut in 1977. He remained at Leeds Road until his release at the end of the 1978-79 season and he signed for Leeds United. Howey is still living in his hometown of Pontefract, working as a painter and decorator.

HOWIE, James 'Jimmy'
Inside-right
Town Years: 1910-1913
Born: *1878 Galston, Ayrshire, Scotland*
Died: *1962 Willesden, Middlesex*
Playing career: *Galston Athletic, Kilmarnock, Kettering Town, Bristol Rovers, Newcastle United, Huddersfield Town (1897-1913)*

Howie joined Town from Newcastle United in 1910 and spent three years at Leeds Road playing in both Dick Pudan and Arthur Fairclough's side before retiring from the game in 1913 and taking the manager's job at Queens Park Rangers. After his time in football had come to an end, Howie became a tobacconist in Willesden, Middlesex before his death in 1963 at the age of 84.

Bobby Hoy

HOY, Robert 'Bobby'

Winger
Town Years: 1965-1975
Born: *1950 Halifax, West Riding of Yorkshire*
Playing career: *Huddersfield Town, Blackburn Rovers, Halifax Town, York City, Rochdale, Macclesfield Town (1965-1981)*
Hoy signed for the club as a youngster in 1965 and made his debut in the 1966-67 season under manager Tom Johnston, though he cemented his place in the first team under Johnston's successor Ian Greaves. Hoy later played a big part in the 1969-70 promotion season and remained at Town during their slide down the divisions before leaving to sign for Blackburn Rovers in 1975. Hoy later became a singer on the club circuit and has also worked delivering car parts for Vauxhall around West Yorkshire. He is now living in Lindley, Huddersfield.

HUDSON, Mark

Midfielder
Town Years: 2005-2007
Born: *1980 Bishop Auckland, County Durham*
Playing career: *Middlesbrough, Chesterfield, Huddersfield Town, Rotherham United, Blackpool, Gainsborough Trinity, Grimsby Town, Worksop Town, Bradford Park Avenue, West Auckland Town, Ashington, Sunderland RCA, Shildon, West Auckland Town (1999-2017)*

Peter Jackson brought 'Huddy' to the club at the start of the 2005-06 season and he was immediately placed in the first team, making his debut against Nottingham Forest in the first game of the season. The former Chesterfield player spent two years at the club before his departure at the end of the 2006-07 season, when he signed for Rotherham United. Hudson signed for Shildon in 2012 and is now First Team Coach at the club.

HUDSON, Mark

Defender, Coach, U23s Manager
Town Years: 2014-2017, 2016-2018 (coach), 2018-present (Under 23s manager)
Born: *1982 Guildford, Surrey*
Playing career: *Fulham, Crystal Palace, Charlton Athletic, Cardiff City, Huddersfield Town (1999-2017)*
Hudson signed for Town from Cardiff City in 2014 and was immediately installed as captain of the first team, replacing Lee Peltier. In 2016, Hudson signed a three year contract which would see him move into a coaching role with the club and after his retirement as a player on the eve of the 2017-18 season, he was appointed as a coach and became the U23's Manager in early 2018. Following David Wagner's departure in January 2019, Hudson was the caretaker manager for a game before the appointment of Jan Siewert. Hudson is now currently a member of Siewert's backroom staff.

HUGHES, Ian

Centre-half
Town Years: 2003-2004
Born: *1974 Bangor, Wales*
Playing career: *Bury, Blackpool, Huddersfield Town, Bacup Borough (1991-2008)*
Hughes signed for Town at the beginning of the 2003-04 promotion season and was a regular starter when it began but ended up falling out of favour and was subsequently dropped from Peter Jackson's side. He was released at the end of the season but returned the following year to receive his play-off winner's medal on the pitch as he had played the required number of games to receive a medal. Hughes later played for non-league Bacup Borough and has since worked for West Lancashire School Sport Partnership.

HULME, Joseph 'Joe'

Right-winger
Town Years: 1938
Born: *1904 Stafford, Staffordshire*
Died: *1991 Winchmore Hill, Buckinghamshire*
Playing career: *Stafford YMCA, York City, Blackburn Rovers, Arsenal, Huddersfield Town (1922-1938)*

After twelve years at Arsenal, Hulme joined Town for a short while in 1938, playing 10 games for Clem Stephenson's side before announcing his retirement in May 1938. He played cricket for Middlesex between 1929 and 1939 before the outbreak of World War Two when he began work as a policeman. Hulme became the Tottenham Hotspur manager in 1945, after a spell as assistant secretary, but left four years later, with little success, although it has since been recognised that he laid the foundations for the First Division winning side of 1950-51 season. After leaving football behind, Hulme became a journalist for The People and retired in 1968. He died in 1991, aged 87.

HUMPSTON, Ronald

Goalkeeper
Town Years: 1951-1953
Born: *1924 Derby, Derbyshire*
Died: *2008 Cheltenham, Gloucestershire*
Playing career: *Portsmouth, Huddersfield Town, Headington United (1947-1953)*

Humpston had spent four years at Portsmouth before joining the club in 1951 where played 5 games for George Stephenson's side during the 1951-52 season. Humpston never managed to play another game for the side and left in 1953 to sign for non-league Headington United. At one stage, the former goalkeeper worked for the Czech FA as a coach but later lived and worked in Cheltenham, where he passed away in 2008 at the age of 83.

HUNT, Jack

Right-back
Town Years: 2009-2013
Born: *1990 Rothwell, West Yorkshire*
Playing career: *Huddersfield Town, Crystal Palace, Barnsley (loan), Nottingham Forest (loan), Rotherham United (loan), Sheffield Wednesday (loan), Sheffield Wednesday, Bristol City (2009-Still Playing)*

Hunt broke into the first team in 2011 after progressing through the academy system but left in 2013 for Crystal Palace after they bid £2 million for him.

He was injured shortly after signing and never played a game at Selhurst Park. Hunt left the club after he was sold to Sheffield Wednesday in 2016 and left Hillsborough in 2018 to sign for Bristol City.

HUNTER, Donald

Right-half
Town Years: 1944-1945 (amateur), 1945-1951
Born: *1927 Thorne,West Riding of Yorkshire*
Died: *2008 Southport, Merseyside*
Playing career: *Luddenfoot, Huddersfield Town, Halifax Town, Southport, Netherfield (1944-1959)*

Hunter arrived at Leeds Road in 1944 as an amateur player from Luddenfoot and remained at the club until 1951. He played 26 games during those seven years but never cemented a place in the first team before signing for Halifax Town in 1951. Died at the age of 81 in 2008.

HURST, Christopher 'Chris'

Midfielder
Town Years: 1997-1998
Born: *1973 Barnsley, West Riding of Yorkshire*
Playing career: *Emley, Huddersfield Town, Halifax Town (loan) (1996-2006)*

Hurst signed from non-league Emley in 1997 and managed four appearances during the 1997-98 season but never featured again following the sacking of Brian Horton. He went on to play in non-league and is now thought to be working as a postman, still living in his home of Barnsley.

HUSBAND, James
Left wing-back
Town Years: 2016 (loan)
Born: *1994 Leeds, West Yorkshire*
Playing career: *Doncaster Rovers, Middlesbrough, Fulham (loan), Huddersfield Town (loan), Norwich City, Fleetwood Town (loan) (2011-Still Playing)*
Husband arrived during the 2015-16 season on loan from Middlesbrough but returned to his parent club during the season. He left 'Boro' in 2017 to sign for Norwich City and had a spell on loan at Fleetwood Town during the 2018-19 season.

HUSLER, Horace
Goalkeeper
Town Years: 1912-1913
Born: *1890 Sheffield, West Riding of Yorkshire*
Died: *1959 Doncaster, West Riding of Yorkshire*
Playing career: *The Wednesday, Huddersfield Town, Doncaster Rovers (1912-1915)*
Husler arrived at the club in 1912 after a period at The Wednesday and played one game for Arthur Fairclough's side in the 1912-13 season before he moved on to sign for Doncaster Rovers in 1913. He was the reason that the FA suspended the club in December 1915 due to Husler not receiving his full wages. Following his departure, Husler worked as a brewery mason and also in property in his native Sheffield. Died in 1959.

HUTCHINGS, Christopher 'Chris'
Left-back
Town Years: 1987-1990
Born: *1957 Winchester, Hampshire*
Playing career: *Chelsea, Brighton , Huddersfield Town, Walsall, Rotherham United (1980-1994)*
A former bricklayer, Hutchings had played for Chelsea and Brighton before heading to Leeds Road in 1987 to sign for Malcolm Macdonald's side. Despite being 30 years of age, he still managed to be a regular in the first team until his departure in 1990. After a stint as youth coach at Millmoor, Hutchings worked as a car salesman before becoming the assistant manager to Chris Kamara at Bradford City in 1996. He stayed on under next manager Paul Jewell and following Jewell's resignation in 2000, Hutchings was given the manager's job.

However, he was sacked after only 12 league games and went on to rejoin Jewell at Wigan Athletic. Hutchings went on to work as assistant manager at Market Drayton Town and also as a coach at Barnsley but is now living in Holmfirth.

HUTCHINSON, George
Outside-right
Town Years: 1945-1947 (amateur), 1947-1948
Born: *1929 Allerton Bywater*
Died: *1996 Sheffield, South Yorkshire*
Playing career: *Huddersfield Town, Sheffield United, Tottenham Hotspur, Guildford City, Leeds United, Halifax Town, (1945-c1958)*
Hutchinson signed from Castleford in 1945 as an amateur but signed professional two years later, only managing one game before leaving in 1948 to join Sheffield United. He remained at Bramall Lane for five years before spending one year at Tottenham Hotspur between 1953 and 1954. Died in 1996, while living in Sheffield.

HUTT, Geoffrey 'Geoff'
Left-back
Town Years: 1965-1976
Born: *1949 Hazelwood, Duffield, Derbyshire*
Playing career: *Huddersfield Town, Blackburn Rovers (loan), Haarlem, York City, Halifax Town (1965-1980)*

HUDDERSFIELD TOWN
GEOFF HUTT
FULL BACK

Hutt joined Town in 1965, and he established himself as the first choice left back in the side and was an ever-present in the 1969-70 promotion season. And whilst many of his teammates came and went as Town tumbled down the leagues, Hutt remained loyal and is one of only a select few to have played for Town in all four divisions. He left in 1976, playing a year in Holland for Haalem and joining York City for a year in 1977. Hutt joined Halifax Town in 1978, remaining for two years before his retirement as a professional. He later worked in the sales department of Tibbett and Britten and the became a delivery driver for Clintons Card before retiring. He now lives in Mirfield and was a Town season ticket holder for many years but is now involved in hospitality on home matchdays at the John Smith's Stadium.

HUWS, Emyr
Midfielder
Town Years: 2015-2016 (loan)
Born: 1993 Llanelli, Wales
Playing career: Manchester City, Northampton Town (loan), Birmingham City (loan), Wigan Athletic, Huddersfield Town (loan), Cardiff City, Ipswich Town (loan), Ipswich Town (2012-Still Playing)
Huws arrived on loan during the 2015-16 season from Wigan Athletic and spent the rest of the season at the club, before he returned to Wigan at the end of the season. David Wagner tried to bring Huws to the club on a permanent basis but Wigan wouldn't budge. He later signed for Cardiff City but is now plying his trade for Paul Lambert's Ipswich Town.

IFIL, Jerel
Defender
Town Years: 2002 (loan)
Born: 1982 Wembley, Greater London
Playing career: Watford, Huddersfield Town (loan), Swindon Town, Aberdeen, Bristol Rovers, Swindon Supermarine (2001-Still Playing)
Ifil spent a short time on loan at the club during the 2001-02 season but returned to Watford after playing a couple of games for Lou Macari's side. After his career ended, Ifil became a personal trainer and now runs his own company Ifil Fit and also works for Iprovefit Ltd as a Mentor. Ifil has since come out of retirement and is playing for non-league Swindon Supermarine.

ILLINGWORTH, Jeremy 'Jez'
Midfielder
Town Years: 1994-1997
Born: 1977 Huddersfield, West Yorkshire
Playing career: Huddersfield Town, Wisbech Town, Ashton United, Altrincham (1994-2008)
After four years as a professional at his home-town club, Illingworth later played non-league football around the North West before ending his career in 2008. He has been the Chief Executive of the Huddersfield based family business Illingworth & Gregory since 2001.

INCE, Thomas 'Tom'
Attacking midfielder / Winger / Forward
Town Years: 2017-2018
Born: 1992 Stockport, Cheshire
Playing career: Liverpool, Blackpool, Crystal Palace (loan), Hull City, Nottingham Forest (loan), Derby County (loan), Derby County, Huddersfield Town, Stoke City (2010-Still Playing)
Ince arrived at the John Smith's Stadium in time for the 2017-18 season. He cost the club £9 million but only lasted one season and he was sold to Stoke City for £12 million including add-ons.

IRELAND, Simon
Midfielder
Town Years: 1990-1992
Born: 1971 Barnstaple, Devon
Playing career: Huddersfield Town, Wrexham (loan), Blackburn Rovers, Mansfield Town, Doncaster Rovers, Boreham Wood (1990-1998)
Ireland began his career at Leeds Road but managed very few appearances before impressing in a cup tie with Blackburn Rovers which led to his transfer to Ewood Park in 1992. He only managed 1 game at Ewood Park before departing and signing for Mansfield Town in 1993. Ireland played at Field Mill for four years preceeding his time at Doncaster Rovers between 1997 and 1998 and eventually played for non-league Boreham Wood before ending his career in 1998. Ireland moved into coaching after his retirement and worked as a coach at Town's academy in the early 2000s, before becoming a coach at Blackburn's academy. In 2013, Ireland joined Brighton as their Under-21s Manager before moving to QPR as Head of Coaching and Coach Education in 2015. Since 2018, he has worked as Nottingham Forest's First Team Coach.

IRONS, Kenneth 'Kenny'
Midfielder
Town Years: 1999-2003
Born: *1970 Liverpool, Lancashire*
Playing career: *Tranmere Rovers, Huddersfield Town, Linfield, NEWI Cefn Druids (1989-2006)*
Steve Bruce signed Irons at the beginning of the 1999-2000 season from Tranmere Rovers, the fee being £500,000. He is best remembered for the goal he scored against Chelsea in the League Cup during his first season and he played under Bruce, Lou Macari and finally Mick Wadsworth before leaving at the end of the 2002-03 season after the club went into administration. He went on to play for Linfield and Caernarfon Town. Irons has since worked as a coach at the Tranmere Rovers Centre of Excellence and also managed Mold Alex FC in the Welsh League. He has also played in the England Master's team, helping England win the 2016 Seniors World Cup which took place in Thailand. Irons is currently living in his native Liverpool and runs his own academy, On S.I.D.E, Sports Academy.

ISAAC, James 'Jimmy'
Outside-right
Town Years: 1934-1935 (amateur), 1935-1945
Born: *1916 Cramlington, Northumberland*
Died: *1993 Huddersfield, West Yorkshire*
Playing career: *Bedlington United, Huddersfield Town, Bradford City, Hartlepools United (1934-1949)*
Isaac began his career at Leeds Road in 1934 and played a number of first team games before World War Two interrupted his playing career in 1939. When the Football League resumed after the end of the War, Isaac signed for Bradford City in 1945 but remained at Valley Parade for just a year ahead of his move to Hartlepools United, where he stayed for two years before retiring from the game. He later died in December 1993 at the age of 77, having returned to Huddersfield after the end of his playing days.

ISLIP, Ernest 'Ernie'
Forward
Town Years: 1911-1923
Born: *1892 Sheffield, West Riding of Yorkshire*
Died: *1941 Huddersfield, West Riding of Yorkshire*
Playing career: *Sheffield Douglas, Huddersfield Town, Birmingham, Bradford City, Kidderminster Harriers, Ashton National, Wrexham (1910-1929)*

Islip arrived at Leeds Road in 1911 when he signed for Dick Pudan's side and he went on to spend twelve years at the club. He was part of the 2nd Division winning side of 1920, the FA Cup winning side of 1922 and was also the leading goalscorer in the 1921-22 season before he moved on to Birmingham in 1923. He later ran the Armitage Arms in Milnsbridge, Huddersfield before passing away in 1941 at the age of 48.

JACKSON, Alexander 'Alec'
Outside-right
Town Years: 1925-1930
Born: *1905 Renton, Scotland*
Died: *1946 Cairo, Egypt*
Playing career: *Aberdeen, Huddersfield Town, Chelsea, Ashton National, Margate, OGC Nice, Le Touquet (1922-1936)*
Jackson was Herbert Chapman's last signing at Leeds Road before he left for Arsenal and he is one of Town's greatest ever players. He played an important part in the third league title winning season of 1925-26 and also helped fire Town to the FA Cup Final against Blackburn Rovers in 1928. Jackson became the first Town player to score at Wembley, a feat that has only been matched by three other players while also playing in the 1930 FA Cup Final against Arsenal before leaving for Chelsea in September of that year. The Scotsman had a successful period at Stamford Bridge but it came to an end during the 1932-33 season after he was approached by French club Nimes. Jackson threatened to accept the lucrative offer unless Chelsea paid him more money, they refused and he could do nothing, ending up finishing his career in non-league playing for clubs such as Margate and Ashton National, although he did later play for French club Nice. Jackson served during the Second World War in North Africa with the Eighth Army and later joined the Pioneer Corps after suffering injury in Libya. He played for the Army football team during the war and stayed on in Africa after the War and was assigned to the Suez Zone. In November 1946, Jackson was driving a truck near his base and lost control, the truck overturned and he suffered serious head injuries, dying before he reached the hospital. Jackson is buried in the war cemetery in Fayid, Egypt.

JACKSON, Mark

Defender
Town Years: 1998 (loan)
Born: *1977 Leeds, West Yorkshire*
Playing career: *Leeds United, Huddersfield Town (loan), Barnsley (loan), Scunthorpe United, Kidderminster Harriers, Rochdale, Farsley Celtic, Farsley (1995-2015)*

Jackson arrived on loan from parent club Leeds United in the 1998-99 season, but only managed a couple of appearances before returning to Elland Road. The Yorkshireman left Elland Road in 2000 and signed for Scunthorpe United. He played at Glanford Park for five years ahead of signing for Kidderminster Harriers in 2005, spending a year at the club before moving to Rochdale in 2006. Jackson left the next year and joined non-league Farsley Celtic and later worked as player-assistant manager alongside Neil Parsley at the club before leaving in 2015. Jackson worked as Head of Football at Leeds City College between 2010 and 2015 before he took the role of Lead Youth Development Phase Coach at Leeds United. He has been the Lead Professional Development Phase Coach at Elland Road since 2016.

Peter Jackson

JACKSON, Peter

Defender, Reserve Team Coach, Manager
Town Years: 1990-1994, 1993-1994 (reserve team coach), 1997-1999 & 2003-2007 (manager)
Born: *1961 Bradford, West Riding of Yorkshire*
Playing career: *Bradford City, Newcastle United, Bradford City, Huddersfield Town (1979-1997)*
Management career: *Huddersfield Town, Lincoln City, Bradford City (1997-2011)*

Jacko' is a Town legend and one of only a select few who have played for and managed the club. He joined from Bradford City in 1990 and quickly became the club captain, impressing the Leeds Road faithful with his committed performances, becoming a cult hero at the club. He excelled under Eoin Hand and was part of the 1991-92 playoff campaign but fell out of favour under Neil Warnock towards the end of the 1993-94 season and moved to Chester City. Jackson later signed for Halifax Town at the beginning of the 1997-98 season but, after Town's disastrous start, Brian Horton was sacked leading to the shock re-appointment of 'Jacko' with Terry Yorath as his Head Coach. 'Jacko' and 'Taff' orchestrated the 'Great Escape' and achieved survival with games to spare. However, after a poor end to the 1998-9 season, 'Jacko' was dismissed and replaced by Steve Bruce. He later worked as a football agent but after Town's administration in 2003 he made a dramatic comeback as manager. At the time, Town found themselves in the fourth tier of English football for the first time since 1980 and promotion was secured in the playoffs at the end of that season. In 2005-6 Town ended up losing to Barnsley in the play-off semi-finals and 'Jacko' never really recovered from this. The 2006-07 season started poorly and then his right hand man, Terry Yorath left the club due to ill health and after more bad results, Jackson was let go in March 2007. He later became the Lincoln City manager in 2007 but took a short break when it was discovered he was suffering from throat cancer. He returned to the job after having the all-clear but was later sacked in 2009. Jackson and his wife went on to run Caremark Calderdale, which was a care home franchise. He did manage his hometown club Bradford City in 2011 but is now back at Town, running hospitality on a matchday at every home game in the Legends Bar.

JAMES, Reece
Defender
Town Years: 2015 (loan)
Born: *1993 Bacup, Lancashire*
Playing career: *Rossendale United, Blackburn Rovers, Preston North End, Manchester United, Carlisle United (loan), Rotherham United (loan), Huddersfield Town (loan), Wigan Athletic, Sunderland (2012-Still Playing)*
James joined the club on a short loan from Manchester United in 2015 and after the loan deal had ended, he returned to his parent club. The Lancastrian later played for Wigan Athletic before being released at the conclusion of the 2017-18 season. He is now playing for Sunderland having signed for the Black Cats at the beginning of the 2018-19 season.

JAMES, Sidney
Centre-half
Town Years: 1913-1917
Born: *1891 Sheffield, West Riding of Yorkshire*
Died: *1917 France (Killed in Action)*
Playing career: *Bird-in-the-Hand F.C., Huddersfield Town (1913-1917)*
James signed for Town in November 1913 but after less than a year at the club, his career was interrupted by the First World War commencing in 1914. The Yorkshireman went to War as a Lance Corporal, but was sadly killed in action in 1917 in France. He is buried in the Cojeul British Cemetery, St. Martin-sur-Cojeul.

JAMESON, John 'Johnny'
Outside-left
Town Years: 1977-1978
Born: *1958 Belfast, Northern Ireland*
Playing career: *Bangor, Huddersfield Town, Linfield, Glentoran (1975-1994)*
Jameson signed from Bangor in 1977 but only managed 1 game at Leeds Road before leaving for Linfield in 1978 and going on to sign for Glentoran in 1980. Jameson was in Northern Ireland's 1982 World Cup squad but didn't make any appearances as he refused to play on a Sunday due to his religious beliefs. After his playing career ended, Jameson has worked in sales including Express Freight and Redhead International. He is now Head of Sales at The Distribution Solution in Belfast.

JEE, Joseph 'Joe'
Outside-left
Town Years: 1909-1919
Born: *1883 Chorlton-cum-Hardy, Lancashire*
Died: *1959 Manchester, Lancashire*
Playing career: *Bolton Wanderers, Brighton & Hove Albion, Huddersfield Town, Nelson (1904-1919)*
Jee signed from Brighton & Hove Albion in 1909 and was part of the team that turned professional in 1910 and played all but one match during that first season under the guidance of Dick Pudan. He continued to be first choice outside-left until League football was suspended in 1915. Jee remained on the books at Leeds Road until 1919, however, by then was considered to be past his best and he was placed on the transfer list. He joined Nelson in October 1919 and Town were fined ten guineas for placing him on the retained list in July. He was also awarded £150 in lieu of a benefit. After his retirement, Jee worked as a packer in a warehouse. He later died in 1959 aged 76 in Manchester.

JENKINS, Stephen 'Steve'
Right-back, Left-winger
Town Years: 1995-2003
Born: *1972 Merthyr Tydfil, Wales*
Playing career: *Swansea City, Huddersfield Town, Cardiff City, Notts County, Peterborough United, Swindon Town, Newport County, Llanelli (1990-2012)*
'Jenks' arrived at the McAlpine in 1995, signed by Brian Horton, originally as a left winger. He was quickly converted to right-back and continued to play there throughout his eight years at the club. Jenkins played over 250 games for Town, leaving in 2003 after the club suffered administration. Since leaving Town, Jenkins has since attended the odd game as a co-commentator for BBC Radio Leeds. He joined Cardiff City in 2003 but signed for Notts County later in the year. A short stint at Peterborough United followed before he joined Swindon Town in 2004. Following two years at the club and a short spell at Worcester City, Jenkins joined Newport County, eventually becoming a player-coach. He joined Andy Legg at Llanelli in 2009 as player-assistant manager before he became the Monmouth Town manager in 2013. Jenkins went on to become manager of Merthyr Town, leaving in 2016 to return as assistant manager at Hereford United. Jenkins left his position in September 2018.

JENNINGS, Dennis
Outside-right
Town Years: 1930-1932
Born: *1910 Habberley Valley, Worcestershire*
Died: *1996 Wadebridge, Cornwall*
Playing career: *Stourport Swifts, Romsley Village, West Bromwich Albion, Kidderminster Harriers, Huddersfield Town, Grimsby Town, Birmingham, Kidderminster Harriers (player-coach), Lockheed Leamington (1928-1953)*

Arriving in 1930, Jennings signed from Kidderminster Harriers but struggled to break into the first team in his first season, but becoming more of a regular during his second season. Jennings only managed a handful of appearances in his final season at the club and transferred to Grimsby Town in 1932. He spent four years in Lincolnshire before heading for Birmingham in 1936. He spent fifteen years at the club and became the oldest player to play for the first team there at 39 years 290 days. During the War, Jennings had worked as a stamp press operator. Jennings then moved to Kidderminster Harriers as player-coach in 1951 before finishing his career at Lockheed Leamington. He ran Little Dinham Caravan Park in Cornwall later in life, passed away aged 85 in 1996.

JEPSON, Ronald 'Ronnie'
Forward, Assistant Manager
Town Years: 1993-1996, 2008 (assistant manager)
Born: *1963 Audley, Staffordshire*
Playing career: *Nantwich Town, Port Vale, Peterborough United (loan), Preston North End, Exeter City, Huddersfield Town, Bury, Oldham Athletic, Burnley (1989-2000)*

'Rocket Ron' signed from Exeter City in 1993 and he went on to form a strike partnership with Andrew Booth. During the 1994-95 promotion season they became the first strike partnership to score over 50 goals for many a year. Following another successful season, Jepson left for Bury in 1996. He later became manager of Gillingham in 2005 but was sacked in 2007. JJepson returned to Town as Stan Ternent's assistant manager in April 2008 but they were both sacked in November 2008 after a terrible start to the season. He joined Neil Warnock at Crystal Palace, QPR, and Leeds United in 2012 before he left the following year. He has been working as the First Team Coach at Cardiff City since 2016.

JEVONS, Philip 'Phil'
Forward
Town Years: 2007-2008 (loan) 2008-2010
Born: *1979 Liverpool, Merseyside*
Playing career: *Everton, Grimsby Town, Yeovil Town, Bristol City, Huddersfield Town (1996-2014)*

Originally a loan signing from Bristol City during the 2007-08 season, Jevons was signed permanently by Andy Ritchie in January 2008. He fell out of favour towards the end of the 2008-09 season and was loaned out to both Bury and Morecambe before signing permanently for the latter in 2010. He became a coach at Everton's academy and is currently the U16s coach, he also ran his own chaffeur business, PJ's Travel between 2012 and 2014.

JOHNSON, Damien
Midfielder
Town Years: 2010-2011 (loan), 2011-2012 (loan)
Born: *1978 Lisburn, Northern Ireland*
Playing career: *Portadown, Blackburn Rovers, Birmingham City, Plymouth Argyle, Huddersfield Town (loan), Fleetwood Town (1994-2013)*

Johnson had two separate loan spells at Town the second being in 2011-12. He played in the middle of midfield for most of the promotion season, although he missed in penalty in the final shootout. Johnson returned to his parent club Plymouth Argyle at the end of the 2011-12 season and they later sold him to Fleetwood Town, where he played until his retirement in 2013. He then worked as U14-U18 Assistant Coach at Everton until 2014 when he joined Blackburn Rovers as U23 Professional Development Phase Lead Coach. He also worked as an Assistant Coach for the Northern Ireland national team between 2014 and 2015 and balanced his role at Blackburn with that of Scout for Northern Ireland, which he has done since 2013.

Ronnie Jepson

JOHNSON, Grant

Midfielder
Town Years: *1997-2000*
Born: *1972 Dundee, Scotland*
Playing career: *Dundee United, Huddersfield Town, Clydebank, Alloa Athletic, Montrose, Brechin City (1990-2007)*

After seven years at Dundee United, Johnson signed for Town in 1997 and played in the 1997-98 Great Escape season, where he was well-liked for his reliable and consistent performances. He later lost his place in the side by the time Steve Bruce became manager in 1999 and he left the club the following year to join Clydebank for a short stint before heading to Alloa Athletic. Johnson left the club in 2001 and joined Montrose, where he played for two years before he headed to Brechin City in 2003. When his four years at Brechin were up, Johnson left the club in 2007 when he left the sport for good. Johnson also worked as a solicitor for Thornton's in Dundee from 2003 until 2015 when he joined Lindsay's.

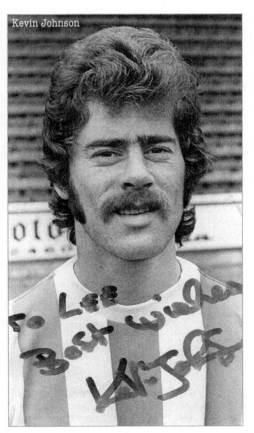

Kevin Johnson

JOHNSON, John 'Jack'

Outside-right
Town Years: *1936-1939*
Born: *1919 Newcastle upon Tyne, Northumberland*
Died: *1975 Leicester, Leicestershire*
Playing career: *Leicester Nomads, Huddersfield Town, Grimsby Town, Shrewsbury Town (1936-1948)*

Johnson began his professional career in 1936 at Leeds Road and managed a small sum of appearances in Clem Stephenson's side before War broke out in 1939. Once the War was over, Johnson signed for Grimsby Town and remained at the club for two years until his departure in 1948. He later had a stint at Shrewsbury Town before finishing his career and passing away in 1975.

JOHNSON, Kevin

Forward
Town Years: *1976-1978*
Born: *1952 Doncaster, West Riding of Yorkshire*
Playing career: *Sheffield Wednesday, Southend United, Gillingham, Workington (loan), Hartlepool United, Huddersfield Town, Halifax Town, Hartlepool United, Gateshead (1970-1984)*

Johnson had been playing for Hartlepool United before Tom Johnston brought him to Leeds Road in 1976. He spent two years at the club and played over 80 games for the club, knocking in over 20 goals as well. He left the club in 1978 after a disagreement with new manager Mick Buxton and he signed for Halifax Town. The Yorkshireman spent two years at The Shay before returning to Hartlepool where he played until 1984. He later played non-league football for Gateshead where he ended his career and is now back living in his hometown of Doncaster.

JOHNSTON, William 'Billy'

Inside-right
Town Years: *1920-1924*
Born: *1901 Edinburgh, Scotland*
Died: *1964 Manchester, Lancashire*
Playing career: *Huddersfield Town, Stockport County, Manchester United, Macclesfield Town, Manchester United, Oldham Athletic, Frickley Colliery (player-manager) (c1918-1936)*

Johnston arrived at the club in 1920, after signing from Selby Town, and was in the side that won both the Charity Shield and FA Cup in 1922. He moved on in 1924 and played for Stockport County before signing for Manchester United in 1928.

Johnston left Old Trafford two years later to sign for non-league Macclesfield Town. He returned to Old Trafford in 1931 but once again left after a year in 1932 to join Oldham Athletic. He went on to sign for Frickley, where he acted as manager/secretary and also played for the first team. Johnston later worked as the Manager of the Cricketer's Arms in Manchester and at a pub in Abergele before his death in November 1964.

JOHNSTON, Thomas 'Tom'

Manager, General Manager
Town Years: 1964-1968 (manager), 1975-1978 (manager and general manager)
Born: *1918 Coldstream, Scotland*
Died: *1994 Nottingham, Nottinghamshire*
Management career: *Rotherham United, Grimsby Town, Huddersfield Town, York City, Huddersfield Town, Huddersfield Town (1958-1978)*
After spending time as manager at Grimsby Town, Johnston arrived at Leeds Road in 1964 to replace Eddie Boot, who had resigned as manager. He almost achieved automatic promotion to the First Division at the end of the 1965-66 season but ultimately missed out by two points, yet he still took Town to the League Cup semi-finals in 1968, the club's best record to date in that competition. Johnston is also remembered by Town fans for changing the club's colours, doing away with blue and white stripes and replacing them with plain blue shirts. He left the club in 1968 to become the manager of York City and spent seven years at Bootham Crescent, achieving promotion twice before shocking the York fans by returning to Leeds Road in 1975. As General Manager, Johnston worked alongside Manager Bobby Collins, but this didn't last very long as Collins resigned citing interference from Johnston. Johnston assumed full control of the team in December 1975, and again changed the shirts back to blue. He remained in charge of the first team until 1977 when he was voted out by the club's board in favour of coach, John Haselden. After very poor results during 1977, Johnston was again voted back in and Haselden demoted to his previous coaching duties. Johnston lasted just a year at his third time in charge of the club, resigning in 1978 with Town 91st in the Football League. The Scotsman quietly retired from the game and lived the rest of his days in Nottingham, dying in 1994 at the age of 75.

JONES, Alan

Midfielder
Town Years: 1967-1973
Born: *1951 Grimethorpe, West Riding of Yorkshire*
Playing career: *Huddersfield Town, Halifax Town, Chesterfield, Lincoln City (1967-1981)*
Jones arrived at the club as an apprentice in 1967 before signing professional in 1970. He played for three years in the first team before he left the club to sign for Halifax Town in 1973. Jones retired from the game in 1981.

JONES, Christopher 'Chris'

Forward
Town Years: 1976-1977
Born: *1945 Altrincham, Lancashire*
Playing career: *Manchester City, Swindon Town, Walsall, York City, Huddersfield Town, Doncaster Rovers, Darlington (loan), Rochdale (1964-1979)*
Jones signed from York City in 1976 but only spent a year at the club and left after playing just 18 games for Tom Johnston's side. Jones retired from professional football in 1979 and became a schoolteacher and now acts as match summariser for all York City games on BBC Radio York. He also released an autobiography in 2015 entitled *The Tale of Two Great Cities*, focusing mainly on his stints at York City and Manchester City.

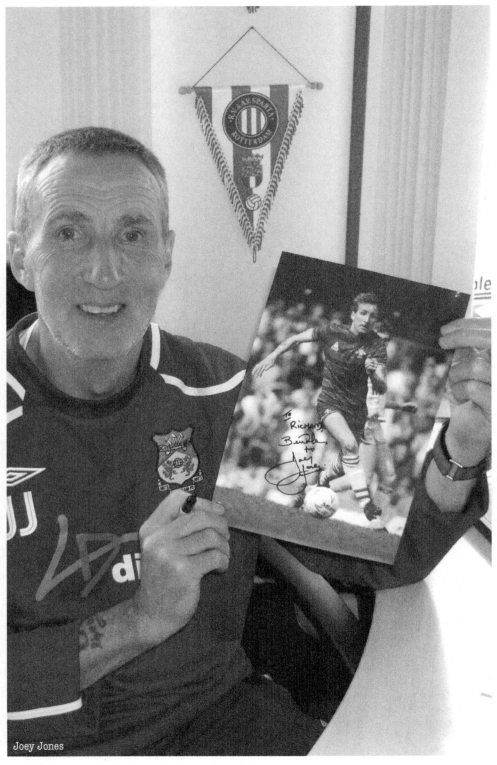

Joey Jones

JONES, Gwyn
Left-half
Town Years: 1933-1934
Born: *1912 Troed-y-rhiw, Wales*
Died: *1968 Littleborough, Lancashire*
Playing career: *Huddersfield Town, Rochdale, Stockport County, Tranmere Rovers (1933-1939)*
After a spell at Merthyr Town, Jones signed for Clem Stephenson's Town side in 1933 but only played 1 game for the club before leaving Leeds Road in 1934. After his time at Town, Jones signed for Rochdale and played almost 100 games at Spotland before he left for Stockport County. Jones went on to live in Littleborough before his death in 1968.

JONES, Joseph 'Joey'
Centre-half
Town Years: 1985-1987
Born: *1955 Llandudno, Wales*
Playing career: *Wrexham, Liverpoo, Chelsea, Huddersfield Town (1973-1992)*
Joey Jones is one of the select few to have won the 1st Division, FA Cup, League Cup and the European Cup and all of these honours were won during his time at Liverpool. He was coming to the end of his career when Mick Buxton brought him to the club in 1985 after playing for Chelsea. Despite beginning his career as a left-back, Jones had converted to centre-half by the time he arrived at Leeds Road. Jones was immediately made captain of the side and was popular with the Town fans thanks to his no-nonsense style and committed, passionate performances. Jones went on to serve Wrexham in a number of roles including caretaker manager and youth coach before he retired in 2017. Jones is still residing in his hometown of Wrexham.

JONES, Paul
Centre-half
Town Years: 1983-1985
Born: *1953 Ellesmere Port, Cheshire*
Playing career: *Bolton Wanderers, Huddersfield Town, Oldham Athletic, Blackpool, Rochdale, Stockport County (1970-1990)*
Paul Jones is considered to be one of the greatest centre-halves that never received an England cap. He had spent thirteen years at Bolton Wanderers before Mick Buxton brought him to Leeds Road in 1983. By fans of a certain age, Jones is considered one of Town's best centre-halves of all time.

He was penalty taker during his two years at Town, even managing to net a hat-trick in one game and also renewed his old Bolton partnership with Sam Allardyce during the 1984-85 season. Jones left the club in 1985 and signed for Oldham Athletic. Jones has since scouted for Bolton Wanderers, Hull City and Crystal Palace and has also coached in China during the 2000s and worked as a judge on a football talent show for Turkish, Vietnamese and Chinese television. Jones was last known to be coaching a Sunday football team called Flyers F.C.

JONES, Robert
Outside-right
Town Years: 1921-1922
Born: *1902 Gateshead, County Durham*
Died: *1958 Gateshead, County Durham*
Playing career: *Huddersfield Town, Walker Celtic, Castleford Town, Washington Colliery (1921-c1929)*
Jones signed from High Fell in 1921 and managed 2 league appearances and a goal during the 1921-22 season before he left. Later played for Castleford Town before he headed home to the North East and played for Washington Colliery. Jones later worked as a builder's labourer in Gateshead before he passed away in March 1958.

JONES, Stephen 'Steve'
Right-winger
Town Years: 2008 (loan)
Born: *1976 Derry, Northern Ireland*
Playing career: *Crewe Alexandra, Burnley, Huddersfield Town (loan) (1995-Still Playing)*
Jones was a winger who was signed on loan from Burnley by Stan Ternent in 2008 and played four games before returning to his parent club. He later played at Walsall, Droylsden, AFC Telford United and Airbus UK Broughton before he signed for Nantwich Town in 2014. He remains at the club and is now player-coach there.

"DID YOU KNOW?"

"Town became the first club in Football League history to be promoted with a negative goal difference in 2017 when they won promotion to the Premier League."

JORDAN, Stephen
Full-back
Town Years: 2011 (loan)
Born: *1982 Warrington, Cheshire*
Playing career: *Manchester City, Cambridge United (loan), Burnley, Sheffield United, Huddersfield Town (loan), Rochdale, Dunfermline Athletic, Fleetwood Town, Chorley (1999-Still Playing)*
Jordan arrived on loan towards the end of the 2010-11 season from Sheffield United and managed 6 appearances before being sent back by manager, Lee Clark. He was released by Sheffield United at the end of that season and he joined Rochdale, he spent a year at the club before he left Spotland in 2012. Jordan then spent a year at Dunfermline Athletic before he joined Fleetwood Town in 2013. He left the club in 2016 and signed for non-league Chorley.

JOY, David
Left-half
Town Years: 1961-1967
Born: *1943 Barnard Castle, County Durham*
Playing career: *Evenwood Town, Huddersfield Town, York City (1961-1968)*
After a stint at York City, Joy worked as a schoolteacher at Rastrick Grammar School teaching PE and English. He now lives in his native Newton Aycliffe in retirement and was a member of Darlington Golf Club at one point.

JUTKIEWICZ, Lukas
Forward
Town Years: 2009 (loan)
Born: *1989 Southampton, Hampshire*
Playing career: *Southampton, Swindon Town, Everton, Plymouth Argyle (loan), Huddersfield Town (loan), Motherwell (loan), Coventry City, Middlesbrough (loan), Middlesbrough, Bolton Wanderers (loan), Burnley, Birmingham City (loan), Birmingham City (1999-Still Playing)*
Jutkiewicz joined Town on loan from Everton during the 2008-09 season but was disliked by Town fans due to a perceived lack of effort and never made the squad again after throwing his training top at Lee Clark as he stormed Town the tunnel to a chorus of boos during a home clash with Cheltenham Town. He later played for Coventry City, Middlesbrough and Burnley before he signed for Birmingham City in 2017. As of 2018, Jutkiewicz remains at St. Andrews.

KADAR, Tamas
Left-back
Town Years: 2011 (loan)
Born: *1990 Veszprém, Hungary*
Playing career: *Zalaegerszeg, Newcastle United, Huddersfield Town (loan), Roda, Diósgyőr, Lech Poznań, Dynamo Kyiv (2004-Still Playing)*
Kadar arrived on loan in January 2011 but was injured after just 2 appearances and was sent back to parent club Newcastle United where he remained until 2012. He has since played for Roda (Holland), Diosgyor (Hungary), Lech Poznan (Poland) and signed for Dynamo Kiev in 2017. Kadar is also a Hungarian international player and has won over 40 caps for his national side.

KAMARA, Malvin
Winger
Town Years: 2007-2009
Born: *1983 Plumstead, Greater London*
Playing career: *West Ham United, Wimbledon, Milton Keynes Dons, Cardiff City, Port Vale, Huddersfield Town (2003-2017)*
Kamara signed from Port Vale in 2007 but was only a regular player in his first season, he was loaned to Grimsby Town during the second season and he was later released. After leaving the club, Kamara had short spells in non-league. He studied at Staffordshire University and then worked for Venquis Ltd in London as a Business Transformation Consultant and is now a Director at Vallum Associates who specialise in recruitment services for the Energy and Utilities industry in London. Whilst at Town, Kamara won an international cap for the Sierra Leone national side in 2007.

KAY, Antony
Centre-half/Central midfielder
Town Years: 2009-2012
Born: *1982 Barnsley, South Yorkshire*
Playing career: *Barnsley, Tranmere R, Huddersfield Town, MK Dons, Bury, Port Vale (1999-Still Playing)*
Lee Clark signed Antony Kay from Tranmere Rovers at the beginning of the 2009-10 season and he was installed in the middle of midfield but was later converted to centre -back. He played for the club for three years and scored both an extra-time equaliser and the winning penalty in the playoff semi-final against AFC Bournemouth in 2011. Kay's contract was ended by mutual consent. He is now club captain at Port Vale.

KAYE, Peter
Forward
Town Years: 1996-1998
Born: *1979 Huddersfield, West Yorkshire*
Playing career: *Huddersfield Town (1996-1998)*
A Huddersfield lad, Peter Kaye progressed through the youth team at Town before signing professional in 1996. He managed 1 game at the end of the 1996-97 season against Swindon Town but never played for the club again and was released in 1998. Kaye is still living and working in Huddersfield.

KELLY, Robert 'Bob'
Inside-forward
Town Years: 1927-1932
Born: *1893 Ashton-in-Makerfield, Lancashire*
Died: *1969 Fylde, Lancashire*
Playing career: *Ashton White Star, Ashton Central, Earlestown Rovers, St Helens Town, Burnley, Sunderland, Huddersfield Town, Preston North End, Carlisle United (1913-1936)*
Kelly was something of a veteran when he arrived at Leeds Road in 1927 and went on to spend five years at Town before leaving the club in 1932. He played over 200 games for the club and was 39 years old when he departed and after some time at Preston North End he retired at Carlisle United in 1936 at the age of 43.

Antony Kay

Kelly had spent two years at Carlisle and the final year was spent as manager of the club. After an eight year absence, while he managed a hotel in Lytham St. Annes, Kelly came back to managed Sporting CP, FC St. Gallen SC Heerenveen, AZ Alkmaar and Barry Town before retiring from the game. Kelly died in 1969 at the age of 75.

KELLY, Gerard 'Gerry'
Outside-right
Town Years: 1929-1932
Born: *1908 South Hylton, Sunderland*
Died: *1986 Ellesmere Port, Cheshire*
Playing career: *Sunderland, Nelson, Huddersfield Town, Charlton Athletic, Chester, Port Vale, Southampton, Shrewsbury Town (1927-1939)*
Kelly was signed by Clem Stephenson from Nelson in 1929 and played for the club for three years. He managed a total of 38 appearances and 15 goals over those years before he left Leeds Road in 1932 to sign for Charlton Athletic. He only spent a year at The Valley before heading to Chester in 1932, he spent four years at the club before he departed in 1936 when Port Vale paid a "substantial fee" for his services. Kelly was immediately installed in the first team but over the 1936-37 season he dropped out of the team and was given a free transfer in 1937. The outbreak of World War Two ended his career Kelly died in 1986 at the age of 77.

KELLY, John
Midfielder
Town Years: 1990 (loan), 1991-1992
Born: *1960 Bebington, Cheshire*
Playing career: *Cammell Laird, Tranmere Rovers, Preston North End, Chester City, Swindon Town, Oldham Athletic, Walsall, Huddersfield Town (loan), Huddersfield Town, Chester City, Rhyl (1978-1995)*
After a long career in the Football League, Kelly arrived at Leeds Road on loan from Walsall towards the end of the 1989-90 season. He returned to the club during the 1990-91 season on a permanent transfer and remained in Eoin Hand's squad until the end of the 1991-92 season when he moved to former club Chester City. Kelly played for Chester for one year before signing for Rhyl in the Welsh League. He remained in Chester and is now running his own business, Kelly's Industrial Clothing, a wholesale of clothing and footwear.

KELLY, Lawrence 'Lawrie'

Left-back
Town Years: 1950-1957
Born: *1925 Wolverhampton, Staffordshire*
Died: *1972 Dudley, Staffordshire*
Playing career: *Wolverhampton Wanderers, Huddersfield Town (1947-1958)*

After three years at hometown club Wolverhampton Wanderers, Kelly arrived at Leeds Road in 1950. He spent the next six years at the club, making over 200 appearances at left-back before he departed from the club in 1957 as the club's policy at the time was to reduce the average age of the side. To note, Kelly was replaced by a young player called Ray Wilson. Kelly became the player-manager of Nuneaton Borough in May 1957 before resigning from the post in December 1958. He later passed away in 1972 whilst living in Dudley.

KELLY, Martin

Defender
Town Years: 2009 (loan)
Born: *1990 Whiston, Merseyside*
Playing career: *Liverpool, Huddersfield Town (loan), Crystal Palace (2008-Still Playing)*

Kelly was signed by Lee Clark in the 2008-09 season from Liverpool on a short-term loan towards the end of the season. He impressed with his magnificent performances all across the back four, managing to play at right back, left back and centre half in his seven appearances. At the end of the season, Kelly returned to his parent club Liverpool and managed a few appearances in their first team and even an England call up in 2012. However, injuries hampered his career and he signed for Crystal Palace in 2014. As of 2018, Kelly has played over 100 games for the Eagles.

KENNEDY, Michael 'Micky'

Midfielder
Town Years: 1980-1982
Born: *1961 Salford, Lancashire*
Playing career: *Halifax Town, Huddersfield Town, Middlesbrough, Portsmouth, Bradford City, Leicester City, Luton Town, Stoke City, Chesterfield, Wigan Athletic (1978-1994)*

Kennedy arrived at Leeds Road in 1980 from his hometown club, Halifax Town and spent two years at the club, playing in midfield and was popular for his tough tackling and hardman image.

He left the club in 1982 to spend two years at Middlesbrough. Kennedy then signed for Portsmouth in 1984 and played over 100 games for 'Pompey' between 1984 and 1988. He is considered a club legend at Fratton Park and was inducted into their Hall of Fame. He retired from the game in 1999 and moved to County Clare, Ireland where he coached a number of junior sides over the years. Died at the age of 57 in February 2019.

KENNON, Neil 'Sandy'

Goalkeeper
Town Years: 1956-1958
Born: *1933 Johannesburg, South Africa*
Died: *2015 Norwich, Norfolk*
Playing career: *Huddersfield Town, Norwich City, Colchester United, Lowestoft Town (1956-1970)*

Kennon was playing international football for Southern Rhodesia in 1956 and he played in a match against England. Town defender Bill McGarry was playing for England at the time and recommended Kennon to Andy Beattie, who later signed him up. Kennon played 80 games for the first team before Bill Shankly let him leave the club in 1959 to join Norwich City on a free transfer. Kennon later became a rep for a whiskey firm and also worked as a window-cleaner before running a number of betting shops in Norwich. He later retired and continued to live in Norwich up until his death in 2015.

KENWORTHY, Ernest

Outside-right
Town Years: 1909-1910
Born: *1888 Matlock, Derbyshire*
Died: *1917 France (Killed in Action)*
Playing career: *Manningham Recreational, Bradford City, Huddersfield Town (1907-1910)*

Kenworthy arrived in 1909 and made 20 appearances for Fred Walker's side during the 1909-10 season. He left the club when they turned professional in time for the 1910-11 season and later worked as Assistant Headmaster at Matlock Town Schools before becoming Headmaster when the previous Headmaster was called up to the First World War. Kenworthy joined up himself in 1916 but met his death November 1917 whilst serving with the 135th Siege Battery. He was killed by a bursting shell and is buried in Coxyde Military Cemetery on the coast of Belgium.

KEOGH, Richard
Centre-half
Town Years: 2007 (loan)
Born: *1986 Harlow, Essex*
Playing career: *Ipswich Town, Stoke City, Bristol City, Huddersfield Town (loan), Carlisle United, Coventry City, Derby County (2004-Still Playing)*
Arriving on loan from Bristol City, Keogh had a very underwhelming loan spell at centre-half during the 2007-08 season. He returned to Bristol City. He signed for Derby County in 2012 where he has played over 250 games and is the captain of the side. Keogh has also played international football for the Republic of Ireland national team and as of 2018, has won 19 caps.

KERRAY, James 'Jim'
Inside-right
Town Years: 1960-1962
Born: *1935 Stirling, Scotland*
Playing career: *Huddersfield Town, Newcastle United, Dunfermline Athletic, St Johnstone, Stirling Albion, Falkirk (1957-1969)*
After a time spent at Dunfermline Athletic, Kerray arrived at Leeds Road in 1960 and managed over 50 appearances for the first team before leaving the club two years later to sign for Newcastle United in 1962. He later returned to Dunfermline before ending his career in 1969.

KILBANE, Kevin
Midfielder
Town Years: 2011 (loan)
Born: *1977 Preston, Lancashire*
Playing career: *Preston North End, West Bromwich Albion, Sunderland, Everton, Wigan Athletic, Hull City, Huddersfield Town (loan), Derby County (loan), Coventry City (1995-2012)*
Kilbane joined on loan from Hull City for the second half of the 2010-11 season and played a part in Town getting to the play-off final that season. His final game at the club was the 3-0 loss to Peterborough United at Old Trafford in the final and he returned to his parent club at the end of the season. Kilbane remained at Hull City until 2012 and had a short stint at Coventry City before leaving the sport later that same year. He is now a pundit for the BBC and on Irish television. To note, Kilbane played international football for the Republic of Ireland between 1997 and 2011, winning a total of 110 caps and playing in the 2002 World Cup Finals.

KILLOCK, Shane
Centre-half
Town Years: 2007-2009
Born: *1989 Huddersfield, West Yorkshire*
Playing career: *Huddersfield Town, Oxford United, Bradford Park Avenue (2005-Still Playing)*
Killock was a youth player at Town before Andy Ritchie played him in an away match against Crewe Alexandra in 2007. This turned out to be his only appearance for the club and he left in 2009 to sign for Oxford United Killock signed for current club Bradford Park Avenue in 2016.

KINDON, Stephen 'Steve'
Forward
Town Years: 1979-1982
Born: *1950 Warrington, Cheshire*
Playing career: *Burnley, Wolverhampton Wanderers, Huddersfield Town (1968-1982)*
'Kindo' signed for Town towards the end of 1979 and proved to be the final piece in the jigsaw that Mick Buxton was looking for, as he helped fire Town to the 1979-80 Fourth Division title. Unfortunately, Kindon suffered from injuries and was forced to retire in 1982. He took on the role of Commercial Manager at Leeds Road, setting up the Town Lottery, Patron's Association and doing a sponsored walk to pay for a new disabled section at the ground. Kindon left the role in 1986 and went on to work as sales manager at Rolyat, a firm of basketware importers before he retired. Now does a lot of after-dinner speaking and has compered the numerous 1979-80 reunions that are hosted at Town. Kindon is now living in Lytham St. Annes.

Steve Kindon

KIRKHAM, Paul
Forward
Town Years: 1987-1989
Born: *1969 Manchester, Lancashire*
Playing career: *Manchester United, Huddersfield Town (1987-1998)*

After a period in Manchester United's youth team, Kirkham signed for Town in 1987 and played one game for the club before leaving in 1989. This started a long career in non-league football. He has since been assistant manager at Abbey Hey, Woodley Sports and New Mills but is now working at Marple Sixth Form College as Head of Football.

KNIGHT, Leon
Forward
Town Years: 2001-2002 (loan)
Born: *1982 Hackney, Greater London*
Playing career: *Chelsea, Huddersfield Town (loan), Brighton & Hove Albion, Swansea City, Barnsley (loan), MK Dons, Wycombe Wanderers (1999-2016)*

'Neon Light' arrived at the club on loan from Chelsea during the 2001-02 season and combined well with Andy Booth, scoring 16 goals in 31 league matches before getting suspended for the end of season playoffs. He later went on to play for Brighton & Hove Albion and Swansea City before playing for a number of non-league or Scottish clubs. Knight later worked as manager of non-league side Barnton between 2015 and 2016 but is perhaps more famous these days for his regular public meltdowns on social media platform, Twitter. He is now running his own company, Weekend King and is also a partner in another company, Trackzy.

KNIGHTON, Albert 'Leslie'
Assistant Manager, Caretaker Manager
Town Years: 1912-1919 (assistant manager), 1912 (caretaker manager)
Born: *1887 Church Gresley, Derbyshire*
Died: *1959 Bournemouth, Hampshire*
Management career: *Huddersfield Town (careatker), Arsenal, Bournemouth and Boscombe Athletic, Birmingham, Chelsea, Shrewsbury Town (1912-1948)*

Knighton was assistant manager at Town between 1912 and 1919 but spent a short amount of time as caretaker manager in 1912 after the departure of Dick Pudan. Knighton went on to have a long career in football, managing Arsenal, Bournemouth and Boscombe Athletic, Birmingham, Chelsea and Shrewsbury Town.

He finally the game in 1948 to become secretary of a golf club and to write his autobiography, *Behind the Scenes in Big Football*. died in 1959 at the age of 72.

KOZLUK, Robert 'Rob'
Right-back
Town Years: 2000 (loan)
Born: *1977 Mansfield, Nottinghamshire*
Playing career: *Derby County, Sheffield United, Huddersfield Town (loan), Wigan Athletic (loan), Preston North End (loan), Barnsley, Sheffield United, Port Vale, Bradford City, Ilkeston (1995-2013)*

Kozluk was loaned to Town by Sheffield United during the 2000-01 season and impressed with his committed performances, earning the Man of the Match award on a number of occasions during his short spell at the club. He remained at Sheffield United until 2007, playing over 200 games before he signed for Barnsley. Kozluk lasted three years at Oakwell before returning to Bramall Lane for a short stint that ended in 2011 after just a year at the club. He later had short spells at Port Vale and Bradford City before ending his career at non-league Ilkeston Town in 2013, later coaching at the club.

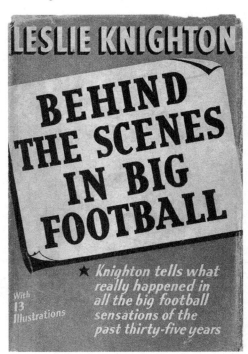

Leslie Knighton's 1948 autobiography

Dick Krzywicki

Kyle arrived on a short-term loan in 2000 from Sunderland and returned to his parent club after playing 4 matches for Lou Macari's side. He played for Sunderland and Coventry City before heading to back to his native Scotland to play for Kilmarnock. He later played for Hearts, Rangers and Ayr United before retiring from the game. The Scotsman has since worked as a storeman on a ship in the Shetland Islands and has been playing darts, competing in BDO events.

"DID YOU KNOW?"

"Town are the only team to have ever won a Play Off Final penalty shoot-out after missing their first three penalties in the 2012 final against Sheffield United."

KRZYWICKI, Ryzard 'Dick'
Forward
Town Years: 1970-1974
Born: *1947 Penley, Flintshire, Wales*
Playing career: *Leek CSOB, West Bromwich Albion, Huddersfield Town, Scunthorpe United (loan), Northampton Town (loan), Lincoln City (1964-1976)*
Krzywicki joined the club late on in the 1969-70 season but played a hand in the promotion at the end of that season. He played during the two seasons spent in the top flight and remained at the club until 1974, Town were relegated to Division Three at the end of that season. Krzywicki signed for Lincoln City in 1974 and spent two years at Sincil Bank before leaving his playing days behind in 1976. After his career in football come to an end, the Welshman later worked David Brown Tractors in Huddersfield before becoming Football Community Officer at Town. He later became the Regional Director for Football in the Community before retiring. Krzywicki still lives in Huddersfield and plays a lot of golf in his spare time.

KYLE, Kevin
Forward
Town Years: 2000 (loan)
Born: *1981 Stranraer, Scotland*
Playing career: *Ayr United, Sunderland, Huddersfield Town (loan), Darlington (loan), Rochdale (loan), Coventry City, Wolverhampton Wanderers (loan), Hartlepool United (loan), Kilmarnock, Heart of Midlothian, Rangers, Ayr United, Newton Stewart (1998-2014)*

LABARTHE, Gianfranco
Forward
Town Years: 2002-2003 (loan)
Born: *1984 Lima, Peru*
Playing career: *Huddersfield Town, Derby County, Universidad San Martin, Deportivo Municipal, Real Garcilaso, Sport Huancayo (2002-Still Playing)*
Labarthe was a Peruvian that signed for Mick Wadsworth's side during the 2002-03 season but only managed to play 3 games before he left the McAlpine Stadium. He later signed for Derby County in 2003 but was released after a year and departed at the end of the 2003-04 season. After leaving Pride Park, Labarthe has since returned to Peru and has played for a number of teams but is now back at his first club Cantolao in the Torneo Descentralizado in Peru.

LAMPKIN, Kevin
Defender
Town Years: 1992-1994
Born: *1972 Liverpool, Lancashire*
Playing career: *Liverpool, Huddersfield Town, Mansfield Town, Ilkeston Town (1992-1996)*
Lampkin joined from Liverpool in 1992 and was described as the 'next Alan Hansen'. It's fair to say that he wasn't and he left the club in 1993 and signed for Mansfield Town. Lampkin later played for Ilkeston Town and Altrincham and is now living in Runcorn and coaches youngsters locally.

LANG, Thomas 'Tommy'

Outside-left
Town Years: 1934-1935
Born: *1906 Larkhall, South Lanarkshire, Scotland*
Died: *1988 Cleland, Scotland*
Playing career: *Larkhall Thistle, Newcastle United, Huddersfield Town, Manchester United, Swansea Town, Queen of the South, Ipswich Town (1925-1947)*
Lang arrived at Leeds Road in 1934 from Newcastle United but only managed 26 appearances for Clem Stephenson's side before he departed in 1935 to sign for Manchester United. After the War, he signed for Ipswich Town in 1946 but retired from the game in 1947. After his retirement, Lang stayed on at Portman Road and worked as the trainer before his death in 1988.

LANGLEY, Ambrose

Secretary-manager
Town Years: 1919-1921
Born: *1870 Horncastle, Lincolnshire*
Died: *1937 Sheffield, West Riding of Yorkshire*
Management career: *Hull City, Huddersfield Town (1905-1921)*
Langley arrived at Leeds Road in November 1919 as the secretary before becoming secretary-manager in December following the resignation of Arthur Fairclough. Langley achieved promotion in 1920, finishing as runners-up of the Second Division and also reachied the FA Cup Final in the same year. He resigned in 1921 and his contract was cancelled, as a gesture from the board of directors, Langley received £500 severance pay.

After his career in football ended, Langley became a licensee and ran the Pheasant Inn, Sheffield and was still in the pub game at the time of his death in 1937 from pneumonia.

LARKIN, Luther

Forward
Town Years: 1908-1909
Born: *1887 Stocksbridge, West Riding of Yorkshire*
Died: *1937 Wakefield, West Riding of Yorkshire*
Larkin played during the club's first ever season and played a couple of games for Fred Walker's side during the 1908-09 season. He left at the end of that season, settled in Skelmanthorpe and worked underground as a machine man. Larkin later passed away in nearby Wakefield in 1937.

LAVERICK, Michael 'Micky'

Midfielder
Town Years: 1979-1982, 1983 (loan)
Born: *1954 Castle Eden, County Durham*
Playing career: *Mansfield Town, Southend United, Huddersfield Town, York City, Huddersfield Town (loan), Boston United (1972-1986)*
Mick Buxton brought Micky Laverick to the club in 1979 after previously working with him at Southend United. Laverick played his part in the 1979-80 promotion season and he remained at the club until 1982. He joined York City but later returned in 1983 for a short loan period. Laverick later played for Boston United and has worked as a prison officer at HMP Ranby for many years.

HMP Ranby

Denis Law

LAW, Denis

Centre-forward
Town Years: 1955-1960
Born: *1940 Aberdeen, Scotland*
Playing career: *Huddersfield Town, Manchester City, Torino, Manchester United (1956-1974)*

Perhaps one of the most famous footballers to play in the blue and white stripes, Denis Law began his career at the club in 1955 and was signed by Andy Beattie. Law made his debut as a 16 year old in 1956 and played in the first team until March 1960 when he signed for Manchester City for £55,000, the club famously spent the money on floodlights for Leeds Road. He spent just one year at Maine Road before he was sold to Italian club Torino in 1961. He left for Manchester United in 1962 and went on to spend eleven years at Old Trafford. He won the FA Cup, First Division (twice), Charity Shield (twice) and the European Cup in those eleven years. Law left for Man City in 1973 and in one of his final games for the club he relegated United by scoring the winning goal in the fixture. He retired from the game in 1974 and has since worked as a pundit on both radio and television and has also done a lot of charity work. Law now lives in Cheshire, successfully battled prostate cancer in 2003 and was awarded a CBE in 2017.

LAWS, Brian

Right-back
Town Years: 1983-1985
Born: *1961 Wallsend, Northumberland*
Playing career: *Burnley, Huddersfield Town, Middlesbrough, Nottingham Forest, Grimsby Town, Darlington, Scunthorpe United (1979-1998)*

Mick Buxton brought Laws to the club in 1983, signing him from Burnley, and he went on to play for the club until 1985. He was sold to Middlesbrough towards the end of the 1984-85 season and he spent three years at Ayresome Park before signing for Brian Clough's Nottingham Forest in 1988. Laws won the League Cup on two occasions at Forest and is considered as one of the club's greatest right-backs. After six years at the club, he left Forest in 1994 on a free transfer to become the player-manager of Grimsby Town. Laws started off well at Grimsby, but was sacked as the result of an incident involving him throwing a plate of chicken wings at Italian midfielder Ivano Bonetti (who the fans had contributed £50,000 of the £100,000 needed to secure his services). He has since managed Scunthorpe United, Sheffield Wednesday and Burnley. Laws now works as co-commentator for BBC Radio Nottingham and is a director of Elite FA Deals, a company that works as a VIP vehicle supplier for professional footballers and members of the entertainment industry.

LAWSON, David

Goalkeeper
Town Years: 1969-1972
Born: *1947 Wallsend, Northumberland*
Playing career: *Newcastle United, Bradford Park Avenue, Huddersfield Town, Everton, Luton Town, Stockport County (1966-1981)*

After playing for Bradford Park Avenue, Lawson signed for the club in 1969. He didn't play many games at Leeds Road but impressed in the ones he did as Everton bought him for £80,000 in 1972, a record fee paid for a gaolkeeper at the time. Lawson played over 100 games for the Toffees before he departed in 1977 and later played for Luton Town and Stockport County before announcing his retirement in 1981. In later life, he worked as a postman before his retirement and is now back living in his home of the North East.

LAWSON, Ian

Forward
Town Years: 1995-1999
Born: *1977 Huddersfield, West Yorkshire*
Playing career: *Huddersfield Town, Blackpool (loan), Bury, Stockport County, Bury (1995-2003)*
Lawson began his career at Town as an apprentice in 1993 and turned professional in 1995. He spent four years on the books as a professional but never really managed to establish himself in the first team and was sold to Bury in 1999. Lawson now sells forklift trucks in Huddersfield and is residing in Kirkburton. His father, Jimmy, played for Town between 1968 and 1976.

LAWSON, James 'Jimmy'

Winger
Town Years: 1968-1976
Born: *1947 Middlesbrough, North Riding of Yorkshire*
Playing career: *Middlesbrough, Huddersfield Town, Halifax Town (1965-1979)*
Lawson arrived at Leeds Road in 1968 from Middlesbrough and went on to play in all four divisions for the club, but most importantly he was part of the 1969-70 Second Division winning side. He later worked as a personal tailor, even advertising his services in Town's matchday programme towards the end of his career at Leeds Road. Lawson then became the manager of Halifax Town in 1976 and worked as a salesman for STILL Materials Handling Ltd and is now living in Kirkburton, Huddersfield. His son Ian also played for the club during the 1990s.

LEDGER, Robert 'Bob'

Winger
Town Years: 1953-1962
Born: *1937 Chester-le-Street, County Durham*
Died: *2015 Doncaster, South Yorkshire*
Playing career: *Huddersfield Town, Oldham Athletic, Mansfield Town, Barrow (1955-1970)*
Ledger began his career at Leeds Road in 1953 but only managed 62 appearances in nine years for the first team before he left the club to sign for Oldham Athletic in 1962. Ledger played over 220 games for the Boundary Park club before he signed for Mansfield Town in 1968. Ledger went on to sign for Barrow in 1969 before he retired from professional football the following year. He later lived and worked in Doncaster before his death in September 2015 whilst residing in a care home.

LEDGER, Robert

Centre-half
Town Years: 1913-1915
Born: *1888 Hamsterley, County Durham*
Died: *1968 Durham, County Durham*
Playing career: *Mickley, Huddersfield Town, Chopwell Villa (1913-c1915)*
Ledger had a short stint at Leeds Road between 1913 and 1915 and played one match at centre-half for Arthur Fairclough's side before the outbreak of World War One. It is thought that Ledger joined the Durham Light Infantry and survived the war. He later lived in Blaydon and worked in the local colliery before he passed away in 1968.

LEE, Alan

Forward
Town Years: 2010-2013
Born: *1978 Galway, Ireland*
Playing career: *Aston Villa, Torquay United (loan), Port Vale (loan), Burnley, Rotherham United, Cardiff City, Ipswich Town, Crystal Palace, Norwich City (loan), Huddersfield Town, Ipswich Town (1994-2014)*
An undisclosed fee brought Alan Lee to the Galpharm Stadium in August 2010 but it took him five months to register a goal for Town, his first goal finally coming against Arsenal in an FA Cup tie in January 2011. Lee flattered to deceive in his three years at Town, scoring more elbows to defender's noses than goals, even missing a penalty in the penalty shoot-out in the 2012 playoff final. He left the club in 2013 to join the academy coaching staff at former club Ipswich Town.

LEGG, William 'Billy'

Defender
Town Years: 1963-1972
Born: *1948 Bradford, West Riding of Yorkshire*
Playing career: *Huddersfield Town, Bradford Park Avenue (1963-1972)*
Billy Legg was a bright prospect when he began his career at Leeds Road and showed some promise in his early appearances. However, a bad car crash ended his career rather prematurely and he had to leave the professional game due to the injuries he had sustained in the accident. He later become a youth coach and has worked all over the North West coaching youngsters. Legg is currently coaching the youngsters at Blackburn Rovers and lives in Bradford.

LEIGHTON, Anthony 'Tony'

Centre-forward
Town Years: 1964-1968
Born: *1939 Leeds, West Riding of Yorkshire*
Died: *1978 Liversedge, West Yorkshire*
Playing career: *Leeds United, Doncaster Rovers, Barnsley, Huddersfield Town, Bradford City (1956-1970)*

Signing from Barnsley in 1964, Leighton spent four years at Leeds Road, managing 44 goals in 97 appearances. He then rounded off his career with a two-year spell at Bradford City before he retired in 1970. Leighton later ran his own sports shop in Liversedge, he also managed Bradford Park Avenue from 1970 to 1973. He later suffered from motor neurone disease and was given a testimonial by Town in 1978. Leighton died not long after this and was only 40.

LEWIS, Dudley

Defender
Town Years: 1989-1992
Born: *1962 Swansea, Wales*
Playing career: *Swansea City, Huddersfield Town, Halifax Town (loan), Wrexham, Halifax Town, Torquay United, Inter Cardiff, Carmarthen Town (1980-1997)*

Lewis had played over 230 games for his hometown club Swansea City when he signed for Eoin Hand's Town side in 1989. He lasted two years at Leeds Road before heading back to Wales to play for Wrexham. Towards the end of his career, Lewis played at Halifax Town and Torquay United and several non-league sides. He is now working as a postman in his hometown of Swansea.

LEWIS, Kevin

Forward
Town Years: 1963-1965
Born: *1940 Ellesmere Port, Cheshire*
Playing career: *Sheffield United, Liverpool, Huddersfield Town, Wigan Athletic, Washington Diplomats (1957-1974)*

Arriving from Liverpool in 1963, Kevin Lewis was in terrific form for a winger, scoring 39 goals in 71 league games over three years at Anfield. He managed 13 goals in 45 league games between 1963 and 1965 at Leeds Road before being offloaded to Wigan Athletic in 1965. He later played abroad for Washington Diplomats before he returned to the UK and was later a pub landlord in Staffordshire.

LEWIS, Wilfred 'Wilf'

Forward
Town Years: 1928-1931
Born: *1903 Swansea, Wales*
Died: *1976 Swansea, Wales*
Playing career: *Baldwin's Welfare, Swansea Amateurs, Swansea Town, Huddersfield Town, Derby County, Yeovil & Petters United, Cardiff City, Haverfordwest Athletic (1925-1936)*

Welshman Lewis signed from Swansea Town in 1928 but managed less than 20 appearances in Clem Stephenson's side before his departure in 1931, when he joined Derby County. He eventually played for Yeovil & Petters United, Cardiff City and Haverfordwest Athletic before his retirement in 1936. Following his depatrure from the game, Lewis worked as a colliery hewer in Nantyglo & Blaina and also as a warehouseman for a rubber and asbestos manufacturing company in Swansea before he passed away in 1976.

LILLEY, Thomas 'Tom'

Right-back
Town Years: 1922-1923
Born: *1900 Newbottle, Houghton-le-Spring, County Durham*
Died: *1964 New Herrington, County Durham*
Playing career: *Methley Perseverance, Huddersfield Town, Nelson, Hartlepools United, Sunderland, St Mirren, Fulham, Annfield Plain, New Herrington Welfare, Shiney Row Swifts, Sunderland District Omnibus Company, Herrington Colliery(1922-c1935)*

Lilley began his professional career at Leeds Road but only managed 3 appearances in Herbert Chapman's side before he left the club in 1923 to sign for Nelson. He spent a year at the club before he signed for Hartlepools United in 1924. Lilley had two seasons at Victoria Park before he transferred to nearby Sunderland in 1927. He only managed one game at Roker Park before heading to St. Mirren in 1928. Two years later, Lilley joined Fulham in 1930 and after just a year at Craven Cottage, retired from professional football in 1931. He went on to play local football in the North East for Annfield Plain, New Herrington Welfare, Shiney Row Swifts and finally Omnibus Company. Lilley later worked as a colliery storeman in Durham before he passed away in 1964.

Mark Lillis

LILLIS, Mark
Midfielder, Forward, Youth Development Coach, Youth Coach, Academy Manager, Caretaker Manager
Town Years: 1977-1985, 1992-1995 (youth development coach), 1995-1996 (youth coach), 2011-2016 (academy manager), 2012, 2013, 2014, 2015 (caretaker manager)
Born: *1960 Manchester, Lancashire*
Playing career: *Huddersfield Town, Manchester City, Derby County, Aston Villa, Scunthorpe United, Stockport County(1977-1995)*
Lillis began his career as a centre-half but was later converted to a forward by Mick Buxton and although he was on the fringes of the first team for the first couple of years at the club, he played a huge part in the 1982-83 promotion season, finishing the season as top scorer with 20 goals in 46 appearances. He was later sold to hometown club, Manchester City in 1985 and also played for Derby County, Aston Villa, Scunthorpe United and Stockport County. After his retirement as a player, Lillis became Youth Development Officer at Town and later became Youth Team Coach in 1995, leaving in 1996 to join Mick Buxton at Scunthorpe as his assistant.

Lillis served as caretaker in 1997 when Buxton was sacked before becoming Halifax Town manager in 1999. After a poor show while in charge of the Shaymen, Lillis lost this position in 2000 and later served as assistant manager at Derby County, Stockport County, Morecambe and Northern Ireland. He also had short stints as caretaker manager at both Derby and Stockport after the departures of John Gregory and Sammy McIlroy respectively. Lillis returned to Town in 2011 and had four separate spells as caretaker manager in 2012, 2013, 2014 and 2015. He worked as John Gregory's assistant manager at Chinese team Chennaiyin FC but left this post in 2018.

LINDSAY, Denis
Goalkeeper
Town Years: 1937-1938
Born: *1916 Benoni, South Africa*
Died: *unknown*
Playing career: *Transvaal FC, Huddersfield Town (1937-1938)*
Denis Lindsay signed from Transvaal FC in 1937 and made 1 appearance in goal for Clem Stephenson's side before he left to return to South Africa at the conclusion of the 1937-38 season. He worked for an engineering firm in Benoni and had also worked in a gold mine.

LINLEY, Harry
Half-back
Town Years: 1912-1921
Born: *1892 Sheffield, West Riding of Yorkshire*
Died: *1975 Sheffield, South Yorkshire*
Playing career: *Huddersfield Town, Halifax Town, (1912-c1935)*
After working at Silverwood Colliery, Linley joined Town in 1912 and played 51 games before joining Halifax Town in 1921. After his football career ended, he later worked as a silversmith in his home of Sheffield before dying in his hometown in April 1975.

"DID YOU KNOW?"

"Town's lowest ever home attendance in the Football League was 1638 v Bournemouth in April 1978. This was at the old Leeds Road Ground."

LLOYD, Anthony
Left-back
Town Years: 2003-2006
Born: *1984 Taunton, Somerset*
Playing career: *Huddersfield Town, Torquay United, York City, Farsley Celtic, York City, Guiseley, Bradford Park Avenue (loan), Stocksbridge Park Steels, North Ferriby United (2003-2011)*

Lloyd began his career at Town in the juniors before turning professional in 2003. He played most of the 2003-04 promotion season at left-wing-back for Peter Jackson's side but he left the club in 2006 to sign for Torquay United. Lloyd later drifted into non-league with York City, Farsley Celtic, Guiseley, Stocksbridge Park Steels and North Ferriby United.

LODGE, Joseph 'Joe'
Half-back
Town Years: 1939-1948
Born: *1921 Skelmanthorpe, West Riding of Yorkshire*
Died: *2002 Skelmanthorpe, West Yorkshire*
Playing career: *Huddersfield Town, St Johnstone, Frickley Colliery (1939-c1952)*

Lodge signed for Town in 1939 but only made two first team appearances for the club before his departure in 1948. Lodge also played cricket for Yorkshire in 1948 and later played football for St. Johnstone between 1950 and 1951 before his retirement as a player, after a time at Frickley Colliery. Lodge moved back to Yorkshire after his career had ended and died in 2002, in his native Skelmanthorpe.

LOGAN, Richard
Midfielder
Town Years: 1993-1995
Born: *1969 Barnsley, West Riding of Yorkshire*
Playing career: *Worsbrough Bridge Athletic, Belper Town, Gainsborough Trinity, Huddersfield Town, Plymouth Argyle, Scunthorpe United, Lincoln City, Gainsborough Trinity (loan) (1989-2003)*

'Logie' signed from Gainsborough Trinity in 1993 and managed to break into Neil Warnock's side towards the end of the 1993-94 season. The Yorkshireman played in the final ever game at Leeds Road and is one of only four Town players to score at Wembley Stadium. Logan returned to his original profession as a bricklayer and now runs his own successful building company, Richard Logan Developments in his native Barnsley.

LOLLEY, Joseph 'Joe'
Winger
Town Years: 2014-2018
Born: *1992 Redditch, Worcestershire*
Playing career: *Littleton, Kidderminster Harriers, Huddersfield Town, Scunthorpe United (loan), Nottingham Forest (2011-Still Playing)*

Lolley signed in 2014 from Kidderminster Harriers but failed to establish himself in the first team for a substantial period of time and was sold to Nottingham Forest in January 2018.

LOPEZ, Cristian
Forward
Town Years: 2013-2014
Born: *1989 Crevillent, Spain*
Playing career: *Alicante, Real Madrid B, Valencia B (loan), Valencia B, Atletico Baleares, Huddersfield Town, Shrewsbury Town (loan), Northampton Town (loan), Burgos, CFR Cluj, Lens, Angers (2008-Still Playing)*

Lopez arrived in Huddersfield in 2013 after signing from Spanish side Atletico Baleares. He only played a couple of games for Mark Robins' side and was loaned out to Shrewsbury Town and then Northampton Town before being released in 2014. Lopez went on to play for Burgos, CFR Cluj and Lens but has played for French side Angers since 2018.

LOW, Gordon
Left-half
Town Years: 1955-1961
Born: *1940 Aberdeen, Scotland*
Playing career: *Huddersfield Town, Bristol City, Stockport County, Crewe Alexandra, Selby Town (1955-1971)*

Low began his career as a junior at Town in 1955 after heading down from Scotland and turned professional in 1957, spending four years in and out of the first team at Leeds Road before leaving the club in 1961 to join Bristol City. He then had seven years at Ashton Gate, playing over 200 games for the club before his departure in 1968. Low spent two years at Stockport County before joining Crewe Alexandra in 1970, later retiring in 1971. He returned to Huddersfield, where he worked as a coach at Town's Centre of Excellence before his retirement. As of 2018, Low is still living in Huddersfield.

LUCKETTI, Christopher 'Chris'

Centre-half
Town Years: 1999-2001, 2008-2010
Born: *1971 Littleborough, Lancashire*
Playing career: *Rochdale, Stockport County, Halifax Town, Bury, Huddersfield Town, Preston North End, Sheffield United (loan), Sheffield United, Southampton (loan), Huddersfield Town (1989-2010)*

Lucketti was signed by Steve Bruce in 1999 and was very popular at the club, so much so that he considered as one of Town's best modern day centre-halves. He was sold to Preston North End in 2001 where he played until 2006 when Neil Warnock signed him for Sheffield United. Two years later, Lucketti returned to Town as one of Stan Ternent's first signings and was immediately installed as club captain. He remained a regular in the side until October 2008 when he was suspended after a red card, in the meantime Ternent was sacked and Lucketti found himself on the sidelines. Although he made a brief reappearance in early 2009 for manager Lee Clark, he never played another game for Town. Lucketti spent the whole of the 2009-10 season on the books but never even featured in a matchday squad or reserve sides. He retired after his departure in 2010 and coached the youngsters at former club Preston. As of May 2018, Lucketti is the assistant manager to Graham Alexander at Salford City.

LUKE, Charles 'Charlie'

Winger
Town Years: 1931-1936
Born: *1909 Esh Winning, County Durham*
Died: *1983 Whitstable, Kent*
Playing career: *Portsmouth, Darlington, Esh Winning, Bishop Auckland, Huddersfield Town, Sheffield Wednesday, Blackburn Rovers, Chesterfield, Whitstable Town (1928-1939)*

After playing for a number of non-league clubs in the North East, Luke signed for Darlington in 1928, time at Esh Winning and Bishop Auckland followed before he eventually arrived at Leeds Road in 1931. He spent five years in Clem Stephenson's side, making over 100 appearances for the club before departing to sign for Sheffield Wednesday in 1936. Luke spent two years at Hillsborough before rounding off his career by playing at Blackburn Rovers, Chesterfield and lastly non-league Whitstable Town. He later died in 1983 at the age of 74.

LUMSDEN, Francis 'Frank'

Outside-right
Town Years: 1933-1935
Born: *1913 Sunderland*
Died: *1965 Leeds, West Riding of Yorkshire*
Playing career: *Shotton Colliery Welfare, Newcastle United (amateur), Trimdon Grange Colliery, Herrington Swifts, Herrington Colliery Welfare, Horden Colliery Welfare, Huddersfield Town, Queens Park Rangers, Burnley, North Shields (1930-1939)*

Lumsden arrived at Leeds Road in 1933, originally as an amateur and went on to play a solitary match for Clem Stephenson's side before he left the club in April 1935 to sign for Queens Park Rangers. Lumsden later worked in Huddersfield as a chemical process worker and passed away in 1965 in nearby Leeds.

LUNN, Frederick 'Fred'

Centre-forward
Town Years: 1920-1921
Born: *1895 Marsden, West Riding of Yorkshire*
Died: *1972 Leeds, West Riding of Yorkshire*
Playing career: *Marsden FC, Huddersfield Town, Sheffield Wednesday, Bristol Rovers, Southend United, Nuneaton Town (1919-1924)*

Lunn arrived at Leeds Road in 1920 after signing from local club Marsden FC. He made a couple of appearances during the 1920-21 season before leaving in August 1921 to sign for Sheffield Wednesday. The Yorkshireman later played for Bristol Rovers, and Southend United before retiring from football and becoming a club steward in Leeds before he died in 1972.

LYNCH, Joel

Centre-half
Town Years: 2012-2016
Born: *1987 Eastbourne, East Sussex*
Playing career: *Brighton & Hove Albion, Nottingham Forest (loan), Nottingham Forest, Huddersfield Town, Queens Park Rangers (2005-Still Playing)*

Lynch signed from Nottingham Forest in 2012 and spent four years at Town, playing 138 games for Simon Grayson, Mark Robins and Chris Powell. He played under new manager David Wagner but left the club at the end of the 2015-16 season amid rumours of a disagreement with the new manager. The defender signed for QPR in the 2016-17 season and remains at Loftus Road. To add, Lynch has 1 cap for Wales, he won this whilst a Town player, in August 2012.

Billy Lynn

LYNN, Joseph 'Joe'
Inside-right
Town Years: 1947-1949 (amateur), 1949-1950
Born: 1925 Seaton Sluice, Northumberland
Died: 1992 Seaton Suice, Northumberland
Playing career: *Cramlington, Huddersfield Town, Exeter City, Rochdale (1947-1956)*
Originally from the North East, Lynn arrived at Leeds Road in 1947 as an amateur, turning professional in 1949. Lynn left the club the following year after playing just five games. Lynn died in June 1992 at the age of 67.

LYON, David 'Dave'
Centre-half
Town Years: 1971-1974
Born: 1951 Market Harborough, Leicestershire
Died: 1999 Cambridge, Cambridgeshire
Playing career: *Bury, Huddersfield Town, Mansfield Town (loan), Cambridge United, Northampton Town, Cambridge City (1968-c1978)*
After playing for Bury, Lyon signed for Town in 1971 whilst the club were in the First Division. He played at Leeds Road for three years before he left the club in 1974 to join Cambridge United. After his retirement as a player, Lyon worked as a builder's labourer, abattoir assistant and glazier before running his own dry cleaning business in Chadderton. He passed away in April 1999 at the age of 48.

LYNN, William 'Billy'
Outside-left
Town Years: 1965-1967
Born: 1947 Newcastle upon Tyne, Northumberland
Died: 2014 Gateshead, Tyne and Wear
Playing career: *Huddersfield Town, Rotherham United (1965-1967)*
Lynn arrived at the club in 1965 and played four first team matches for Tom Johnston's side. After Lynn left Leeds Road in 1967, he returned to Gateshead and began working at Clark Chapmans whilst also playing for the local side. He spent a number of years at the club, eventually leaving and turning out for a local pub team called The Tavern. Lynn later worked at Boyd's with central heating ducts whilst also turning out for Washington, where he picked up the Player of the Year award. He also spent a time at the Fairholme Club in Newcastle who ended up in the Guinness Book of Records for winning 98 games in a row! In his later years, Lynn was a family man and doted on his grandchildren, never missing a game that his grandson played in, he also enjoyed gardening and going on holiday with his wife, Lorraine. Billy Lynn died in 2014.

LYTHGOE, Alfred 'Alf'
Centre-forward
Town Years: 1934-1938
Born: 1907 Nantwich, Cheshire
Died: 1967 Stockport, Cheshire
Playing career: *Crewe Alexandra, Whitchurch, Sandbach Ramblers, Congleton Town, Ashton National, Stockport County, Huddersfield Town, Stockport County (1927-1939)*
After two years at Stockport County, Lythgoe arrived at Leeds Road in 1934 and spent four years at the club before he departed in 1938 to return to Stockport. His career was ended just a year later when the Second World War broke out and the Football League was suspended. Lythgoe later worked as a horseman on a farm in Warrington and also as a railway worker. He later worked as the manager of non-league Altrincham between 1953 and 1955 and played cricket locally in Stockport before he died in April 1967 at the age of 60.

Lou Macari

MACARI, Luigi 'Lou'

European Scout, Caretaker Manager, Manager

Town Years: 1999-2000 (European scout), 2000 (caretaker manager), 2000-2002 (manager)
Born: *1949 Edinburgh, Scotland*
Management career: *Swindon Town, West Ham United, Birmingham City, Stoke City, Celtic, Stoke City, Huddersfield Town (1984-2002)*

Macari had been a manager at Swindon Town, Celtic, West Ham United and Stoke City before Steve Bruce made him a scout at Sheffield United. When Bruce left Bramall Lane to take the Town job in 1999, he brought Macari with him to the McAlpine Stadium as European Scout. When Bruce was dismissed in October 2000 due to a disastrous start to the season, Macari was offered the job on a temporary basis but didn't want it and only took the job after Bruce gave him his blessing. After 4 games in charge, the Scotsman was given the job on a permanent basis and came close to saving the club from relegation in the 2000-01 season. However, due to results going against the club on the final day of the season, Town were relegated to the third tier for the first time since the 1987-88 season. Macari took Town to the playoffs the season after but were beaten by Brentford in the semi-finals. He was controversially sacked, the club informing the press before Macari himself. Macari has not had a job in football since and now does after dinner speaking and works for MUTV on a regular basis.

MACARI, Paul

Forward

Town Years: 2001-2003
Born: *1976 Manchester, Greater Manchester*
Playing career: *Stoke City, Sheffield United, Huddersfield Town (1992-2010)*

Son of Lou, Paul Macari signed on a free transfer from Sheffield United in 2001 and spent two years at the club before he was released at the end of the 2002-03 season after the club went into administration. During his time at the club, Macari only made a few substitute appearances and never started a match. He later played non-league football for both Leek Town and Alsager Town and after retirement, Macari worked as a retail store manager at Terraces Menswear in Stoke before working for Domino's Pizza, running some of their franchises around Stoke. He is currently a franchisee for Creams Cafe in Stockport and is also a landlord with a number of properties.

MACAULAY, James

Inside-left

Town Years: 1910-1913
Born: *1888 Portarlington, County Laois, Ireland*
Died: *1945 Preston, Lancashire*
Playing career: *Cliftonville, Rangers, Huddersfield Town, Preston North End, Leicester City, Grimsby Town, Lancaster Town, Morecambe (1905-1925)*

Macaulay arrived at Leeds Road in 1910 and played 97 games for the club under Dick Pudan and Arthur Fairclough before he departed in 1913 to sign for Preston North End. His career ended in 1925 and he went on to work as a paint & plumbing goods salesman but is listed on the 1939 Register as living at Preston Royal Infirmary. Irishman Macaulay passed away six years later, in 1945.

MACDONALD, Malcolm

Manager

Town Years: 1987-1988
Born: *1950 Fulham, London*
Management career: *Fulham, Huddersfield Town (1980-1988)*

After a spending time as manager of former club Fulham, 'Supermac' had been the licensee of a pub in Worthing before the call came for him to become the manager at Leeds Road in October 1987, after the demotion of Steve Smith.

Although results started to improve under the new manager, a 10-1 thrashing at Manchester City's Maine Road in November set the team back and by the end of the season the team had won just 6 matches and conceded 100 goals. Macdonald was sacked with one game to go at the end of the season and replaced by his assistant manager, Eoin Hand. 'Supermac' later ran a hotel in Berwick-upon-Tweed but when this venture went bankrupt, he moved to Italy in 1992 and worked in telecommunications for a while, running his own phone-line business before it was closed down by the Italian government and he returned to England. He worked for a radio station in Newcastle and in 1997 was charged with drink-driving, thus losing his radio show and admitting he was an alcoholic. Macdonald has since worked in local radio and as an after-dinner speaker and is now living in the North East.

MACFADYEN, William 'Willie'

Centre-forward
Town Years: 1936-1939
Born: *1904 Overtown, Scotland*
Died: *1971 Birmingham, Warwickshire*
Playing career: *Motherwell, Clyde (loan), Huddersfield Town, Clapton Orient (1920-1939)*

Before signing for Town in 1936, MacFadyen had spent 15 years playing for Motherwell. He played in the 1938 FA Cup Final, where Town lost to Preston North End, and left to sign for Clapton Orient at the end of the 1938-39 season. During the Second World War, MacFadyen served in the RAF and also guested for Blackpool, Nottingham Forest, Rochdale as well as Town. He became secretary-manager of Dundee United in 1945, lasting nine years in the job before he resigned. This job proved to be his last in football and he later worked as a physiotherapist and chiropodist before his death in 1971.

MACHIN, Melvyn 'Mel'

Technical Advisor, Manager
Town Years: 2003 (technical advisor), 2003 (manager)
Born: *1945 Newcastle-under-Lyme, Staffordshire*
Management career: *Manchester City, Barnsley, Bournemouth, Huddersfield Town (1987-2003)*

Machin was brought in by manager Mick Wadsworth as Technical Advisor in January 2003 but after Wadsworth was sacked in March, the club's board of directors turned to Machin and gave him the manager's job. Although he managed to win a couple of games, relegation to the bottom tier was confirmed with one game to go at the end of the 2002-03 season. Machin's weekly contract was not renewed and he parted company with the club. Machin has lived in Bournemouth in retirement since he left the club in 2003 and had actually retired in 2002 but had been tempted out of retirement by the offer to work at Town with Mick Wadsworth, who had coached for him at Barnsley in the early 1990s.

MACLEOD, Alasdair 'Ally'

Inside-left
Town Years: 1974 (loan)
Born: *1951 Glasgow, Scotland*
Playing career: *St. Mirren, Southampton, Huddersfield Town (loan), Hibernian, Stenhousemuir, Hamilton Academical, Queen of the South (1970-1984)*

MacLeod has the distinction of being Town's first ever loan player and he arrived in 1974 from Southampton. He played 4 matches and scored 1 goal before he returned to The Dell, later leaving the club in the same year and signing for Hibernian. MacLeod played over 200 games for Hibs before leaving in 1982 and ended his career at Queen of the South in 1984. MacLeod later worked as a financial advisor for AML Associates in Kincardine for many years but is now thought to be retired.

MADRICK, Carl

Forward
Town Years: 1985-1988
Born: *1968 Bolton, Lancashire*
Playing career: *Huddersfield Town, Peterborough United, Chorley (1985-1989)*

Madrick signed for the youth team in 1985, before he turned professional in 1987. Probably best remembered for scoring the goal that beat Manchester City 1-0 in the 1987-88 season, a particular significance as City had beaten Town 10-1 at Maine Road earlier that season. He left for Peterborough United in 1988 but lasted just a year at London Road before he departed the club in 1989. Madrick later played for non-league Chorley and since he retired from the game has been working at Richard Hough Ltd in his hometown Bolton.

MAGNER, Edward 'Ted'

Manager

Town Years: 1938-1944 (coach), 1942-1943 (manager)
Born: *1891 Newcastle-upon-Tyne, Northumberland*
Died: *1948 Derby, Derbyshire*
Management career: *Lille, Metz, Denmark, Huddersfield Town, Derby County, Metz (1935-1947)*

After previously working as the Denmark national team manager, Magner arrived at Leeds Road in 1938 and worked as Town's first ever specialist coach, also assisting Clem Stephenson with his managerial duties. After Stephenson left his post in 1942, Magner served the club as caretaker manager. He was replaced by former Town player David Steele in 1943 and reverted back to his previous role as coach. Magner left Leeds Road in 1944 to become the manager of Derby County. In December 1947, he was about to take the manager's job for the Denmark national football team before being taken seriously ill. Magner died in July 1948 in his Derby home and is buried in the Nottingham Road cemetery.

MAGUIRE, Peter

Forward

Town Years: 1989-1991
Born: *1969 Holmfirth, West Riding of Yorkshire*
Playing career: *Leeds United, IFK Osby (loan), Huddersfield Town, Stockport County (loan), Emley, Elgin City, Forres Mechanics, Lossiemouth (1986-2002)*

After beginning his career at Leeds United, Eoin Hand brought Maguire to Leeds Road in 1989. He spent two years at the club but only managed a small quantity of appearances for the club before heading into non-league. Maguire later played for Emley before he moved to Scotland, where he played for Elgin City, Forres Mechanics and Lossiemouth amongst others. He is now thought to be working as a fireman and is living in Elgin with his wife.

MAHON, John 'Jack'

Outside-right

Town Years: 1938-1945
Born: *1911 Gillingham, Kent*
Died: *1993 Hull, Humberside*
Playing career: *New Brompton Excelsior, Doncaster Grammar School, Doncaster Rovers, Leeds United, West Bromwich Albion, Huddersfield Town, York City (1928-1946)*

Mahon arrived at Leeds Road in 1938 from West Bromwich Albion and played 6 games at outside-right during the 1938-39 season. The outbreak of World War Two interrupted his career at Leeds Road but he remained on the club's books until 1945. Mahon did play in a few games in the Wartime League over those six years but joined York City, where he played for just a year before he retired in 1946. Mahon then coached in Denmark with IFK Elsborg between 1947 and 1950, in Sweden with IFK Gothenberg between 1950 and 1954 and then joined Leeds United as a coach. He also ran a youth club in Leeds and, for a time, became coach at York City followed by starting as a trainer at Hull City before he retired from the game in 1954. Mahon later passed away in 1993 and was living in Hull at the time of his death.

MAHONEY, Brian

Inside-right

Town Years: 1967-1972
Born: *1952 Tantobie, County Durham*
Playing career: *Huddersfield Town, Barnsley (1967-1975)*

Mahoney signed for the club in 1967 from his local club Tantobie and first appeared in Ian Greaves' side in 1970 and made 22 appearances at Leeds Road before his departure in 1972. He signed for Barnsley and played three years at Oakwell before his departure. Mahoney still lives in Huddersfield and is now retired.

MAITLAND, Lloyd

Winger

Town Years: 1972-1977
Born: *1957 Coleshill, Warwickshire*
Playing career: *Huddersfield Town, Darlington (1972-1979)*

Originally from Birmingham, Maitland joined Town in 1972 and was part of the Youth Team that progressed to the FA Youth Cup Final in 1974. He became the first ever black player to play a professional game for Town in 1975 and played over 40 games for the first team. Two years later, Maitland departed for Darlington in 1977 before a car accident ended his footballing career. He did turn out for many local sides in Huddersfield and worked as a plasterer but is now living in Thackley and works in Honley making granite worktops.

MAJEWSKI, Radoslaw

Midfielder
Town Years: 2014-2015 (loan)
Born: *1986 Pruszków, Poland*
Playing career: *Znicz Pruszków, Dyskobolia Grodzisk, Polonia Warsaw, Nottingham Forest, Huddersfield Town (loan), Veria, Lech Poznań (2002-Still Playing)*

Majewski signed on loan from Nottingham Forest during the 2014-15 season and was involved in a bizarre incident on his debut where he was substituted by Mark Robins and the Town fans began to boo. Majewski was in tears in the dressing room, not realising the Town faithful were booing the decision to take him off, not his performance. Ultimately, he managed very few appearances for the club before returning to the City Ground. Majewski later signed for Veria in Greece in 2015 before leaving for Lech Poznan in 2016.

MAKEL, Lee

Midfielder
Town Years: 1995-1998
Born: *1973 Sunderland, County Durham*
Playing career: *Newcastle United, Blackburn Rovers, Huddersfield Town, Bradford City, Plymouth Argyle, Dunfermline Athletic, Livingston, Östersunds FK, East Fife, Östersunds FK, Cowdenbeath (1991-2013)*

After initially playing at Blackburn Rovers, Brian Horton brought Makel to the McAlpine in 1995 and he became a regular in his first season but fell out of favour by the time his departure in 1998. He spent three years at Hearts and after a short spell at Bradford City in 2001, signed for Livingston. Makel later joined Plymouth Argyle, Dunfermline Livingston (again) before he moved to Sweden in 2008, to play for Östersunds FK. He later managed the club between 2009 and 2010 but returned to Scotland to play for Cowdenbeath between 2011 and 2013 before he announced his retirement from the game. Makel is now working as an academy coach at Hibernian's academy.

"DID YOU KNOW?"

"Clem Stephenson is the longest serving manager in the club's history with his reign lasting 13 years and 12 days."

MALAM, Albert

Inside-forward
Town Years: 1934-1936
Born: *1913 Liverpool, Lancashire*
Died: *1992 Kendal, Cumbria*
Playing career: *Chesterfield, Huddersfield Town, Doncaster Rovers, Wrexham, Runcorn (1934-1947)*

Malam arrived at Leeds Road in 1934 after signing from Chesterfield, and he spent two years in Clem Stephenson's side. He managed 11 goals in 23 games before leaving for Doncaster Rovers. Although the War had stalled six years of his football career, Malam remained on the books at 'Donny' until 1946. He became the player-manager of Runcorn. Died in February 1992, whilst living in Kendal.

MALONE, Scott

Left-back
Town Years: 2017-2018
Born: *1991 Rowley Regis, West Midlands*
Playing career: *Wolves, Újpest (loan), Bournemouth, Millwall, Cardiff City, Fulham, Huddersfield Town, Derby County (2009-Still Playing)*

After impressing in performances against Town in the 2016-17 season, Malone was signed from Fulham in 2017 for the club's first ever Premier League campaign. He played a number of games at left-back and helped achieve survival but was sold to Derby County after just one year at the club, on the eve of the 2018-19 season.

MANGNALL, David 'Dave'

Centre-forward
Town Years: 1929-1934
Born: *1905 Wigan, Lancashire*
Died: *1962 Penzance, Cornwall*
Playing career: *Doncaster Rovers, Leeds United, Huddersfield Town, Birmingham, West Ham United, Millwall, Queens Park Rangers (1921-1944)*

Mangnall arrived at Leeds Road in late 1929, signing from nearby Leeds United and during his time at the club he scored 73 goals in 90 first team matches. He left the club in 1934 to sign for Birmingham and later played for West Ham United, Millwall and Queens Park Rangers, where he became manager in 1944. Mangnall managed the club to their first ever promotion when he won the Third Division South in 1948. He never managed in the Football League again, becoming a publican in Penzance, later dying there in 1962, at the young age of 56.

MANN, Frank
Forward
Town Years: 1912-1923
Born: *1891 Newark, Nottinghamshire*
Died: *1966 Huddersfield, West Riding of Yorkshire*
Playing career: *Lincoln City, Aston Villa, Huddersfield Town, Manchester City, Manchester United, Mossley, Meltham Mills (1909-1930)*

Mann signed from Aston Villa and this began an eleven year affiliation with Huddersfield Town. He originally signed for Dick Pudan's side in 1911 but spent most of his Town career playing for Arthur Fairclough. Although the First World War disrupted four years of his career, Mann remained at Leeds Road after the War and remained a regular once Ambrose Langley became the manager in 1919. He was part of the Division Two runners-up side of 1920 and won the FA Cup and Charity Shield in 1922 under manager Herbert Chapman. Mann left the club in 1923 to sign for Manchester City and later played for Manchester United and Mossley before he ended his career at Meltham Mills in 1930. He settled in Huddersfield and later ran the Zetland Hotel in the town centre and before his death in July 1966.

MANU, Elvis
Winger
Town Years: 2016 (loan)
Born: *1993 Dordrecht, Netherlands*
Playing career: *SC Amstelwijck, SSW, Feyenoord, Feyenoord, Brighton & Hove Albion, Huddersfield Town (loan), Akhisarspor (2012-Still Playing)*

Manu arrived from Brighton & Hove Albion on a short loan in the 2015-16 season but only managed 5 appearances in David Wagner's side. He left Brighton in 2017 and was last known to be playing for Akhisarspor in Turkey.

MARGETSON, Martyn
Goalkeeper
Town Years: 1999-2002
Born: *1971 Neath, Wales*
Playing career: *Manchester City, Southend United, Huddersfield Town, Cardiff City (1992-2007)*

Steve Bruce brought Margetson to the McAlpine in 1999 as goalkeeping cover for Nico Vaesen. Once Vaesen was sold to Birmingham City in 2001, Margetson became first choice and was No. 1 during the 2001-02 season where Town reached the playoffs.

He left at the end of that season to sign for Cardiff City, where he stayed for five years until his retirement in 2007. Margetson had taken the job of goalkeeping coach the previous season and remained in the role until 2011. He later joined Sam Allardyce at West Ham United and combined these duties with his job as Wales goalkeeping coach. Margetson returned to Cardiff City in 2014 but re-joined Sam Allardyce at his various managerial stops, Everton being the most recent. Margetson is also a property developer in his native Wales.

MARLOW, Leonard 'Len'
Centre-forward
Town Years: 1922
Born: *1899 Putney, London*
Died: *1975 Huddersfield, West Yorkshire*
Playing career: *Huddersfield Town, Torquay United, Grays Town, Thurrock Athletic (1922-1928)*

Marlow arrived in January 1922 from Old Kingstonians but played just one game for the club during the 1921-22 season before he transferred to Torquay United in 1922. He remained at Torquay for five years before he departed the club in 1927 and retired from the game shortly after spells at Grays Town, Thurrock Athletic and Thames Mills. Marlow went on to work as a foreman for Fiberite in Thurrock, Essex before he later passed away in 1975, whilst living in Huddersfield. The Southerner had served with the 1/5th Battalion East Surrey Regiment during World War One.

MARRIOTT, John 'Jackie'
Outside-right
Town Years: 1955-1957
Born: *1928 Scunthorpe, Lincolnshire*
Died: *2016 Scunthorpe, Lincolnshire*
Playing career: *Scunthorpe United, heffield Wednesday, Huddersfield Town, Scunthorpe United (1944-1963)*

After a long time playing at Sheffield Wednesday, Marriott signed for the club in 1955 and spent two years at Leeds Road playing at outside-right for Andy Beattie's side. He left Town in 1957 to sign for hometown club Scunthorpe United and had seven years at the Old Showground, playing over 200 games at outside-right. Marriott retired from professional football in 1963 and went on to work as a rep for Petrol Fina before his death in 2016 at the age of 87.

MARSDEN, Christopher 'Chris'

Midfielder
Town Years: 1988-1994
Born: *1969 Sheffield, West Riding of Yorkshire*
Playing career: *Sheffield United, Huddersfield Town, Coventry City (loan), Wolves, Notts County, Stockport County, Birmingham City, Southampton, Busan I'Park, Sheffield Wednesday (1987-2005)*

After a short stint at hometown club Sheffield United, Marsden arrived at Leeds Road in 1988. The Yorkshireman spent the next six years at the club and played over 100 games for the first team including the 1991-92 playoff campaign and the 1992-93 season where Town achieved a 'Great Escape' after being rooted to the bottom before Mick Buxton returned as coach and helped steer Town to safety. He fell out of favour during the 1993-94 season and was sold to Wolves by Neil Warnock in 1994. Marsden later played for Notts County, Stockport County and Birmingham City before signing for Southampton in 1999. He was a fan's favourite at the club and captained them to the 2003 FA Cup Final.

MARSHALL, Brian

Left-half
Town Years: 1971-1975
Born: *1954 Bolton-on-Dearne, West Riding of Yorkshire*
Playing career: *Huddersfield Town, Scunthorpe United (loan) (1971-1975)*

Marshall signed for the club as an apprentice in 1970 and turned professional in 1972. The Yorkshireman played over 30 games at Leeds Road, mostly for Ian Greaves' side before he was released from the club in 1975. Marshall later played for Bradley Rangers and Almondbury in Huddersfield but is now living in retirement in Sheffield.

MARTIN, Lee

Goalkeeper, Physiotherapist, Goalkeeping Coach
Town Years: 1985-1992, 2003, 2003-2008 (physiotherapist), 2003-2006 (goalkeeping coach)
Born: *1968 Huddersfield, West Riding of Yorkshire*
Playing career: *Huddersfield Town, Blackpool, Bradford City (loan), Rochdale, Halifax Town, Macclesfield Town (1987-2004)*

Martin was part of the youth team that was coached by Steve Smith before he made his debut for the senior side in 1987. He remained at Leeds Road until 1992 before he signed for Blackpool and had the distinction of playing in the final ever game at Leeds Road, albeit playing for the Seasiders. Martin returned to Town as physiotherapist and goalkeeping coach under new manager Peter Jackson in time for the 2003-04 season. Martin also remained registered as a player which came in handy when Ian Gray injured his hand and the club only had one keeper on the books, Martin spent six matches on the bench as cover. He remained at the club until 2008 as physio, relinquishing his role as goalkeeping coach in 2006. Martin was later replaced by Ian Liversedge and moved on to the role as physio for Tranmere Rovers, covering Les Parry who had been appointed caretaker manager. He also ran his own physiotherapy practice next to the Galpharm Stadium, but is now based in Outlane, Huddersfield.

MARTIN, Lee

Left-back
Town Years: 1997 (loan)
Born: *1968 Hyde, Cheshire*
Playing career: *Manchester United, Celtic, Bristol Rovers, Huddersfield Town (loan), Glossop North End, Bangor City, NEWI Cefn Druids (1982-2008)*

Martin is perhaps most famous for scoring the winning goal in the 1990 FA Cup Final replay for his team Manchester United. He was playing for Bristol Rovers by the time he arrived at Town on loan in 1997, returning to his parent club later on in the season. Martin left Bristol in 1998 and drifted into non-league playing for Glossop North End. He has since coached Chester's youth team and worked for MUTV but is now working with young people in Chester, helping them to gain qualifications and gain employment.

MARTIN, William

Left-back
Town Years: 1911-1912 (amateur)
Born: *1886 Poplar, London*
Died: *unknown*
Playing career: *Huddersfield Town (1911-1912)*
Martin was a left-back that signed for the club in 1911 from non-league Ilford and he played for Town between 1911 and 1912. The Southerner played just 5 league games for Dick Pudan's side, covering the injured Fred Bullock before his release from the club at the conclusion of the 1911-12 season. Martin was also a Gold Medalist in the 1912 London Olympics.

MASKELL, Craig

Centre-forward
Town Years: 1988-1990
Born: *1968 Aldershot, Hampshire*
Playing career: *Southampton, Swindon Town (loan), Huddersfield Town, Reading, Swindon Town, Bristol City (loan), Brighton & Hove Albion, Happy Valley, Leyton Orient, Hampton & Richmond Borough, Aylesbury United, Staines Town (1986-2012)*
Maskell arrived at Leeds Road in 1988 from his first club Southampton and although he only spent two seasons at Town, Maskell managed 54 goals in 108 appearances, including scoring 33 goals in the 1988-89 season. He left for Reading in 1990, and then signed for Swindon Town in 1992, helping them to promotion to the Premier League in 1993. The former striker is now working for Protec Football Academy as a football coach.

MASON, Keith

Goalkeeper
Town Years: 1982-1986
Born: *1958 Leicester, Leicestershire*
Playing career: *Leicester City, Huddersfield Town, Colne Dynamoes, Witton Albion, Workington Reds (1981-2001)*
Mason began his career at Leicester City before signing for Town in 1982 and he remained at Leeds Road for four years before his departure in 1986. He left the club as he felt he was not getting enough game team and he joined Colne Dynamoes. Whilst he was playing for Colne, Mason won the 1988 FA Vase against Emley. After turning out for Colne, Mason later played for Witton Albion and won the Northern Premier League at the club and was also voted Player of the Year on at least one occasion.

Mason later played for Workington Reds at the age of 43 due to a shortage of goalkeepers and was also involved in managing the new Colne F.C. side. He is a qualified heating engineer and has worked within sales in the plumbing and heating industry for over thirty years and worked for Uponor between 2000 and 2012, before he joined UFW Ltd as area sales manager. Mason now works for himself designing and supplying underfloor heating and is based in Carlisle.

MASSIE, Leslie 'Les'

Forward
Town Years: 1953-1966
Born: *1935 Aberdeen, Scotland*
Playing career: *Huddersfield Town, Darlington, Halifax Town, Bradford Park Avenue (1953-1973)*
Massie arrived at Leeds Road in 1953 and he spent thirteen years at the club, playing 363 matches and scoring 108 goals. He played for Andy Beattie, Bill Shankly, Eddie Boot and Tom Johnston during his time at the club and finally left in 1966 to sign for Darlington. He advanced, going on to play for Halifax Town, Bradford Park Avenue, Workington and Drogheda United before ending his career in 1973. After his playing days were up, Massie worked in the haulage business, at Holsets in Huddersfield and also ran a garage in Waterloo, Huddersfield for a time. He is now living in retirement and occasionally attends Town games as a guest of the club.

MATMOUR, Karim

Forward
Town Years: 2016
Born: *1985 Strasbourg, France*
Playing career: *Borussia Mönchengladbach, Eintracht Frankfurt, 1. FC Kaiserslautern, Al-Arabi, Huddersfield Town, Munich (2005-2017)*
David Wagner signed Matmour in January 2016 on a short term contract until the end of the 2015-16 season. He is perhaps best remembered for scoring in the 4-1 win over local rivals Leeds United before he left the club at the end of the season. Matmour went on to play for 1860 Munich and Adelaide United before beginning work as assistant manager at German side Kehler FV. To add, Matmour played 30 games for the Algerian national side between 2007 and 2012.

MATTIS, Dwayne

Midfielder
Town Years: 1998-2004
Born: *1981 Huddersfield, West Yorkshire*
Playing career: *Huddersfield Town, Huddersfield Town, Bury, Barnsley, Walsall (loan), Walsall, Chesterfield, Macclesfield Town (1998-2012)*

Mattis came through the youth ranks at Town and made a handful of appearances between 1998 and 2004 before being released. He later played for Bury, Barnsley, Chesterfield, Walsall and Macclesfield Town before his career came to an end in 2012. Mattis has been coaching local football around Huddersfield for a number of years and now runs his own driving school, Mattis School of Motoring.

MAY, Andrew 'Andy'

Midfielder
Town Years: 1987-1990
Born: *1964 Bury, Lancashire*
Playing career: *Manchester City, Huddersfield Town, Bolton Wanderers (loan), Bristol City, Millwall, Larne (loan), Welling United (1980-1995)*

Andy May signed in 1987 from his hometown club Manchester City and is perhaps best remembered by Town fans for scoring the consolation goal in the 10-1 defeat to Man City in November 1987. He played at Leeds Road for three years before leaving for Bristol City in 1990 and spent two years at Ashton Gate before signing for Millwall in 1992, later retiring from professional football all together in 1995. May later worked as a youth coach at Wigan Athletic, is now living in Dorchester and thought to be working in the logistics industry.

MAY, David

Centre-half
Town Years: 1999-2000 (loan)
Born: *1970 Oldham, Lancashire*
Playing career: *Blackburn Rovers, Manchester United, Huddersfield Town (loan), Burnley, Bacup Borough (1988-2006)*

More famous for spending a long career at both Blackburn Rovers and Manchester United and one of a select few European Cup winners to play for the club, May was signed on loan during the 1999-00 season by his old teammate Steve Bruce but was injured on his debut and returned to Old Trafford shortly after.

He remained at the club until 2003, leaving for a one year spell at Burnley. May later played for Bacup Borough in non-league before he retired from the game and he is now a regular on MUTV, has coached in Dubai and has also worked as a wine importer.

McALISKEY, John

Forward
Town Years: 2004-2007
Born: *1984 Huddersfield, West Yorkshire*
Playing career: *Huddersfield Town, Torquay United (loan), Wrexham (loan), Mansfield Town, Alfreton Town, Salford City, Witton Albion, Altrincham, Northwich Victoria, Matlock Town (loan), Royal Dolphins, Golcar United, Huddersfield YMCA (2004-2016)*

Another one of Gerry Murphy's academy graduates, McAliskey scored on his debut against Macclesfield Town in a 4-0 win but is most famous for scoring 2 goals in 2 minutes against Scunthorpe United which turned a 2-1 scoreline into a 3-2 win. McAliskey never pushed on and struggled to cement a first team place before finally being released in 2007. He had a short spell for Mansfield Town and played in non-league for Alfreton Town, Salford City, Witton Albion, Altrincham, Northwich Victoria and Matlock Town before he dropped down into the Huddersfield District League with spells at Golcar United, Royal Dolphins and Huddersfield YMCA. McAliskey now works as a chemical process technician at Syngenta in Huddersfield.

McCAFFREY, James 'Jim'

Winger
Town Years: 1977-1978
Born: *1951 Luton, Bedfordshire*
Playing career: *Nottingham Forest, Mansfield Town, Huddersfield Town, Portsmouth, Northampton Town (1969-1980)*

McCaffrey had played over 200 games for Mansfield Town before he arrived at Leeds Road in 1977. He managed 32 games for the club before leaving in 1978 to sign for Portsmouth. After a small number of games at Portsmouth, McCaffrey left Fratton Park in 1979 to join Northampton Town, retiring after just one year with the Cobblers in 1980. After his career ended, McCaffrey ran a newsagents in Rothley and went on to run one at Glenfield Hospital in Leicester.

McCALL, Andrew 'Andy'
Inside-forward
Town Years: 1939
Born: *1908 Cumnock, Ayr, Scotland*
Died: *1979 unknown*
Playing career: *Cumnock Juniors, Cymnock Townhead Thistle, Ayr United, St Johnstone, Huddersfield Town, Nottingham Forest, Dundee, Huntly (player-coach) (1927-1946)*
McCall had a short spell at Leeds Road after signing from St. Johnstone just before the Second World War and after his departure later played for Nottingham Forest and Dundee. He later became a coach at Dundee for a number of years and later began at Dundee United. McCall died in 1979.

McCANN, John
Left-winger
Town Years: 1960-1962
Born: *1934 Glasgow, Scotland*
Playing career: *Barnsley, Bristol City, Huddersfield Town, Derby County, Darlington (1955-1966)*
McCann signed for the club in 1960 from Bristol City and play for Eddie Boot's side for two years before leaving in 1962 to sign for Derby County. He had a short spell at Darlington after leaving in 1964 before joining Chesterfield the same year. McCann spent two years at Saltergate before retiring from professional football in 1966. Since beginning his career at Barnsley in the late 1950s, he has remained in the area and up until recently was still living with wife, Eileen, although was unfortunately suffering from ill health. McCann is a now a resident at Deangate Care Home, Barnsley.

McCOMBE, Jamie
Centre-half
Town Years: 2010-2012
Born: *1983 Pontefract, West Yorkshire*
Playing career: *Scunthorpe United, Halifax Town (loan), Lincoln City, Bristol City, Huddersfield Town, Doncaster Rovers, Stevenage, Lincoln City (player-coach) (2001-Still Playing)*
'Boom Boom' arrived in 2010 from Bristol City and was immediately installed at centre-half by manager Lee Clark but eventually fell out of favour in 2011 and was loaned out to Preston North End after a red card against Leyton Orient. He was brought back by new manager Simon Grayson soon after but was released at the end of the 2011-12 season. McCombe has played for Lincoln City since 2016 and is also on the backroom staff in a player-coach role.

McCOMBE, John
Centre-half
Town Years: 2003-2007
Born: *1985 Pontefract, West Yorkshire*
Playing career: *Huddersfield Town, Torquay United (loan), Hereford United, Port Vale, Mansfield Town, York City, Macclesfield Town (2003-Still Playing)*
McCombe progressed through the youth ranks at Town before making his debut in the last game of the 2002-03 season. After this, McCombe never really managed to get into the first team and left the club in 2007 to sign for Hereford United. He signed for Boston United in 2018. He is also a director of his own coaching school, Pro Player Football Academy based in Wakefield (http://www.proplayerfootball.com).

John McCombe

McCUBBIN, Alexander 'Sandy'
Inside-forward
Town Years: 1910-1912
Born: *1887 Greenock, Scotland*
Died: *1971 San Francisco, USA*
Playing career: *Greenock Morton, Bristol Rovers, Huddersfield Town, Lincoln City, New Land Athletic, Lincoln Corinthians (1904-1921)*
McCubbin spent time playing at Greenock Morton and Bristol Rovers before he signed for Fred Walker's side in 1910. He was part of Town's first professional side and knocked in 5 goals in 11 matches before heading for the exit door in 1912, he later played for Lincoln City before emigrating to America in 1921. McCubbin lived in San Francisco until his death in September 1971.

McDERMOTT, Brian
Forward
Town Years: 1986 (loan)
Born: *1961 Slough, Berkshire*
Playing career: *Arsenal, Fulham (loan), IFK Norrköping (loan), Oxford United, Huddersfield Town (loan), Djurgårdens IF (loan), Cardiff City, Exeter City, Yeovil Town, South China, Slough Town (1977-1995)*

McDermott joined a short loan from Oxford United in 1986, playing 4 games and scoring 1 goal. He left Oxford in 1987 to sign for Cardiff City and later had spells with Exeter City and Yeovil Town before heading to Hong Kong in 1992 to sign for South China. McDermott returned to the UK in 1995 and played for Slough Town, becoming the manager in 1996. McDermott became the chief scout at Reading after a brief stint as manager at Woking. He also worked as the Under 19s Manager and Reserve Team Manager before becoming Caretaker Manager in 2009 after Brendan Rodgers left the club. After impressing in the role, he got the job full time, later taking Reading to the Premier League in 2012 but was sacked in March 2013. He took the Leeds United job in April 2013, and although he was sacked in January 2014, he was reinstated the following month. At the end of the season he was replaced by Dave Hockaday and he became the chief scout at Arsenal in 2014, leaving the following year when he returned to Reading as Manager. McDermott was sacked at the end of the 2015-16 season.

McDERMOTT, Donal
Forward
Town Years: 2011-2012
Born: *1989 Dublin, Ireland*
Playing career: *Manchester City, Milton Keynes Dons (loan), Scunthorpe United (loan), Bournemouth (loan), Huddersfield Town, Bournemouth, Rochdale, Swindon Town (2006-Still Playing)*

McDermott signed from Manchester City in 2011 and although he was put straight into the first team for the 2011-12 season, he failed to impress and was quickly offloaded to AFC Bournemouth in January 2012. He spent two years at Bournemouth before signing for Dundalk and after stints at non-league Salford City and Ramsbottom, Rochdale and Swindon Town in 2017. McDermott was released by the Wiltshire club at the end of the 2017-18 season.

McDONAGH, James 'Seamus'
Goalkeeper
Town Years: 1988 (loan)
Born: *1952 Rotherham, West Riding of Yorkshire*
Playing career: *Rotherham United, Manchester United (loan), Bolton Wanderers, Everton, Bolton Wanderers, Notts County, Scarborough, Huddersfield Town (loan), Charlton Athletic, Galway United, Spalding United, Grantham Town, Telford United, Grantham Town, Arnold Town (1970-1994)*

McDonagh signed on a short term loan from Scarborough in the 1987-88 season and made 6 appearances for Malcolm Macdonald's failing side. He later played for Charlton Athletic before becoming the player-manager of Galway United. Since his retirement as a player, McDonagh has worked as goalkeeping coach at Coventry, Mansfield, Notts Forest, Millwall, Rotherham, Leicester, Aston Villa, Plymouth Argyle, Hull City and was appointed the goalkeeping coach at Sunderland in 2011. He followed Martin O'Neill to the Republic Of Ireland national team when he was appointed goalkeeping coach in 2013 and left the role in 2018. He is now the goalkeeping coach at Nottingham Forest.

McDONALD, Scott
Forward
Town Years: 2002 (loan)
Born: *1983 Melbourne, Australia*
Playing career: *Gippsland Falcons, Casey Comets, Southampton, Huddersfield Town, Bournemouth (loan), Wimbledon, Motherwell, Celtic, Middlesbrough, Millwall, Motherwell, Dundee United (1998-2018)*

McDonald arrived on loan from Southampton at the start of the 2002-03 season, he played 14 games but only managed 1 goal during his time at the club. he returned to Southampton before moving to Wimbledon. He signed for Motherwell in 2004 before getting a move to Celtic in 2007. He played over 100 games at Celtic Park, scoring over 60 goals before moving to Middlesbrough in 2010. He left for Millwall in 2013 before returning to Motherwell in 2015. He signed a one-year deal at Dundee United in 2017, later being released at the end of the 2017-18 season and retiring from the game to concentrate on his career as a football pundit. McDonald won 26 caps for the Australian national side between 2006 and 2012 but failed to score in any of those appearances for his country.

McEVOY, Donald 'Don'
Centre-half
Town Years: 1945-1947 (amateur), 1947-1954
Born: *1928 Golcar, Huddersfield*
Died: *2004 Halifax, West Yorkshire*
Playing career: *Huddersfield Town, Sheffield Wed, Lincoln City (player-coach), Barrow (1945-1962)*
McEvoy was a Huddersfield boy and he began his career at his hometown club in 1945 as an amateur, after a period playing at local club Bradley United. He turned professional in 1947 and played at centre-half for 155 matches, including the 1952-53 promotion season where he was among seven ever-presents in the side. A transfer in 1954 took him to Sheffield Wednesday. Managerial roles later included Halifax Town, Barrow, Grimsby Town, two years at Southport before returning to Barrow in 1970. After leaving football, McEvoy ran the Crown Hotel in Brighouse and also worked for Pennine Radio as a match summariser until his retirement. He died in a Halifax care home in 2004 at the age of 75.

McGARRY, William 'Bill'
Right-half
Town Years: 1951-1961
Born: *1927 Stoke-on-Trent, Staffordshire*
Died: *2005 South Africa*
Playing career: *Northwood Mission, Port Vale, Huddersfield Town, Bournemouth (1945-1963)*
After a six year spell at Port Vale, McGarry arrived at Leeds Road in 1951 and went straight into George Stephenson's side, playing at right-half. He played every game during the 1952-53 promotion season along with six other players and managed to win four England caps during his time at Town. McGarry eventually left the club in 1961 to become the player-manager at Bournemouth but it was at Wolves that he tasted most success, winning the Texaco Cup in 1971, qualifying for the UEFA Cup and finishing runners up in 1972 and winning the League Cup in 1974. Later managed a number of sides including Power Dynamos (Zambia) and the Zambian national side before returning to Wolves in 1985. However, after just 61 days, he resigned after falling out with the owners of the club. McGarry later coached in South Africa and made his home there before he passed away in 2005 after a long battle against illness.

McGIFFORD, Grahame
Right-back
Town Years: 1970-1976
Born: *1955 Carshalton, Surrey*
Playing career: *Huddersfield Town, Hull City, Port Vale, Northwich Victoria (1970-1978)*
McGifford signed as a junior in 1970 and eventually progressed into the first team in 1972, remaining for four years and playing over 40 games at right-back for Ian Greaves, Bobby Collins and then Tom Johnston. He left the club in 1976 and retired from the game in 1978. McGifford moved into the finance industry and worked for Freedom Finance as Group Compliance Director for nine years before taking on the same role at Debt Advisory Line. He has worked at Quint Group Limited as Group Compliance Director since February 2013.

McGILL, James 'Jimmy'
Inside-left
Town Years: 1967-1971
Born: *1946 Partick, Scotland*
Died: *2015 Huddersfield, West Yorkshire*
Playing career: *Arsenal, Huddersfield Town, Hull City, Halifax Town, Frickley Athletic (1965-1978)*
After two years at Arsenal, McGill signed for Town in 1967 and he spent four years at Leeds Road, including playing a vital role in the 1969-70 promotion season. He left the club in 1971 to join Hull City and later joined Halifax Town in 1975, spending two years at The Shay before a short spell at Frickley Athletic, where McGill ended his career in 1978. McGill later worked as a welder at ICI in Huddersfield before his retirement and his death in Longwood, Huddersfield in March 2015.

McGINLEY, William 'Billy'
Inside-left
Town Years: 1974-1975
Born: *1954 Dumfries, Scotland*
Playing career: *Leeds United, Huddersfield Town, Bradford City, Crewe Alexandra (1972-1978)*
After starting his career at Leeds United, McGinley signed for Town in 1974 and spent just one year at the club before signing for Bradford City in 1975. He spent two years at Valley Parade ahead of enjoying a one year spell at Crewe Alexandra in 1978, announcing his retirement in the game in the same year. McGinley is still living in Crewe and has done since his playing days.

McGRELLIS, Frank

Forward
Town Years: 1978
Born: *1958 Falkirk, Scotland*
Playing career: *Coventry City, Huddersfield Town (loan), Hereford United (1977-1988)*

McGrellis signed on loan from Coventry City in 1978 and made his professional debut during this time. He later played for Hereford United between 1978 and 1982 and also spent three years playing for Wits University in South Africa. McGrellis later emigrated to Australia. He has coached in Oz for many years and is currently Bentleigh Greens technical director.

McHALE, John 'Kevin'

Outside-right
Town Years: 1956-1968
Born: *1939 Darfield, West Riding of Yorkshire*
Playing career: *Huddersfield Town, Crewe Alexandra, Chester, Hastings United (1955-1972)*

McHale began his career at Town in the youth team and made his debut as a 17 year old in 1956. He spent the next twelve years in the first team, playing 375 first team matches. McHale played his entire Town career in the Second Division but is still considered a legend at Town and is still warmly received on his rare visits to the club. He left for Crewe Alexandra in 1968, helping them achieve promotion at the end of the 1967-68 season. After he ended his playing days, went on to work for David Brown Tractors in Huddersfield for many years before retirement and is now living in Honley.

McINERNEY, Ian

Outside-left
Town Years: 1988-1989
Born: *1964 Liverpool, Lancashire*
Playing career: *Newcastle Blue Star, Huddersfield Town, Stockport County, Morecambe (1988-1990)*

McInerney signed for Eoin Hand's side in 1988 from Newcastle Blue Star and played 10 games in the first team before being released in 1989. He left professional football in 1991 and is now back living and working in his hometown of Liverpool.

McINTOSH, Martin

Centre-half
Town Years: 2005-2007
Born: *1971 East Kilbride, Scotland*
Playing career: *Tottenham Hotspur, St Mirren, Clydebank, Hamilton Academical, Stockport County, Hibernian, Rotherham United, Rotherham United (loan), Huddersfield Town, Grimsby Town (loan), Mansfield Town (1988-2011)*

After a long career in both the Scottish and English Football Leagues, Martin McIntosh arrived at Town in 2005 after signing from Rotherham United. He spent two years at the club before joining Mansfield Town in 2007. McIntosh later had a stint at Guiseley before becoming the manager of Worksop Town in 2010. He left the club in 2011 and later took the Buxton job the following year, where he spent six years before resigning in early 2018. Most recently, had a short spell as manager of non-league Ilkeston Town in 2018 but has since left the post and is now managing Frickley Athletic.

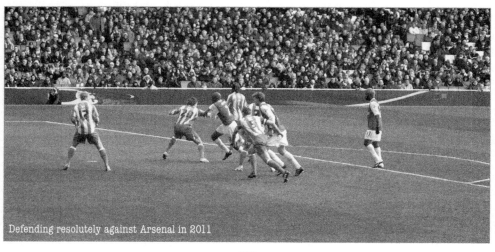

Defending resolutely against Arsenal in 2011

McKAY, Colin
Wing-half
Town Years: 1920-1922
Born: *1896 Kilmarnock, Scotland*
Died: *unknown*
Playing career: *Heart of Midlothian, Sheffield Wednesday, Huddersfield Town, Bradford City, Aberavon (1919-1924)*

Colin played 18 games for both Ambrose Langley and Herbert Chapman before he left the club in 1922 to sign for Bradford City. McKay. He retired from the game after a spell at Aberavon in 1924.

McKENNA, Johnny
Outside-right
Town Years: 1948-1954
Born: *1926 Belfast, Northern Ireland*
Died: *1980 Blackpool, Lancashire*
Playing career: *Linfield, Huddersfield Town, Blackpool, Southport, Wisbech Town (1945-1959)*

After playing for Linfield in Northern Ireland, McKenna arrived at Leeds Road in 1948 and spent six years at Leeds Road, playing 139 games for George Stephenson and Andy Beattie before he signed for Blackpool in 1954. He also played for Southport and Wisbech Town in non-league before his retirement as a player and later passed away in 1980.

MCLAREN, William 'Willie'
Wing-half
Town Years: 1913-1915
Born: *1887 Fauldhouse, Scotland*
Died: *unknown*
Playing career: *Cowdenbeath, Burnley, Huddersfield Town, Cowdenbeath (1910-1915)*

McLaren had been playing for Burnley before he arrived at Leeds Road in 1913. He played 32 matches at wing-half for Arthur Fairclough's Town side before he was released in 1915. The Scotsman later returned to his former club Cowdenbeath before retiring from the professional game.

"DID YOU KNOW?"

"John Haselden is the shortest serving full-time manager, lasting just 5 months in 1977 before he was demoted and replaced by his predecessor, Tom Johnston!"

McLEAN, George
Inside-forward
Town Years: 1930-1935
Born: *1897 Forfar, Angus, Scotland*
Died: *1970 Forfar, Angus, Scotland*
Playing career: *Forfar Athletic, Bradford Park Avenue, Huddersfield Town (1920-1939)*

After a nine years at Bradford Park Avenue, McLean arrived at Leeds Road in 1930 and during his time at the club, played 131 games for Town in the five years he spent at the club. He later returned to his previous club Forfar Athletic in 1935 and ended his career there in 1939, when World War Two broke out. McLean later ran a fish and chip shop. Died in Forfar in 1970.

McMANUS, Brendan
Goalkeeper
Town Years: 1945-1947
Born: *1923 Kilkeel, Northern Ireland*
Died: *2010 Oldham, Lancashire*
Playing career: *Newry City, Huddersfield Town, Oldham Athletic, Bradford City, (1945-1956)*

Goalkeeper that played one game during the 1946-47 season before leaving the club to join Oldham Athletic. He spent a season at Boundary Park before leaving for Bradford City in 1948. He lived the rest of his life in Oldham and died there in September 2010 at the age of 86.

Bob McNab

McNAB, Robert 'Bob'
Left-back
Town Years: 1962-1966
Born: *1943 Huddersfield, West Riding of Yorkshire*
Playing career: *Huddersfield Town, Arsenal, Wolverhampton Wanderers (1962-1984)*

McNab signed for his hometown club in 1962 and played at Leeds Road for four years before joining Arsenal for £50,000. He didn't make his debut at Highbury until 1968 but from then on played over 300 games for the first team and also gained four England caps. McNab left Arsenal in 1975 to join Wolverhampton Wanderers but this was an unhappy spell and he left to play for San Antonio Thunder in America. Later joined Vancouver Whitecaps, going on to coach them after his playing career had come to an end. McNab emigrated to Los Angeles, California and has worked as a property developer. He was also part of a consortium that bought Portsmouth in 1999 and he acted as caretaker manager for a month during this period. McNab is still living in LA.

McNAB, Neil
Midfielder
Town Years: 1992 (loan)
Born: *1957 Greenock, Scotland*
Playing career: *Greenock Morton, Tottenham Hotspur, Bolton Wanderers, Brighton and Hove Albion, Leeds United (loan), Portsmouth (loan), Manchester City, Tranmere Rovers, Huddersfield Town (loan), Ayr United, Darlington, (1972-1994)*

After a long career in the Football League, McNab arrived on loan in 1992 from parent club Tranmere Rovers. He played 11 first team matches for Eoin Hand's side before returning to the Wirral. He later had short periods at Ayr United, Darlington, Derry City, Witton Albion and Long Island Rough Riders before his retirement as a player in 1994. McNab then began work as Youth Team Coach at Manchester City in the same year, later losing his job in 1997 after a managerial upheaval. He later coached the Portsmouth youth team before becoming Exeter City manager in 2002, losing his job after only four months. McNab then emigrated to America and coached at Chiefs Futbol Club and since 2008 has been the director of coaching. In 2017, McNab was coaching and suffered a stroke on the playing field and is currently in recovery as of 2018.

Harry McShane with wife and son, the actor Ian.

McNEILL, Alan
Right-half
Town Years: 1968-1969
Born: *1945 Belfast, Northern Ireland*
Playing career: *Middlesbrough, Huddersfield Town, Oldham Athletic, Stockport County, (1967-1982)*

McNeill arrived at Leeds Road in 1968 from Middlesbrough but only managed two games before leaving in 1969. McNeill later played for Witton Albion and in the Huddersfield District League and after retiring as a player, became a sports centre supervisor for Kirklees Metropolitan Council in 1977, later progressing to operations manager, being responsible for six sports centres in the area. He is now retired but still lives in Huddersfield and bowls for Kirkheaton Conservative Club.

McSHANE, Henry 'Harry'
Outside-left
Town Years: 1946-1947
Born: *1920 Holytown, Lanarkshire, Scotland*
Died: *2012 Urmston, Lancashire*
Playing career: *Blackburn Rovers, Huddersfield Town, Bolton Wanderers, Manchester United, Oldham Athletic, (1937-1958)*

Father of actor Ian McShane, Harry joined Town in 1946 from Blackburn Rovers, playing at outside-left and managed around 15 appearances at Leeds Road before leaving for Bolton Wanderers in 1947. McShane also had spells at at Bolton, Manchester United and Oldham. He later worked as a personnel officer for Massey Ferguson in Stretford and also at Old Trafford in a number of capacities such as stadium announcer and as a talent scout. He passed away in 2012 at the age of 92 after suffering from Alzheimer's.

McSTAY, William 'Willie'
Defender
Town Years: 1987-1988
Born: *1961 Hamilton, Scotland*
Playing career: *Celtic Boys Club, Celtic, Huddersfield Town, Notts County, Hartlepool United (loan), Partick Thistle (loan), Kilmarnock, Sligo Rovers (1981-1994)*

After six years at Celtic, McStay signed for Town in 1987, with many believing that Town had signed the wrong McStay and that they had actually meant to sign his brother, Paul. The Scotsman only managed a handful of appearances for Malcolm Macdonald's side before he left for Notts County in 1988. He retired as a player after in 1994 to become youth coach at Celtic. He was later appointed the manager of Celtic Reserves in 2007, a job he kept hold of until 2009 when he became the manager of Ujpest in Hungary. McStay didn't last long in Hungary and returned to the UK in April 2010, again taking the job of managing Celtic Reserves, although he left only two months into his second spell. McStay then became manager of Ross County in November 2010 but was sacked early in the New Year due to poor results. He later worked as Dietmar Hamann's assistant manager at Stockport County and worked as a youth coach at Bristol City before becoming manager of Celtic Nation in 2013. He resigned just a year later after the club was sold and retuirned to Celic as Head of U21s Recruitment.

MEADS, Thomas 'Tommy'
Wing-half
Town Years: 1927-1928
Born: *1900 Grassmoor, Derbyshire*
Died: *1983 Chesterfield, Derbyshire*
Playing career: *Claycross Town, Matlock Town, Stockport County, Huddersfield Town, Reading, Tottenham Hotspur, Notts County (1920-1937)*

Meads signed from Stockport County in 1927 and played over 40 games for Jack Chaplin's side before his departure a year later in 1928. A one-year stint at Reading followed, before he signed for Tottenham Hotspur in 1929, going on to make over 180 appearances for Spurs. After his football career came to an end, Meads later worked at Sloane School, as a boarding house keeper in Scarborough, as Scarborough's trainer-coach, Chesterfield's reserve team coach and a coach for Middlesex AFA before he passed away in 1983.

MEAGAN, Michael 'Mick'
Left-half
Town Years: 1964-1968
Born: *1934 Dublin, Ireland*
Playing career: *Everton, Huddersfield Town, Halifax Town, Drogheda, Bray Wanderers (1952-1976)*

Meagan had spent twelve years at Everton before he was signed by Tom Johnston in 1964. The Irishman spent four years in Town's first team, playing over 100 games before leaving to sign for Halifax Town in 1968. He then held the role of Republic of Ireland's manager for two years, eventually leaving having failed to qualify for Euro 72. He had also been managing Drogheda as player-manager between 1969 and 1973 and had a further spell as player-manager at Shamrock Rovers between 1974 and 1976. Meagan later worked in a Dublin hospital but is now retired in Churchtown.

MEASHAM, Ian
Right-back
Town Years: 1981-1986
Born: *1964 Barnsley, West Riding of Yorkshire*
Playing career: *Huddersfield Town, Cambridge United, Burnley, Barnet, Doncaster R (1981-1996)*

Measham progressed through the youth team at Town before making his debut in a West Riding Cup tie in 1981. Measham later spent six years at Burnley, making over 200 appearances for the club before ending his career, after two years at Doncaster Rovers, in 1996. He went on to work for Vauxhall but is now working as Commercial Vehicles Manager at Vindis Group and is still living in Cambridge.

MELLOR, Robert 'Brett'
Centre-half
Town Years: 1976-1980
Born: *1960 Huddersfield, West Riding of Yorkshire*
Playing career: *Huddersfield T, Barnsley (1976-1980)*

Mellor began his career at his hometown club in 1976 and turned professional in 1978. He made a solitary appearance for Town during the 1977-78 season and remained with the club until 1980. Mellor played local non-league football around Huddersfield and began work as a police officer. He was in the police force for 18 years before leaving to become a pub landlord in New Mill. Believed to be back living in Huddersfield after spending time in Bridlington.

MENDES, Junior
Forward
Town Years: 2004-2006
Born: 1976 Balham, Greater London
Playing career: Chelsea, St Mirren, Carlisle United (loan), Dunfermline Athletic, Mansfield Town, Huddersfield Town, Northampton Town (loan), Grimsby Town (loan), Notts County, Lincoln City (loan), Aldershot Town, Stevenage Borough (loan), Ilkeston Town, Ayr United, (1993-2015)

After impressing Town boss Peter Jackson in games against Town during the 2003-04 season, Mendes signed at the beginning of the 2004-05 season from Mansfield Town. His time at Town was a bit hit and miss and he was loaned out a couple of times before leaving to join Notts County. Now works as a sports scientist and as a fitness coach at Partick Thistle. His full name is Albert Junior Hillyard Andrew Mendes and is probably the only league player to have represented Montserrat at international level.

MERCER, William 'Billy'
Goalkeeper
Town Years: 1924-1928
Born: 1888 Prescot, Lancashire
Died: 1956 Worthing, Sussex
Playing career: Grosvenor, Prescot, Prescot Athletic, Huddersfield Town, Prescot Athletic, Hull City, Huddersfield Town, Blackpool (1908-1930)

Goalkeeper that signed from Hull City in 1924, he played in two of the three First Division winning seasons and remained at the club for another two seasons, both of which which saw Town finish runners-up. He left in 1928 and had a short spell at Blackpool before retiring from the game in 1930. Mercer later ran a sports outfitting business before passing away in 1956.

METCALF, George
Right-half
Town Years: 1910-1911
Born: 1885 Easington, County Durham
Died: 1963 Durham, County Durham
Playing career: Sunderland, North Shields, Huddersfield Town (1909-1911)

Metcalf signed in 1910 from North Shields and played 6 games in the club's first ever professional season, under manager Dick Pudan. He was released in 1911 at the end of the season and returned to his home of Durham to work in the local colliery. Died in 1963.

METCALFE, Victor 'Vic'
Outside-left, Youth Coach
Town Years: 1940-1958, 1961-1964 (youth coach)
Born: 1922 Barrow-in-Furness, Lancashire
Died: 2003 Huddersfield, West Yorkshire
Playing career: Ravensthorpe Albion, Huddersfield Town, Hull City (1940-1960)

Metcalfe signed for Town in 1940 as an amateur from Ravensthorpe Albion, later turning professional in December 1945. He played over 450 games for the club before leaving in June 1958 to sign for Hull City. Metcalfe only lasted just over a year there before retiring in February 1960. He returned to Leeds Road the following year to work as a youth coach and remained on the payroll until December 1964 when he accepted similar role with Halifax Town. It was with the Shaymen that he held his only management position, from June 1966 to November 1967. Metcalfe remained in Huddersfield and later lived in retirement in Golcar and also turned out for Broad Oak Cricket Club for many years before passing away in 2003 at the age of 81.

MIDWOOD, Michael
Forward
Town Years: 1993-1994, 1997-1998
Born: 1976 Burnley, Lancashire
Playing career: Huddersfield Town, Halifax Town, Accrington Stanley (loan), Happy Valley (loan), Glentoran (loan), Halifax Town, Emley, Doncaster Rovers, Happy Valley, Instant-Dict, Ossett Town, Farsley Celtic, Stainland United (1993-2007)

Midwood began his career at Town in 1993 but was released in 1994 and later had a spell at Halifax Town before Brian Horton brought him back to the club in 1997. He played just 1 game during the 1997-98 season before being released at the end of that season by Peter Jackson. Midwood later enjoyed a long career in non-league at a number of clubs including Emley, Doncaster Rovers, Ossett Town and Farsley Celtic but now works as a team leader for Northern Care in Elland and also plays cricket and football locally.

"DID YOU KNOW?"

"In 2017, Town became the 49th club to play in the Premier League since its formation in 1992."

MIELCZAREK, Raymond 'Ray'

Centre-half
Town Years: 1967-1971
Born: 1946 Caernarfon, Wales
Died: 2013 Rhosddu, Wales
Playing career: Wrexham, Huddersfield Town, Rotherham United (1964-1974)

Signing from Wrexham in 1967, Mielczarek was never a first team regular but played a couple of games in the 1969-70 promotion season. Mielczarek became a cake salesman and later worked at Plas Madoc Leisure Centre as an attendant followed by sixteen years in Brymbo Steelworks security department before its closure in 1990. In later life, he spent time as a lorry driver and driving instructor. His last job was as an ambulance driver Died in 2013, aged 67.

MILLER, Ishmael

Forward
Town Years: 2015-2016
Born: 1987 Moston, Greater Manchester
Playing career: Manchester City, West Bromwich Albion, Nottingham Forest, Blackpool, Huddersfield Town, Bury, Oldham Athletic (2005-Still Playing)

Signing from Blackpool in 2015, Miller played 37 games before being released in 2016 by new manager, David Wagner. He had a short time at Bury and also played for Oldham Athletic but he is now plying his trade for Tranmere Rovers.

MILLER, Thomas 'Tommy'

Midfielder
Town Years: 2011-2012
Born: 1979 Shotton Colliery, County Durham
Playing career: Hartlepool United, Ipswich Town, Sunderland, Ipswich Town, Sheffield Wednesday, Huddersfield Town, Swindon Town, Bury, Hartlepool United, Halifax Town (1997-2015)

Signed by Lee Clark in 2011, Miller played a part in the 2011-12 promotion season, missing a penalty in the Playoff Final shootout against Sheffield United. He left that summer to sign for Swindon Town and was installed as their caretaker player manager in the 2012-13 season. He currently works at both Hartlepool College of Further Education and Stillington Community Primary School as a football coach. Miller is a busy man as he combines all of this with his role as assistant manager at Spennymoor Town and running his own business TM8 in Wynyard, Stockton-on-Tees.

MILLS, Henry 'Harry'

Goalkeeper
Town Years: 1948-1955
Born: 1922 Blyth, Northumberland
Died: 1990 Blyth, Northumberland
Playing career: Blyth Spartans, Huddersfield Town, Halifax Town, Blyth Spartans (1947-1957)

Mills arrived at Leeds Road in 1948, after a spell at Blyth Spartans, and went on to play over 150 games as goalkeeper for the club before leaving in 1956 to sign for nearby Halifax Town. He spent just one year at The Shay before heading back to Blyth Spartans in 1957. The decision was made to retire from the game which enabled him to look after game to look after his wife, who was suffering from ill health. Mills died at the age of 67 in 1990.

MILLS, William 'Willie'

Inside-forward
Town Years: 1938-1940
Born: 1915 Alexandria, Scotland
Died: 1991 Aberdeen, Scotland
Playing career: Bridgeton Waverley, Aberdeen, Huddersfield Town, Clyde, Lossiemouth, Huntly, Hamrun Spartans (1931-1950)

After six years at Aberdeen, Mills signed for Clem Stephenson's side in 1938 and managed to make 27 league appearances before football was suspended due to the outbreak of World War Two. He left the club in 1940 and later played for Clyde, Lossiemouth and Huntly in his native Scotland before his career came to an end in 1950. Mills passed away in 1991 in Aberdeen.

MILLWARD, Ernest 'Ernie'

Outside-left
Town Years: 1910-1913
Born: 1887 Hartshill, Staffordshire
Died: 1962 Christchurch, Dorset
Playing career: Cobridge Church, Biddulph Mission, Glossop, Wrexham, Stoke, Hanley Swifts, Port Vale, Stoke, Huddersfield Town, Crewe Alexandra (1903-1913)

Dick Pudan signed Ernie Millward from Stoke in 1910 and the Staffordshire born outside-left made only 2 appearances for the first team before his departure in 1913 to sign for Crewe Alexandra. Millward later worked as an engineering manager in Newcastle-under-Lyme. Died in 1962, whilst living in Christchurch, Dorset.

MILNER, John
Wing-half
Town Years: 1959-1963
Born: *1942 Huddersfield, West Riding of Yorkshire*
Playing career: *Huddersfield Town, Lincoln City, Bradford Park Avenue, Boston Beacons, Denver Dynamos (1959-1974)*

Milner began his career at his hometown club in 1959, turning professional in 1960. He only managed around 20 appearances at Leeds Road before moving on to Lincoln City in 1963. Milner later moved to America and played for Boston Beacons and Denver Dynamoes in the North American Soccer League.

MILNES, Charles 'Charlie'
Right-half
Town Years: 1912-1913
Born: *1885 Manchester, Lancashire*
Died: *1956 Bradford, West Riding of Yorkshire*
Playing career: *Bradford Park Avenue, Huddersfield Town, Rochdale, Halifax Town, Rochdale, Pontypridd, Tranmere Rovers, Rochdale (1905-1923)*

After a time at Bradford Park Avenue, Milnes signed for Town in 1912, playing a few matches during the 1912-13 season before being released. Manchester born Milnes spent his later days in Bradford and took up work as a Customs and Excise officer. Died in November 1956.

MIRFIN, David
Centre-half
Town Years: 2003-2008
Born: *1985 Sheffield, South Yorkshire*
Playing career: *Huddersfield Town, Scunthorpe United, Watford, Scunthorpe United, Hartlepool United (loan), Mansfield Town (2003-Still Playing)*

A product of the academy system, Mirfin made his debut as a substitute in the final game of the 2002-03 season under then-manager Mel Machin. He scored an important goal as a makeshift forward against York City in early 2004 and found the back of the net in the first Play-off Semi-Final and played in the Final. He was a mainstay in the defence for the next few seasons before being sold by Stan Ternent in 2008 despite being voted Player's Player of the Year in the previous May. Mirfin was snapped up by Scunthorpe United where he enjoyed a couple of spells, playing for Watford briefly in between the two. He has been at Mansfield Town since May 2017.

Graham Mitchell

MITCHELL, Graham
Centre-half, Youth Coach, U18s Coach, Caretaker Assistant Manager, Caretaker Manager, Academy Manager
Town Years: 1986-1994, 2002-2006 (youth coach), 2006-2009 (u18s coach), 2007, 2008, 2008 (caretaker assistant manager) 2008 (caretaker manager), 2009-2011 (academy manager)
Born: *1968 Shipley, West Riding of Yorkshire*
Playing career: *Huddersfield Town, Bradford City, Raith Rovers, Cardiff City, Halifax Town (1983-2004)*

Originally from Shipley, Graham Mitchell joined Town as a youth player in 1986 and quickly rose through the ranks to break into the first team. He didn't really get established until the late 1980s but by the 1990s, he was a regular in the side. He retired from professional football in 2002 but did play for non-league Bradford Park Avenue and Farsley Celtic whilst briefly working as a postman. He became a youth coach at Town in 2002 and was asked to assist caretaker manager Gerry Murphy in 2007 following the sacking of Peter Jackson. He reverted back to his role as U18's Coach but was back to assist to Murphy a year later after Andy Ritchie's sacking and once again in November 2008 after Stan Ternent's sacking, even taking charge of one match. He returned to the role of Under 18's Coach once again before becoming Academy Manager in 2009 following the retirement of Gerry Murphy. Mitchell was replaced by Mark Lillis in 2011 and after a spell as caretaker manager of Eccleshill United, is now the Regional Manager for the North West EFL Coaching Department.

Ken Monkou

MONKOU, Kenneth 'Ken'

Centre-half
Town Years: 1999-2001
Born: *1964 Nickerie, Suriname*
Playing career: *Feyenoord, Chelsea, Southampton, Huddersfield Town (1985-2001)*
Monkou was brought to the club by Steve Bruce in 1999 from Southampton and was quite a popular signing at the time, putting in a number of cultured performances, but disagreements with Bruce led to a rift and Monkou hardly ever played for the first team again. He left in 2001 and lived in Amsterdam, opening a pancake house, which later went bankrupt. Monkou now works as an ambassador for Show Racism The Red Card, is a representative for PFA schemes and has also had involvements with football education and property. The Dutchman currently lives in Harrogate.

MOONEY, Thomas

Midfielder
Town Years: 1990-1993
Born: *1973 Newry, Northern Ireland*
Playing career: *Huddersfield Town, Ballymena United (1990-1993)*
Tommy Mooney began his career at the club in 1990 and played a couple of games in the first team before his departure in 1993. He returned to his home of Northern Ireland where he now lives and works.

MORGAN, Lawrence 'Lol'

Left-half
Town Years: 1949-1954
Born: *1931 Rotherham, West Riding of Yorkshire*
Playing career: *Sheffield United (amateur), Huddersfield Town, Rotherham United, Darlington (1949-1966)*
Morgan began his professional career at Leeds Road in 1949 and after spending five years at Town, left the club in 1954 to sign for Rotherham United. He spent ten years at Millmoor and made over 300 appearances for the club. After his playing career wound down, Morgan became the player-manager at Darlington in 1964 but resigned in 1966 after the club's chairman refused to offer him anymore than a £10 a week pay rise. He later managed Norwich City before being sacked in 1970 which prompted him to take up employment as a work study officer and then a spell in a brewery. During this time, Morgan turned down job offers from former club Darlington and Bradford City and he also scouted for Tottenham Hotspur. He is still alive and living in retirement in Rotherham.

MORRIS, Charles 'Charlie'

Left-back
Town Years: 1910-1911
Born: *1880 Oswestry, Shropshire*
Died: *1952 Chirk Bank, Shropshire*
Playing career: *Chirk, Derby County, Huddersfield Town, Wrexham, Chirk (1899-1912)*
After spending ten years at Derby County, Morris joined Dick Pudan's Town in 1910. This was Town's first season as a professional side and Morris left the following year after playing 16 league games in that first season. He left the club in 1911 and signed for Wrexham where he spent a year before he re-joined first club Chirk before his retirement in 1912. Morris was the Duke of Westminster's private cricket professional between 1910 and 1916 and became a Methodist lay preacher and was a member of Churk Rural District Council. By the late 1930s, Morris was in charge of the Parish Hall in Chirk, Ceiriog in his native Wales and he later passed away in 1952 at the age of 71. Between 1900 and 1911, Charlie Morris won 28 international caps for Wales, 3 of them were won during his spell at Leeds Road.

MORRIS, Lee

Forward

Town Years: 2001 (loan)
Born: *1980 Blackpool, Lancashire*
Playing career: *York City, Sheffield United, Derby County, Huddersfield Town (loan), Leicester City, Yeovil Town, Burton Albion (1997-2015)*

Morris arrived on loan in the 2000-01 season from Derby County, playing 5 games and scoring 1 goal. He left Derby in 2004 to sign for Leicester City but only managed a handful of games in his two years at the club and signed for Yeovil Town in 2006. Morris also played for Burton Albion, Hereford United and Kidderminster Harriers before becoming player-coach at Eastwood Town in 2011. He coached the Under 15s at former club Derby in 2012 and later took on roles in the Development Centre at Pride Park until he became the Under 16s coach in 2015. Morris gained his UEFA A License at this time and had a spell as joint manager of Loughborough Dynamo between 2014 and 2015. He has since managed Goole, Frickley Athletic and Worsborough Bridge. In 2017, he took the manager's job at SC United Bantams in America in 2018 after previously having a spell as their boss the year before. These days, he combines this role with that of Director of Player Development.

MORRIS, Seymour

Forward

Town Years: 1933-1935
Born: *1913 Ynyshir, Wales*
Died: *1991 Ynyshir, Wales*
Playing career: *Lovells Athletic, Aberaman Athletic, Huddersfield Town, Birmingham (c1932-1945)*

Morris was a miner who joined the army and served in the Welsh Regiment. He was spotted by Town scouts whilst playing for little known Aberaman Athletic and was persuaded to sign a professional contract in 1933. Howver, having failed to really break into the first team in the two years that followed, Morris left for Birmingham in 1935. During the Second World War, he serviced aircraft at Elmdon aerodrome but left Birmingham in 1945 and returned to his native Wales, for whom he had earned 5 international caps between 1936 and 1939, to work in a tool factory. He coached the work's football team and he and his wife later ran a children's home. Died at the age of 78 in October 1991.

MORRISON, Andrew 'Andy'

Centre-half

Town Years: 1996-1998
Born: *1970 Inverness, Scotland*
Playing career: *Plymouth Argyle, Blackburn Rovers, Blackpool, Huddersfield Town, Manchester City, Blackpool (loan), Crystal Palace (loan), Sheffield United (loan) (1987-2001)*

Morrison arrived in 1996 after signing from Blackpool and was unveiled as a triple signing along with Marcus Stewart and Andy Payton. He was well liked by the Town faithful but was plagued by injuries and after a falling out with Peter Jackson in 1998 he transferred to Manchester City. Again, injuries hampered his time at City but he is a cult hero at the club and is now a Fan Ambassador at the Etihad. After his retirement as a player in 2002, Morrison joined Andy Preece at Worcester City, working as his assistant manager. Upon leaving Worcester City he joined Northwich Victoria, again as Preece's assistant manager until their resignations in 2012 to join Airbus UK Broughton. Morrison resigned in 2015 amid rumours of a bust up with the directors and is now Director of Football at Connah's Quay Nomads in the Welsh Premier League.

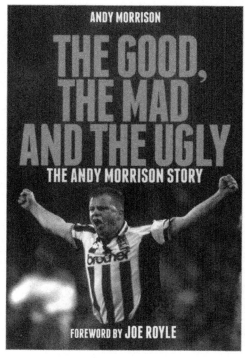

ANDY MORRISON

THE GOOD, THE MAD AND THE UGLY

THE ANDY MORRISON STORY

FOREWORD BY JOE ROYLE

MORRISON, Sean
Centre-half
Town Years: 2011, 2012 (loan)
Born: *1991 Plymouth, Devon*
Playing career: *Swindon Town, Southend United (loan), Reading, Huddersfield Town (loan), Cardiff City (2008-Still Playing)*

Morrison signed on loan from Reading in the 2010-11 season but returned to his parent club without making an appearance. The 6ft 4in defender came back on loan again the following season and played a huge part in the 2011-12 promotion season with his committed performances and conversion of a penalty in the shootout. Morrison remained at Reading until 2014, when he signed for Cardiff City. Was crowned the Bluebirds' 'Player of the Year' for 2017-2018.

MORTON, Arthur
Right-half
Town Years: 1945-1948
Born: *1925 Thurcroft, West Riding of Yorkshire*
Died: *1961 Barnsley, West Riding of Yorkshire*
Playing career: *Huddersfield Town (1945-1948)*

Although he spent three years at Town between 1945 and 1948, Morton only played 2 games in the FA Cup before he left the club in 1948 and seemingly hung up his boots. The Yorkshireman passed away in 1961 in Barnsley.

MOSES, Adrian 'Adie'
Centre-half
Town Years: 2001-2003
Born: *1975 Doncaster, South Yorkshire*
Playing career: *Barnsley, Huddersfield Town, Crewe Alexandra, Lincoln City, Mansfield Town, Gainsborough Trinity (1993-2009)*

Moses joined from Barnsley in 2001 and played centre-half at the McAlpine for two seasons under Lou Macari and Mick Wadsworth. Due to economy measures at the club, Moses was released and signed for Crewe Alexandra where he played until 2006. He also had a two year spell at Lincoln City between 2006 and 2008 and rounded off his career with spells at Mansfield Town and Gainsborough Trinity before retiring from the game in 2009. After his playing days came to an end, Moses worked for Paul Kerr Associates as a financial consultant between 2009 and 2013. Adie is now working in a similar role and director for Onside Financial Management.

Adie Moses

MOULDEN, Paul
Forward
Town Years: 1995
Born: *1967 Farnworth, Lancashire*
Playing career: *Bolton Lads' Club, Manchester City, A.F.C. Bournemouth, Oldham Athletic, Birmingham City, Huddersfield Town, Rochdale, Accrington Stanley, Bacup Borough (1984-1999)*

Moulden joined Town on a short term deal from Birmingham City in 1995 and made 2 appearances towards the end of the 1994-95 season. He was involved in a goal against former club, Birmingham in one of those games where the ball deflected off him and into the goal, but it was ultimately credited to Darren Bullock. Moulden later played for Rochdale, Accrington Stanley and Bacup Borough before retiring from the game in 1999. The Farnworth native now runs a fish and chip shop, Paul's Chippy, in Bolton. One strange claim to fame is that he was once listed in the Guiness Book of Records following a record haul of 289 goals in 40 games for an under-15s side!

MOUNTAIN, Robert 'Bob'
Forward
Town Years: 1972-1975
Born: *1956 Wombwell, West Riding of Yorkshire*
Playing career: *Huddersfield Town, Frickley Colliery, Mexborough Town, Bridlington Trinity, Grantham Town, Matlock Town, Alfreton Town (1972-1986)*

Mountain played in the youth team that reached the FA Youth Cup final in 1974 and played one professional match for the club in the 1973-74 season. He didn't manage to play another game for the club and left in 1975. After his career ended, Mountain became a miner but is now working at Beatson Clark in Rotherham, a glass packaging manufacturers, as a line leader.

MOUNTFORD, Robert 'Bob'

Centre-forward
Town Years: 1977-1978
Born: *1952 Stockton Brook, Stoke-on-Trent*
Died: *2008 Adamstown, Australia*
Playing career: *Brown Edge, Port Vale, Scunthorpe United (loan), Crewe Alexandra (loan), Rochdale, Huddersfield Town, Halifax Town, Crewe Alexandra, Stockport County, Newcastle KB United, Brisbane City FC, Blacktown City (1969-1981)*
Mountford joined Town from Rochdale in 1977 but only played for one season in Tom Johnston's side, before heading to nearby Halifax Town in 1978. After two years at the club, he left The Shay in 1980 and had a short spell at Stockport County before moving to Australia. Mountford played for Newcastle KB United and also served at the club as assistant coach. In 2007, Mountford took over as manager of Adamstown Rosebud but passed away from cancer in August 2008 while still in charge. He was also working as a prison warder, having been in the service since 1988.

MOUNTFORD, Reginald 'Reg'

Full-back
Town Years: 1929-1946
Born: *1908 Darlington, County Durham*
Died: *1994 Brighton, East Sussex*
Playing career: *Darlington, Huddersfield Town (1928-1946)*
After a spell at Darlington, Mountford arrived at Leeds Road in 1929 and played for the club for seventeen years, including the 1938 FA Cup Final. Reg retired from the professional game in 1946 and worked as a school master in Huddersfield before moving to Denmark to coach football in Copenhagen. He also managed the Denmark national team during the 1948 Olympics and remained in the country until 1952, when he returned to England. Mountford passed away in 1994 after settling in Brighton, Sussex.

MURPHY, Gerald 'Gerry'

Youth Coach, Academy Manager, Caretaker Manager, Director of Football Development
Town Years: 2007, 2008, 2008 (caretaker manager)
Born: *1943 Dublin, Ireland*
Murphy had worked at the club since 1988 and was manager of the youth team from the early 1990s, working with Kevin Blackwell between 1993 and 1995 and then on his own from then onwards. He became Academy Manager in 1999 and was first appointed caretaker manager towards the end of the 2006-07 season after Peter Jackson had been sacked. Murphy had 6 games in charge before the appointment of Andy Ritchie at which time he stepped up to become Director of Football Development. Was called upon to act as caretaker manager again towards the end of the 2007-08, famously beating local rivals Leeds United in a 1-0 game. He reverted to his previous duties following the appointment of Stan Ternent at the end of the 2007-08 season but after Ternent was sacked in November 2008, Murphy took over as caretaker manager for a third spell and took charge of 5 matches, beating local rivals Leeds United again, 2-1 at Elland Road. After Lee Clark was appointed manager in December 2008. Gerry retired in in early 2009 but still lives in Huddersfield and does some scouting for the Irish Football Association.

"DID YOU KNOW?"

"In 1990, Peter Withe and Jason Withe became the first father and son pairing to play in a game for Town, albeit in the reserves."

MURPHY, Joseph 'Joe'

Goalkeeper
Town Years: 2014-2017
Born: *1981 Dublin, Ireland*
Playing career: *Tranmere Rovers, West Bromwich Albion, Sunderland, Scunthorpe United, Coventry City, Huddersfield Town, Bury (1998-Still Playing)*
Mark Robins signed Murphy in 2014 as goalkeeping cover for Alex Smithies but he only made a couple of appearances during his time at Town. The Irishman was loaned to Bury in 2017 and signed permanently at the end of the 2016-17 season.

MUTCH, Alexander 'Sandy'
Goalkeeper
Town Years: 1910-1922
Born: *1884 Inverurie, Scotland*
Died: *1967 Newcastle-upon-Tyne, Northumberland*
Playing career: *Inverurie Locos, Aberdeen,*
Huddersfield Town, Newcastle United (1906-1924)
Mutch signed from Aberdeen in 1910, the
first season as a professional club, and
went on to spend twelve years at Town.
The Scotsman's time at the club included a
Second Division runners-up season and two
FA Cup Finals, including one win, before he
left for Newcastle United in 1922. Two years
later he retired as a player and became their
first team coach. He became the groundsman
at St. James Park before being forced into
retirement by ill health. Died due as a result
of kidney failure in 1967, at the age of 82.

NAYLOR, James 'Jimmy'
Half-back
Town Years: 1928-1930
Born: *1901 High Crompton, Lancashire*
Died: *1983 Shaw, Lancashire*
Playing career: *Huddersfield Town, Newcastle*
United, Manchester City, Macclesfield Town, Nelson,
Wigan Athletic (1920-c1937)
Naylor spent two years at Leeds Road,
playing over 40 games for the club under
Jack Chaplin and then Clem Stephenson.
The Lancastrian later found work as a clerk
for the local authorities in his hometown of
Crompton before passing away in 1983.

NAYSMITH, Gary
Left-back
Town Years: 2010-2012
Born: *1978 Edinburgh, Scotland*
Playing career: *Heart of Midlothian, Everton,*
Sheffield United, Huddersfield Town, Aberdeen, East
Fife (player-manager) (1996-2016)
Former Scottish international Naysmith
was brought to the Galpharm Stadium by
Lee Clark in 2010 from Sheffield United
but suffered an injury to his toe in a cup tie
with former club Everton in August and
spent five months in the treatment room.
Naysmith did play in the 2011 Play-off Final
against Peterborough United and made a
handful of appearances in the 2011-12 season
before being released. He went on to become
East Fife's player/manager in 2013. He left
the club in 2016 and is currently manager of
Queen of the South.

Peter Ndlovu

NDLOVU, Peter
Forward
Town Years: 2001 (loan)
Born: *1973 Bulawayo, Rhodesia*
Playing career: *Coventry City, Birmingham City,*
Huddersfield Town (loan), Sheffield Utd (1988-2011)
Ndlovu was loaned to Town during
the 2000-01 season and made an instant
impression by socring four goals in his
first six games. This coincided with an
upturn in Town's progress in the relegation
battle they were involved in at the time.
Sadly, Birmingham City manager Trevor
Francis recalled him and refused to either
loan him back or sell him. The Zimbabwe
international left England in 2004 and
headed for South Africa where he played
for Mamelodi Sundowns, Thanda Royal
Zulu, Highfield United and Black Mambas
before hanging up his boots in 2011. Ndlovu
became the Zimbabwe assistant manager
in 2011, remaining in the post until 2013.
He was involved in a serious car accident
in December 2012 and two passengers, his
brother and a female, were killed in the
collision. A trial in March 2013 found him
not guilty of for culpable homicide due to
lack of evidence and is now back living in
his native Zimbabwe.

NEWBOLD, Alfred 'Alf'
Right-back
Town Years: 1945-1946
Born: *1921 Hartlepool, County Durham*
Died: *2001 Birmingham, West Midlands*
Playing career: *Huddersfield Town (1945-1951)*
Newbold signed in 1945 from Ouston
Wanderers and played a couple of games
for David Steele's side before leaving Leeds
Road the following year to sign for Welsh
side Newport County. Died in 2001.

NEWBY, Jonathan 'Jon'

Forward
Town Years: 2003-2004
Born: *1978 Warrington, Merseyside*
Playing career: *Liverpool, Huddersfield Town, Wrexham, Southport, Morecambe (1998-2016)*
After starting his career at Liverpool, Newby joined Town in time for the 2003-04 season. He was originally intended to be the club's main goalscorer, however he never managed a goal for the club and left at the end of the season to rejoin former club Bury. Spells at Wrexham, Southport, Morecambe, Greenock Morton and Northwich Victoria followed before becoming the player-manager of Colwyn Bay in 2012. He is now working as a coach in Liverpool's academy and is also a season ticket holder at Anfield.

NEWTON, Robert 'Bob'

Forward
Town Years: 1973-1977
Born: *1956 Chesterfield, Derbyshire*
Playing career: *Huddersfield Town, Hartlepool United, Port Vale, Chesterfield, Hartlepool United, Stockport County (loan), Bristol Rovers (1973-1987)*
Newton was part of the youth team that reached the 1974 final of the FA Youth Cup and broke into the first team earlier than most of his youth team teammates. He left for Hartlepool United in 1977 and spent five years at Victoria Park, scoring over 50 goals in over 150 appearances at the club before spending a year at Port Vale. Newton then joined hometown club Chesterfield in 1983 and spent two years at Saltergate, before heading back to Hartlepool and finished his career at Bristol Rovers in 1987. Still considered a legend at Chesterfield, Hartlepool and Port Vale, he used to do matchday hospitality at Chesterfield but is now working as a long distance lorry driver.

"DID YOU KNOW?"

"Five players have gone on to become the manager at Town and they are; Clem Stephenson, David Steele, Eddie Boot, Steve Smith and Peter Jackson. Mark Lillis and Graham Mitchell have also had caretaker spells in charge."

NGONGE, Michel

Forward
Town Years: 2000 (loan)
Born: *1967 Huy, Belgium*
Playing career: *Watford, Huddersfield Town (loan), Queens Park Rangers, Kilmarnock (1986-2002)*
Ngonge joined on a short loan from Watford during the 1999-2000 season and played a couple of matches for Steve Bruce's side. The Belgian forward never quite made his mark in England and retired as a professional in 2002. Ngonge returned to his native Belgium and took employment as a French Law Manager for Cyrmax in Brussels until 2013. He later worked for a company called Together4yoursucess but since 2016 has been a football coach at St. John's International School, a private English school in Brussels.

NICHOLSON, James 'Jimmy'

Midfielder
Town Years: 1964-1973
Born: *1943 Belfast, Northern Ireland*
Playing career: *Manchester United, Huddersfield Town, (1960-1977)*
Already a Northern Ireland international when he arrived at the club, 'Jimmy Nic' signed from Manchester United in 1964. He played for the club for nine years, captaining the side to the Second Division title in 1970 and was at the club during the two seasons spent in the top flight before leaving in 1973 having suffered a second successive relegation. Nicholson settled in Sale, Cheshire and opened up a sports centre in the town during the late 1970s. Nicholson still works at the sports centre but has reduced his hours as he has got older.

NIELSEN, Martin

Midfielder
Town Years: 1998
Born: *1973 Denmark*
Playing career: *F.C. Copenhagen, Huddersfield Town (loan), FC Midtjylland (1996-2011)*
Peter Jackson signed Nielsen towards the end of the 1997-98 season but he only played a couple of substitute appearances. He returned to his home country, Denmark and worked as a coach. After his career in football ended, Neilsen began work as an insurer and has worked as a Key Account Manager for a number of companies in Denmark, working for Netsøg since 2013.

NIGHTINGALE, Albert

Inside-forward
Town Years: 1948-1951
Born: *1923 Rotherham, West Riding of Yorkshire*
Died: *2006 Liverpool, Merseyside*
Playing career: *Sheffield United, Huddersfield Town, Blackburn Rovers, Leeds United (1941-1956)*

Although he only spent three years at Leeds Road, Albert Nightingale certainly made his mark and was popular for his ability to earn penalties by diving in the box. A move to Blackburn Rovers in 1951 for £12,000 led to what was arguably his most successful period. However, Nightingale suffered from injury problems that forced his retirement at the age of 32. Became a storeman at a firm in Huddersfield and went on to work as a green keeper at Woodsome Hall Golf Club until his retirement. He passed away in 2006 in Liverpool but lived in Almondbury, Huddersfield for many years and had bowled for the Liberal Club in the area.

NORMAN, Anthony 'Tony'

Goalkeeper
Town Years: 1995-1997
Born: *1958 Mancot, Wales*
Playing career: *Burnley, Hull City, Sunderland, Huddersfield Town (1976-1997)*

The former Welsh international was signed by Brian Horton in 1995 and was brought in as goalkeeping cover for Steve Francis, remaining until 1997 before his retirement as a professional. He became a police officer but had to leave the force after being diagnosed with a rare heart condition. The Welshman has since coached the goalkeepers at Sunderland's Academy, Darlington, Blyth Spartans and but is now running his own goalkeeping coaching school in Durham.

NORWOOD, Oliver

Midfielder
Town Years: 2012-2014
Born: *1991 Burnley, Lancashire*
Playing career: *Manchester United, Huddersfield Town, Reading, Brighton & Hove Albion, Fulham (loan), Sheffield United (loan) (2009-Still Playing)*

Norwood signed from Manchester United in 2012 and spent two years at Town before leaving for Reading in 2014. He has played for Brighton & Hove Albion since 2016. Spent the 2017-18 season on loan at Fulham and 2018-19 on loan at Sheffield United.

Lee Novak

NOVAK, Lee

Forward
Town Years: 2009-2013
Born: *1988 Newcastle-upon-Tyne, Tyne and Wear*
Playing career: *Huddersfield Town, Birmingham C, Charlton Athletic, Scunthorpe U (2006-Still Playing)*

Novak was signed by Lee Clark in 2009 from non-league Gateshead and spent four years in the first team playing alongside Jordan Rhodes for most of that time. Clark later took him to Birmingham City in 2013 where he remained until 2016. A spell at Charlton followed before joining Scunthorpe in 2017.

O'CONNELL, Brendan

Midfielder
Town Years: 1990 (loan)
Born: *1966 Lambeth, London*
Playing career: *Portsmouth, Exeter City, Burnley, Huddersfield Town (loan), Barnsley, Charlton Athletic, Wigan Athletic, (1985-2003)*

O'Connell arrived on a short term loan in 1990 and played 11 games, scoring once. He returned to his parent club Barnsley and stayed there until 1996 The London-born midfielder is now coaching in Canada, having emigrated in the early 2010s.

O'CONNOR, Derek

Goalkeeper
Town Years: 1994-1998
Born: *1978 Dublin, Ireland*
Playing career: *Crumlin United, Huddersfield Town, Bradford Park Avenue, Frickley Athletic, St Patrick's Athletic (1994-2001)*

Irishman O'Connor only managed one game in the first team during his four year spell at Town. After his departure in 1998, he played non-league football in the North of England and worked as a gardener for Grace Landscapes in Mirfield. O'Connor has since left Yorkshire and is now living in his hometown of Dublin, Ireland.

O'DOHERTY, Kenneth 'Ken'

Centre-half
Town Years: 1988-1992
Born: *1963 Dublin, Republic of Ireland*
Playing career: *University College Dublin, Crystal Palace, Huddersfield Town, Exeter City (loan), Shelbourne (1980-1995)*

O'Doherty signed from Crystal Palace in 1988 and spent four years at Leeds Road, playing for Eoin Hand and Ian Ross. He returned to Ireland in 1992 to play for Shelbourne and is now working as Staff Relations Manager at Trinity College in Dublin.

Billy Lynn's player pass from 1965/6

OGILVIE, Duncan

Outside-right
Town Years: 1936
Born: *1911 Glasgow, Scotland*
Died: *1977 Stirling, Scotland*
Playing career: *Huddersfield Town, Falkirk, Hamilton Academical, Dundee United (1930-1950)*

Ogilvie signed from Motherwell in 1936 and spent just nine months at Leeds Road, playing at outside-right. The Scotsman later served as a director at Falkirk before passing away in 1977 at the age of 65.

O'GRADY, Michael 'Mike'

Outside-left
Town Years: 1958-1965
Born: *1942 Leeds, West Riding of Yorkshire*
Playing career: *Huddersfield Town, Leeds United, Wolverhampton Wanderers, Birmingham City (loan), Rotherham United, Cork Hibernians (1958-1975)*

After beginning his career at Leeds Road, O'Grady transferred to Leeds United in 1965 and also had a four year spell at Wolverhampton Wanderers between 1969 and 1973. He retired from the game in 1975, after short spells at Rotherham United and Cork Hibernians. O'Grady had also played twice for England and scored three goals for the national side. Remarkably, his appearances were seven years apart! After retirement as a player, O'Grady worked as a grip for Yorkshire Television for eighteen years until being made redundant. He then worked behind the bar of the Royal Oak public house in Aberford until his retirement. He is still living in Aberford and still attends the occasional Town game.

O'NEIL, Brian

Midfielder
Town Years: 1974-1976
Born: *1944 Bedlington, Northumberland*
Playing career: *Burnley, Southampton, Huddersfield Town, Bideford A.F.C. (1962-1976)*

O'Neil joined the club from Southampton in 1974 and played over 60 matches in his two year spell under Bobby Collins and Tom Johnston. He left the club in 1976, later playing for Bideford A.F.C. in non-league before becoming a civil engineer. A serious accident left him unable to work and he now lives in Hedge End, Hampshire and has an interest in racehorses.

O'REGAN, Kieran
Midfielder
Town Years: 1988-1993
Born: *1963 Cork, Ireland*
Playing career: *Tramore Athletic, Brighton & Hove Albion, Swindon Town, Huddersfield Town, West Bromwich Albion, Halifax Town(1982-1998)*

O'Regan joined Eoin Hand's side from Swindon Town in 1988, thus beginning a five year spell at Leeds Road. He was signed by his former Ireland manager Hand and went straight into the first team, going on to make over 200 appearances for the club and chipping in with a number of goals. O'Regan moved on to West Bromwich Albion in 1993 before heading back to Yorkshire in 1995 when he joined Halifax Town. He was then joint manager with George Mulhall from 1997 until 1998 during which time the Shaymen were crowned champions of the Conference. O'Regan became the sole manager in August 1998 after Mulhall retired but he didn't last long and was sacked in 1999 after rumours of a rift between him and player-coach Peter Butler. The Irishman became match summariser for BBC Radio Leeds in 1999, covering all Town games both home and away and continued in this role up until the end of the 2015-16 season, when he gave it up to concentrate on his golf. He is now working at Lockwood Carpet Clearance Centre in Huddersfield and lives in Honley.

OLDFIELD, John
Goalkeeper
Town Years: 1961-1969
Born: *1943 Carlton-in-Lindrick, Nottinghamshire*
Died: *2002 Leeds, West Yorkshire*
Playing career: *Huddersfield Town, Wolverhampton Wanderers, Crewe Alexandra (loan), Bradford City (1961-1973)*

Oldfield began his career at Leeds Road in 1961 as an amateur before signing professional a year later in 1962 and he went on to play over 150 matches in goal before leaving the club in 1969. He enjoyed a two year spell at Wolverhampton Wanderers before signing for Bradford City in 1971. Oldfield retired as a professional in 1973 and went into the pub trade after his retirement as a player, running a sports and social club in West Yorkshire. Died in 2002.

OLIVER, Peter
Left-back
Town Years: 1976-1977
Born: *1948 Dunfermline, Scotland*
Playing career: *Heart of Midlothian, York City, Huddersfield Town (1969-1977)*

Oliver was a defender that signed from York City in 1976 and he spent the 1976-77 season at Leeds Road. The Scotsman later worked as a printer back home in Scotland for many years but is now thought to have retired.

ONIBUJE, Folawiyo 'Fola'
Forward
Town Years: 2003 (loan)
Born: *1984 Lagos, Nigeria*
Playing career: *Charlton Athletic, Preston North End, Huddersfield Town (loan), Barnsley, Peterborough United, Cambridge United, Swindon Town, Brentford (loan), Wycombe Wanderers (loan), Wycombe Wanderers, Shrewsbury Town, St Albans City, Macclesfield Town, Accrington Stanley, Weymouth, Woking, Grays Athletic, Southport, Boreham Wood, Tooting & Mitcham United, Cheshunt (2002-2016)*

Onibuje came to Town on a short loan from Preston North End at the end of 2003, making two appearances. He went on to play for a plethora of clubs in both league and non-league football including Barnsley, Swindon Town, Accrington Stanley, Woking, Greys Athletic, Wycombe Wanderers, Shrewsbury Town, Southport, Macclesfield Town and Weymouth. Onibuje is now living in Malta and works as Director of Recruitment for IGaming Elite.

ONUORA, Ifem 'Iffy'
Forward
Town Years: 1989-1994, 2004
Born: *1967 Glasgow, Scotland*
Playing career: *Everton, Huddersfield Town, Mansfield Town, Gillingham, Swindon Town, Sheffield United, Grimsby Town, Tranmere Rovers, Huddersfield Town, Walsall (1988-2004)*

After graduating from Glasgow University, Iffy wrote to many Football League clubs asking for a trial but without success. He first came to Town's attention after Dai Jones had seen him playing in an FA Coaching Scheme Course and he recommended Onuora to Peter Withe and Eoin Hand who quickly snapped him up in 1988. He broke into the first team and played 165 games before a move in 1994 took him to Mansfield Town.

Onuora later played for Gillingham and Sheffield United amongst other clubs before returning towards the end of the 2003-04 season, he even chipped in with an important goal in the play-offs but left at the end of the season. He later had coaching roles at Walsall, Swindon Town, Gillingham and was then Peter Jackson's assistant manager until 2009 when they were both sacked. He took the Ethiopian national team manager's job in 2010 but left in 2011 having told the media that he had had to remove some cows from the training pitch in order to begin training. Onuora now works as Equalities Coach for the PFA and is part of the England U21 coaching staff.

PAGE, Robert 'Rob'

Centre-half
Town Years: 2008
Born: *1974 Llwynypia, Wales*
Playing career: *Watford, Sheffield United, Cardiff C, Coventry C, Huddersfield T, Chesterfield (1985-2011)*
Page signed from Coventry City in early 2008 on a short-term deal and he impressed the Town faithful in his short time at the club but refused to sign another contract at the end of the 2007-08 season. Later became a coach at Port Vale until 2014 when he was given the manager's job at Vale Park. Page left for Northampton Town in 2016 but was sacked in January 2017 after describing his team's performance as "men against girls". After a brief spell as a coach at Nottingham Forest, the Welshman was given the job of managing the Welsh U21 side in March 2017.

PALMER, Kasey

Midfielder
Town Years: 2016-2017 (loan), 2017-2018 (loan)
Born: *1996 Lewisham, Greater London*
Playing career: *Chelsea, Huddersfield Town (loan), Derby County (loan), Blackburn Rovers (loan) (2016-Still Playing)*
Palmer arrived on loan from Chelsea for the 2016-17 season and played regularly in the first team until he picked up a hamstring injury. He returned to the side for the Playoff Final against Reading and for the 2017-18 season, but due to the persistent injury problems he returned to Chelsea in January 2018. Palmer was later loaned out to Derby County and spent the 2018-19 season on loan at Blackburn Rovers.

PARKER, Keigan

Forward
Town Years: 2008-2009
Born: *1982 Livingston, Scotland*
Playing career: *St Johnstone, Blackpool, Huddersfield Town, Hartlepool United (loan), Oldham Athletic, Bury (loan), Mansfield Town, Fleetwood Town (loan), Stockport County, A.F.C. Blackpool, A.F.C. Fylde, Ayr United, Cork City, Irvine Meadow, Shettleston, Airdrieonians, Clyde, Wyre Villa, Thorniewood United (1998-Still Playing)*
One of Stan Ternent's signings, Parker had a very uneventful spell at Town, scoring only two goals during his stay. He was released at the end of the 2008-09 season and joined Oldham Athletic. Brief spells at Mansfield Town, Stockport County, A.F.C. Blackpool and Fylde followed before he headed back to Scotland. Last known to be playing for Thorniewood United.

PARKER, Robert 'Bob'

Full-back
Town Years: 1954-1965
Born: *1935 Seaham, County Durham*
Playing career: *Murton Colliery, Huddersfield Town, Barnsley (1954-1969)*
Parker signed as a youth player in 1954 and then turned professional in 1959, remaining until 1965 when he signed for Barnsley. In 1969, after four years at Oakwell, Parker retired and later worked as a coach at the club. He still lives in Barnsley and is now retired.

PARKIN, Derek

Right-back
Town Years: 1963-1968
Born: *1948 Newcastle-upon-Tyne, Northumberland*
Playing career: *Huddersfield Town, Wolverhampton Wanderers, Stoke City (1963-1983)*
Parkin began his career at Leeds Road and spent four years as a professional at the club but he is best remembered for his 14 year spell at Wolverhampton Wanderers between 1968 and 1982. He holds the record for most appearances at Molineux (609) and is still considered to be a legend there. Parker finished his career with a one year spell at Stoke City before hanging up his boots in 1983. He later worked as a landscape gardener and is now living in retirement in Telford.

PARKIN, Jonathan 'Jon'
Forward
Town Years: 2011-2012 (loan)
Born: *1981 Barnsley, South Yorkshire*
Playing career: *Barnsley, Hartlepool United (loan), York City (loan), York City, Macclesfield Town, Hull City, Stoke City (loan), Stoke City, Preston North End (loan), Preston North End, Cardiff City, Doncaster Rovers (loan), Huddersfield Town (loan), Scunthorpe United (loan), Fleetwood Town, Forest Green Rovers, Newport County, York City (1998-Still Playing)*
The 'Beast' arrived on loan in 2011 from his parent club Cardiff City and made 3 appearances for Lee Clark's side. He later had spells at Fleetwood Town, Forest Green Rovers and Newport County before signing for York City in 2017. Parkin released his autobiography, *Feed The Beast*, in 2018.

PARSLEY, Neil
Full-back
Town Years: 1990-1993
Born: *1966 Liverpool, Lancashire*
Playing career: *Leeds United, Chester City (loan), Huddersfield Town, Doncaster Rovers (loan), West Bromwich Albion, Exeter City, Witton Albion, Guiseley, Witton Albion (1985-2001)*
Parsley joined Town from Leeds United in 1990 and won the Player of the Year award in 1993. He left the later that year to join West Bromwich Albion where he spent for two years before moving into non-league where he played for Witton Albion and Guiseley before becoming manager of Guiseley in 2001. Parsley later took the Farsley Celtic manager's job in 2008 and remained with them when they reformed as Farsley AFC in 2010. He spent seven years at Throstle Nest before he left the club in 2017 and has worked as a builder and site manager since his professional career ended.

PATERSON, Jamie
Winger
Town Years: 2015-2016 (loan)
Born: *1991 Coventry, West Midlands*
Playing career: *Walsall, Nottingham Forest, Huddersfield Town (loan), Bristol City (2010-Still Playing)*
Paterson spent the 2015-16 season on loan at Town from Nottingham Forest. Although the club tried to sign him permenantly, Forest wouldn't budge and he was eventually sold to Bristol City in 2016. As of 2019, Paterson remains at Ashton Gate.

PATERSON, Martin
Forward
Town Years: 2013-2015
Born: *1987 Tunstall, Stoke-on-Trent, Staffordshire*
Playing career: *Stoke City, Scunthorpe United, Burnley, Huddersfield Town, Blackpool, Port Vale, Tampa Bay Rowdies, ATK (2005-2018)*
Signed from Burnley in 2013, Paterson is probably best remembered for a training ground bust-up with Adam Clayton that was re-inacted as a celebration when a goal was scored against Sheffield Wednesday in 2013. He left the club in 2015 and has since had spells at Orlando City, Blackpool, Port Vale, Tampa Bay Rowdies and ATK in the Indian Super League. Paterson returned to Tampa in 2018 as a coach.

PAUREVIĆ, Ivan
Defensive midfielder
Town Years: 2016-2017
Born: *1991 Essen, Germany*
Playing career: *Borussia Dortmund, Fortuna Dusseldorf, Ufa, Huddersfield Town, Ufa (2010-date)*
German born Croat Paurević arrived at the club in 2016 from Ufa in Russia but only managed 2 appearances before returning to Ufa in 2017. He had previously played under David Wagner at Borusia Dortmund but could not recapture the form that prompted his acqisition.

PAYTON, Andrew 'Andy'
Forward
Town Years: 1996-1998
Born: *1967 Whalley, Lancashire*
Playing career: *Hull City, Middlesbrough, Celtic, Barnsley, Huddersfield Town, Burnley, (1985-2002)*
The 'Padiham Predator' was snapped from Barnsley for £325,000 in 1996 and his goals kept Town up during the 1996-97 season, but after Brian Horton's sacking in 1997, he fell out of favour with new manager Peter Jackson and was sold to Burnley in a swap deal for Paul Barnes less than 12 months later. He played at Burnley for five years and is considered a club legend at Turf Moor but fell on hard times after he left the game. In 2009, his house was raided when police heard that he had a cannabis farm in the property. Payton later worked as assistant manager at Colne, Padiham and latterly Northwich Victoria but is now football coach at Burnley College and is a UEFA 'A' Qualified Football Coach.

PEARSON, Stanley 'Stan'
Outside-right
Town Years: 1921-1922
Born: 1895 Sheffield, West Riding of Yorkshire
Died: 1988 Sheffield, South Yorkshire
Playing career: Sheffield Wednesday, Huddersfield Town, Denaby United (1917-c1923)
Pearson joined from Malin Bridge Old Boys in November 1921 but only managed 1 appearance in the first team. He was released at the end of that particular season and returned to his native Sheffield to work in industry. Pearson was later the manager of a steel rolling mill. Died in 1988.

"DID YOU KNOW?"

"Two World Cup winners have played for Town, Ray Wilson (1952-1964) won it with England in 1966 and Erik Durm (2018-2019) won it with Germany in 2014."

PELTIER, Lee
Right-back / Centre-half
Town Years: 2009-2011, 2014-2015
Born: 1986 Liverpool, Merseyside
Playing career: Liverpool, Yeovil Town, Huddersfield Town, Leicester City, Leeds United, Huddersfield Town, Cardiff City (2004-Still Playing)
Signed by Lee Clark in 2009, Peltier impressed with his performances at right-back and this attracted a £750,000 bid from Leicester City which was accepted in 2011. He remained at Leicester until 2012 before signing for Leeds United where he spent two years before returning to Town in 2014. Unfortunately, this failed spectacularly and left at the end of the 2014-15 season having only made a handful of appearances and has been playing for Cardiff City since 2015.

PERCIVAL, Ronald 'Jack'
Centre-half
Town Years: 1948-1950
Born: 1924 Ealing, Greater London
Died: 2011 Ipswich, Suffolk
Playing career: Huddersfield Town, Chesterfield, Cambridge United (1947-1951)
Percival played for non-league Tunbridge Wells before signing for Town in 1948. He only managed a few league starts before leaving in 1950. Percival later played for Chesterfield, then Cambridge United and passed away in 2011 in his late 80s.

PERRETT, Robert 'Bob'
Outside-left
Town Years: 1936-1939
Born: 1919 Bournemouth, Hampshire
Died: 1994 Bournemouth, Hampshire
Playing career: Bournemouth & Boscombe Athletic, Huddersfield Town, Southampton (1936-1942)
After a spell at Bournemouth & Boscombe Athletic, Perrett signed for Town in 1936 and made one solitary appearance in Clem Stephenson's side before his career at Town was interrupted by the outbreak of the Second World War in 1939. He served in the Navy on HMS Illustrious during the War but returned to the game to play for Southampton before retiring in 1942. Later worked as a coach at his home town club, Bournemouth. He also found work as an insurance salesman and in the gas meter industry before passing away in 1994.

PHILLIPS, David
Midfielder
Town Years: 1997-1999
Born: 1963 Wegberg, Germany
Playing career: Plymouth Argyle, Manchester City, Coventry City, Norwich City, Nottingham Forest, Huddersfield Town, Lincoln City (1981-2001)
By the time Phillips joined Town during the 1997-98 season he had already enjoyed a long successful career in professional football, turning out for Plymouth Argyle, Manchester City, Coventry City, Norwich City and Nottingham Forest. He spent two years at the club and, along with Barry Horne, were christened the "Old Gits". He left in 1999 after playing over 50 games and had short spells at Lincoln City and Stevenage Borough before calling time on his career in 2001. Phillips is a UEFA A Licence coach and has been working as Head of Football for the Warwickshire College Group since 2003 and also freelances as a co-commentator for Sky Sports on occasion.

PICKERING, William 'Bill'
Right-back
Town Years: 1927-1929
Born: 1904 Birmingham, Warwickshire
Died: 1971 Warley, Warwickshire
Playing career: Latch & Batchelors, Sunderland, Merthyr Town, Gillingham, Huddersfield Town, Reading, Colwyn Bay United, Bristol Rovers, Accrington Stanley , (1924-1938)

Pickering arrived at Leeds Road in 1927 from Sunderland but only managed a single appearance for Jack Chaplin's side before agreeing to sign for Reading in 1929. He left the Berkshire club for Colwyn Bay United in 1930 and later joined Bristol Rovers in 1931, spending six years in Bristol, making over 200 appearances in their first team. Pickering served in the Second World War as a Royal Marine Commando and was stationed in the Far East. He died in February 1971.

PIERCE, Gary
Goalkeeper
Town Years: 1971-1973
Born: *1951 Bury, Lancashire*
Playing career: *Bury, Bolton Wanderers, Mossley, Huddersfield Town, Wolves, Barnsley, Blackpool, Accrington S, Rossendale United, Chorley (1971-1984)*
Pierce signed for Town in 1971 from Mossley and played over 20 games in goal before leaving the club for Wolves in 1973. He spent six years at Molineux, making over 100 appearances, but is best remembered for playing in the 1974 League Cup Final. Pierce went on to spend four years at Barnsley and then a spell at Blackpool before retiring from professional football. He later played for Accrington Stanley, Rossendale United and Chorley in non-league and worked as a youth coach at Bury. Pierce took employment as a delivery driver but is now living in retirement in Ainsworth.

PILKINGTON, Anthony
Winger
Town Years: 2009-2011
Born: *1988 Blackburn, Lancashire*
Playing career: *Atherton Collieries, Stockport County, Huddersfield Town, Norwich City, Cardiff City (2006-Still Playing)*
'Pilks' arrived in January 2009 from Stockport County and impressed the Town faithful with his performances on the wing, until he broke his leg in March 2011 in a fixture against Rochdale. He never played for the club again and was sold to Premier League side Norwich City in the summer of that year, spending three years at Carrow Road before signing for Cardiff City in 2014. 'Pilks' joined Wigan Athletic in the 2019 January transfer window.

POOLE, Joseph 'Joe'
Forward
Town Years: 1941-1947
Born: *1923 Huddersfield, West Riding of Yorkshire*
Died: *1990 Huddersfield, West Yorkshire*
Playing career: *David Brown's Works, Huddersfield Town, Bradford City (1941-1949)*
Originally from Huddersfield, Joe Poole joined his hometown club in 1941 during the Second World War and made a couple of appearances in the first team but left in 1947 to join local rivals Bradford City. Poole spent two years at Valley Parade and remained in Huddersfield until his death in 1990.

POOLE, Terence 'Terry'
Goalkeeper
Town Years: 1968-1977
Born: *1949 Chesterfield, Derbyshire*
Playing career: *Manchester United, Huddersfield Town, Bolton Wanderers, (1967-1981)*
Poole began his career at Manchester United before arriving at Leeds Road in 1968 and went on to spend nine years at Town, mostly as first choice keeper. He had played over 200 games for the club by the time of his departure and had appeared in all four divisions. Poole signed for Bolton Wanderers but never really cemented a place in their first team and left in 1981 to retire from professional football. He has since run a video shop and had his own taxi business, TP Travel in Wingerworth, Chesterfield.

Terry Poole

POTTER, Cecil
Secretary-manager
Town Years: 1925-1926
Born: *1888 West Hoathly, West Sussex*
Died: *1975 Sutton, Greater London*
Management career: *Derby County, Huddersfield Town, Norwich City (1920-1929)*

After a spell as manager of Derby County, Potter arrived at Leeds Road in 1925 to replace the outgoing Herbert Chapman. Potter was the last boss to assume the role of secretary-manager and guided the club to win theri third First Division title in a row. However, he was asked to resign in the close season for unspecified reasons and later became the manager of Norwich City. Potter later worked as an insurance agent in Sussex. Died in 1975 at the age of 86, whilst living in Sutton, Surrey

POWELL, Christopher 'Chris'
Manager
Town Years: 2014-2015
Born: *1969 Lambeth, Greater London*
Management career: *Leicester City (caretaker), Charlton Athletic, Huddersfield Town, Derby County (caretaker), Southend United (2010-present)*

After winning promotion with Charlton Althletic, Powell was the ideal candidate to replace Mark Robins in 2014. Unfortunately, Powell's appointment lasted just over a year before he was sacked and replaced by David Wagner in November 2015. Powell was appointed assistant manager at Derby County for the 2016-17 season but was made caretaker following the sacking of Nigel Pearson. When Steve McClaren was given the job in late 2016, Powell left and has been the manager of Southend United since 2018.

POYET, Diego
Midfielder
Town Years: 2014 (loan)
Born: *1995 Zaragoza, Spain*
Playing career: *Charlton Athletic, West Ham United, Huddersfield Town (loan) Pafos (2013-Still Playing)*

Son of Gus Poyet, Diego arrived at the club in 2014 on loan from West Ham United and managed 2 appearances before returning to his parent club. He left the Hammers in 2016 and later played for Godoy Cruz in Argentina and signed for Cypriot side Pafos in 2017. Interestingly, he played for the England Under 16 and 17 sides but then for Uruguay at under 20 level!

Chris Powell

PRICE, Albert 'Billy'
Centre-forward
Town Years: 1937-1947
Born: *1917 Wellington, Shropshire*
Died: *1995 Bradford, West Yorkshire*
Playing career: *Wrockwardine Wood, Huddersfield Town, Reading, Hull City, Bradford City, Winsford United (1936-1952)*

Billy Price began his professional career at Leeds Road in 1937, after a spell at Wrockwardine Wood in Shropshire. Unfortunately, it was interrupted by the Second World War in 1939 but after the end of the War he played 51 games and scored 23 goals before being transferred to Reading. He lasted just a year at Elm Park before signing for Hull City in 1948 and then Bradford City in 1949 before retiring in 1952. Price later played for non-league Winsford United and passed away in 1995.

PROCTOR, James
Inside-forward
Town Years: 1911-1912
Born: *1892 West Ham, London*
Died: *1976 Barking, Essex*
Playing career: *Custom House FC, Huddersfield Town, Leicester Fosse (1911-1913)*

Proctor arrived at Leeds Road in 1911 after being brought to the club by Dick Pudan and he played 4 matches up front in the first team during the 1911-12 season before being released at the conclusion of it. He later played for Leicester Fosse for a short time before leaving professional football. Worked as a plastic welder in Barking before his death in January 1976.

PUDAN, Albert 'Dick'
Full-back (Player-manager)
Town Years: 1910-1912 (player-manager)
Born: 1881 West Ham, Essex
Died: 1957 London
Playing career: West Ham United, Bristol Rovers, Newcastle United, Leicester Fosse, Huddersfield Town (player-manager), Leicester Fosse (1899-1914)
Management career: Huddersfield T (1910-1912)
Pudan arrived at the club as a player from Leicester Fosse in 1910 but he ended up as the club's first professional manager. He took charge of the club's first campaign in the Football League and achieved a very respectful 13th position. He took charge for most of the 1911-12 season but he stepped down as manager in April in favour of a more knowledgeable person, a gesture that was greatly appreciated by the board of directors. He remained at the club until November 1912 as a player and returned to Leicester Fosse and carried on playing up until 1914. In 1919 when Fosse became Leicester City, he took a seat on the board of directors and also had a spell as chairman of the club. Away from football, Pudan established himself as a very successful hosiery manufacturer in the West Midlands. Passed away at the age of 75 whilst living in London and he died from coronary thrombosis.

PUGH, Daral
Winger
Town Years: 1982-1985
Born: 1961 Crynant, Wales
Playing career: Doncaster Rovers, Huddersfield Town, Rotherham United, Cambridge United (loan), Torquay United, Bridlington Town (1977-1990)
Pugh impressed while playing for Doncaster Rovers and spent three years at Town, including the 1982-83 promotion season. He left for Rotherham United in 1985 and then spent two years at Torquay United before hanging up his boots and becoming Football in the Community Officer at Town. He left Leeds Road in 1991 to work for Wakefield District Council as Football Development Officer. He then spent three years at Leeds Council before becoming the Assistant Academy Manager at Leeds United and then Leicester City. Pugh later worked as Rotherham and Leeds before taking up his current job of Head of Academy Coaching at Sheffield Wednesday.

PUGH, John 'Graham'
Midfielder
Town Years: 1972-1975
Born: 1948 Chester, Cheshire
Playing career: Sheffield Wednesday, Huddersfield Town, Chester C, Barnsley, Scunthorpe U (1965-1981)
After a number of years at Sheffield Wednesday, Pugh arrived at Leeds Road in 1972 and played over 80 matches for the first team before his departure in 1975. Pugh later played for Matlock Town and went into the pub trade, running a number of pubs in Sheffield and the surrounding areas but is now the landlord of Lockwood and Salford Conservative Club in Huddersfield.

PURDIE, Bernard
Left-back
Town Years: 1979-1982
Born: 1949 Wrexham, Wales
Playing career: Wrexham, Chester, Crewe Alexandra, Huddersfield Town, Crewe Alexandra (1968-1983)
Signed in 1980 from Crewe Alexandra as cover for the first choice left-back Fred Robinson, Bernard Purdie was almost immediately called upon when Robinson was injured. The Welshman made the position his own and didn't miss another game during the 1979-80 promotion season. He left Town in 1982 and returned to Crewe for a short spell before joining non-league Bangor City. Purdie became a postman in his hometown of Wrexham and although retired, he still resides there.

QUESTED, Wilfred 'Len'
Left-half
Town Years: 1951-1957
Born: 1925 Folkestone
Died: 2012 Queensland, Australia
Playing career: Fulham (amateur), Huddersfield Town, Auburn, Hakoah, Awaba (1943-1965)
After a spell at Fulham, Quested was signed by Town in 1951 and for the next seven years he was a regular in the first team, making over 220 appearances and playing during the 1952-53 promotion season, then emigrated to Australia with his Australian wife. Quested had a spell at Cumberland United on 1964 as a coach before he came out of retirement to play for Awaba. He also won an international cap for Australia at some point and later worked coaching youngsters before he later passed away in Queensland in 2012 at the age of 87.

QUIGLEY, John 'Johnny'

Inside-left
Town Years: 1965-1966
Born: *1935 Glasgow, Scotland*
Died: *2004 Nottingham, Nottinghamshire*
Playing career: *Nottingham Forest, Huddersfield Town, Bristol City, Mansfield Town (1957-1970)*

After a long spell at Nottingham Forest, Quigley arrived at Leeds Road in 1965 but left just a year later in 1966 to join Bristol City. He later coached at Mansfield and in the Middle East before returning to the UK and live in Nottingham. He passed away in December 2004 at the age of 69.

QUINLAN, Philip 'Phil'

Forward
Town Years: 1991 (loan)
Born: *1971 Madrid, Spain*
Playing career: *Everton, Huddersfield Town (loan), Southport FC (1989-1993)*

Quinlan began his career at Everton but never managed a game in the first team. He was loaned to Town during the 1990-91 season where he impressed the Town faithful with his goals and committed performances. He later played for Southport and Doncaster Rovers and is still living in Southport. Quinlan was last known to be working in Ladbrokes in Formby village.

RACCHI, Daniel 'Danny'

Defender / Midfielder
Town Years: 2005-2008
Born: *1987 Elland, West Yorkshire*
Playing career: *Huddersfield Town, Bury, Wrexham, York City, Kilmarnock, Valur, Hyde, F.C. Halifax Town, Tamworth, Torquay United (2005-2016)*

Racchi came through the youth ranks at Town but was released in 2008 after only making a couple of substitute appearances for managers Peter Jackson and Andy Ritchie. He joined Bury and spent two years at Gigg Lane before short spells at Wrexham and York City before heading up to Scotland to play for Kilmarnock. After, two years at the club, Racchi left in 2013 and had later enjoyed short spells at Valur, Hyde, Halifax Town, Tamworth, Torquay United and finished his football career at F.C. United of Manchester in 2016. He now works as a hairdresser at Gary Pearce Men's Hair in Waterloo, Huddersfield, after a short time at a barbers in Oldham, and lives in Greetland.

Paul Rachubka

RACHUBKA, Paul

Goalkeeper
Town Years: 2004, 2004 (loan), 2004-2007
Born: *1981 San Luis Obispo, California, United States*
Playing career: *Manchester United, Huddersfield Town (loan), Blackpool, Leeds United, Oldham Athletic, Crewe A, Bolton W Bury (2000-2018)*

Rachubka arrived on loan from Charlton Athletic towards the end of the 2003-04 season where he was immediately installed as the first choice goalkeeper, replacing Phil Senior. He kept goal during the Play-off Final that season where Town triumphed over Mansfield Town at the Millennium Stadium but returned to the Addicks at the end of the season. Rachubka was loaned out to MK Dons and Northampton Town during the 2004-05 season before he returned to Town on loan during the same season. He only only played 3 matches before being signed permanently. Rachubka continued to be the number 1 until he lost his place in the side to Matt Glennon and he later joined Blackpool in 2007. He played over 100 matches for the club until his departure in 2011. The former England Under-20 keeper last played for Kerala Blasters but since 2019 has been working for EY in Manchester in the field of Personal Performance.

RAITT, George
Left-half
Town Years: 1911-1912
Born: *1880 Glasgow, Scotland*
Died: *1960 Sydney, Australia*
Playing career: *Shettleston, Cambuslang Rangers, Huddersfield Town (1909-1912)*

Raitt was a left-half that joined the club in 1911 and played 6 league games during the 1911-1912 season before being released at the end of the season. The Scotsman later emigrated to Sydney, Australia where he lived and worked before his death in 1960.

RANDALL, Charles
Half-back
Town Years: 1908-1910
Born: *1884 Bearpark, County Durham*
Died: *1916 Killed in Action*
Playing career: *Hobson Wanderers, Newcastle United, Huddersfield Town, Castleford Town (loan), Woolwich Arsena, North Shields Athletic (1908-1914)*

Randall was part of the Town side that played its first ever season as a club, albeit an amateur club, and Randall was actually a Newcastle United player but played for Town as an amateur, including 2 appearances in the FA Cup. After Town turned professional in 1910, Randall left for Castleford Town and later played for Woolwich Arsenal. He went to War in 1914 and he was a Private in the Coldstream Guards and died in action in September 1916. Private Randall is buried at Dantzig Alley British Cemetery in Mametz.

RANKIN, Andrew 'Andy'
Goalkeeper
Town Years: 1979-1982
Born: *1944 Bootle, Lancashire*
Playing career: *Everton, Watford, Huddersfield Town (1963-1982)*

Rankin signed from Watford as a 36 year old as cover for the injured Alan Starling and ended up playing for the rest of the 1979-80 promotion season. He made the No. 1 jersey his own and played two more years before retiring from the game in 1982 and later found work tarmacking roads, driving a mobile clinic and then worked as a forklift truck driver at a printers in Denby Dale for 18 years. Rankin is now retired and living in Thongsbridge and his 1979-80 medal has been on exhibition at Town's training ground complex, Canalside.

RAW, Henry 'Harry'
Inside-forward
Town Years: 1923-1931
Born: *1903 Tow Law, County Durham*
Died: *1965 Tow Law, County Durham*
Playing career: *Tow Law Town, Huddersfield Town, West Bromwich Albion, Lincoln City (1923-1938)*

Raw signed from Tow Law Town in 1923 and played during the third championship winning season in 1925-26, under Cecil Potter, and also in the 1930 FA Cup Final under Clem Stephenson. Just a year later, Raw left in 1931 to sign for West Bromwich Albion and later played for Lincoln City and Spennymoor United. After his career in football came to an end, Raw later worked as a grocer's assistant in Durham before working in the steelworks in the North East. He had a spell as manager of Crook Town in the 1940s before he passed away in 1965.

RAWLINGS, James 'Sid'
Outside-right
Town Years: 1934-1935
Born: *1913 Wombwell, West Riding of Yorkshire*
Died: *1956 Penarth, Wales*
Playing career: *Preston North End, Huddersfield Town, WBA, Northampton Town, Millwall, Everton, Plymouth Argyle, Tavistock (1931-1948)*

Rawlings signed from Preston North End in 1934 and managed a handful of games in the first team before leaving the following year for a one year stay at West Bromwich Albion in 1935. Before the outbreak of World War Two, Rawlings had spells with Northampton Town and Millwall and resumed his football career in 1946, where he turned out for Plymouth Argyle for two years before retiring from the game after a spell at Tavistock in 1948. Rawlings later played local football for Tavistock before managing them and passed away in 1956 after suffering from leukemia.

RAY, Richard 'Dick'
Full-back
Town Years: 1908-1909
Born: *1876 Ruth Lane, Staffordshire*
Died: *1952 Leeds, West Riding of Yorkshire*
Playing career: *Macclesfield, Burslem Port Vale, Crewe Alexandra, Macclesfield, Manchester City, Coventry City, Stockport County, Chesterfield, Leeds City, Huddersfield Town (1893-1909)*

After a long career in the Football League, Ray arrived at Leeds Road in 1908 from

Leeds City and played a number of games during the Town's first season as a club. He left at the end of the 1908-09 season and worked as a fruit salesman in Leeds after his retirement as a player and also went on to serve in the First World War in the Royal Army Service Corps. In 1919, he was invited to become a member of the original committee that was elected to manage the new Leeds United club after the expulsion of Leeds City. Ray became the club's first manager until 1920 and then became assistant manager until 1923 when he left to manage Doncaster Rovers and spent four years in South Yorkshire before he returned to Leeds after Fairclough's resignation in 1927. He spent another eight years at Elland Road before resigning in March 1935 and becoming manager of Bradford City in April of the same year. Ray lasted until his resignation in 1937 and after his spell at Valley Parade he later worked as Millwall's chief scout and also ran a garage business and a number of billiard clubs in Leeds before passing away at the age of 76 in December 1952.

RAYNOR, Paul
Forward
Town Years: 1985-1987
Born: *1966 Nottingham, Nottinghamshire*
Playing career: *Nottingham Forest, Bristol Rovers (loan), Huddersfield Town, Swansea City, Wrexham (loan) , Cambridge United, Preston North End, Guangdong Hongyuan, Leyton Orient, Kettering Town, Ilkeston Town, Boston United, King's Lynn, Hednesford Town, Gainsborough Trinity, Ossett Albion, King's Lynn, Crawley Town (1984-2009)*
Raynor began his career at Nottingham Forest before Mick Buxton signed him in 1985, and he spent two years at the club, playing over 50 games. He left for Swansea City in 1987, his time there spanning five years and over 200 first team appearances and also had a spell at Cambridge United between 1992 and 1993 before two years at Preston North End. Raynor re-signed for Cambridge in 1995 before again leaving the club in 1997 and following this, he then embarked on a long career in the lower leagues including spells at Leyton Orient, Kettering Town, Ilkeston Town and Boston United before he became player-manager of Hednesford Town in 2001. He left the same year and had further spells at Ossett Albion

and Gainsborough Trinity before he was appointed assistant manager to Steve Evans at Boston United in 2004. Raynor later took charge of the team when Evans was sacked in 2006 and he later followed Evans to Crawley Town in 2007, remaining until they both moved to Rotherham United in 2012. He has since acted as assistant manager to Evans at Leeds United and Mansfield Town was lastly assistant manager to Evans at Peterborough United before being sacked in 2019.

REDFERN, Levi
Half-back
Town Years: 1927-1932
Born: *1905 Burton upon Trent, Staffordshire*
Died: *1976 Ferndown, Dorset*
Playing career: *Bolton Albion, Conisbrough Discharged Soldiers, Denaby United, York City, Huddersfield Town, Bradford City, Rochdale, Sheffield United (1923-1935)*
Redfern joined the club in May 1927, signing from York City, and spent five years at Leeds Road, playing over 50 games in the first team before leaving for Bradford City in December 1932. He left Valley Parade in 1934 and signed for Rochdale in September 1934 and spent a year at the club before he signed for Sheffield United in August 1935. After just 2 appearances in the first team at Bramall Lane, Redfern retired and later worked as a schoolteacher and had a lifelong interest in horseracing, owning a number of racehorses before he passed away in 1976.

REID, Robert 'Bob'
Full-back
Town Years: 1914-1919
Born: *1889 Newtongrange, Midlothian, Scotland*
Died: *1964 Lasswade, Midlothian, Scotland*
Playing career: *Newtongrange Star, Heart of Midlothian, Cowdenbeath, Burnley, Huddersfield Town, Southend United (1906-1921)*
Bob Reid joined Town in 1914 from Burnley and played during the 1914-15 season, usually at right-back but on occasion at left-back. After the suspension of league football in 1915, Reid never played another game at Leeds Road and after League football resumed in 1919, he signed for Southend United, where he played until 1921. The Scotsman passed away in 1964.

REID, Francis 'Frank'

Inside-forward
Town Years: 1946-1949
Born: *1920 Mauchline, Scotland*
Died: *1970 unknown*
Playing career: *Cumnock Juniors, Huddersfield Town, Stockport County, Mossley (1946-1951)*

Reid signed from Cumnock Juniors in 1946 and played a couple of games for the first team before joining Stockport County in 1949. He spent two years at Stockport before leaving professional football and turning out for for non-league Mossley and Stalybridge Celtic. The Scotsman passed away in 1970.

REID, Paul

Midfielder
Town Years: 1994-1997
Born: *1968 Oldbury, Worcestershire*
Playing career: *Leicester City, Bradford City (loan), Bradford City, Huddersfield Town, Oldham Athletic, Bury, Swansea City (1986-2005)*

Reid signed from Bradford City in 1994 and was immediately picked for the first team and scored two goals in the opening 4-2 win over Blackpool in the 1994-95 season. After Phil Starbuck left the club, Reid was installed as captain of the side although he was injured towards the end of the season and missed the playoffs, which Town won. He remained at the club until 1997 until he signed for Neil Warnock at Oldham Athletic and then followed Warnock to Bury in 1999, playing for three years and making over 100 first team appearances. Reid had a one year spell at Swansea City before heading into the Welsh League to play for Carmarthern Town and later Afan Lido. He later coached Port Talbot Town and had a spell as manager of former club Afan Lido but is now currently coaching at Swansea City's academy.

Jordan Rhodes

RHODES, Jordan

Forward
Town Years: 2009-2012
Born: *1990 Oldham, Lancashire*
Playing career: *Ipswich Town, Huddersfield Town, Blackburn Rovers, Middlesbrough, Sheffield Wednesday, Norwich City (loan) (2007-Still Playing)*

Rhodes was signed by Lee Clark at the beginning of the 2009-10 season and made an immediate impact by scoring on his debut. He was top scorer for each of his three seasons at Town including 40 in the 2011-12 promotion season but he later forced a move to Blackburn Rovers in 2012 and was sold to the club for £8 million. Rhodes left Ewood Park in 2015 and after spells at Middlesbrough and Sheffield Wednesday. He is now playing for Norwich City, on loan from the Owls.

RICHARDS, Ashley 'Jazz'

Left-back
Town Years: 2013 (loan)
Born: *1991 Swansea, Wales*
Playing career: *Swansea City, Crystal Palace (loan), Huddersfield Town (loan), Fulham (loan), Fulham, Cardiff City (2009-Still Playing)*

Richards arrived on loan from Swansea City during the 2013-14 season and played a few matches at left-back before returning to his parent club. He signed for Fulham in 2015 and spent a year at Craven Cottage before signing for Cardiff City in 2016.

RICHARDSON, George E

Outside-right
Town Years: 1914-1923
Born: *1891 Seaham, County Durham*
Died: *1969 Huddersfield, West Riding of Yorkshire*
Playing career: *Huddersfield Town, Hull City, Hartlepools United, Lancaster Town (1910-1928)*

Richardson began his professional career at Town in 1914 but his first four years coincided with the First World War. Richardson remained in Huddersfield after his career ended and worked as a billiard hall manager. He also worked as trainer at Town in 1946 for the Yorkshire League team and was appointed assistant trainer to the first team in November 1955. Richardson later became licensee of the Red Lion in Lockwood. Passed away in 1969 at the age of 68 and was still living in Huddersfield at the time of his death.

RICHARDSON, George

Centre-forward
Town Years: 1933-1934
Born: *1912 Worksop, Nottinghamshire*
Died: *1968 Worksop, Nottinghamshire*
Playing career: *Huddersfield Town, Sheffield United, Hull City, Bangor City (1931-1948)*

Richardson began his professional career at Town in 1933 and played 1 game for Clem Stephenson's side. He later played for Sheffield United and Hull City for ten years. Later returned to his native Worksop and worked as Worksop Town's manager in 1961. Died in 1968.

RICHARDSON, James 'Jimmy'

Centre-forward
Town Years: 1910-1912
Born: *1885 Glasgow, Scotland*
Died: *1951 Cathcart, Scotland*
Playing career: *Huddersfield Town, Sheffield Wednesday, Sunderland, Ayr United, Partick Thistle (loan), Millwall (1904-1922)*

Richardson signed in 1910 from Third Lanark and managed 24 league goals in 42 league games over the next two seasons before headed off to Sunderland. Later played for Ayr United before being posted to France to fight for his country. He returned to the UK in 1918 with stomach troubles but this did not stop him signing for Millwall in 1921 and spent a year at The Den before he retired from professional football in 1922. After his retirement, Richardson became the Ayr United manager in 1923 but left a year later to join Cowdenbeath in the top job. Although he was popular at Cowdenbeath, he resigned in 1925. Richardson was still seen on occasion at Ayr United as a supporter and was spotted at a game just a few months before his death in August 1951.

"DID YOU KNOW?"

"A total of 8 managers have achieved promotion in the club's history. They are; Ambrose Langley (1920), Andy Beattie (1953), Ian Greaves (1970), Mick Buxton (1980 and 1983), Neil Warnock (1995), Peter Jackson (2004), Simon Grayson (2012) and David Wagner (2017)."

RICHARDSON, James 'Jimmy'

Inside-forward
Town Years: 1934-1937
Born: *1911 Ashington, Northumberland*
Died: *1964 Bexley, Kent*
Playing career: *Blyth Spartans, Newcastle United, Huddersfield Town, Newcastle United, Millwall, Leyton Orient (player-coach) (1925-1948)*

After playing for Newcastle United, Richardson signed for Town in 1934 and played in the first team at Leeds Road for three years and over 120 appearances before he rejoined former club Newcastle for a short spell in 1937. He transferred to Millwall in the same year, remaining on the books until 1946, but only managing around 55 appearances due to the outbreak of World War Two in 1939. Richardson had a short spell at Leyton Orient in 1948 as player-coach before he retired from professional football and became the assistant trainer at the club. He was later promoted to trainer in 1951 and remained in the role until 1955, before becoming Millwall's assistant trainer in 1956 before he retired on health grounds. Ashington-born Richardson passed away at the age of 53 in 1964.

RICHARDSON, Lee

Midfielder
Town Years: 1997-2000
Born: *1969 Halifax, West Riding of Yorkshire*
Playing career: *Halifax Town, Watford, Blackburn Rovers, Aberdeen, Oldham Athletic, Huddersfield Town, Chesterfield (1987-2004)*

Originally from Halifax, Richardson signed from Oldham Athletic in 1997 but over his three years at the club, Richardson only managed around 40 appearances before leaving in 2000. He had a short spell at Livingston before signing for Chesterfield where he spent four years including a spell as caretaker manager in 2003. The Yorkshireman is now a qualified psychologist. He studied a Bachelor's Degree in Psychology at the Open University between 1997 and 2004 and then a Master's degree in Sports and Exercise Psychology between 2012 and 2015. He has since founded his own company, AIM For and has also worked at West Ham United, Crystal Palace, Wigan Athletic and the England U21s but now combines roles as a psychologist at both Hull City and Lancashire C.C.C. and lives in his hometown of Halifax.

RICHARDSON, George Edward 'Ted'

Winger
Town Years: 1923-1924
Born: *1901 Easington, County Durham*
Died: *unknown*
Playing career: *Easington Colliery Welfare, South Shields, Newcastle United, Huddersfield Town, Sheffield Wednesday, South Shields, York City, Bradford City, Easington Colliery Welfare, Ashington, Whitburn, Easington Colliery Welfare (1919-1933)*

After a spell at Newcastle United, Richardson went South and signed for Herbert Chapman's Town side in 1923. He only managed 6 appearances for the first team before he left in 1924 and later enjoyed short spells at Sheffield Wednesday, South Shields and York City before signing for Bradford City in 1926. Richardson spent two years at Valley Parade before leaving professional football and turning out for Easington Colliery, Ashington and Whitburn in non-league.

RICHMOND ROOSE, Leigh

Goalkeeper
Town Years: 1911 (amateur)
Born: *1877 Holt, Wales*
Died: *1916 Killed in Action*
Playing career: *UCW Aberystwyth, Aberystwyth Town, Druids, London Welsh, Stoke, Everton, Stoke, Sunderland, Celtic, Port Vale, Huddersfield Town, Aston Villa, Woolwich Arsenal, Aberystwyth Town, Llandudno Town (1895-1914)*

After a long career in English football, Roose arrived at Leeds Road in 1910 and played 5 games in goal during the 1910-11 season before he left the club for Aston Villa. He also played for Woolwich Arsenal and drifted into the Welsh leagues. When the First World War broke out in 1914, Roose joined up and served in the Royal Army Medical Corps in France and Gallipoli. He enlisted as a private of the Royal Fusiliers in 1916 and served on the Western Front and it is quite fitting that his goalkeeping abilities helped him become a noted grenade thrower. Roose was awarded the Military Medal for bravery and was later promoted to the rank of lance corporal before he was killed near the end of the Battle of the Somme. His body has never been recovered and his name appears on the War Memorial to missing soldiers at Thiepval.

RIDEHALGH, Liam

Left-back
Town Years: 2009-2014
Born: *1991 Halifax, West Yorkshire*
Playing career: *Huddersfield Town, Swindon Town (loan), Chesterfield (loan), Rotherham United (loan), Tranmere Rovers (loan), Tranmere Rovers (2009-Still Playing)*

Ridehalgh began his career in the youth team at Town and turned professional in 2009. He broke into the first team during the 2010-11 season and impressed with his performances at left-back before being struck down with glandular fever. Ridehalgh never regained his place in the first team and he left the club in 2014 after loan spells at Swindon Town, Chesterfield, Rotherham United and Tranmere Rovers before he made the move to Tranmere permanent in 2014.

RIPLEY, Keith

Winger
Town Years: 1978-1979
Born: *1954 Normanton, West Riding of Yorkshire*
Playing career: *Huddersfield Town, Doncaster Rovers, Gainsborough Trinity (1978-1980)*

Ripley signed from Gainsborough Trinity in 1978 and played a few matches for Tom Johnston's side but after Johnston's resignation, coach Mick Buxton was appointed manager and he deemed Ripley surplus to requirements which prompted a move to Doncaster Rovers in 1979. Ripley is now an independent financial advisor from his base in Pontefract.

RITCHIE, Andrew 'Andy'

Manager
Town Years: 2007-2008
Born: *1960 Manchester, Lancashire*
Management career: *Oldham Athletic, Barnsley, Huddersfield Town (1998-2008)*

After the sacking of Peter Jackson, the board of directors agreed terms with Phil Parkinson but he dropped out at the last minute and Ritchie was appointed towards the end of the 2006-07 season. Ritchie had an unspectacular spell in charge of the club and was sacked on April Fool's Day 2008, quite fitting for a man who spent most of his time at the club leaning on the dugout looking out of his depth. He has since worked on MUTV and as a match summariser for BBC Radio Leeds.

Gary Roberts

However, Neil Warnock didn't rate him and he was soon off-loaded to Leicester City in 1993. Roberts signed for Norwich City in 1997, starting a seven year association with the East Anglian club where he became a firm fan's favourite. He now does media work, including the Welsh language commentary for Sky Sports and Radio Cymru. He also works for BBC Wales and still lives in Norwich.

ROBINS, Ian
Forward
Town Years: 1978-1982
Born: *1952 Bury, Lancashire*
Playing career: *Oldham Athletic, Bury, Huddersfield Town (1969-1982)*

Ian Robins signed in 1978 from Bury and was converted back to his original position as a centre forward by manager, Mick Buxton. He was top scorer in the 1979-80 promotion season and managed to score the 100th and 101st goals of the season in the final game against Hartlepool United, which secured the Fourth Division title. He has since run a newsagent's, managed the sales team at Port Petroleum and run a pub in Wigan, where he still lives. Robins comes to watch Town when he is available and was present at Wembley when Town clinched promotion to the Premier League in 2017.

ROBERTS, Gareth 'Gary'
Winger
Town Years: 2008-2012
Born: *1984 Liverpool, Merseyside*
Playing career: *Liverpool, Denbigh Town, Bala Town, Rhyl, Bangor City, Welshpool Town, Accrington Stanley, Ipswich Town (loan), Ipswich Town, Crewe Alexandra (loan), Huddersfield Town, Swindon Town, Chesterfield, Portsmouth, Wigan Athletic (2000-Still Playing)*

Stan Ternent brought Roberts to Town at the beginning of the 2008-09 season and was a mainstay in the team until his departure in 2012 to Swindon Town. The popular Scouser signed for Chesterfield in 2013 and then helped Portsmouth win promotion to Div 1. He spent two years at Portsmouth before following manager Paul Cook to Wigan Athletic in 2017.

ROBERTS, Iwan
Forward
Town Years: 1990-1993
Born: *1968 Bangor, Wales*
Playing career: *Watford, Huddersfield Town, Leicester City, Wolves, Norwich City, Gillingham, Cambridge United (loan) (1986-2005)*

Roberts arrived at Leeds Road in 1990, although he wasn't popular to begin with, he managed to win over the supporters after scoring 35 goals in the 1991-92 season.

Ian Robins

ROBINS, Mark
Manager
Town Years: 2013-2014
Born: *1969 Ashton-under-Lyne, Lancashire*
Management career: *Rotherham United, Barnsley, Coventry City, Huddersfield Town, Scunthorpe United, Coventry City (2007-present)*
Robins arrived in 2013 from Coventry City to replace the sacked Simon Grayson. He managed to keep the club in the Championship on the last day of the 2012-13 season. He resigned after the first game of the 2014-15 season after a humiliating opening day battering by Bournemouth, who put four goals past the hapless Terriers. He later became manager of Scunthorpe United in 2014 but has managed Coventry City since 2017.

ROBINSON, Anton
Midfielder
Town Years: 2011-2014
Born: *1986 Harrow, Greater London*
Playing career: *Millwall, Exeter City, Eastbourne Borough, Fisher Athletic, Grays Athletic, Weymouth, Bournemouth, Huddersfield Town, Gillingham (loan), Coventry City (loan) (2004-2014)*
After impressing Lee Clark in performances for AFC Bournemouth, Robinson was signed at the beginning of the 2011-12 season. Since being released by Town, Robinson has invested in a number of companies and has been a scout at former club, Bournemouth since 2016.

ROBINSON, Frederick 'Fred'
Left-back
Town Years: 1979-1982
Born: *1954 Rotherham, West Riding of Yorkshire*
Playing career: *Rotherham United, Doncaster Rovers, Huddersfield Town (1973-1982)*
Fred Robinson signed for Town in 1979 from Doncaster Rovers and was immediately installed as the first choice left-back in Mick Buxton's side. He did make a recovery but couldn't get back into the side due to the performances of Bernard Purdie. However, the following season Robinson played almost every game but was forced to retire in 1982 due to a knee injury sustained in a testimonial. The Rotherham born defender then worked at engineering firm Holsets for over 20 years before retiring but still lives in Huddersfield and is a regular at Town home games.

ROBINSON, Jack
Defender
Town Years: 2014-2015 (loan)
Born: *1993 Warrington, Merseyside*
Playing career: *Liverpool, Queens Park Rangers, Huddersfield Town (loan), Nottingham Forest (2010-Still Playing)*
Robinson joined on loan during the 2014-15 season from his parent club Queens Park Rangers before returning towards the end of the season. He remained with QPR until 2018, when he signed for Nottingham Forest.

ROBINSON, Liam
Forward
Town Years: 1982-1986
Born: *1965 Bradford, West Riding of Yorkshire*
Playing career: *Nottingham Forest, Huddersfield Town, Bury, Bristol City, Burnley (1982-2004)*
Robinson began his career at Town in 1982 and spent four years on the books at Leeds Road before he left in 1986 to sign for Bury. He later played for Burnley, Bristol City, Tranmere Rovers and Scarborough and later went into non-league. Robinson now runs his own tree surgeon business, A Cut Above and is based in Bolster Moor, Huddersfield.

Fred Robinson

ROBINSON, Philip 'Phil'
Midfielder
Town Years: 1992-1994
Born: *1967 Stafford, Staffordshire*
Playing career: *Aston Villa, Wolverhampton Wanderers, Notts County, Huddersfield Town, Chesterfield, Notts County, Stoke City (1985-2007)*
Robinson arrived at Leeds Road in 1992. He played over 70 matches for the club, including the final game at Leeds Road and the 1994 Autoglass Final. The former Aston Villa junior left the club in 1994 to join Chesterfield and later had spells with former club Notts County, Stoke City and Hereford United before signing for Stafford Rangers in 2000. He later became their manager and coached at Cheltenham Town before joining Birmingham City to oversee recruitment in the academy. A return to first club Aston Villa to work as Head of Talent Identification followed but Phil is now working at Manchester City as International Youth Scouting and Recruitment Manager.

ROBINSON, Reginald 'Reg'
Defender
Town Years: 1933-1935
Born: *1910 Sheffield, West Riding of Yorkshire*
Died: *1993 Scunthorpe, Lincolnshire*
Playing career: *Scunthorpe United, Huddersfield Town, Exeter City, Watford (1933-1939)*
Robinson had a spell at Scunthorpe United before signing for Town in 1933 and he only played 2 first team matches before he left in 1935. He later played for Exeter City and Watford before his career was interrupted by World War Two. Robinson later returned to Scunthorpe to work at a steel plate mill in the area. Died in 1993 at the age of 83.

"DID YOU KNOW?"

"Despite appearing at Wembley in seven finals, only four Town players have scored at the national stadium. They are; Alec Jackson (1928), Richard Logan (1994), Andy Booth (1995) and Chris Billy (1995). Town also played a league game at Wembley in 2018 against Tottenham Hotspur but failed to find the scoresheet."

ROBINSON, Ronald 'Ronnie'
Defender
Town Years: 1994 (loan)
Born: *1966 Sunderland, County Durham*
Playing career: *Ipswich Town, Leeds United, Doncaster Rovers, West Bromwich Albion, Rotherham United, Peterborough United, Exeter City, Huddersfield Town (loan), S(1984-1995)*
Robinson signed on loan from Exeter City in 1994 but only managed 2 games for Neil Warnock's side before he returned to his parent club. Since his retirement as a player, Robinson has been working as a car salesman and was last known to be working for Mercedes Benz in Stockton.

ROBINSON, Theo
Forward
Town Years: 2009-2011, 2013 (loan)
Born: *1989 Birmingham, West Midlands*
Playing career: *Watford, Millwall, Derby County (loan), Derby County, Huddersfield Town (loan), Doncaster Rovers, Motherwell, Port Vale, Lincoln City, Southend United (2006-Still Playing)*
Lee Clark brought Robinson to the club in 2009 and he managed 16 goals in 45 appearances before joining Millwall in 2011. He then played for Derby County between 2011 and 2013 (including spending a time on loan at Town under Mark Robins) before eventually signing for Doncaster Rovers. The Brummie played for Motherwell and Lincoln City before signing for former club Southend United in 2017.

ROBSON, James 'Jimmy'
Reserve Team Manager, Coach, Caretaker Manager
Town Years: 1979-1988 (coach), 1987 (caretaker)
Born: *1939 Pelton, County Durham*
Mick Buxton brought former teammate Jimmy Robson to the club as Reserve Team Coach in 1979 and he remained at the club throughout the reign of Mick Buxton and when Steve Smith became manager in 1986, Robson worked as his assistant manager and coach. He remained as a coach under next manager Malcolm Macdonald but was sacked by Eoin Hand in 1988, just before what would have been his testimonial year at Leeds Road. After leaving Town, Robson worked as head of youth development at Rochdale and also at Burnley's Centre of Excellence and has remained in Burnley and now lives there in retirement.

ROBSON, Joseph 'Joe'

Forward
Town Years: 1930-1932
Born: *1903 Gateshead, County Durham*
Died: *1969 Bradford, West Riding of Yorkshire*
Playing career: *Craghead United, Saltwell Villa, Grimsby Town, Huddersfield Town, Bradford Park Avenue, Gainsborough Trinity, Nuneaton Town, Burton Town (1922-c1936)*

Robson joined from Grimsby Town in 1930, playing over 30 games before leaving in 1932. Bradford Park Avenue, Gainsborough Trinity, Nuneaton Town and Burton Town were his clubs prior to retiring from the game in the late 1930s. Robson remained in Bradford with his wife Alice and worked as a boiler engineer. Also ran a poultry farm before he passed away in 1969.

RODGERS, Arnold

Centre-forward
Town Years: 1942-1949
Born: *1923 Rotherham, West Riding of Yorkshire*
Died: *1993 Bristol*
Playing career: *Wickersley, Huddersfield Town, Bristol City, Shrewsbury Town (1946-1956)*

Before his career in football, Rodgers was an apprentice draughtsman. He signed for Town in 1942, turning professional in 1946. The Rortherham born striker knocked in 17 league goals in 28 league matches before heading to Bristol City in 1950 and went on to spend six years at Ashton Gate, playing over 200 games and scoring over 100 goals. Rodgers had a short spell at Shrewsbury Town in 1956 before retiring from the game and working as manager at Welton Rovers and Bath City. Passed away in 1993 in Bristol.

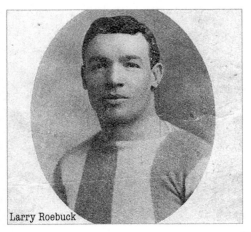

Larry Roebuck

RODGERSON, Ralph

Full-back
Town Years: 1913-1921
Born: *1893 Sunderland, County Durham*
Died: *1939 Durham, County Durham*
Playing career: *Pallion Institute, Seaham Harbour, Burnley, Huddersfield Town, Leeds United, Dundee, Spennymoor United, Carlisle United, Spennymoor United, Sunderland West End, Hetton United, Thornley Albion (1912-c1931)*

Rodgerson arrived at the club in 1913 from Burnley but his playing career was interrupted by the outbreak of World War One. He did eventually make his professional debut for the club during the 1919-20 season but did play in the Wartime League at Leeds Road as well. Rodgerson left in 1921 to join nearby Leeds United, where he lasted for just a year. Later played for Dundee, Spennymoor United and Carlisle United. Rodgerson passed away in early 1939 just before the outbreak of World War Two.

ROEBUCK, Larrett 'Larry'

Left-back
Town Years: 1913-1914
Born: *1889 Jump, West Riding of Yorkshire*
Died: *1914 Killed in Action*
Playing career: *Silverwood Colliery, Huddersfield Town (1912-1914)*

Larrett Roebuck joined Town in 1913 from Silverwood Colliery but only managed a handful of appearances before the First World War broke out in 1914. Roebuck was called up to fight but was later killed in action, becoming the first player from the Football League to perish during the First World War. Lance-Corporal Roebuck was one of forty men that were listed as killed or missing in action near Beaucamps-Ligny following an attack on an enemy position. Town had been sending Roebuck's wife Marie £1 a week since he had been called up but Arthur Fairclough wrote to her on 26 February 1915 to inform her that the club would have to cease payments due to the club's weak financial state. He told Marie in his letter that the club would grant her ten shillings a week for four weeks and also forwarded £2 and five shillings that had been collected from the players. Larrett Roebuck's remains have never been found.

ROSS, Ian
Assistant manager, Manager
Town Years: 1991-1992 (assistant manager), 1992-1993 (manager)
Born: 1947 Glasgow, Scotland
Management career: Valur, KR Reykjavik, Huddersfield Town, Keflavik, Berwick Rangers (1985-1996)

Ian Ross joined the club during the 1990-91 season as Eoin Hand's assistant, after the departure of Peter Withe. and he later took over the manager's role in March 1992 after Hand was sacked due to poor results. Town reached the play-offs under Ross but lost in the semi-final to Peterborough United. However, the following season saw his side languishing in the drop zone before Mick Buxton was brought in as First Team Coach in early 1993. Buxton's appointment coincided with Town moving up the division and avoiding relegation with games to spare. Ross later left in 1993 after Mick Buxton's decision to leave the club and he later managed in Iceland before settling back in Lancashire where he enjoyed retirement and watched Liverpool regularly. Passed away in February 2019 after a short illness.

ROUGHTON, William 'George'
Full-back
Town Years: 1928-1936
Born: 1909 Manchester, Lancashire
Died: 1989 Southampton, Hampshire
Playing career: Droylsden, Huddersfield Town, Manchester United, Exeter City (player-manager) (1928-1945)

After beginning his career at his local club, Droylsden, Roughton signed for Town in 1928 and played at full-back, helping Town to second place in the 1933-34 season. He left for Manchester United in 1936, but only managed less than 100 appearances in nine years due to the outbreak of World War Two in 1939. After the War, Roughton took the manager's job at Exeter City and although he didn't really achieve any success in terms of trophies, he managed to keep them in the Third Division (South) throughout his seven years at the club. He became the manager of Southampton in 1952, remaining for three years before he was asked to resign by the board. After leaving The Dell, Roughton worked part-time for the Hampshire F.A. Died in 1989.

ROWE, Rodney
Forward
Town Years: 1993-1997
Born: 1975 Huddersfield, West Yorkshire
Playing career: Huddersfield Town, Scarborough (loan), Bury (loan), York City, Halifax Town (loan), Gillingham, Hull City (1993-2006)

Rowe began his career at his hometown club and played for us until 1997, when he joined York City. He spent two years with the Minstermen, playing over a hundred games for the club. He then spent two years at Gillingham before leaving for Hull City in 2002 and after only one year in Humberside, Rowe left the club and spent the rest of his career in non-league turning out for clubs such as Wakefield and Emley, Ashton United, Ossett Town, Farsley Celtic and Bradford Park Avenue. He has since worked at Reinwood Junior School as a learning mentor and has coached football locally for many years including at Dalton Dynamoes and DRAM Community.

ROWLEY, Jack
Half-back
Town Years: 1909-1910
Born: 1885
Died: unknown
Playing career: Bolton Wanderers, Huddersfield Town (1909-1910)

Rowley signed for Fred Walker's side in 1909 after a spell at Bolton Wanderers and played 5 FA Cup games for the club as well as 17 Midland League appearances during 1909-10. Rowley later worked as trainer.

RUDGE, Andrew 'Andy'
Midfielder, Assistant Trainer
Town Years: 1908-1910
Born: Circa 1879 Egremont, Cheshire
Died: 1950 Birkenhead, Cheshire
Playing career: Huddersfield Town (1908-1910)

Rudge had been playing for Mirfield United before he signed for the club in 1908 and made 1 appearance during the 1908-09 season. He was also the Assistant Trainer at Leeds Road until the end of the 1910-11 season as well as working as the groundsman at Leeds Road before he later took as a job as a chemical worker near his home in Mirfield. Rudge is thought to have passed away in 1950 whilst living in Birkenhead, Cheshire.

RUDGE, John
Forward
Town Years: 1960-1966
Born: *1944 Wolverhampton, Staffordshire*
Playing career: *Wolverhampton Wanderers, Huddersfield Town, Carlisle United, Torquay United, Bristol Rovers, Bournemouth (1960-1977)*

Rudge began his career at Leeds Road as an apprentice, later signing professional forms, but only made a couple of appearances for Eddie Boot's side and ended up moving on to Carlisle United in 1966. He remained in Cumbria until 1969 before he left for Torquay United. Played for Bristol Rovers and Bournemouth before retiring in 1977. Rudge was given the Port Vale manager's job in 1983 and managed the Valiants for sixteen years before being controversially sacked in 1999. Upon his departure from Vale Park, Rudge was offered the role of Director of Football at the club but he turned them down and took the same role at rivals Stoke City. He was suspended twice during his fourteen year spell at Stoke due to fallouts with managers and eventually left the post in May 2013. Rudge later scouted for Hull City but is now back working at Port Vale as Director of Football alongside manager and former Port Vale player, Neil Aspin.

RUSSELL, Colin
Forward
Town Years: 1982-1984
Born: *1961 Liverpool, Lancashire*
Playing career: *Liverpool, Huddersfield Town, Stoke City (loan), Bournemouth, Doncaster Rovers, Scarborough, Wigan Athletic, (1977-1990)*

Russell began his career at hometown club Liverpool but only made a single professional appearance before Mick Buxton brought him to the club in 1982. He spent two years at Leeds Road, playing 81 matches and scoring an impressive 25 goals in the process. After a loan spell at Stoke City during the 1983-84 season, Russell signed for Bournemouth and spent two years at Dean Court before returning to the North and signing for Doncaster Rovers in 1986. He later left the club to sign for Scarborough in 1988 and later played for Wigan Athletic, Colne Dynamoes, Bangor City, Morecambe, Droylsden and Warrington Town all in non-league. The Liverpudlian is now believed to be living in his native Liverpool and runs a double glazing business.

RYAN, Robert 'Robbie'
Left-back
Town Years: 1994-1998
Born: *1977 Dublin, Republic of Ireland*
Playing career: *Huddersfield Town, Millwall, Bristol Rovers (1993-2008)*

Ryan began his career at Town in 1994, after playing in the youth team. After four years, he left the club in 1998 to sign for Millwall, after being deemed surplus to requirements by Peter Jackson. Ryan played for the Lions for six years and perhaps most famously played in the 2004 FA Cup Final for the club, where he was marking Manchester United's Cristiano Ronaldo. Ryan left the club shortly afterwards and signed for Bristol Rovers, playing for the Gas for three years until his departure in 2007. He had short spells at non-league clubs Welling United, Ashford Town, Fisher Athletic and Croydon Athletic before calling time on his career for good. Ryan has since coached at Millwall's academy and has worked as a cable linesman for London Underground.

SANDERCOCK, Philip 'Phil'
Defender
Town Years: 1977-1979
Born: *1953 Plymouth, Devon*
Playing career: *Torquay United, Huddersfield Town, Northampton Town, Nuneaton Borough (1969-1981)*

After eight years at Torquay United, Sandercock joined the club in 1977, playing two years in Town's back four. After being deemed surplus to requirements by Mick Buxton, Sandercock left Leeds Road in 1979 to sign for Northampton Town, remaining at the club until 1981. After a spell at Nuneaton Borough, he retired from football for good and has since changed his name to Phil Grant and moved to Milton Keynes, where he has worked at Tesco in the area.

"DID YOU KNOW?"

"A total of 7 managers have led the club to relegation. They are; Andy Beattie (1952 and 1956), Ian Greaves (1972 and 1973), Bobby Collins (1975), Malcolm Macdonald (1988), Lou Macari (2001), Mel Machin (2003) and Jan Siewert (2019)."

SAUNDERS, John

Centre-half
Town Years: 1972-1976
Born: *1950 Worksop, Nottinghamshire*
Died: *1998 Worksop, Nottinghamshire*
Playing career: *Mansfield Town, Huddersfield Town, Barnsley, Lincoln City, Doncaster Rovers (1969-1981)*
Saunders arrived in 1972 from his first club Mansfield and broke into Ian Greaves' side during the 1972-73 season, He retired from professional football in 1981 and later served as as Chairman of Worksop Town, and was also the owner of their Tigers Club but when they moved to a new ground in the town, he retained ownership of the old social club and ran it until his death in January 1998.

SAWARD, Patrick 'Pat'

Right-half
Town Years: 1961-1963
Born: *1928 Cobh, County Cork, Ireland*
Died: *2002 Newmarket, Suffolk*
Playing career: *Millwall, Aston Villa, Huddersfield Town (1951-1963)*
Pat Saward was coming to the end of his football career when he arrived at Leeds Road in 1961, but Town got two good years out of the veteran before he retired in 1963. He worked as Jimmy Hill's assistant manager at Coventry City during the late 1960s and became the manager of Brighton & Hove Albion in 1970, remaining for three years before getting the sack.

The Irishman later managed Al Nasr in Dubai but then left football to run a holiday business in Majorca although he returned to the UK and retired in Newmarket before he passed away in September 2002 after suffering from Alzheimer's disease.

SCANNELL, Sean

Winger
Town Years: 2012-2018
Born: *1990 Croydon, Greater London*
Playing career: *Crystal Palace, Huddersfield Town, Bradford City (2007-Still Playing)*
Simon Grayson brought 'Scanz' to the club in 2012 from Crystal Palace but was in and out of the team under managers Grayson and Mark Robins. The appointment of Chris Powell changed this and Scannell impressed with his performances but unfortunately suffered an injury halfway through the 2016-17 promotion season and apart from one appearance in 2017-18, never played for the club again. He left in the pre-season of 2018-19 to sign for local rivals Bradford City.

SCHOFIELD, Daniel 'Danny'

Winger
Town Years: 1998-2008
Born: *1980 Doncaster, South Yorkshire*
Playing career: *Huddersfield Town, Yeovil Town, Millwall, Rotherham United, Accrington Stanley (loan), Stockport County (loan) (1997-2016)*
Schofield had been playing Brodsworth Miners Welfare before Peter Jackson paid them £2,000 and a set of goal nets for his services in 1998. He didn't make his debut until the final match of the 1998-99 season but he did eventually break into the first team in the 2001-02 season and was a regular up until his departure at the end of the 2007-08 season. Schofield was part of the 2003-04 promotion winning team, including scoring a vital penalty in the playoff semi-final and also in the shootout in the final. After ten years at the club, Schofield left for Yeovil Town in 2008. He has since had spells coaching at Barnsley and Bradford Park Avenue before he started working as an academy coach at Leeds United in December 2016. Schofield has been the Development Phase Coach at Elland Road since August 2017 and had been working as an estate agent before he graduated from Manchester Metropolitan University in July 2016 with a bachelor's degree in Sports Science.

SCOTT, Paul
Right-back
Town Years: 2002-2004
Born: *1979 Wakefield, West Yotkshire*
Playing career: *Huddersfield Town, Bury, Morecambe (1997-2012)*

Scott began his career in Town's academy in 1997 and eventually made his debut in the 2002-03 season, he played a number of matches during that season and also a couple in the following season which saw Town promoted in 2003-04. Wakefield-born Scott left the Galpharm Stadium at the end of the 2003-04 season season to join Bury and remained at Gigg Lane for six years, playing over 200 matches for the Shakers. Scott later had a two year spell at Morecambe before he retired from professional football in 2012.

SCULLY, Patrick 'Pat'
Centre-half
Town Years: 1994 (loan), 1994-1996
Born: *1970 Dublin, Ireland*
Playing career: *Arsenal, Southend United, Huddersfield Town, Shelbourne, Shamrock Rovers, Drogheda United (1987-2003)*

Scully originally arrived on loan from Southend United towards the end of the 1993-94 season and signed permanently in time for the 1994-95 season, playing at centre-half in a partnership with Lee Sinnott during the promotion season. He left Town in 1996 after falling out of favour with Brian Horton and returned to Ireland to sign for Shelbourne, where he spent five years and then one with Shamrock Rovers in 2001. Scully later finished his career at Drogheda United in 2003 and went on to manage Kilkenny City in 2005, Shamrock Rovers between and finally Limerick between 2009 and 2012. The Irishman now works as a taxi driver in Castlegregory, Ireland.

Scott Sellars: Ex-footballer sentenced for death crash

🕐 10 January 2013   f 💬 y ✉ ≺ Share

Ex-professional footballer Scott Sellars has been sentenced after he fell asleep while driving his car and killed a motorcyclist.

Sellars, 47, who played for Newcastle and Blackburn, pleaded guilty to causing death by careless driving.

He was driving home from work after returning from Dubai, where he had been coaching Manchester City's youth team.

Sellars played for Blackburn, Newcastle and Bolton

SELLARS, Scott
Midfielder
Town Years: 1999-2002
Born: *1965 Sheffield, West Riding of Yorkshire*
Playing career: *Leeds United, Blackburn Rovers, Leeds United, Newcastle United, Bolton Wanderers, Huddersfield Town, Mansfield Town (1983-2003)*

Sellars had been playing for Bolton Wanderers when Steve Bruce brought him to the club in 1999 going on to spend two seasons before he left and spent a short time at Danish club AGF Aarhus in 2001. He retired from professional football in 2003 and worked as assistant manager to Lee Richardson at Chesterfield between before becoming Academy Coach at Manchester City's in 2009. The Yorkshireman is now Head of Academy Player Development at Molineux. In 2013 he escaped a jail sentence despite pleading guilty to causing an accident in which a motorcyclist died due to his careless driving.

SENIOR, Colin
Left-half
Town Years: 1945-1951
Born: *1927 Dewsbury, West Riding of Yorkshire*
Died: *2011 Leicester, Leicestershire*
Playing career: *Huddersfield Town, Accrington Stanley, Peterborough United (1945-1954)*

After a spell at Stocksbridge, Senior signed for Town in 1945 but didn't make a professional appearance until the 1950-51 season. Senior later played for Corby Town and Peterborough United before he left professional football in 1954. Died in 2011.

SENIOR, Michael
Midfielder
Town Years: 1999-2002
Born: *1981 Huddersfield, West Yorkshire*
Playing career: *Huddersfield Town, Wakefield & Emley, Halifax Town, Ossett Albion (1999-2004)*

Senior, brother of Phil, began his career at Town in the juniors before he made it into the first team squad during the 1999-2000 season. He only made a couple of appearances under Steve Bruce and Lou Macari before he was released at the end of the 2001-02 season by Macari. Senior then went into non-league and played for Wakefield & Emley, Halifax Town, Ossett Town and then Ossett Albion before hung up his boots in the early 2010s. He is still living in Huddersfield.

SENIOR, Philip 'Phil'

Goalkeeper
Town Years: 1999-2006
Born: *1982 Huddersfield, West Yorkshire*
Playing career: *Huddersfield Town, (1999-2006)*
Peter Jackson brought Senior into the first team squad for a game during the 1998-99 season but he didn't make make it off the bench and his professional debut didn't come until the 2002-03 season. After Ian Gray suffered an injury early on in 2003-04 season, Senior became the No. 1 but lost his place towards the end of the season when Paul Rachubka came in on loan. He remained at the club until his release in 2006 and later played for Northwich and Halifax Town. Senior has worked as a schoolteacher in Leeds for a number of years.

SHANKLY, William 'Bill'

Assistant Manager, Reserve Team Coach, Manager
Town Years: 1955-1956 (assistant manager and reserve team coach), 1956-1959 (manager)
Born: *1913 Glenbuck, Scotland*
Died: *1981 Liverpool, Merseyside*
Management career: *Carlisle U, Grimsby Town, Workington, Huddersfield , Liverpool (1949-1974)*
'Shanks' arrived at Leeds Road in 1955 to assist his former Preston teammate Andy Beattie and also took the reserve side between 1955 and 1956. He assumed the role of manager after Beattie's resignation in 1956 and after average seasons in the Second Division, Shankly left the club in 1959 to join fellow Second Division side Liverpool. He won the Second Division in 1962 and won three First Division titles with Liverpool in 1964, 1966 and 1973 and also won the FA Cup twice in 1965 and 1974 and the UEFA Cup in 1973. After those triumphs, Shankly retired in 1974 but had laid the foundations for the Liverpool team that went on to dominate Europe in the 1970s and 1980s. Shankly later regretted his retirement and would still turn up at Liverpool's training ground until being told he wasn't welcome. Later worked as a consultant at Wrexham and Tranmere Rovers and presented his own chat show on Radio City 96.7.'Shanks' passed away in 1981 at the age of 68 after suffering from a heart attack. He has been honoured at Anfield by the erection of the Shankly Gates and there is also a museum dedicated to his memory in the city.

SHARP, Kevin

Left-back
Town Years: 2002-2003
Born: *1974 Sarnia, Ontario, Canada*
Playing career: *AJ Auxerre, Leeds United, Wigan Athletic, Wrexham, Huddersfield Town, Scunthorpe United, Shrewsbury Town, Guiseley, Hamilton Academical, Northwich Victoria (1991-2009)*
Mick Wadsworth brought left-back Sharp to the club for the 2002-03 season, he had been playing for Wrexham before he signed for the club. He played most of the 2002-03 season but the club was bogged down with financial difficulties and administration and Town were relegated at the end of the season. Sharp left the club and joined Scunthorpe United where he played for two years before he spent a year at Shrewsbury Town and then signed for Guiseley in 2006. After a short spell at the club, Sharp then signed for Hamilton Academical where he played until 2007. He then became the player-assistant manager at Northwich Victoria until 2008 and became player-assistant manager at Harrogate Town in 2009. Sharp has worked for First E11even Sports Management as a Football Consultant since 2011.

SHAW, George 'David'

Forward
Town Years: 1967-1969
Born: *1948 Huddersfield, West Riding of Yorkshire*
Playing career: *Huddersfield Town, Oldham Athletic, West Bromwich Albion, Oldham Athletic (1966-1978)*

Shaw began his career at his hometown club and spent three years at Leeds Road before leaving in 1969 after rarely playing in the first team. He spent four years at Oldham Athletic before leaving in 1973 for West Brom but returned to Oldham in 1975 and stayed there until his retirement as a player in 1978. Shaw then ran a pub and later worked at Hopkinson's in Huddersfield as a driver before retiring. He now lives in retirement in Fenay Bridge with his wife, Sylvia. Shaw is the grandson of former Town player and manager David Steele.

SHAW, George

Full-back
Town Years: 1924-1926
Born: *1899 Swinton, West Riding of Yorkshire*
Died: *1973 Doncaster, West Riding of Yorkshire*
Playing career: *Bolton-on-Dearne, Rossington Main Colliery, Gillingham, Doncaster Rovers, Huddersfield Town, West Bromwich Albion, Stalybridge Celtic, Worcester City (player-manager) (1920-1939)*

Prior to his football career, Shaw had served in the First World War as a seaman on board the HMS Victory in 1918 and had also worked as a miner before and after the War before he signed for Gillingham in 1920. He returned to Yorkshire, playing for Rossington Main Colliery in 1921 and then later signed for Doncaster Rovers. Shaw arrived at Leeds Road in February 1924 and played a handful of games during each of three title winning years over 1924, 1925 and 1926 before he left the club in December 1926 to join West Bromwich Albion, who had paid a record breaking £4,100 for his services. He played at the Hawthornes for twelve years before leaving the club in 1938 to join Stalybridge Celtic as player-manager. After just a year at the club, Shaw left in 1939 to become the player-manager of Worcester City before the outbreak of World War Two ended his football career. Whilst playing part time, Shaw had worked as an assurance agent and later moved to Malta and coached a number of teams there in the 1940s and 1950s before he passed away in Doncaster in 1973, at the age of 73.

SHEARER, Duncan

Forward
Town Years: 1986-1988
Born: *1962 Fort William, Scotland*
Playing career: *Clachnacuddin, Chelsea, Huddersfield Town, Swindon Town, Blackburn Rovers, Aberdeen, Inverness Caledonian Thistle (1979-2002)*

Mick Buxton acquired Shearer in 1986 from Chelsea and he scored a hat-trick on his debut against Barnsley. The Scotsman remained at the club for two seasons before he left at the end of the disastrous 1987-88 season but not before scoring 10 of Town's 41 goals that season. He retired as a player in 2002 to become the assistant manager at Aberdeen and then manager at Buckie Thistle, wherre he won the Aberdeenshire Cup on two occasions before being sacked in April 2008 after poor results. He later coached at former club Inverness Caledonian Thistle, and had a spell as caretaker manager in 2013 after Terry Butcher's sacking. He remained at Caley Thistle, coaching the development side before his departure in 2017 and he also writes a column for the Press and Journal newspaper. Shearer also played seven times for the Scotland national side between 1994 and 1995.

SHIEL, John

Inside-left
Town Years: 1938-1939
Born: *1917 Seahouses, Northumberland*
Died: *2013 Seahouses, Northumberland*
Playing career: *North Shields, Newcastle United, Huddersfield Town, North Sunderland (1936-1949)*

Shiel signed from Newcastle United in 1938 and although he managed to feature for the reserves on many occasions, he only managed 1 appearance in the first team before he was released just before the Second World War. He joined the services, serving in the Royal Navy and after returning from the War he returned to fish from his local village of Seahouses and also returned to playing football, turning out for North Sunderland until 1949. Shiel later assisted with Farne Island cruises and his favourite moment was in 1977 when he escorted Queen Elizabeth II to visit the Farne Islands on her Silver Jubilee tour. He remained in Seahouses for the rest of his life and at the time of his death in November 2013, he was the oldest living former Newcastle United player and probably Town's too.

SHIELDS, Ralph

Forward
Town Years: 1914-1920
Born: *1892 Newbiggin, Northumberland*
Died: *1944 Sandakan Death Camp, Borneo*
Playing career: *Newbiggin Athletic, Choppington Alliance, Newcastle United, Huddersfield Town, Exeter City, Brentford (1913-1927)*

Signing from Newcastle United in 1914, Shields spent six years at Leeds Road and scored 22 goals in 47 games for Arthur Fairclough and Ambrose Langley's sides, before moving on to Exeter City in 1920. After just a year at the club, Shields signed for Brentford. After his retirement as a player, Shields and his family emigrated to Australia in 1927 to start a new life in Concord, New South Wales. During the Second World War he served with the Australian Army Service Corps in Malaysia and was captured by the Imperial Japanese Army and became a Prisoner of War in the Sandakan Prisoner of War Camp in North Borneo. Shields died on the 21st of November 1944 and is buried in the Labuan War Cemetery, Malaysia.

SHINER, Roy

Centre-forward
Town Years: 1951-1955
Born: *1924 Ryde, Isle of Wight*
Died: *1988 Ryde, Isle of Wight*
Playing career: *Cheltenham Town, Huddersfield Town, Sheffield Wednesday, Hull City (1948-1962)*

Shiner had been playing for Cheltenham Town before he arrived at Leeds Road to sign for George Stephenson's side. After a four year spell at Leeds Road, Shiner joined Sheffield Wednesday in 1955 and later had a short spell at Hull City between 1959 and 1960 before he hung up his boots in 1962 after a spell at Cheltenham Town. Following his retirement from the game, Shiner moved back to the Isle of Wight, managed Newport I.O.W., East Cowes and St. Helens Blue Star and became a building contractor on the island before he passed away in 1988.

"DID YOU KNOW?"

"Eoin Hand became the club's first non-British manager when he took charge in 1988."

SHORT, Christopher 'Chris'

Defender
Town Years: 1994-1995 (loan)
Born: *1970 Munster, West Germany*
Playing career: *Pickering Town, Scarborough, Manchester United (loan), Notts County, Huddersfield Town (loan), Sheffield United, Stoke City, Scarborough, Hinckley United (1988-2001)*

Short spent time on loan at Town during the 1994-95 season before returning to his parent club Notts County. He left Meadow Lane in 1995 to join Sheffield United and later had short spells at Stoke City and Scarborough before he finished his career in 2001, at non-league Hinckley United. After his football career ended, Short became a fitness coach and had worked with Blackburn Rovers, Crystal Palace, Derby County, Leicester City and Sheffield United before he rejoined Neil Warnock at Leeds United in 2012. He left with Warnock a year later and in 2016 became the fitness coach at Bradford City, first team coach at Blackpool, and is now Head of Sports Science at Oxford United.

SHOTTON, Malcolm

Defender
Town Years: 1988
Born: *1957 Newcastle upon Tyne, Northumberland*
Playing career: *Leicester City, Atherstone Town, Nuneaton Borough, Oxford United, Portsmouth, Huddersfield Town, Barnsley, Hull City, Ayr United, Barnsley (1974-1996)*

Shotton joined Town in February 1988 from Portsmouth and was later made captain of the side but his time at the club was a short one as he was sold to Barnsley in exchange for centre-half Andy Duggan in September of the same year. He played at Oakwell for two years before spending two years at Hull City and then signing for Ayr United in 1992. Shotton spent another two years at Ayr before heading back to Barnsley in 1994, retiring as a player in 1996 and becoming assistant manager at Oakwell. He became the Oxford United manager in 1998 but spent just a year in the post before his departure in 1999. He later worked at Bradford City as assistant manager and coached at both Loughborough University and Barnsley College. Shotton was last known to be selling cars at Mercedes Benz in Huddersfield and is now living in Penistone.

SIDEBOTTOM, Arnold 'Arnie'
Defender
Town Years: 1976-1978
Born: *1954 Shawlands, Barnsley, West Riding of Yorkshire*
Playing career: *Manchester United, Huddersfield Town, Halifax Town (1972-1979)*

Sidebottom arrived at Leeds Road in 1975 from Manchester United and spent three years at the club before heading to Halifax Town in 1978 and retiring from the game completely in 1979. He had combined his football career with his cricketing career which had begun in 1973, when he started to turn out for Yorkshire. Sidebottom finally played test match cricket for England in 1982 but was banned for three years as he was part of the rebel tour to went to South Africa. He also played for Orange Free State between 1981 and 1984 and after his three year ban he returned to test cricket in 1985 where he was called up for the Trent Bridge Test against Australia but he only took 1 for 65 before he limped off with an injury. The Yorkshireman continued to play for Yorkshire until 1991 when he became a coach at the club, remaining for another twelve years before finally leaving the club in 2003. He has since coached football and cricket at Woodhouse Grove School and has also coached young cricketers at Thongsbridge Cricket Club and his son Ryan's academy. Sidebottom has also worked on the after-dinner speaking circuit and is currently living in Wetherby.

SIMPKIN, Christopher 'Chris'
Left-half
Town Years: 1975-1976
Born: *1944 Hull, East Riding of Yorkshire*
Playing career: *Hull City, Blackpool, Scunthorpe United, Huddersfield Town, Baltimore Comets (loan), Hartlepool United, Scarborough (1962-1978)*

After a long career in the Football League, Simpkin arrived at Town in 1975 from Scunthrope United and played during the 1975-76 season before he moved on to Hartlepool United in 1976. He spent two years at Victoria Park before heading into non-league with Scarborough and after his retirement as a player, Simpkin worked in the motor industry for many years before his retirement. He currently lives in Hull and spends a lot of time in Spain with his daughter during the summer months.

SIMPSON, John
Full-back
Town Years: 1939-1948
Born: *1918 Hedon, East Riding of Yorkshire*
Died: *2000 Market Weighton, East Yorkshire*
Playing career: *Bridlington Trinity, Huddersfield Town, York City, Grantham (1939-1953)*

Simpson was a left-back that joined the club in 1939 as an amateur from Bridlington Trinity and turned professional seven years later, in 1946, but only managed 7 games before leaving for York City in 1948. He played over 200 matches for York's first team before retiring from professional football in 1953. Simpson became the physiotherapist-coach at Hull City in 1954 and spent nine years at Boothferry Park before heading to Hartlepool United in 1963, again working as coach. He later managed Hartlepool between 1970 and 1971 before heading to Cambridge United in the same year to work as coach and physiotherapist at the club. Simpson later joined York as physiotherapist in 1977, remaining until 1983. He moved to live in Market Weighton with his wife Dorothy, where he still worked part time as a physio, before passing away in June 2000 at the age of 81.

SIMPSON, Robbie
Forward
Town Years: 2009-2012
Born: *1985 Poole, Dorset*
Playing career: *Norwich City, Cambridge City, Cambridge United, Coventry City, Huddersfield Town, Brentford (loan), Oldham Athletic (loan), Oldham Athletic (loan), Oldham Athletic, Leyton Orient, Cambridge United, Exeter City, Milton Keynes Dons (1995-Still Playing)*

Lee Clark signed Simpson for the 2009-10 season but after starting the season as a first choice forward, he lost his place in the side and spent time on loan at Brentford and Oldham Athletic before finally leaving the club in 2012 to sign for Oldham on a permanent deal. He went on to play for Leyton Orient and Cambridge United before signing for Exeter City in 2016. Whilst at Exeter, Simpson set up his own business which helps former footballers find employment after their playing days have ended. After Paul Tisdale left Exeter to join Milton Keynes Dons in 2018, Simpson followed him to Stadium MK.

SIMPSON, Ronald 'Ron'
Inside-forward
Town Years: 1950-1958
Born: *1934 Carlisle, Cumberland*
Died: *2010 Carlisle, Cumbria*
Playing career: *Huddersfield Town, Sheffield United, Carlisle United, Queen of the South (1950-1967)*
Simpson began his career as a 16 year old in 1950 and made his debut the following year, going on to play 118 games for the club before leaving to sign for Sheffield United in 1958. He helped the Blades to promotion from Division Two in 1961 and then played over 230 games for Carlisle United. Simpson later worked for Pearl Assurance Company and the family retail business before retiring. Died in November 2010 at the age of 76.

SINCLAIR, Frank
Right-back
Town Years: 2007 (loan), 2007-2008
Born: *1971 Lambeth, Greater London*
Playing career: *Chelsea, West Bromwich Albion (loan), Leicester City, Burnley, Huddersfield Town (loan), Huddersfield Town, Lincoln City, (1990-2015)*
By the time he arrived on Town, Sinclair had enjoyed a long career in professional football, playing the majority of it in the Premier League, including winning the FA Cup, League and Cup Winners' Cup with Chelsea and the League Cup with Leicester. He originally joined on loan towards the end of the 2006-07 season from Burnley and impressed with his performances at right-back and was signed on a permanent contract for the 2007-08 season. The Jamaican international is now assistant manager at Radcliffe Borough. Sinclair also works as a pundit for Chelsea TV, works as a coach for Edukick England and is also a consultant for Rubix Sports Management, run by former Town player Adnan Ahmed.

Frank Sinclair

SINCLAIR, Wiliam 'Willie'
Inside-forward
Town Years: 1958-1960
Born: *1934 Coatbridge, Scotland*
Playing career: *Aberdeen, Falkirk, Huddersfield Town, Tranmere Rovers (1950-1962)*
Sinclair signed from Falkirk in 1958and spent two years at Leeds Road. He had short spells with Tranmere Rovers, Halifax Town and Stirling Albion before he moved to Australia where he played for Adelaide Polonia and APIA. Sinclair is now back in the UK and currently lives in his native Fife.

SINNOTT, Jordan
Midfielder
Town Years: 2012-2015
Born: *1994 Bradford, West Yorkshire*
Playing career: *Huddersfield Town, Altrincham (loan), Bury (loan), Altrincham, Halifax Town, Chesterfield (2012-Still Playing)*
Son of Lee, Jordan Sinnott began his career at Town as a junior before turning professional in 2012 but made just two appearances before leaving the club in 2015 to sign for his father at Altrincham. He signed for current club, non-league Alfreton Town In 2018.

SINNOTT, Lee
Centre-half
Town Years: 1994-1997
Born: *1965 Aldridge, Staffordshire*
Playing career: *Walsall, Watford, Bradford City, Crystal Palace, Bradford City, Huddersfield Town, Oldham Athletic, Scarborough (1982-2000)*
Neil Warnock brought Sinnott to the club in the 1994-95 season and he was immediately installed at centre-half and captained the side to play-off triumph in 1995, infamously dropping the trophy on his head. He ended his career at Scarborough in 2000, before becoming the manager at Farsley Celtic in 2003. His exploits at Throstle Nest impressed Port Vale, who gave him the manager's job in 2007. Sinnott was sacked just a year later and became the manager of Bradford Park Sinnott joined Altrincham in 2011 as manager and managed to secure promotion in 2014 but was later sacked in March 2016 with 'Alty' in the relegation zone. Lee has been the manager of Gainsborough Trinity since February 2018 and lives in Hull. His son, Jordan, also played for the club.

SKARZ, Joseph 'Joe'

Left-back
Town Years: 2006-2010
Born: *1989 Huddersfield, West Yorkshire*
Playing career: *Huddersfield Town, Bury, Rotherham United, Oxford United, Bury (2006-Still Playing)*
Skarz began his career as a junior at Town before he was brought into the first team in 2007 to fill in at left-back after Peter Jackson had released Danny Adams. He signed professional later on in 2007 and won the League One Apprentice of the Year whilst at the club. SKarz played for the club until his departure in 2010, when he joined Bury, and he played at Gigg Lane for three years before he signed for Rotherham United. He spent two years at the New York Stadium before signing for Oxford United in 2015 and after two years there, he signed for former club Bury in 2017.

SKELTON, George

Inside-left
Town Years: 1945-1947
Born: *1919 Thurcroft, West Riding of Yorkshire*
Died: *1994 Rotherham, South Yorkshire*
Playing career: *Thurcroft Welfare, Huddersfield Town, Leyton Orient (1945-1948)*
Skelton spent two years at Leeds Road but only managed 1 appearance for the first team before his departure in 1947 to sign for Leyton Orient. He left Orient the following year after making just 3 appearances and later passed away in Rotherham in September 1994.

SLADE, Charles 'Charlie'

Midfielder
Town Years: 1914-1922
Born: *1891 Bath, Somerset*
Died: *1971 Doncaster, West Riding of Yorkshire*
Playing career: *Bath City, Stourbridge, Aston Villa, Huddersfield Town, Middlesbrough, Darlington, Folkestone (1910-1927)*
Slade began his career at the club in 1914, signing from Aston Villa, and played over 100 matches in the first team, including the 1920 and 1922 FA Cup Finals, winning the latter. He left the club in 1922 to sign for Middlesbrough and remained at Ayresome Park for two years before he signed for Darlington. Slade then signed for Folkestone in 1927 when he career ended and Slade announced his retirement from the game. He later worked as a coach in Spain, Venezuela,

Mexico and Sweden before he became the Rotherham United coach in 1929, and then the Aldershot coach in 1930. He later worked as Middlesex Schools coach in 1934 and took a coaching job in Belgium in 1936 before working as a scout at Crystal Palace before he was appointed joint-manager with Fred Dawes in 1950. Just a year later, they were both removed and Slade reverted to his role of chief scout until he eventually left the club in 1955. He retired and resided in Doncaster until his death in 1971 at the age of 80.

SLICER, John 'Jacky'

Midfielder
Town Years: 1925-1927
Born: *1902 Bramley, Leeds, West Riding of Yorkshire*
Died: *1979 Huddersfield, West Yorkshire*
Playing career: *Doncaster Rovers, Mexborough Town, Huddersfield Town, Norwich City, Luton Town, Ashton National, York City (1925-1933)*
Slicer spent two years at Leeds Road, managing 7 appearances and 2 goals before he left the club in 1927 to sign for Norwich City, where he played between 1927 and 1930. After his departure from the Canaries, Slicer signed Luton Town and retired from the game sometime in the early 1930s before he passed away in 1979 in Huddersfield.

SMAILES, James 'Jimmy'

Outside-left
Town Years: 1927-1931
Born: *1907 Tow Law, County Durham*
Died: *1986 Tow Law, County Durham*
Playing career: *Huddersfield Town, Tottenham Hotspur, Blackpool, Grimsby Town, Stockport County, Bradford City, Waterhouses Sports Club (1926-1939)*
Signing from Tow Law Town in 1927, Smailes played around 30 games as an outside-left before he left for Tottenham Hotspur in 1931. He spent just a year at White Hart Lane before he departed the club in 1931 to sign for Blackpool. Smailes enjoyed a two year spell at Blackpool, before leaving for Grimsby Town and he later played for Stockport County and ended his professional career at Bradford City in 1939. However, Smailes did play as a guest player during the War at teams such as Bradford Park Avenue, Hartlepool United and he even played a few games back at Leeds Road. He later joined Waterhouse Sports Club as a coach in 1946 before he passed away in Durham in May 1986.

SMITH, Albert 'Bertie'

Half-back
Town Years: 1922-1926
Born: 1898 Camberwell, London
Died: 1957 Streatham, London
Playing career: Huddersfield Town, Bradford City, Bangor City, Bournemouth (c1917-c1934)

After a spell at Nunhead, Smith signed for Town in 1922 and although he was on Town's books whilst they won three First Division titles in succession, he only made a handful of appearances across those three seasons. He left the club in 1926 and signed for Bradford City, leaving the club a year later in 1927. After leaving Valley Parade, Smith joined non-league Rhyl Athletic and later played for Bangor City and Bournemouth & Boscombe Athletic before he was appointed to the backroom staff at the latter. He later joined Tilling Athletic and also played for Streatham Town and London Transport Sports Association before he retired from the game. Smith later passed away while he was living in Streatham in 1957.

SMITH, Alexander 'Alec'

Full-back
Town Years: 1968-1970
Born: 1947 Thornhill, West Riding of Yorkshire
Playing career: Ossett Albion, Bradford City, Huddersfield Town, Southend United, Colchester United, Halifax Town (1964-1976)

Smith signed from Bradford City in 1968 and he played at the club for two years before he left to join Southend United in 1970. He later played for Colchester United and Halifax Town between before retiring as a player. Smith then refereed and ran the line in the Central League whilst working in asphalting at Competent Asphalt in Mirfield. He then went on to work as a coach driver for Stanley Baths in Dewsbury and his final job was at K Steels in Lockwood. Smith has now retired but still lives in Huddersfield.

"DID YOU KNOW?"

"Ronnie Jepson was the first Town player to score at the new Alfred McAlpine Stadium against Scunthorpe United in August 1994."

SMITH, Alexander 'Alex'

Left-back
Town Years: 1997-1998
Born: 1976 Liverpool, Merseyside
Playing career: Everton, Swindon Town, Huddersfield Town (loan), Chester City, Port Vale, Reading, Shrewsbury Town (loan), Chester City, Wrexham, Southport (1994-2007)

After starting his career at Swindon Town, Smith signed on a free transfer towards the end of the 1997-98 season. He played a handful of games towards the end of the 'Great Escape' season before joining Chester City. Smith spent just one year at the club before joining Port Vale in 1999, going on to spend two seasons at Vale Park before heading to Elm Park in 2001 to sign for Reading. He spent two years at the club but hardly played a game before returning to his former club Chester City in 2003. Smith later had spells at Wrexham and Southport before his career seemingly ended in 2007.

SMITH, Bertram 'Bert'

Inside-forward
Town Years: 1913-1919
Born: 1892 Higham, Kent
Died: 1969 Biggleswade, Bedfordshire
Playing career: Huddersfield Town, Tottenham Hotspur, Young Boys (player-coach) (1910-1934)

Smith signed from non-league Metrogas in 1913 and his spell at Town was interrupted by the outbreak of WW1 but he remained on Town's books throughout the War, leaving in 1919 when league football resumed. He signed for Tottenham Hotspur and spent eleven years at White Hart Lane, playing over 300 games in the process and also won the 1921 FA Cup. Smith was involved in an incident in 1922 against rivals Arsenal - after Spurs had scored, the referee was pulled by players, blows with fists were exchanged and the referee was trampled on. Smith was found to have used "filthy language" and was suspended for a month. He won two England caps and after his playing career ended he worked as a coach at Northfleet United. He later coached Young Boys in Switzerland, Harwich and Parkeston, Hitchin and Stevenage Borough before taking the job of trainer and groundsman at Hitchin Town, a role he performed from 1937 until his retirement in 1966. Smith was residing in Biggleswade when he passed away in 1969.

Billy Smith

SMITH, William H. 'Billy'
Outside-left
Town Years: 1913-1934
Born: *1895 Tantobie, County Durham*
Died: *1951 Doncaster, West Riding of Yorkshire*
Playing career: *Huddersfield , Rochdale (1914-1935)*
W.H. Smith is one of the biggest legends in Huddersfield Town's history and he signed for Arthur Fairclough's side in 1913 from Hobson Rovers. Smith spent twenty-one years at Leeds Road and during that time he played in the 1920 Second Division runners-up side, the 1920, 1922, 1928, 1930 FA Cup Finals, the 1924, 1925 and 1926 Division One winning sides and played 574 games, scoring 126 goals for the side. He is one of the most decorated players in the club's history and finally left the club in 1934 to became the player-manager of Rochdale. Smith lasted just one year at the club before he left football and became a newsagent in Doncaster with his wife, Nellie. He later became the landlord of the Wellington Inn in Elland before he passed away in 1951 whilst living in Doncaster. Smith had had his leg amputated previously and sadly died from cancer. To add, Smith's son Conway Smith also played for Town in the 1940s.

SMITH, William 'Conway'
Inside-forward
Town Years: 1945 (amateur), 1945-1951
Born: *1926 Huddersfield, West Riding of Yorkshire*
Died: *1989 Huddersfield, West Yorkshire*
Playing career: *Huddersfield Town, Queens Park Rangers, Halifax Town, Nelson (1945-1962)*
Son of Billy Smith, Conway began his Town career in 1945. Smith retired as a professional in 1962. Interestingly, Conway and his father became the first father and son pairing to score 100 Football League goals. He later worked for March Tailors in Huddersfield, ran the Unit 2 bar at the Starlight Nightclub and also worked for Kirklees Council before passing away after suffering a heart attack in 1989.

SMITH, Daniel 'Dan'
Left-back
Town Years: 2006 (loan)
Born: *1986 Sunderland, Tyne and Wear*
Playing career: *Sunderland, Huddersfield Town (loan), Aberdeen, Darlington (2004-2014)*
Smith played for part of the 2005-06 season on loan from Sunderland. He only played three games at Roker Park and is perhaps best known for breaking Abou Diaby's leg in a game against Arsenal. Smith enjoyed a two year spell at Aberdeen before joining non-league Gateshead in 2008. He played for a number of non-league teams in the North East including; Blyth Spartans, Chester-le-Street, Darlington, Seaham Red Star and Holland Park Hawks and was last known to be working as an energy consultant for Utility Wise.

SMITH, David 'Dave'
Forward
Town Years: 1967-1974
Born: *1950 Sheffield, West Riding of Yorkshire*
Playing career: *Huddersfield Town, Stockport County (loan), Halifax Town (loan), Cambridge United, Hartlepool United, Gateshead (1967-1976)*
Smith began his career at Town as a junior in 1967 before he turned professional in 1971, playing a number of games in the First Division but by the time he left in 1974, Town were in the Third Division. He signed for Cambridge United in 1974, leaving the following year to join Hartlepool United and retired from professional football in 1976. Smith later played for Gateshead and is now residing in Wakefield.

SMITH, Jack
Centre-forward
Town Years: 1932-1934
Born: *1915 Batley, West Riding of Yorkshire*
Died: *1975 Urmston, Lancashire*
Playing career: *Huddersfield Town, Newcastle United, Manchester United, Blackburn Rovers, Port Vale, Macclesfield Town (player-manager) (1930-1955)*

After playing local football for Whitehall Printers and Dewsbury Moor Welfare, Smith signed for Town in 1932, beginning his professional footballing career. As a centre-forward, he scored 4 league goals in 45 league games before signing for Newcastle United in 1934, playing over 100 games and scoring over 70 goals at St. James Park. Smith signed for Manchester United in 1938 and remained on their books throughout the Second World War but left for Blackburn almost immediately after the hostilities had come to an end. He later played in non-league football and became the player-manager of Macclesfield in 1951 and won the Cheshire County League title in 1953 before he left Moss Rose in 1955 and never worked in football again. Smith later passed away in 1975 at the age of only 60 whilst living in Urmston.

Mark Smith

SMITH, Leslie 'Les'
Right-half
Town Years: 1946-1949
Born: *1920 Manchester, Lancashire*
Died: *2001 Hazel Grove, Greater Manchester*
Playing career: *Stockport County, Huddersfield Town, Oldham Athletic (1946-1956)*

After a spell at Stockport County, Smith joined Town in 1946 and remained at Leeds Road for three years until his departure in 1949. He later played for Oldham Athletic for seven years before leaving returning to his occupation of carpet salesman. Smith had served as an Army sergeant during World War Two and was stationed in Egypt. Died in 2001

"DID YOU KNOW?"

"Phil Starbuck was the last Town player to score at the old Leeds Road ground against Blackpool in April 1994. "

SMITH, Mark
Left-winger
Town Years: 1989-1991
Born: *1961 Sheffield, West Riding of Yorkshire*
Playing career: *Sheffield United, Scunthorpe United, Kettering Town, Rochdale, Huddersfield Town, Grimsby Town, Scunthorpe United (1980-1995)*

Smith began his career at Sheffield United in 1980 but failed to brak into their first. After a trial period at Town during the 1981-82 season, he drifted into non-league with Worksop Town and Gainsborough Trinity before he signed for Scunthorpe United in 1985. Smith later signed for Rochdale in 1988 before he moved to Leeds Road in 1989 when Eoin Hand brought him to the club. Smith spent two years at the club and played over 100 games for Town before he left the club in 1991 and transferred to Grimsby Town, where he spent two years. He then played for former club Scunthorpe United before his professional career ended in 1995. He spent a long while in non-league turning out for Boston United, Gainsborough, Matlock Town, Sheffield FC, Hallam and Maltby Main and later managed Buxton and former club Maltby Main in the early 2000s. Smith is still living and working in his native Sheffield.

SMITH, Mark
Defender
Town Years: 1993 (loan)
Born: *1960 Sheffield, West Riding of Yorkshire*
Playing career: *Sheffield Wednesday, Plymouth Argyle, Barnsley, Notts County, Huddersfield Town (loan), Chesterfield (loan), Lincoln City (1977-1994)*

Smith arrived on loan in 1993 from parent club Notts County and played five games for Ian Ross' side before returning. He later played for Lincoln City as player-coach between 1993 and 1994 before retiring from professional football. Smith became the Youth Coach at Lincoln in 1994 before leaving to take up a similar role at Notts County in 1995. He acted as caretaker manager between December 1996 and January 1997 before Sam Allardyce was appointed at Meadow Lane. Smith became the assistant manager to Allardyce but left in 1998 to coach at Barnsley's Academy, where he guided his side to the FA Youth Cup semi-final in 2002 and to win the competition in 2003. Smith left his post as in 2003 and became the Academy Under-19 Coach at Sheffield Wednesday. He later became the assistant manager at Ilkeston Town before being appointed International Youth Director at Sheffield United in 2007. He then became the youth team coach at Chesterfield in May 2013 before leaving this post in the summer of 2018.

SMITH, Martin
Forward
Town Years: 2000-2003
Born: *1974 Sunderland, Tyne and Wear*
Playing career: *Sunderland, Sheffield United, Huddersfield Town, Northampton Town, Darlington, Blyth Spartans, Kettering Town (1992-2010)*

After a short spell at Sheffield United, Steve Bruce brought Smith to the McAlpine in 2000 to replace the outgoing Marcus Stewart. He suffered injury problems during his first couple of seasons at the club but he was a regular in the side when relegation occurred during the 2002-03 season. Smith left the club at the end of that season to join Northampton Town where he spent three years until his departure in 2006 and returned to the North East to sign for Darlington and later had spells at non-league Blyth Spartans and Kettering Town. He is now back living and working in the North East.

SMITH, Norman
Half-back
Town Years: 1923-1927
Born: *1897 Newburn, Newcastle upon Tyne, Northumberland*
Died: *1978 Newcastle upon Tyne, Tyne and Wear*
Playing career: *Mickley, Ryton United, Newburn, Huddersfield Town, Sheffield Wednesday, Queens Park Rangers, Kreuzlingen (player-coach) (c1923-1932)*

Smith began his career at Leeds Road in 1923 but only managed a handful of appearances before leaving for Sheffield Wednesday in 1927. In 1939, Smith became Stan Seymour's assistant manager at Newcastle United and he remained in this position throughout the 1940s and 1950s and was given the manager's job in 1961 after Charlie Mitten was sacked. He only lasted 35 matches before resigning at the end of the 1961-62 season but still remained at the club in various capacities for many more years. Smith passed away in 1978 whilst travelling home from watching a game at St. James Park, he was 80 years old.

SMITH, Paul
Midfielder
Town Years: 1970-1974
Born: *1954 Thorne, West Riding of Yorkshire*
Playing career: *Huddersfield Town, Cambridge United (1970-1976)*

Smith began his career at Leeds Road as an apprentice in 1970 and signed professional in 1972. He only managed 2 appearances in the first team before he left the club in 1974 to sign for Cambridge United and spent two years at the club before leaving professional football for good in 1976. Smith is now back living in his native South Yorkshire.

SMITH, Stephen 'Steve'

Left-Back, Midfielder, Chief Scout, Coach, Youth Coach, Caretaker Manager, Manager, Head of Academy Recruitment, Academy Scout

Town Years: 1963-1977, 1979-1987 (non contract player), 1979-1987 (chief scout, coach, youth coach), 1986-1987 (caretaker manager), 1987 (manager), 1987-1988 (youth coach), 2012-2013 (head of academy recruitment)

Born: *1946 Huddersfield, West Riding of Yorkshire*

Playing career: *Huddersfield Town, Bolton Wanderers (loan), Halifax Town (1961-1987)*

Steve Smith is the only man to manage his home-town club but began his Town career in 1961 as an apprentice. Smith spent sixteen years at Leeds Road and was part of the 1969-70 promotion season and was in the side that was relegated in 1972, 1974 and 1975, thus becoming one of a select few players to play in all four divisions for the club. Tom Johnston allowed Smith to leave in 1977 to join Halifax Town but he returned two years later to become Mick Buxton's chief scout. Smith was also a regular in the reserves from 1979 onwards before he returned to the first team in 1981 to play in an FA Cup game. Smith later took the youth team before he was appointed caretaker manager after Mick Buxton was sacked, getting the job full time in January 1987. He lasted less than a year in the top job before resigning and reverting to his previous role of youth coach. Smith was sacked in 1988 for economy reasons and went on to work at Bradford City as Youth Development Officer. He later returned to Town in 2012 as Head of Academy Recruitment before stepping down just a year later. Smith is now suffering from dementia but is invited to every Town home game as a guest of the club.

SMITH, Thomas 'Tommy'

Centre-forward

Town Years: 1979-1981

Born: *1959 Wolverhampton, Staffordshire*

Playing career: *Bromsgrove Rovers, Sheffield United, Huddersfield Town, Emley (1978-1981)*

After a spell at Sheffield United, Smith signed for Town in 1978 but was mostly a reserve player. He remained in the reserves until he left in 1981 and later played for local club Emley. Smith is now living and working in Chorley, Lancashire.

SMITHIES, Alexander 'Alex'

Goalkeeper

Town Years: 2007-2015

Born: *1990 Huddersfield, West Yorkshire*

Playing career: *Huddersfield Town, Queens Park Rangers, Cardiff City (2007-Still Playing)*

A bright prospect from the club's academy, Smithies made his full debut in the 4-0 defeat to Leeds United in the 2007-08 season, having come on as a substitute in the game before against Southend United. He was Matt Glennon's understudy until Gerry Murphy dropped Glennon in 2008 and gave Smithies the goalkeeper's jersey. Smithies was the first choice goalkeeper at Town until Ian Bennett forced him out of the side in the 2010-11 season, although an injury to Bennett in the second leg of the 2012 Playoff semi-final saw Smithies regain his place in the team for the final, saving a couple of penalties and scoring the winning one to achieve promotion to the Championship. He remained the first choice until he was controversially sold during the 2015-16 season to Queens Park Rangers and became a fan's favourite at Loftus Road until he transferred to Cardiff City on the eve of the 2018-19 season.

SODJE, Akpoeyere 'Akpo'

Centre-forward

Town Years: 2004-2005

Born: *1980 Greenwich, Greater London*

Playing career: *Dynamos, QPR, Huddersfield Town, Darlington, Port Vale, Sheffield Wednesday, Charlton Athletic, Hibernian, Tianjin Teda, Preston NE, Scunthorpe United, Tranmere Rovers (2001-2014)*

Brother of Efe, Akpo signed in 2004 on a short term deal and made a couple of appearances for Peter Jackson's side but did not manage to find the net. He left in 2005 to join Darlington and later joined Port Vale in 2006 and then Sheffield Wednesday in 2007. Sodje later became something of a journeyman, turning out Charlton Athletic, Hibernian, Tianjin Teda, Preston North End, Scunthorpe United, Tranmere Rovers and Macclesfield Town (loan). He has been without a club since Tranmere released him in 2014 and in 2017 was suspected to have been part of a money laundering scheme with his brothers. Sodje was asked to return from Dubai, where is now living, to be interviewed but he refused and the case later collapsed in September 2017.

Efe Sodje

SODJE, Efetobore 'Efe'
Centre-half
Town Years: 2003-2005
Born: *1972 Greenwich, Greater London*
Playing career: *Macclesfield Town, Luton Town, Crewe Alexandra, Huddersfield Town, Yeovil Town, Southend United (loan), Southend United, Gillingham, Macclesfield Town (1994-2015)*
Sodje had played for Nigeria in the 2002 World Cup, just a year before he arrived at Town from Crewe Alexandra. Well known for wearing a bandana, Sodje was a fan's favourite during his time at the club. Later became team captain during the 2003-04 promotion season. Peter Jackson cancelled Sodje's contract near the end of the 2004-05 season due to his bad disciplinary record and he signed for Yeovil Town. He joined former club Macclesfield Town in 2013 as assistant manager but after a disagreement with a staff member, was unfairly sacked in November 2015. Sodje, his brothers and cousins were taken to court accused of money laundering but were acquitted when the case collapsed in September 2017. It was revealed in January 2019 that Sodje had been jailed in September 2017 for defrauding a children's charity but reporting restrictions had been imposed at that time and only lifted when his brother Sam was acquitted.

"DID YOU KNOW?"

"Town have won 3 Play Off Finals despite not scoring a goal in any of them. They won finals in 2004, 2012 and 2017 all on penalties. "

SOUTHERN, Keith
Midfielder
Town Years: 2012-2014
Born: *1981 Gateshead, Tyne and Wear*
Playing career: *Everton, Blackpool (loan), Blackpool, Huddersfield Town, Fleetwood Town, Shrewsbury Town (loan) (1997-2015)*
Simon Grayson brought Southern to the club at the beginning of the 2012-13 season and he spent two years at Town before signing for Fleetwood Town in 2014. He retired from professional football in 2015 and moved into coaching. Southern holds the UEFA B Licence and has since worked as youth coach at Blackburn Rovers and Warrington Town.

SPEDDING, James 'Jim'
Centre-half
Town Years: 1936-1937
Born: *1912 Keighley, West Riding of Yorkshire*
Died: *1982 Connah's Quay, Wales*
Playing career: *Rosehill Villa, Gateshead, Huddersfield Town, Chesterfield, Darlington, Worksop Town (1933-1939)*
After a three year spell at Gateshead, Spedding arrived at Leeds Road in 1936 but only managed 4 appearances for Clem Stephenson's side before he departed for Chesterfield in 1937. He spent two years at Saltergate before heading to Darlington in 1939 and he later had a spell at Worksop Town before announcing his retirement from the game. Spedding is listed on the 1939 Register as an unemployed professional footballer and later passed away in December 1982.

SPENCE, Marshall 'Bon'
Defender
Town Years: 1923-1933
Born: *1899 Ferryhill, County Durham*
Died: *1982 Huddersfield, West Yorkshire*
Playing career: *Ferryhill Celtic, Ferryhill Athletic, Sunderland (amateur), Spennymoor United, Ferryhill Athletic, Huddersfield Town (1920-1933)*
Originally hailing from Ferryhill, Spence arrived at Leeds Road in 1923 from Ferryhill Athletic. He spent ten years at the club and played over 80 games for the first team before he retired from professional football in 1933. Spence settled in the area and later worked as a school teacher in Huddersfield before he passed away in early 1982.

SPENCER, James 'Jimmy'

Forward
Town Years: 2009-2014
Born: *1991 Leeds, West Yorkshire*
Playing career: *Huddersfield Town, Notts County, Cambridge U, Plymouth A, Mansfield T (2009-date)*

Spencer had been at the club since he was seven years old, turning professional in 2009. He was loaned out to Northwich Victoria, Morecambe, Cheltenham Town, Brentford, Crawley Town and Scunthorpe United before eventually leaving the club in 2014. Spencer joined Notts County but has been turning out for Mansfield Town since 2017.

SPRIGGS, Steven 'Steve'

Inside-right
Town Years: 1971-1975
Born: *1956 Armthorpe, Doncaster*
Playing career: *Huddersfield Town, Cambridge United, Middlesbrough (loan) (1971-1987)*

Spriggs joined the club as an apprentice in in March 1971 and later turned professional in 1974. He spent a year as a professional at the club before he left to sign for Cambridge United in 1975. Spriggs became a record holder at the club with 416 first team appearances to his name when he left in 1987, he is now living in Cambridgeshire, running his own building firm.

STANIFORTH, Ronald 'Ron'

Right-back
Town Years: 1952-1955
Born: *1924 Newton Heath, Lancashire*
Died: *1988 Barrow, Cumbria*
Playing career: *Newton Albion, Stockport County, Huddersfield Town, Sheffield Wednesday, Barrow (player-manager) (1946-1961)*

Staniforth arrived in 1952 from Stockport County and spent three years at Leeds Road, playing in defence including during the 1952-53 promotion season. He was also called up to the England squad eight times at Town and later left for Sheffield Wednesday in 1955. Later worked as player-manager at Barrow before retiring from the game in 1961 and left the club in 1964. He joined the Wednesday coaching staff in 1970, became the chief scout in 1971 and then the youth coach. After leaving Hillsborough in 1976, Staniforth then moved back to Barrow, where he worked in a local shipyard and also coached the work's football team before he passed away in October 1988 aged 64.

STANT, Philip 'Phil'

Forward
Town Years: 1991
Born: *1962 Bolton, Lancashire*
Playing career: *Camberley Town, Reading, Hereford United, Notts County, Blackpool (loan), Lincoln City (loan), Huddersfield Town (loan), Fulham, Mansfield Town, Cardiff City, Mansfield Town (loan), Bury, Lincoln City, Brighton & Hove Albion, Worcester City, Dover Athletic, Hayes, Hinckley United, Gainsborough Trinity, Ilkeston Town (1981-2004)*

Falklands veteran Stant had enjoyed a long career before he arrived at Leeds Road in 1991, on loan from Notts County. He played 5 matches and scored 1 goal for Eoin Hand's side before he returned to his parent club. Stant signed for Fulham in 1991 but left the same year to join Mansfield Town, a club he spent two years at before he signed for Cardiff City in 1993. Stant signed for Lincoln City in 1997 and spent four years at the club, becoming the manager in 2000, before being sacked a year later. After a short spell at Brighton & Hove Albion, Stant moved into non-league and turned out for Worcester City, Dover Athletic, Hayes and Hinckley United before being given the player-manager's job at Gainsborough Trinity in 2002 In 2003 Stant is now working for the Football League in youth coaching and has also run the Newark & Sherwood College Football Academy.

STANTON, Brian

Midfielder
Town Years: 1979-1986
Born: *1956 Liverpool, Lancashire*
Playing career: *Bury, Huddersfield Town, Wrexham (loan), Rochdale (1976-1988)*

After originally working as a carpenter, Stanton signed professional for Bury in 1976 and signed for Town early on in the 1979-80 promotion season. Stanton played a key part in the 1979-80 and 1982-83 seasons and remained at the club until 1986. He also wrote a place in football history when he scored 4 goals against Bradford City in a 6-3 result, holding the record for the fastest hat-trick scored by a player who isn't a forward. Stanton left the club in 1986 and spent two years at Rochdale before retiring going on to work for Bury Council as a gypsy liaison officer, later taking on the same role at Bolton Council. He is still at Bolton Council but is now working as a housing officer.

Frank Stapleton

STAPLETON, Frank

Forward
Town Years: 1991 (player-coach)
Born: *1956 Dublin, Ireland*
Playing career: *Arsenal, Manchester United, Ajax, Anderlecht (loan), Derby County, Le Havre, Blackburn Rovers, Aldershot, Huddersfield Town (player-coach), Bradford City (player-manager), Brighton & Hove Albion (1974-1995)*

Following Peter Withe's exit to Aston Villa, Stapleton was brought in by Eoin Hand as player coach. However, he only played 5 games before leaving Leeds Road to become the player-manager at local rivals Bradford City, much to the dismay of the Town faithful who let their feelings be known to Stapleton when the two sides met later on in the season. Stapleton was sacked at Valley Parade in 1994 and after a short spell at Brighton & Hove Albion he called time on his career in 1995. He later became the manager of New England Revolution in 1996 and also worked as a Forward's coach during the 2003-04 season at Bolton Wanderers. Stapleton has since acted as assistant manager to Ray Wilkins, when he was the manager of Jordan in 2014, and is a regular on MUTV and does a lot of after-dinner speaking.

STARBUCK, Philip 'Phil'

Forward
Town Years: 1991-1994
Born: *1968 Nottingham, Nottinghamshire*
Playing career: *Nottingham Forest, Huddersfield Town, Sheffield United, Bristol City (loan), Oldham Athletic, Plymouth Argyle, Cambridge City, Burton Albion, Arnold Town (1984-2006)*

Starbuck signed from Nottingham Forest in 1991 and was immediately installed in the first team and chipped in with a number of goals in the 1991-92 and 1992-93 seasons. He later played as a sweeper and midfielder during Neil Warnock's time as manager, captained the side in the 1994 Autoglass Final, and even the last ever goal at the old Leeds Road ground in 1994. Starbuck later fell out with Warnock after he found out that the captaincy had been taken off him by reading the local newspaper. He became player-manager of Hucknall Town in 2001. Starbuck remained there until 2003 when he took the Leigh RMI job, again as player-manager. He only lasted a year in that post and spells as manager of Arnold Town, Hednesford Town and Grantham Town followed. Starbuck is now living in Loughborough and runs his own building business Starbuck & Son Builders, runs his own charity New4Old and since 2012 has been part of the ministry team at New Springs City in Loughborough.

STARLING, Alan

Goalkeeper
Town Years: 1976-1980
Born: *1951 Dagenham, Essex*
Playing career: *Luton Town, Torquay United (loan), Northampton Town, Huddersfield Town, Bradley Rangers, Bradford City (1969-1983)*

Starling joined Town from Northampton Town in 1975 and is perhaps the only Town player that was fined for indecent exposure on the field of play! This came in a game against Scunthorpe United when he had, as usual, responded to the chants of "Starling, show us your arse!". Starling retired in 1980 from professional football but came out of retirement for a short spell at local side Bradley Rangers and also as goalkeeping cover at Bradford City in 1983. He is still residing in Huddersfield and he works as national account manager for the Huddersfield based Miles Group.

STEAD, Jonathan 'Jon'

Forward
Town Years: 2002-2004, 2013-2015
Born: *1983 Huddersfield, West Yorkshire*
Playing career: *Huddersfield Town, Blackburn Rovers, Sunderland, Sheffield United, Ipswich Town, Bristol City, Notts County (2002-Still Playing)*

After playing in Gerry Murphy's youth team, Stead made the step up to the first team in the 2002-03 season, forming a partnership with club legend Andy Booth. He didn't pull up any trees during that season but the season after, 2003-04, he was a revelation. Stead and Booth combined perfectly as Town shot up the league and Stead had been attracting attention from Premier League clubs including Sunderland. He was sold to Blackburn Rovers in early 2004 for over £1 million and ended up scoring the goals that kept Blackburn in the league that season. Stead signed for Sunderland in 2005 for £1.8 million and went on to play for Sheffield United, Ipswich Town (where Stan Ternent had tried to sign him for Town in the 2008-09 season) and Bristol City before he returned to Town in June 2013. He spent two years at the club before leaving for Notts County in 2015, after previous loan spells at Oldham Athletic and Bradford City. Stead is currently contracted at Notts County and has played over 100 games for the club since he signed.

Alan Starling

STEELE, David

Wing-half, Manager
Town Years: 1922-1929, 1943-1947 (manager)
Born: *1894 Carluke, Scotland*
Died: *1964 Huddersfield, West Riding of Yorkshire*
Playing career: *Armadale, St Mirren, Douglas Water Thistle, Bristol Rovers, Huddersfield Town, Preston North End, Bury, Bradford Park Avenue (1913-1930, 1942)*
Management career: *Bradford Park Avenue, Huddersfield Town, Bradford City (1936-1952)*

Steele signed from Bristol Rovers in 1922 for £2,500 and began a seven year playing association with Town. He won three league championships and also played in the FA Cup Final against Blackburn Rovers in 1928 before he departed for Preston North End in 1929, but after just a year at the club, he retired from professional football in 1930. Steele later coached at Bury, Sheffield United and Bold Klubben F.C. in Denmark before he was appointed manager at Bradford Park Avenue in 1936. In 1942, Steele re-registered as a player because of an injury crisis and later returned to Leeds Road in 1943 as manager and even played a match in the Wartime League. Steele's first season in post Wartime football saw Town finish just one spot above the relegation zone and saw him resign as Town manager. He left football and began to work on his family's fruit farm before being tempted back into to football to work as Bradford City's manager in 1948. He managed Bradford for four years and left in 1952 with the club struggling. Steele later returned to Town as a scout and also ran a pub in Stanningley before he passed away in May 1964 at the age of 69.

STEER, Jed

Goalkeeper
Town Years: 2015, 2015, 2016 (loan)
Born: *1992 Norwich, Norfolk*
Playing career: *Norwich City, Yeovil Town (loan), Cambridge United (loan), Aston Villa, Doncaster Rovers (loan), Yeovil Town (loan), Huddersfield Town (loan), Charlton Athletic (loan) (2010-Still Playing)*

In his ten year career so far, Jed Steer has become a bit of a loan specialist and had three separate spells at Town during the 2015-16 season. In total he played 40 games between the sticks after Alex Smithies was sold. Steer returned to his parent club, Aston Villa, at the end of the season and as of 2018 he is still there.

STEPHENSON, Clement 'Clem'

Inside-forward, Manager
Town Years: 1921-1929, 1929-1942 (manager)
Born: *1890 Seaton Delaval, Northumberland*
Died: *1961 Huddersfield, West Riding of Yorkshire*
Playing career: *Aston Villa, Huddersfield Town (1905-1929)*
Management career: *Huddersfield Town (1929-1942)*

After a ten year spell at Aston Villa, Stephenson joined Town in 1920 and was Herbert Chapman's first signing as manager of the club, costing £4,000. He won the FA Cup with Town in 1922, beating Preston North End 1-0 and played during each season of the thrice Champions era between 1923 and 1926, gaining an England cap in 1924. He also played during the 1928 FA Cup Final loss to Blackburn Rovers. Following his retirement as a player, Stephenson immediately replaced manager Jack Chaplin in 1929 and went on to become the longest serving manager in the club's history (a record that has stood since 1942). He spent thirteen years in the top job at Leeds Road and oversaw the club's record victory (10-1 over Blackpool in 1930), an FA Cup Final appearance in 1938 where Town lost 1-0 to Preston (a reversal of the 1922 result) and finished in 2nd place during the 1933-34 season. Stephenson remained at Leeds Road until his departure in 1942 and settled into retirement in the town before passing away in 1961, aged 71.

STEPHENSON, George

Manager
Town Years: 1947-1952
Born: *1900 New Delavel, Northumberland*
Died: *1971 unknown*
Management career: *Huddersfield T (1947-1952)*

Brother, of Clem, George Stephenson arrived at the club in 1947 following the resignation of former manager, David Steele. He was the successful candidate out of sixty applicants and his main job was to avoid relegation from the First Division. Stephenson spent five years at Leeds Road before resigning in March 1952 when relegation from the First Division seemed certain. He became the landlord of the Sportsman Inn in Halifax before leaving in the early 1960s to become the coach of Derby County's 'A' Team. Stephenson later worked as a blacksmith. Died in 1971 at the age of 70.

STEWART, Alan

Left-back
Town Years: 1940-1949
Born: *1922 Newcastle-upon-Tyne, Northumberland*
Died: *2004 Acomb, North Yorkshire*
Playing career: *Huddersfield T, York C (1940-1957)*

Stewart arrived at the club as an amateur in 1940, having to wait a full five years before he made his first appearance for the club. Stewart later went on to work as a brewery representative before he passed away in 2004 at the age of 81.

STEWART, Henry

Full-back
Town Years: 1948-1951
Born: *1925 Wigan, Lancashire*
Died: *1996 Doncaster, South Yorkshire*
Playing career: *Thorne Colliery, Goole Town, Huddersfield Town, Frickley Colliery (1946-c1951)*

After playing for Goole Town and Thorne Colliery, Stewart signed in 1948 and later became a professional, making over 50 appearances for the club before leaving in 1951, rather unexpectedly, and returned to work in the Thorne area of Doncaster in the local colliery. He later worked at Bullcroft Colliery and then at Richard Dunston's Shipyard before his retirement. Stewart also played local football in Thorne and was later a referee as well before he passed away in April 1996 aged 70.

Marcus Stewart

STEWART, Marcus

Forward
Town Years: 1996-2000
Born: *1972 Bristol, Gloucestershire*
Playing career: *Bristol Rovers, Huddersfield Town, Ipswich Town, Sunderland, Bristol City, Preston North End (loan), Yeovil Town (loan), Yeovil Town, Exeter City (player-coach) (1991-2011)*

'Stewie' arrived at the McAlpine in 1996 from his first club Bristol Rovers and was already well known to Town fans after an impressive display in the 1995 play-off final which Town ended up winning. He spent four years at the club, and played a major part in the 1997-98 Great Escape season and was part of the Town side that topped Division One during the 1999-2000 season. Stewart was controversially sold by manager Steve Bruce in January 2000 and replaced by Martin Smith. He was sold to Ipswich Town and a few weeks later played his former club and scored. Stewart's goals contributed to Ipswich's promotion push and they were promoted to the Premiership at the end of the season, whilst Town missed out on the playoffs, finishing eight. The sale of Stewart was partly blamed for this failure and many Town fans cite his sale as the start of Town's downfall, later being relegated twice in three years and facing financial meltdown within three years. He finished the 2000-01 season as the second highest scorer in the Premiership, behind top scorer Thierry Henry. Stewart retired from professional football and continued in his coaching role at the club until 2012 when he returned to Bristol Rovers as first team development coach. A year later, Stewart was promoted to the role of assistant manager, a role he continued in until his departure in 2019.

STOKES, Derek

Forward
Town Years: 1960-1966
Born: *1939 Normanton, West Riding of Yorkshire*
Playing career: *Bradford City, Huddersfield Town, Bradford City, Dundalk (1957-1967)*

Stokes began his career at Bradford City before signing for Town in 1960. In each of his four seasons at Leeds Road, Stokes was the leading scorer. He returned to Bradford City in 1966 in exchange for defender Roy Ellam. He retired in 1967 and worked as a golf club steward but is now living in retirement in West Yorkshire.

STONEHOUSE, Kevin

Forward
Town Years: 1983-1984
Born: *1959 Bishop Auckland, County Durham*
Playing career: *Blackburn Rovers, Huddersfield Town, Blackpool, Darlington, Carlisle United (loan), Rochdale, Bishop Auckland (1979-1990)*

Stonehouse began his career at Blackburn Rovers and joined Town in 1983, he spent a year at Leeds Road before spending two years at Blackpool and then signed for Darlington in 1986. He also had spells at Rochdale and Bishop Auckland before hanging up his boots in the early 1990s. Stonehouse began working as Community Manager for Football in the Community at Darlington until 2012 and he is now National International Scout at Newcastle United.

STOUTT, Stephen 'Steve'

Defender
Town Years: 1980-1985
Born: *1964 Halifax, West Riding of Yorkshire*
Playing career: *Bradley Rangers, Huddersfield Town, Wolverhampton Wanderers, Grimsby Town, Lincoln City, Boston United, Grantham Town (1980-1996)*

Stoutt, originally from Halifax, began his career at Town in the youth team in 1980 and made his first professional appearance for the club in 1984. He made 9 other first team appearances before leaving the club to sign for Alan Buckley's Wolverhampton Wanderers in April 1985. Stoutt spent three years at Molineux and made over 100 appearances for the club before leaving in 1988 to play for Grimsby Town. He spent two years there but only made a couple of appearances before signing for Lincoln City in 1990, leaving the following year. Stoutt drifted into non-league and played for Boston United and Grantham Town and also had a spell as caretaker manager of Grantham in 1996. The Yorkshireman worked for over twenty years as a milkman in Brighouse but is now believed to be living in Spain.

"DID YOU KNOW?"

"Terry Dolan was the first winner of the Hargreaves Memorial Trophy (Player of the Year) in 1975."

STUART, Mark
Midfielder
Town Years: 1992-1993
Born: *1966 Hammersmith, Greater London*
Playing career: *Charlton Athletic, Bradford City, Huddersfield Town, Rochdale, Chesterfield (loan), Southport, Stalybridge Celtic, Guiseley (1984-2002)*
Stuart spent a year at Leeds Road before signing for Rochdale in 1993 and played at Spotland for six years and is a cult hero at the club after playing over 200 games and scoring over 40 goals. He later played for Southport, Stalybridge Celtic and Guiseley and has since worked as a fireman and is residing in Rochdale, having lived there since his playing days.

SUMMERILL, Phil
Forward
Town Years: 1973-1974
Born: *1947 Birmingham, Warwickshire*
Playing career: *Birmingham City, Huddersfield Town, Millwall, Wimbledon (1963-1979)*
Summerill had been playing for hometown club Birmingham City before he signed for Town in 1973. He spent just over a year at the club, playing over 50 games before his transfer to Millwall in 1974. Summerill spent three years with the Lions and then two years at Wimbledon before announcing his retirement in 1979. Summerill worked as a football development officer at Birmingham City Council and later delivered cars before retirement. He now lives in Solihull, West Midlands.

SUTTON, David 'Dave'
Centre-half
Town Years: 1978-1985
Born: *1957 Tarleton, Lancashire*
Playing career: *Plymouth Argyle, Reading (loan), Huddersfield Town (loan), Bolton Wanderers, Rochdale (1973-1989)*
Sutton originally signed on loan from Plymouth Argyle in 1978 before making a permanent switch a few months later. He was immediately installed in a centre-half pairing with Keith Hanvey and they went on to play in both the 1979-80 and 1982-83 promotion seasons. Sutton remained at the club until 1985 when he joined Bolton Wanderers, spending three years at the club before he left in 1988 to join Rochdale, retiring in 1989 and becoming the physiotherapist at Spotland.

Following the departure of manager Danny Bergara, Sutton was appointed caretaker manager in 1989 before Terry Dolan was given the job. Dolan later offered Sutton a position on his staff when he took the Hull City job in 1991 but Sutton decided to stay and became manager of Rochdale. He remained in the role until 1994 after he was sacked due to a run of heavy defeats. Sutton later ran Sooty's Plants in Tarleton with his father but sold the business, although he still works there and lives next door. He is also Director of Football at non-league club, Burscough.

SWANN, Jack
Inside-forward
Town Years: 1919-1921
Born: *1893 Easington, County Durham*
Died: *1990 Hendon, Greater London*
Playing career: *Seaham Colliery, Huddersfield Town, Leeds United, Watford, Queens Park Rangers, Thames Association, Lovells Athletic (1914-1929)*
Swann signed from Seaham Colliery in 1919, leaving two years later after scoring 36 goals in 74 games. He joined Leeds United in 1921 and played at Elland Road for four years before heading South to join Watford in 1925. After two years at Vicarage Road, Swann joined Queens Park Rangers in 1927, later retiring from the game after spells at Thames Association and Lovells Athletic. Many years later, Swann was a VIP guest at Wembley for the centenary FA Cup Final because he was the oldest surviving footballer to play in an FA Cup Final. He later passed away in 1990, well into his 90s.

SWEENEY, Alan
Right-back
Town Years: 1972-1978
Born: *1956 Glasgow, Scotland*
Playing career: *Huddersfield Town, Emley, Hartlepool United (1972-1982)*
'Toddy' was in the youth team that reached the FA Youth Cup final in 1974, eventually losing to Tottenham Hotspur. He was the first choice right-back in Tom Johnston's side until Mally Brown arrived in 1977. After a short spell at Emley he joined Hartlepool United in 1979. Sweeney remained with the Monkey Hangers until 1982 but is now working as a caretaker of a school in Huddersfield and watches Town regularly.

TANNER, John
Outside-right
Town Years: 1946-1948
Born: *1921 Harrogate, West Riding of Yorkshire*
Died: *1987 Bradford, West Yorkshire*
Playing career: *Yorkshire Amateur, Huddersfield Town, Yorkshire Amateur (1946-1948)*
Originally from Harrogate, Tanner signed for the club in April 1946 from Yorkshire Amateur and turned professional in 1948, playing just 1 game for the club and scoring 1 goal during the 1948-49 season. Tanner returned to Yorkshire Amateur in September 1948 and was also a cricketer and who played first-class cricket for Oxford University between 1947 and 1949, playing a few matches during each season as a lower-order right-handed batsman and wicketkeeper. Tanner also played for Marylebone Cricket Club in 1955 and had represented Oxfordshire in the Minor Counties Championship in 1951 before he later passed away in 1987 at the age of 56.

TAYLOR, Andrew 'Andy'
Left-back
Town Years: 2007 (loan)
Born: *1986 Blackburn, Lancashire*
Playing career: *Blackburn Rovers, Huddersfield Town (loan), Tranmere Rovers (loan), Tranmere Rovers, Sheffield United, Walsall, Blackpool, Oldham Athletic (2004-Still Playing)*
After a left-back crisis at the club, Peter Jackson brought in Andy Taylor on loan from Blackburn Rovers during the 2006-07 season. He only played 8 league games before returning to his parent club. He signed for Walsall in 2012 and played over 150 games at the Bescot Stadium before he left in 2016. After a two year spell at Blackpool, Taylor signed for Oldham Athletic in 2018.

TAYLOR, Archibald 'Archie'
Right-back, Trainer
Town Years: 1910-1911, 1926-1929 (trainer)
Born: *1879 Dundee, Scotland*
Died: *1966 Dundee, Scotland*
Playing career: *Dundee, Raith Rovers, East Craigie, Bolton Wanderers, Bristol Rovers, Brentford, West Ham United, Falkirk, Huddersfield Town, Barnsley, York City (player-manager) (1900-1914)*
After a spell at Falkirk, Archie Taylor arrived at Leeds Road in 1910 in time for the club's first professional season.

He played throughout 1910-11, before he left the club at the end of the season to join Barnsley. Taylor won the FA Cup with Barnsley in 1912 and had previously won it with Bolton Wanderers in 1904. He later enjoyed a one year spell at York City as player-manager before the First World War interrupted his football career. Taylor later worked for Dundee United as their trainer and later worked as trainer at Town between 1926 and 1929 before he left to become the trainer at Birmingham in June 1929. He later passed away in March 1966 at the age of 86.

TAYLOR, Richard 'Dick'
Goalkeeper
Town Years: 1972-1982
Born: *1957 Huddersfield, West Riding of Yorkshire*
Playing career: *Huddersfield Town, York City (loan) (1972-1982)*
Dick Taylor was well thought of during his time at Town and played in the successful 1974 Youth Team that reached the FA Youth Cup final. He was also selected for England Schoolboys during this time and played his first game for Town's first team in 1974 as a 16 year old. Taylor remained on the books at Leeds Road until 1982 but missed a few years through injury and along with Peter Fletcher, was granted a testimonial at the club in 1982 when he had to retire due to a recurring back injury which had blighted his Town career. Taylor left football completely and is currently working for Honda Halifax as a car salesman and lives in Shepley, Huddersfield.

TAYLOR, Harold 'Harry'
Inside-right
Town Years: 1910-1912
Born: *1892 Fegg Hayes, Staffordshire*
Died: *1960 unknown*
Playing career: *Chell Heath, Fegg Hayes, Newcastle United, Fulham, Stoke, Huddersfield Town, Port Vale, Manchester City (1909-1921)*
After spells at Newcastle United, Fulham and Stoke City, Taylor arrived at Leeds Road in 1910 and played a handful of games during the 1911-12 season before leaving for Burslem Port Vale in 1912. He never played a game at Vale Park before signing for Manchester City for £300. Taylor played at Maine Road for nine years before leaving in 1921 and passed away in 1960.

TAYLOR, Jeffrey 'Jeff'
Centre-forward
Town Years: 1947-1949 (amateur), 1949-1951
Born: *1930 Huddersfield, West Riding of Yorkshire*
Died: *2010 Holmfirth, West Yorkshire*
Playing career: *Huddersfield Town, Fulham, Brentford (1947-1956)*

Brother of Ken, Jeff Taylor began his career at Leeds Road in 1947 and played 71 games for the club and scored 29 times playing as a centre-forward. He retired from professional football in 1956 and became an opera singer. During his footballing career, Taylor had paid for studies in singing and piano at the Royal Academy of Music and had performed opera under the name "Neilson Taylor" and was a bass baritone. In 1962, Taylor became the understudy to Michel Roux in Pelléas et Mélisande and Walter Alberti and John Shirley-Quirk in L'incoronazione di Poppea at Glyndebourne. Taylor toured the world after this and later worked as the Professor of Singing at the Royal Scottish Academy of Music in Glasgow for eighteen years until 1992. After retiring as a teacher, Taylor lived in Holmfirth before his death in 2010 at the age of 80.

Ken Taylor

TAYLOR, Kenneth 'Ken'
Half-back
Town Years: 1950-1965
Born: *1935 Huddersfield, West Riding of Yorkshire*
Playing career: *Huddersfield Town, Bradford Park Avenue, Sligo Rovers (1950-1968)*

Kenneth Taylor began his career at Leeds Road in 1950 and spent fifteen years at the club, playing over 250 matches for the first team. He left for Bradford Park Avenue in 1965 and played for the club for two years before a short spell at Sligo Rovers in 1968 brought an end to his football career. Alongside his football career, Taylor was an accomplished cricketer and played for Yorkshire between 1953 and 1968. Taylor also played test cricket for England, making his debut in 1959 and playing his final test in 1964, breaking his finger in his final match against Australia. After his retirement from football and cricket, Taylor became a professional artist, having studied art at Huddersfield Art School and the Slade School of Fine Art, and taught art in Norfolk for over thirty years. He has since released a book in 2006 and still draws and paints regularly from his base in Melton Constable.

TAYLOR, Raymond 'Ray'

Left-winger
Town Years: 1949-1953
Born: *1930 Jump, Barnsley, West Riding of Yorkshire*
Died: *2012 Southport, Merseyside*
Playing career: *Wolverhampton Wanderers, Wath Wanderers, Huddersfield Town, Southport, Denaby United, Frickley Colliery, Stocksbridge Works, Rockingham (1946-1960)*

After a spell at Wath Wanderers, Taylor arrived at the club in 1949 but only managed a couple of appearances before his departure in 1953. He spent two years at Southport before finishing his professional career in 1955, later enjoying spells at Denaby United, Frickley Colliery, Stocksbridge Works and Rockingham before he passed away in August 2012.

TAYLOR, Samuel 'Sammy'

Inside-forward
Town Years: 1913-1921
Born: *1893 Sheffield, West Riding of Yorkshire*
Died: *1973 Sheffield, West Riding of Yorkshire*
Playing career: *Atlas & Norfolk Works, Silverwood Colliery, Huddersfield Town, Sheffield Wednesday, Mansfield Town, Southampton, Halifax Town, Grantham, Chesterfield, Llanelli, Loughborough Corinthians (1911-1933)*

Taylor signed for the club in 1913 but didn't turn professional until after the First World War ended. He was part of the team that were promoted as runners-up of Division Two in 1920 and also played in the FA Cup Final that year. Taylor left the club in 1921 to sign for Sheffield Wednesday and spent four years at the club, playing over 100 games at Hillsborough. He then had short spells at Mansfield Town and Southampton before signing for Halifax Town in 1928, leaving the following year. Spells at Grantham and Chesterfield followed before he ended his career at Grantham Town, after a spell at Loughborough Corinthians in 1933. Taylor later worked as an ambulance driver in Sheffield before his death in early 1973 at the age of 79.

"DID YOU KNOW?"

"To date, Adnan Ahmed is the only Pakistani international to have played for the first team."

TAYLOR, Edward 'Ted'

Goalkeeper
Town Years: 1922-1927
Born: *1887 Liverpool, Lancashire*
Died: *1956 Huddersfield, West Riding of Yorkshire*
Playing career: *Liverpool Balmoral, Oldham Athletic, Huddersfield Town, Everton, Wrexham (1910-1929)*

After playing for Oldham Athletic, Taylor arrived at Leeds Road in 1922 for the fee of £2,500 and played over 120 matches before he moved to Everton in February 1927. After playing for The Toffees for over a year, Taylor left League football to play for non-league Ashton National in September 1928 and left for Wrexham in November of the same year and finally retired from football in 1929 at the end of the 1928-29 season. Taylor later worked as a schoolboys' coach at Altrincham Grammar School, as a colliery hewer in Hemsworth, and in the cotton trade in Manchester before passing away in July 1956 in Huddersfield at the age of 69.

TAYLOR-FLETCHER, Gary

Forward
Town Years: 2005-2007
Born: *1981 Widnes, Cheshire*
Playing career: *Northwich Victoria, Hull City (loan), Leyton Orient, Grays Athletic (loan), Dagenham & Redbridge (loan), Lincoln City, Huddersfield Town, Blackpool, Leicester City, Sheffield Wednesday (loan), Millwall (loan), Tranmere Rovers, Accrington Stanley, Bangor City (1999-Still Playing)*

After a spell at Lincoln City, Taylor-Fletcher was brought to the club by Peter Jackson, who had represented him as an agent before taking the Town job in 2003. He spent two years at the club, including the 2006 playoff semi-final losing side and also scored the Football League's 500,000th goal in 2006. Taylor-Fletcher left in 2007 to join Blackpool, gaining promotion the Premier League with the Seasiders in 2010 and remained at the club until 2013, when he joined Leicester City. He left Leicester after two years, in 2015, and had short spells at Tranmere Rovers and Accrington Stanley before joining Bangor City in 2017. Taylor-Fletcher had a short spell as player-manager at Bangor before becoming assistant manager when Kevin Nicholson was appointed in May 2017. Taylor-Fletcher and Nicholson left the club in May 2018 after the club was relegated after failing to obtain a tier one license.

TEMPEST, Dale

Forward
Town Years: 1984-1986
Born: *1963 Leeds, West Riding of Yorkshire*
Playing career: *Fulham, Huddersfield Town, Gillingham (loan), Lokeren, Colchester United, South China AA, Eastern AA, Kitchee SC, South China AA (1980-1998)*

After a four year spell at Fulham, Leeds born Tempest arrived at Leeds Road in 1984 and played for Mick Buxton's side for two years and was leading scorer in both seasons he spent at the club. He left in 1986 and left the country to sign for Lokeren in Belgium but after just a year, Tempest returned to England in 1987 to sign for Colchester United, a club he remained at until 1989. He again left the country and moved to Hong Kong where he played for South China AA, Eastern AA and Kitchee SC in a nine year spell. Tempest also played 6 matches and scored 2 goals for the Hong Kong national side between 1996 and 1998. He returned to England and began working for Town as Public Relations Officer in 1999 but later left the club and now works for Sky Bet as a betting expert and their PR Guru.

TERNENT, Francis 'Stan'

Manager
Town Years: 2008
Born: *1946 Gateshead, County Durham*
Management career: *Blackpool, Hull City, Bury, Burnley, Gillingham, Huddersfield Town (1979-2008)*

After a long career in football management, Ternent was working at Derby County as assistant manager before he arrived at the club towards the end of the 2007-08 season to become the manager. He was backed by new chairman Dean Hoyle and signed a lot of new players for big money. However, Ternent's spell at the club was a complete disaster and fans were growing restless with the poor performances and rumours of behind the scenes rumblings before Ternent was sacked in November 2008 after just 15 games in charge of the club. He later scouted for Sunderland before becoming the Chief Recruitment Officer at Hull City in 2012. Five years later, Ternent was sacked by the club in January 2017 following the exit of the manager, Mike Phelan. Ternent currently resides in Cliviger, Lancashire.

THACKERAY, Andrew 'Andy'

Midfielder
Town Years: 1986-1987
Born: *1968 Huddersfield, West Riding of Yorkshire*
Playing career: *Huddersfield Town, Newport County, Wrexham, Rochdale, Halifax Town, Nuneaton Borough, Ashton United, Mossley (1986-2007)*

Thackeray came through the youth ranks at Manchester City before he signed for Town in 1986 and made 2 appearances for the club before he was released and he headed to Newport County in 1987, spending just a year at the club before he signed for Wrexham in 1988, remaining until 1992 when he signed for Rochdale. Thackeray remained at Spotland until 1997 when he signed for Halifax Town, playing a major part in their Conference winning team of 1997-98. He later had spells at Nuneaton Borough, Ashton United and Mossley and was a first team regular for each club he played for except Town and finished his career at Mossley in 2007. Thackeray now works as a chiropodist in Huddersfield and worked as Town's chiropodist when Lee Martin was the physio during the mid-2000s.

Stan Ternent's autobiography - 'Stan The Man'

THOMPSON, Arthur

Inside-forward
Town Years: 1941-1949
Born: *1922 Dewsbury, West Riding of Yorkshire*
Died: *1996 Mirfield, West Yorkshire*
Playing career: *Thornhill Edge SC, Huddersfield Town (1941-1949)*

Originally from Dewsbury, Thompson signed for Town in 1941 from Thornhill Edge SC and played a number of matches during the 1946-47 season and also a couple during the 1947-48 and 1948-49 seasons before he retired from professional football in 1949. Thompson later passed away at the age of 74 in July 1996 and was living in Mirfield at the time of his death.

THOMPSON, Tyrone

Winger
Town Years: 2003-2004
Born: *1982 Sheffield, South Yorkshire*
Playing career: *Sheffield United, Lincoln City (loan), Doncaster Rovers (loan), Huddersfield Town, Scarborough, Halifax Town, Crawley Town, Torquay United, Mansfield Town, Grimsby Town, FC Halifax Town, Lincoln City, Sheffield, Gainsborough Trinity (2000-2014)*

Thompson was signed by Peter Jackson in 2003, but only managed 2 appearances for the club before he departed at the end of the 2003-04 season. He drifted into non-league football and played for Scarborough, Halifax Town, Crawley Town, Mansfield Town, Torquay United, Grimsby Town, Lincoln City, Sheffield F.C. and Gainsborough Trinity. Thompson is now running TB8 Management, a company whose purpose is to provide an environment where players are able to maintain an elite level of sporting performance.

THOMSON, Robert

Left-back
Town Years: 1911-1912
Born: *1890 Glasgow, Scotland*
Died: *unknown*
Playing career: *St. Anthony's Glasgow, Huddersfield Town (1911-1912)*

Robert Thomson signed for Town in 1911 and made 5 appearances during the 1911-12 season, as cover for first choice left-back Fred Bullock, before he left the club in 1912. He later enjoyed a short trial spell at Manchester United before he left the game completely.

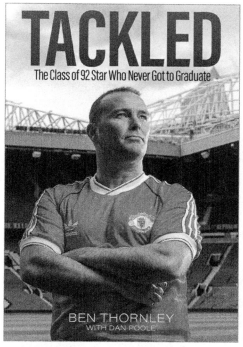

TACKLED
The Class of 92 Star Who Never Got to Graduate

BEN THORNLEY
WITH DAN POOLE

THORNLEY, Benjamin 'Ben'

Winger
Town Years: 1996 (loan), 1998-2001
Born: *1975 Bury, Lancashire*
Playing career: *Manchester United, Stockport County (loan), Huddersfield Town (loan), Huddersfield Town, Aberdeen, Blackpool, Bury, Halifax Town, Bacup Borough, Salford City, Wilmslow Albion, Witton Albion (1993-2010)*

Ben Thornley is said to have had the most potential of the Class of 92 at Manchester United but he suffered an injury which hampered his time at Old Trafford. He was loaned to Town in 1996, impressing with his performances and was later signed permanently two years later when Peter Jackson was the manager. Thornley played over 100 games during his second spell at the club before transferring to Blackpool in 2001. He later played for Bury, Halifax Town, Bacup Borough, Salford City, Wilmslow Albion and Witton Albion and combined his time in non-league with working as a taxi driver. Thornley now lives down South with his girlfriend and is also a regular on MUTV and is usually co-commentator on their coverage of Manchester United games. He also released his autobiography, *Tackled*, in October 2018.

THORPE, George
Goalkeeper
Town Years: 1932-1933
Born: *1909 Farnworth, Bolton, Lancashire*
Died: *1986 Bolton, Lancashire*
Playing career: *Pendlebury, Leeds United, Huddersfield Town, Chester City (c1930-1933)*

After a spell at Bradford City, Thorpe arrived at Leeds Road in 1932 and made a few appearances for Clem Stephenson's side, deputising for Hugh Turner when he went through a lean spell, before he departed the club in 1933. He later played for Chester City and worked as a tailor's presser in Worsley, Lancashire before he passed away in 1986 in Bolton.

THORRINGTON, John
Midfielder
Town Years: 2001-2004
Born: *1979 Johannesburg, South Africa*
Playing career: *Manchester United, Bayer Leverkusen, Huddersfield Town, Grimsby Town, Chicago Fire, Vancouver Whitecaps FC, D.C. United (1997-2013)*

Thorrington arrived at the McAlpine in 2001 after a spell at Bayer Leverkusen and was a first team regular during the 2001-02 and 2002-03 seasons but ended up losing his place during the 2003-04 promotion season. He left the club in 2004 to sign for Grimsby Town, later leaving the country to emigrate to America in 2005 and he signed for Chicago Fire. Thorrington spent five years at the club before signing for Vancouver Whitecaps in 2011, leaving the following year in 2012 and he finished his career at D.C. United in 2013. He is now the general manager and executive vice president of soccer operations at Los Angeles FC in the MLS in America. Thorrington was an American international during his time at the club and earned one cap in 2001.

TICKELL, Brian
Forward
Town Years: 1956-1959
Born: *1939 Carlisle, Cumberland*
Playing career: *Raffles United, Huddersfield Town, Carlisle United, Gateshead, Ballymena United (1956-c1960)*

Tickell joined the club in the month that Andy Beattie left and played 1 game for the club during the 1958-59 season. After leaving Town in 1959, Tickell played for Carlisle United, Gateshead and Ballymena before a knee injury forced his retirement from the game. Tickell inituially worked for the Ministry of Agriculture Food and Fisheries but decided to open a hair salon with his wife Jean. He later became a property developer before retiring in 1991 and is back living in Carlisle.

TISDALE, Paul
Forward
Town Years: 1996 (loan)
Born: *1973 Valletta, Malta*
Playing career: *Southampton, Northampton Town (loan), Huddersfield Town (loan), Bristol City, Exeter City (loan), Dundee United (loan), FinnPa, Panionios, Yeovil Town, Exeter City (1987-2014)*

Arrived in 1996 for a 2 match loan spell from parent club Southampton. Tisdale had a very lacklustre career as a footballer and is more famous for his exploits as a manager. He took charge of Team Bath in 2001 and took them to the first round of the FA Cup in 2002, the first University side since 1881 to do so. He left for Exeter City in 2006 and was renowned for both his snappy dressing and his results on the football field. He achieved two promotions at Exeter City and attracted a lot of attention from bigger clubs but always turned them down. After growing frustration from the fans at St. James Park, Tisdale left for Milton Keynes Dons in 2018 after twelve years in charge of the Grecians.

TOMPKIN, Maurice
Inside-forward
Town Years: 1946-1947
Born: *1919 Countesthorpe, Leicestershire*
Died: *1956 Leicester, Leicestershire*
Playing career: *Countesthorpe United, Leicester City, Bury, Huddersfield Town, Kettering Town (1937-1947)*

Tompkin had served in the Second World War in India beforre he enjoyed a short spell at Leeds Road between 1946 and 1947, where he managed 10 league appearances for David Steele's side. He was a middle-order batsman for Leicestershire between 1938 and 1956 and toured Pakistan with the Marylebone Cricket Club in the mid 1950s. Upon his return, Tompkin suffered from ill-health and he passed away in 1956 from pancreatic cancer at the age of 37.

TOMPKIN, Percy

Outside-left
Town Years: 1919-1920
Born: *1894 Salford, Lancashire*
Died: *1948 Countesthorpe, Leicestershire*
Playing career: *Countesthorpe United, Leicester Imperial, Sutton Junction, Hinckley United, Nuneaton Town, Huddersfield Town, Leicester Fosse, Nuneaton Town (1910-1925)*

Tompkin joined Town from the Army and played one solitary game in the 1919-20 season before he left at the end of the season to sign for Leicester Fosse and remained at the club until 1925, when he returned to former club Nuneaton Town. Tompkin later lived in Blaby, Leicestershire and worked as a hosiery manufacturer before he died in 1948.

TOPPING, Christopher 'Chris'

Centre-half
Town Years: 1978-1981
Born: *1951 Bubwith, East Riding of Yorkshire*
Playing career: *York City, Huddersfield Town, Scarborough (1968-1982)*

After a ten year career at York City, where he played over 400 matches (over 300 of them consecutively), Tom Johnston brought Topping to Leeds Road in 1978. He was usually employed as cover for first choice centre-halves Dave Sutton and Keith Hanvey and played 49 matches for the club before leaving in July 1981 to join Scarborough. Topping retired from professional football in 1982 and later worked as a postman and a mushroom farmer in Selby before retirement.

TRENHAM, Robert

Left-back
Town Years: 1908-1910
Born: *1887 Bradford, West Riding of Yorkshire*
Died: *1958 Leeds, West Riding of Yorkshire*
Playing career: *Leeds City, Huddersfield Town (1907-1910)*

Signing from Leeds City in July 1908, Robert Trenham has the distinction of playing in the club's first ever league match, against South Shields on the 5th of September 1908. Trenham was a left-back and he played 28 matches in the club's first ever season and was later released from the club in July 1910, once Town turned professional. Trenham passed away in 1958 and had been residing in Leeds at the time of his death.

TREVITT, Simon

Right-back
Town Years: 1984-1995
Born: *1967 Dewsbury, West Riding of Yorkshire*
Playing career: *Huddersfield Town, Hull City, Swansea City, Guiseley (1984-1998)*

Trevitt began his career at Leeds Road in 1984, turning professional in 1986, eventually becoming first choice right-back in the first team. He played during the 1991-92 failed promotion campaign and also played in the 1995 Playoff Final at Wembley, which saw Town gain promotion. Trevitt left the club in 1995 to join Hull City where he remained until 1998 and he also later played non-league football for Guiseley. He is now a postman and lives in Liversedge, he has also played cricket for Liversedge Cricket Club. To note, Trevitt was granted a testimonial in 1995, one of the last Town players to be granted one.

TROTMAN, Neal

Centre-half
Town Years: 2010 (loan)
Born: *1987 Levenshulme, Manchester*
Playing career: *Burnley, Oldham Athletic, Halifax Town (loan), Preston North End, Colchester United (loan), Southampton (loan), Huddersfield Town (loan), Oldham Athletic (loan), Rochdale, Chesterfield (loan), Chesterfield, Plymouth Argyle, Bristol Rovers (2004-2015)*

Trotman was loaned to Town in 2010 from Preston North End, initially playing poorly, his performances improved towards the end of the 2009-10 season. He left the club to return to his parent club who released him in 2011 and he signed for Rochdale in before he left for Chesterfield in 2012. At the end of the 2012-13 season, Trotman was released by Chesterfield and he joined Plymouth Argyle after a trial with Partick Thistle. He left in 2014 to sign for Bristol Rovers, leaving in 2015 due to persistent injury problems and Trotman has worked as an FA Licensed Intermediary since 2016.

DID YOU KNOW?"

"Huddersfield Town are the only team in English football to play in all four divisions in two different grounds."

TUCKER, Gordon

Defender
Town Years: 1987-1989
Born: *1968 Manchester, Lancashire*
Playing career: *Derby County, Huddersfield Town, Scunthorpe United, Goole Town, Hyde United (1986-1998)*

After a spell at Derby County, Tucker signed for Town in 1987 and is considered of Town's worst ever players. He played almost 40 games in the first team before being released in 1989 and was signed by Mick Buxton at Scunthorpe United. Tucker lasted a year in Lincolnshire before he signed for non-league Goole Town and he later left Goole in 1994 to sign for Hyde United. Whilst playing for Hyde United, Tucker was sent to prison for drug offences, later being released in 1998. He is currently living and working in Oldham.

TURNER, Andrew 'Andy'

Winger
Town Years: 1995 (loan)
Born: *1975 Woolwich, Greater London*
Playing career: *Tottenham Hotspur, Portsmouth, Crystal Palace, Wolverhampton Wanderers, Rotherham United, Yeovil Town, Tamworth, Northampton Town, Northwich Victoria, Cinderford Town, Belper Town, Banbury United, Chasetown (1992-2008)*

After starting his career at Tottenham Hotspur, Turner arrived on a short loan in the 1995-96 season. He left Spurs in 1996 and played for Portsmouth, Crystal Palace, Wolverhampton Wanderers, Rotherham United, Yeovil Town, Tamworth, Northampton Town and a number of non-league clubs before finally hanging up his boots at Chasetown in 2008. Turner had been working as under 10s coach at Wolverhampton Wanderers before coaching Chasetown and Kidsgrove Athletic. He was then appointed manager of Alsager Town in 2012 before resigning in January 2014 to take the role of assistant manager at Coalville Town. He then worked for Nottingham Forest as the under 15s coach before being appointed manager of Romulus in 2015. Turner spent two years at the club before leaving in November 2017. After this, he worked as a coach at Shepshed Dynamo before he took the job of head coach at Port Vale's Football and Education Academy in April 2018 and is also the manager of non-league Alsager Town.

TURNER, Hugh

Goalkeeper
Town Years: 1926-1937
Born: *1904 Wigan, Lancashire*
Died: *1996 Huddersfield, West Yorkshire*
Playing career: *Felling Colliery, Darlington (amateur), High Fell FC, Huddersfield Town, Fulham, Hurst (1923-1946)*

After playing for High Fell FC, Turner arrived at the club in 1926. He played over 370 matches for the club between 1926 and 1937 before transferring to Fulham. He later played for Town during the War as a guest and also played for non-league Hurst after the War, later finishing his career at the club. Turner passed away in 1996 and had been back at the club as a guest for a game against Peterborough United in 1992.

TURNER, John

Goalkeeper
Town Years: 1975 (loan)
Born: *1954 Gateshead, County Durham*
Playing career: *Derby County, Doncaster Rovers (loan), Brighton & Hove Albion (loan), Huddersfield Town (loan), Reading, Torquay United, Chesterfield, Torquay United, Weymouth, Burnley, Peterborough United (1970-1986)*

Turner began his career at Derby County in 1972 and was loaned to Town in 1975, playing 1 game between the sticks. He left the 'Rams' in the same year to sign for Reading, playing at Elm Park until 1978 when he moved on to Torquay United. Turner remained at Plainmoor until 1980 when he transferred to Chesterfield and he played over 130 games during his three years at Saltergate before he returned to Torquay. He later played for Weymouth, Burnley and ended his career after a two year spell at Peterborough United in 1986. Turner and his wife Amanda entered the pub trade in 1987 and ran The Fortune of War in Torquay and have run the Jolly Sailor in Newton Abbot since the year 2000. John's brother Robbie played at Leeds Road between 1983 and 1985.

DID YOU KNOW?"

"Joey Gudjonsson's dad managed Stoke City, Notts County, Barnsley and the Icelandic national team "

TURNER, Kenneth 'Ken'

Full-back
Town Years: 1957-1963
Born: *1941 Great Houghton, West Riding of Yorkshire*
Died: *2017 Barnsley, South Yorkshire*
Playing career: *Huddersfield Town, Shrewsbury Town, York City, Sligo Rovers (1957-1969)*

Turner began his career at Town in 1957, remaining on the books until 1963 before he transferred to Shrewsbury Town. He spent three years at Gay Meadow before he signed for York City in 1966, leaving the following year and joining Sligo Rovers as a player in 1968, later becoming manager in 1969. Turner spent two years in charge of the club before his departure in 1971 and he returned to his native Barnsley, working for the Post Office for thirty years before his retirement at the age of 60. Turner later passed away at the age of 76 in 2017.

TURNER, Robert 'Robbie'

Forward
Town Years: 1983-1985
Born: *1966 Easington, Greater London*
Playing career: *Huddersfield Town, Cardiff City, Hartlepool United (loan), Bristol Rovers, Wimbledon, Bristol City, Plymouth Argyle, Notts County, Shrewsbury Town (loan), Exeter City, Cambridge United, Hull City (loan), Taunton Town, Newton Abbot (1984-2006)*

Turner began his career at Leeds Road as an apprentice in 1983 and remained at the club until 1985 when he transferred to Cardiff City. He left the Bluebirds the following year to sign for Bristol Rovers in 1986. He left in 1987 to join Wimbledon, playing during the season that they won the FA Cup in 1988 and he later played for Bristol City, Plymouth Argyle, Notts County, Exeter City, Cambridge United and Taunton Town before retiring in the late 1990s. Turner carried on playing local football with Newton Abbot at the age of 40 and has run his own plumbing business in the area for many years.

UNSWORTH, David

Left-back
Town Years: 2008-2009
Born: *1973 Chorley, Lancashire*
Playing career: *Everton, West Ham United, Aston Villa, Everton, Portsmouth, Ipswich Town (loan), Sheffield United, Wigan Athletic, Burnley, Huddersfield Town (1992-2009)*

After a successful trial period, Stan Ternent offered Unsworth a one-year contract at the club. He played in just four matches at the beginning of the 2008-09 season and missed a penalty against Millwall in his last game for the club. Later on in that season, Unsworth's contract was paid up and he retired from professional football shortly afterwards to become the Development Coach at Preston North End, later being promoted to First Team Coach. He then acted as caretaker manager at Deepdale on two occasions before he was sacked in 2012. Unsworth joined Sheffield United as Head of Academy Coaching but left the following year. He was appointed Assistant Manager of the Everton U21 team in September 2013 and was given the Manager's job in 2014. Unsworth acted as caretaker manager of Everton on the final day of the 2015-16 season, reverting to his previous role once Ronald Koeman was appointed as boss. When Koeman was sacked during the 2017-18 season, Unsworth was again appointed caretaker manager and was tipped for the job before Sam Allardyce was given it. Unsworth remains at Goodison Park as the manager of Everton U23s.

VAESEN, Nico-Jos 'Nico'

Goalkeeper
Town Years: 1998-2001
Born: *1969 Hasselt, Belgium*
Playing career: *Tongeren, Cercle Brugge, K.S.C. Eendracht Aalst, Huddersfield Town, Birmingham City, Lierse, K.F.C. Verbroedering Geel (1990-2008)*

Experienced keeper Vaesen arrived in 1998 from K.S.C. Eendracht Aalst and was sent off for deliberate handball in his debut match at the beginning of the 1998-99 season. He played for the club until 2001 and played over 140 first team matches. Vaesen then became first-choice goalkeeper at Birmingham and kept goal during the 2002 play-offs which saw the club promoted to the Premier League. He later suffered a cruciate injury and his replacement Maik Taylor made the No. 1 jersey his own. As a result, Vaesen left St. Andrews in 2006 and returned to Belgium before retiring from the game in 2008. The Belgian is now working for Star Factory Football Management and also runs his own business, VN Consulting & Management from his base in his home country.

VALENTINE, Peter

Defender
Town Years: 1979-1983
Born: *1963 Huddersfield, West Riding of Yorkshire*
Playing career: *Huddersfield Town, Bolton W, Bury, Carlisle United, Rochdale (1979-1996)*

Valentine began his career as an apprentice at Leeds Road in 1979, turning professional in 1981. He spent two years in and out of the first team, making just over 20 appearances for the club before he signed for Bolton Wanderers in 1983. Valentine played for them for two years before signing for Bury in 1985, going on to play over 320 times for the Shakers. He later played for Carlisle United and Rochdale before retiring from the game in 1996. Valentine is still living and working in Huddersfield.

VAUGHAN, James

Forward
Town Years: 2012-2013 (loan), 2013-2016
Born: *1988 Birmingham, West Midlands*
Playing career: *Everton, Norwich City, Huddersfield Town (loan), Huddersfield Town, Birmingham City, Bury, Sunderland, Wigan Athletic (2004-Still Playing)*

Vaughan originally arrived on loan during the 2012-13 season and impressed enough to be signed permanently in 2013. He spent three years at the club but suffered from injury problems and when David Wagner introduced double training sessions in 2015, Vaughan complained that he was getting stuck in traffic on his way home. Vaughan was loaned out to Birmingham City and was later sold to them in 2016. He later had spells at Bury and Sunderland before signing for Wigan Athletic in 2018.

VAUGHTON, Willis

Half-back
Town Years: 1929-1934
Born: *1911 Sheffield, West Riding of Yorkshire*
Died: *2007 Sheffield, South Yorkshire*
Playing career: *Huddersfield Town, Sheffield United, Boston United (player-manager) (1929-1939)*

Vaughton was a defender who only played twice for Town but did manage to score a goal before leaving for Sheffield United in 1934. Vaughton was forced to retire from the professional game due to injuries while in the role of player-manager at Boston United. Later worked as a furnace bricklayer in Wortley and passed away in a care home in Sheffield in 2007.

VEALL, Raymond 'Ray'

Left-wing
Town Years: 1965-1968
Born: *1943 Skegness, Lincolnshire*
Playing career: *Skegness Town, Doncaster Rovers, Everton, Preston North End, Huddersfield Town, Los Angeles Wolves, Maritzburg, Gisborne City (1960-1974)*

Veall arrived at Leeds Road in 1965 after a short spell at Preston North End and remained at the club until 1968, when he moved to America to play for Los Angeles Wolves. He later moved to New Zealand in the early 1970s and he still resides in Gisborne.

VINCENT, Jamie

Left-back
Town Years: 1999-2001
Born: *1975 Wimbledon, London*
Playing career: *Crystal Palace, Bournemouth, Huddersfield Town, Portsmouth, Derby County, Millwall, Yeovil Town, Swindon Town, Walsall, Aldershot Town, Didcot Town (1993-2012)*

Peter Jackson brought Vincent to the club halfway through the 1998-99 season and immediately played him at left-back. He played during the 1999-2000 and 2000-01 seasons before he was sold to Portsmouth in 2001. Vincent spent three years at 'Pompey' before he moved to Derby County for a year in 2004. He also played for Millwall, Yeovil Town, Swindon Town, Walsall and Aldershot Town before heading into non-league with a short spell with Didcot Town, which ended in 2012. Vincent is now working as a Maintenance Director for Adept London in Surrey.

WADE, Thomas 'Tom'

Left-back
Town Years: 1927-1929 (amateur), 1929-1930
Born: *1909 Leeds, West Riding of Yorkshire*
Died: *1960 Leeds, West Riding of Yorkshire*
Playing career: *Methley Perseverance, Huddersfield Town, Darlington, Dartford (1926-1933)*

Wade signed from Methley Perseverance in 1927 as an amateur and later signed professional in 1929. He played once during the 1929-30 season before he was released from the club in 1930. He later played for Darlington and after his career in football ended, Wade worked as a crane driver in Darlington before he passed away in 1960 at the age of 51.

WADSWORTH, Ian

Forward
Town Years: 1983-1986
Born: *1966 Huddersfield, West Riding of Yorkshire*
Playing career: *Huddersfield Town, Doncaster Rovers (1983-1986)*

Wadsworth progressed through the youth ranks at Town and made a solitary appearance for the first team in 1984. He left the club in 1986 and had a short spell at Doncaster Rovers and later played for a number of clubs in Germany but is now living in Holmfirth and runs his own tiling business. At one point, Wadsworth was heavily involved with local club, Holmfirth Town with former Town players Andrew Watson and Robbie Edwards, however Holmfirth Town no longer exists.

WADSWORTH, Michael 'Mick'

Manager
Town Years: 2002-2003
Born: *1950 Barnsley, West Riding of Yorkshire*
Management career: *Matlock Town, Carlisle United, Scarborough, Colchester United, Oldham Athletic, Huddersfield Town, DR Congo, Beira-Mar, Gretna (caretaker), Chester City, Hartlepool United, Celtic Nation, Sheffield F.C. (1985-2014)*

After the sacking of Lou Macari, the board of directors brought in former Oldham Athletic manager Wadsworth on the recommendation of Sir Bobby Robson, as Wadsworth had worked with him at Newcastle United. Wadsworth's appointment coincided with the dire financial situation the club found itself in and he wasn't paid for most of his tenure at the club. After poor results throughout the season, Wadsworth was sacked in January 2003. However, the board of directors couldn't afford his payout and he was reinstated, bringing in Mel Machin as an advisor. Two months later, the results had not improved on the pitch and he was sacked once again, this time for good. November 2003 saw Wadsworth appointed manager of the Democratic Republic of Congo national side. He took charge of the team in the 2004 African Nations Cup, losing three out of three matches. He was sacked from his role and was forced to leave the country. A few months later, Wadsworth was appointed manager of Beira-Mar in Portugal but was sacked after just three months.

He had a spell as assistant manager at Shrewsbury Town before being appointed Director of Club Development at Scottish club Gretna, later becoming the Director of Football and assistant manager in July 2007. The club went under in 2008 and Wadsworth was laid off. A year later, he surfaced at Chester City as manager, later getting sacked after just thirteen games. He took the job of First Team Coach at Hartlepool United in June 2010, becoming caretaker manager in August and becoming permanent manager later on in the season. He was sacked in December 2011 and later worked at Sheffield United in 2013 as caretaker first team coach. He has since managed non-league clubs Celtic Nation and Sheffield FC before becoming Senior Youth Development Coach at Sheffield United in 2015.

WADSWORTH, Samuel 'Sam'

Left-back
Town Years: 1921-1929
Born: *1896 Darwen, Lincolnshire*
Died: *1961 Eindhoven, Holland*
Playing career: *Darwen, Blackburn Rovers, Nelson, Huddersfield, Burnley, Lytham (1913-1931)*

After a trial at Nelson, Wadsworth was signed by Town in 1921 and he won the FA Cup in 1922 with Town and played in each of the three successive First Division winning sides of 1924, 1925 and 1926. He was also part of the side that finished runners-up in 1927 and 1928. Wadsworth even managed to get called up for the England squad in 1922, and played on 6 occasions between then and 1926. He remained at Town until 1929 and after eight years, one FA Cup winners medal and three First Division titles, he left the club. Wadsworth later played for Burnley and Lytham. After retirement, Wadsworth and his wife lost everything after a failed garage venture. He was offered the manager's job at Dutch club Delft in 1934 before being offered the PSV job in 1935, lasting three years there before heading to DWS where he remained for two years. Wadsworth later managed PSV for a second spell between 1945 and 1951, and then spent a four year spell at Brabantia before spending a year at BVC Amsterdam in 1956. Wadsworth later passed away in September 1961, having lived in Eindhoven since the 1930s.

David Wagner

WAGNER, David
Manager
Born: *1971, Geinsheim am Rhein, West Germany*
Previous managerial history: *Borussia Dortmund II, Huddersfield Town (2011-2019)*

After a spell as the head coach of Borussia Dortmund II, Wagner arrived at the club in 2015 after Chris Powell's dismissal. In just a few short weeks, he'd revolutionised the way the team played, employing a style of play known as "gegenpressing". Although the club narrowly avoided relegation to League One at the end of the 2015-16 season, he set about bringing in his own players that he believed fitted his style of play. Almost every footballing "expert" predicted Town to get relegated but Town topped the Championship table in the early season and didn't drop below 8th position all season. Wagner turned down offers from Aston Villa, Wolfsburg and Leicester City during the season and stated that he was happy at Town. Wagner eventually steered Town to the playoffs and, against all the odds, to promotion. This feat also earned him the Championship Manager of the Year award. Again, most of the football "experts" were certain that Wagner would leave soon after the promotion but he soon signed an improved contract and remained at the club for the 2017-18 season, the club's first ever season in the Premier League. After bringing in new signings, Town started the campaign well and after an opening day win at Crystal Palace, topped the Premier League. The good form continued but ended up dying down as the season progressed, but Wagner pulled it out of the bag and after good results against Watford, Manchester City and finally Chelsea, Town avoided relegation with one game to spare. He signed another improved deal and brought in reinforcements but the season started badly, with losses against Chelsea and Manchester City and it never really improved. It was thought that the club had turned a corner but it was downhill from there on. Town went on an 8 match losing streak before finally managing a 0-0 draw against relegation rivals Cardiff City in January 2019 to stop the horrendous run. This turned out to be Wagner's final game in charge as he resigned two days later and left the club by mutual consent.

WALFORD, Stephen 'Steve'
Centre-half
Town Years: 1987 (loan)
Born: *1958 Highgate, London*
Playing career: *Tottenham Hotspur, Arsenal, Norwich City, West Ham United, Huddersfield Town (loan), Lai Sun, Wycombe Wanderers (1975-1989)*

Walford was brought to the club during the 1987-88 season to help plug the leaky defence. He played at centre-half during the 10-1 Man City game and played 11 other matches before returning to his parent club, West Ham United. Walford left Upton Park in 1989 and later played for Lai Sun (Hong Kong), Wealdstone and Wycombe Wanderers before his retirement as a professional. Walford has worked as Martin O'Neill's assistant manager since 1990, working at Wycombe Wanderers, Norwich City, Leicester City, Celtic, Aston Villa, Sunderland and has been the Republic of Ireland assistant manager since 2013. He also worked as assistant to Neil Lennon at Bolton Wanderers between 2015 and 2016.

WALKER, Frederick 'Fred'
Centre-half, Player-secretary-manager
Town Years: 1908-1910
Born: *1884 Barrow-in-Furness, Lancashire*
Died: *1963 Barrow-in-Furness, Lancashire*
Playing career: *Barrow, Leeds City, Huddersfield Town (1905-1910)*

Walker was playing for Leeds City when he received the offer to play for Town prior to the 1908-09 season. He played in Town's first ever match and he was appointed secretary-manager, combining these roles with that as captain of the side. Walker was a centre-half and he achieved 16th position in the North Eastern League before the club switched to the Midland League in 1909-10. He achieved 5th position in his second season at the helm. He was released when the club turned professional and it was decided a more experienced man was required to lead the club. It seems that Walker began work as an office boy in Barrow-in-Furness whilst playing for Barrow. He was then snapped up by Leeds City in 1905, playing at centre-half for three years, before becoming secretary-manager at Leeds Road. After he left the club, he returned to his native Barrow and worked as a clerk. Fred Walker is thought to have passed away in 1963 and was still living in his native Barrow.

WALKER, Paul

Midfielder
Town Years: 1976-1977
Born: *1949 Bradford, West Riding of Yorkshire*
Playing career: *Wolverhampton W, Peterborough United, Barnsley, Huddersfield Town (1968-1977)*

After playing for Wolves, Peterborough and Barnsley, Walker arrived at Leeds Road in 1976. He only managed a single game for the first team but was a regular in the reserves until his departure in 1977. Walker left football in the late 1970s and started a travel business which catered for American and Canadian tourists in the UK. After about ten years he sold the company to an American travel company. He then took on senior roles at Ley Wilkinson and Federal Express before setting up his own business in contract packaging, CPS Packaging and CPS Finishing. After seventeen years in the industry, Walker retired in 2012 and is now living in Leeds.

WALLACE, Robert 'Bob'

Inside-right
Town Years: 1963-1967
Born: *1948 Huddersfield, West Riding of Yorkshire*
Playing career: *Huddersfield Town, Halifax Town, Chester, Aldershot (1963-1977)*

Wallace spent four years at Leeds Road tbefore leaving in 1967 to join Halifax Town. He remained at The Shay until 1972 and then turned out for Chester City, Aldershot. Wallace left the Hampshire club in 1977 and later retired from professional football before he became a landlord in Huddersfield, running, in no particular order, The Black Bull in Berry Brow, The Angel in Paddock, The Traveller's Rest in Brockholes, The Wappy Springs in Lindley, The Scape House in Scapegoat Hill and The Crossroads in Holmfirth.

WALLACE, Murray

Centre-half
Town Years: 2012-2016
Born: *1993 Glasgow, Scotland*
Playing career: *Rangers, Falkirk, Huddersfield Town, Falkirk (loan) , Scunthorpe United (loan), Scunthorpe United, Millwall (2009-Still Playing)*

Wallace was signed from Falkirk in 2012 by Lee Clark and after four years at Town, he signed for Scunthorpe United, after a loan spell, in 2016 and since 2018 has played for Millwall.

Ronnie Wallwork under police surveillance

WALLWORK, Ronald 'Ronnie'

Midfielder
Town Years: 2007-2008
Born: *1977 Newton Heath, Greater Manchester*
Playing career: *Manchester United, Carlisle United (loan), Stockport County (loan), Royal Antwerp (loan), West Bromwich Albion, Bradford City (loan), Barnsley (loan), Huddersfield Town (loan), Sheffield Wednesday, Ashton United (1993-c2014)*

Wallwork spent a short time on loan at Town during the 2007-08 season from West Bromwich Albion. He left West Brom in 2008 and spent a short time at Sheffield Wednesday before retiring in the same year. He later ran D&R Designers, a clothes business in Failsworth before he was charged with concealing criminal property in connection with offence relating to stolen cars in January 2011. He was sentenced in December 2011 for 15 months after pleading guilty. He later avoided jail in 2014 after pleading guilty to stealing a car and signed for Ashton United in the same year.

WALSH, Alan

Forward
Town Years: 1991-1992
Born: *1956 Hartlepool, County Durham*
Playing career: *Middlesbrough, Darlington, Bristol City, Beşiktaş, Walsall, Huddersfield Town, Shrewsbury Town, Cardiff City, Michelotti, Hartlepool United, Bath City (1977-1995)*

After a long career in the Football League,

Walsh spent a short time at Leeds Road during the 1991-92 season after signing from Walsall. He left for Shrewsbury Town in 1992 and spent a short time at the club before rounding off his career with short spells at Cardiff City, Hartlepool United and Bath City before hanging up his boots in 1995. After his retirement, Walsh spent eleven years at former club Bristol City in a coaching capacity before his departure in 2011. He then joined rivals Bristol Rovers in 2012 as youth team coach, before leaving four years later in 2016.

WALTER, Joseph 'Joe'
Outside-right
Town Years: 1922-1925
Born: *1895 Eastville, Bristol, Gloucestershire*
Died: *1995 Bristol, Avon*
Playing career: *All Hallows, Cliftonians, Gloucestershire Regiment, Horfield United, Bristol Rovers, Huddersfield Town, Taunton United, Blackburn Rovers, Bristol Rovers, Bath City, Kingswood (1914-1931)*
One of Town's Thrice Champions, Joe Walter arrived at Leeds Road from Bristol Rovers in 1922 and played in two of the three championship winning seasons. He left for Taunton United in 1925 and had spells at Blackburn Rovers, Bristol Rovers (again) and Bath City before retiring after a short spell at Kingswood. He worked as a groundsman after his playing career ended, firstly for the Bristol Co-Operative Society and then Bristol City. He also worked as a proprietor of a cooked meat shop in Bristol in the late 1930s. Bristol Rovers later gave him a job as assistant coach in 1960. By the early 1990s, Walter was thought to have died but was incredibly tracked down and was found to be living in Bristol. This discovery coincided with Town's final season at Leeds Road and he was invited to watch Town play Bristol Rovers at Twerton Park. He was also interviewed for Town's Final Whistle VHS and was the guest of honour at Town's final game at the old Leeds Road ground. Joe Walter passed away in May 1995, just three months short of his 100th birthday. Neil Warnock and the entire first team squad attended his funeral. Joe Walter had served in the Gloucestershire Regiment during World War One and he represented the Third Battalion of the Glorious Glosters.

WARD, Daniel 'Danny'
Left-winger/Forward
Town Years: 2011 (loan), 2011-2015
Born: *1991 Bradford, West Yorkshire*
Playing career: *Leeds United, Bolton Wanderers, Swindon Town (loan), Coventry City (loan), Huddersfield Town (loan), Huddersfield Town, Rotherham United (loan), Rotherham United, Cardiff City (2005-Still Playing)*
Ward originally arrived on loan towards the end of the 2010-11 season and impressed that much that he was later signed permanently. He spent four years at the club before he was sold to Rotherham United in 2015. David Wagner tried to sign Ward in the January 2017 transfer window but his offer was turned down. Ward signed for Cardiff City in 2017.

WARD, Daniel 'Danny'
Goalkeeper
Town Years: 2016-17 (loan)
Born: *1993 Wrexham, Wales*
Playing career: *Wrexham, Tamworth (loan), Liverpool, Morecambe (loan), Aberdeen (loan), Huddersfield Town (loan), Leicester City (2011-Still Playing)*
Ward signed on loan from Liverpool for the 2016-17 season and he was in goal when Town were promoted to the Premier League in 2017, saving crucial penalties in the shootouts in both the semi-final and final. He returned to Liverpool at the end of the season and was later sold to Leicester City in 2018.

WARD, Elliott
Centre-half
Town Years: 2015 (loan) [two spells]
Born: *1985 Harrow, Greater London*
Playing career: *West Ham United, Norwich City, Nottingham Forest (loan), Bournemouth, Huddersfield Town (loan), Blackburn Rovers, Milton Keynes Dons (loan) (2001-Still Playing)*
Ward arrived on loan from AFC Bournemouth in 2015, he played 5 games for the club before sustaining a knee injury and returning to his parent club. He returned for a second spell on loan in December but returned at the end of the month after making no appearances. Ward signed for Blackburn Rovers in 2016 before being released in 2018 after a loan at MK Dons. Ward has been playing for Notts County since the summer of 2018.

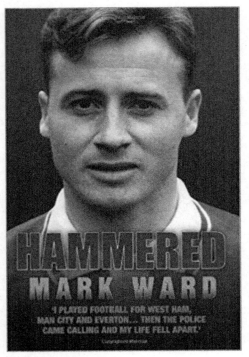

WARD, Mark

Right-winger
Town Years: 1996
Born: *1962 Huyton, Liverpool, Lancashire*
Playing career: *Northwich Victoria, Oldham Athletic, West Ham United, Manchester City, Everton , Birmingham City, Huddersfield Town, Ayr United, Wigan Athletic, Dundee (1977-1999)*

After playing for a number of Premier League clubs, Mark Ward arrived at the McAlpine Stadium in 1996 after previously playing for Birmingham City. He only spent a short time at the club before playing for Ayr United, Wigan Athletic, Dundee, Valur, Altrincham and Leigh RMI before retiring. He had a spell as manager of Altrincham but was sacked in 2001 an he later went to America to coach but this coincided with the 9/11 terrorist attacks and he was soon back home in Merseyside. Ward fell on hard times and was later jailed in 2005 after 4 kilograms of cocaine was found during a raid at a house he owned. After four years, Ward was released from HM Prison Kirkham in 2009 and also wrote a book about his career whilst he was inside. He is now involved on a match day at former clubs West Ham United and Everton and is also working to set up a floristry business with his wife.

WARD, Peter

Forward
Town Years: 1986-1989
Born: *1964 Chester le Street, County Durham*
Playing career: *Newcastle United, Chester-Le-Sreet Town, Huddersfield Town, Rochdale, Stockport County, Wrexham, Morecambe (1982-1999)*

After playing for his local side, Chester-le-Street Town, Ward was signed by Mick Buxton in November 1986. He played at Leeds Road for three years before he left for Rochdale in 1989 and he left Spotland two years later to join Stockport County, where he played over 150 games. Ward then transferred to Wrexham in 1995 and he spent four years at the Racecourse Ground, playing over 100 matches. He then had a short spell at Morecambe in 1999 before his retirement as a player. Ward moved into coaching and began coaching at Stockport County's Centre of Excellence in 2000 as the U15s and U16s coach. Ward also coached in China between 2002 and 2003 and also worked as Stockport County Under 18s assistant coach between 2004 and 2005. He was promoted to assistant manager at Edgeley Park in 2006, remaining in the role until 2009 when he followed Jim Gannon to Motherwell as his assistant manager. Following Gannon's dismissal in 2010, Ward left the club with him and returned to Stockport as assistant manager. Later acting as caretaker manager in 2011 after Paul Simpson was sacked. He later left the club in July 2011 but returned in 2012 to work as Chief Scout and Talent Identification Officer, leaving in 2013. He then worked for Leyton Orient as a scout between 2013 and 2015 and then scouted for Colchester United between 2015 and 2016. Ward is an A-Licensed coach and is currently living in Ashton-under-Lyne.

WARD, Richard

Midfielder
Town Years: 1993-1994
Born: *1973 Scarborough, North Riding of Yorkshire*
Playing career: *Notts County, Huddersfield Town (1991-1994)*

Ward signed from Notts County and made a couple of appearances for the first team, but was mainly a reserve player, he has since worked for Cleveland Potash and is heavily involved with Staithes Athletic and Staithes Cricket Club in Saltburn-by-the-sea.

WARNOCK, Neil
Manager
Town Years: 1993-1995
Born: *1948 Sheffield, West Riding of Yorkshire*
Management career: *Burton A, Scarborough, Notts Co, Torquay , Huddersfield T, Plymouth Oldham A, Bury, Sheffield U, Crystal P, QPR, Leeds, Crystal P, Rotherham, Cardiff (1980-date)*

After a short spell at Torquay United, Neil Warnock arrived at Leeds Road in 1993 to replace the outgoing manager, Ian Ross. He led the club to two Wembley finals in his two years at the club, firstly the Autoglass Final in 1994 and then gaining promotion in 1995 in the end of season Play Off Final. He left the club soon after the promotion to join Plymouth Argyle. He has since managed Oldham Athletic, Bury, and Sheffield United, where he spent eight years and won promotion to the Premier League in 2006. He then took charge of Crystal Palace between 2007 and 2010 before he left for Queens Park Rangers after Palace were placed into administration. He achieved promotion to the Premier League before managing Leeds United, Palace and QPR. He then joined Rotherham United towards the end of the 2015-16 season and performed a Great Escape where he saved Rotherham from relegation. Warnock joined Cardiff City in October 2016. He took them to the Premier League at the end of the 2017-18 season, thus achieving a record breaking eighth promotion in his career.

Neil Warnock

WATSON, Albert
Half-back
Town Years: 1935-1937 (amateur) 1937-1948
Born: *1918 Bolton on Dearne, West Riding of Yorkshire*
Died: *2009 Sunderland, Tyne and Wear*
Playing career: *Huddersfield Town, Oldham Athletic (1935-1950)*

Watson began his professional career at Town in 1937 after spending two years as an amateur. He only played 18 matches at Leeds Road during his eleven years as a professional due to the outbreak of World War Two. Watson left the club in 1948 and joined Oldham Athletic, where he spent two years before retiring from professional football in 1950. He later ran a sports shop in Sunderland before he passed away in 2009 at the age of 91.

WATSON, William 'Billy'
Left-half, Trainer
Town Years: 1912-1928, 1928-1929 (trainer)
Born: *1893 Bolton on Dearne, West Riding of Yorkshire*
Died: *1962 Sunderland, County Durham*
Playing career: *Bolton United, Huddersfield Town (1911-1927)*

Watson signed from non-league Bolton United and spent his entire professional career at Huddersfield Town. He arrived in 1912 and made his debut just three months later, he established himself in the side after the end of World War One and League football resumed in 1919. Watson was part of the 1919-20 promotion winning side and also played in each of the three First Division winning sides and also won the FA Cup in 1922. He finally retired from professional football in 1928 after sixteen years at the club and he remained on the payroll as a member of the training staff and also captained the reserve side. Watson left the club altogether in July 1929 but his two sons Albert and Willie later played for the club. He later worked as a caterer for school children in Golborne before passing away in April 1962 at the age of 68.

DID YOU KNOW?"

"Neil Danns recorded a single called 'Survive' in 2010 but it was never released."

WATSON, Edwin
Midfielder
Town Years: 1938-1939
Born: *1914 Pittenweem, Scotland*
Died: *1944 unknown*
Playing career: *Blackburn Rovers, Partick Thistle, Huddersfield Town, Bradford PA (c1935-1939)*

Watson had been playing for Partick Thistle before he arrived at Leeds Road in 1938 and played a couple of games for the first team before leaving in 1939 to sign for Bradford Park Avenue. The Scotsman died in 1944.

WATSON, James 'Jimmy'
Inside-forward
Town Years: 1952-1957
Born: *1924 Plean, Stirlingshire, Scotland*
Died: *1996 Dunfermline, Scotland*
Playing career: *Huddersfield Town (1946-1951)*

After starting his career at Motherwell, Watson arrived at Leeds Road in 1952, signed by fellow Scotsman Andy Beattie. He spent five years at the club, playing over 140 matches at inside-forward, including the 1952-53 promotion season. Watson returned to Scotland and became a licensee in Dunfermline. He remained in the town as a businessman before passing away in April 1996 at the age of 72.

WILLIE WATSON

LEICESTER & ENGLAND

WATSON, William 'Willie'
Outside-left
Town Years: 1937-1946
Born: *1920 Bolton on Dearne, West Riding of Yorkshire*
Died: *2004 Johannesburg, South Africa*
Playing career: *Huddersfield Town, Sunderland, Halifax Town (1937-1956)*

Watson began his career at Town in 1937 but only made a few appearances before World War Two broke out in 1939. He left for Sunderland in 1946 and spent eight years and played over 200 matches at Roker Park before becoming player-manager of Halifax Town. Watson is perhaps more famous for his cricket career and was a left-handed batsman who made his debut for Yorkshire in 1939 and played for them up until 1958, appearing in 23 Test matches for England during that time. He joined Leicestershire in 1958 as assistant-secretary and captain and became Halifax manager soon after for a second spell, remaining at The Shay for two years before heading to Bradford City to become their manager in 1966. He emigrated to South Africa in 1968 to coach the Wanderers and after his career in football ended, Watson worked as a poultry farmer. Died in Johannesburg in 2004.

WATTS, Julian
Centre-half
Town Years: 1998 (loan)
Born: *1971 Sheffield, West Riding of Yorkshire*
Playing career: *Rotherham United, Sheffield Wednesday, Leicester City, Huddersfield Town (loan), Bristol City, Lincoln City (loan), Blackpool (loan), Luton Town, Northern Spirit (1990-2004)*

Watts arrived on loan during the 1997-98 season from Leicester City and played 8 matches before being recalled to Filbert Street. He later played for Bristol City, Luton Town and Northern Spirit before retiring in 2004. After his retirement as a player, Watts later worked as Commercial Manager of Approved Food in Dinnington before being promoted to Business Unit Manager. He reverted to his previous role in February 2016 before leaving the company in June 2018. He has since worked for Player Trader as Head of UK/Global Development and has also had spells as manager of non-league sides Hallam FC, Shirebrook Town and Rainworth Miners Welfare. Watts is now working as a financial advisor.

WEATHERHEAD, Shaun
Centre-half
Town Years: 1986-1989
Born: *1970 Halifax, West Riding of Yorkshire*
Playing career: *Huddersfield Town, York City, Accrington Stanley (1987-c1994)*
Weatherhead began his career at Leeds Road as an apprentice in 1986 and left three years later in 1989, one year after turning professional, after suffering from injury problems. He later played for York City before he moved to Hong Kong and played professionally there until 1993, when he returned to the UK to play for Accrington Stanley. Weatherhead worked as a health insurance agent before becoming a personal trainer. Later became a performance/ life coach, specialising in business and education sectors. From 2006 to 2017, Weatherhead was the owner of U Can Shine, a company that delivered motivational programmes to children across the North of England, raising aspirations and changing the lives of young people. Since 2017, he has been a motivational coach, running his own company SW Coaching. Weatherhead also coaches football and runs numerous soccer camps for children in Huddersfield.

WEBSTER, Simon
Centre-half
Town Years: 1985 (loan) 1985-1988
Born: *1964 Hinckley, Leicestershire*
Playing career: *Tottenham Hotspur, Exeter City (loan), Norwich City (loan), Huddersfield Town (loan), Huddersfield Town, Sheffield United, Charlton Athletic (loan), Charlton Athletic, West Ham United, Oldham Athletic (loan), Derby County (loan), St Albans City (1981-1997)*
Webster joined on loan from Tottenham Hotspur in 1985 before later signing permanently. He played for three years at Leeds Road before heading to Sheffield United in 1988. He spent two years at Bramall Lane before signing for Charlton Athletic in 1990 and three years later he moved to West Ham United, but suffered an injury in training which is what eventually ended his professional career. Webster later trained as a physiotherapist and became the Academy Physiotherapist at West Ham in 1997, remaining until 2001 when he became the First Team Physio. He also worked as a Junior and then Senior Physiotherapist for Bromley NHS Trust during this time.

Webster left Upton Park in 2004 to join Gillingham as their Physiotherapist, remaining until 2006. He has worked as a physiotherapist for Nuffield Health since 2006 and combines this with his role as Charlton Athletic Women's team's physiotherapist.

WELLS, Mark
Defender
Town Years: 1993-1994
Born: *1971 Leicester, Leicestershire*
Playing career: *Notts County, Huddersfield Town, Scarborough, Dagenham & Redbridge (loan), Gateshead, Worcester City, Harrogate Town, Hinckley Town, Pickering Town (1990-2003)*
Neil Warnock brought Mark Wells to the club in 1993 from Notts County and he managed to make over 20 appearances for the first team during the 1993-94 season but he left the club after that and signed for Scarborough. He spent three years at the McCain Stadium before leaving in 1997 and later played for Gateshead, Worcester City, Harrogate Town, Hinckley Town and Pickering Town before hanging up his boots. Towards the end of his career he changed his name to Mark Tyrrell. Wells/Tyrrell now works as a tiler in York, where he settled once his playing days ended.

WELLS, Nahki
Forward
Town Years: 2014 (loan), 2014-2017
Born: *1990 Hamilton, Bermuda*
Playing career: *Dandy Town Hornets, Bermuda Hogges, Eccleshill United, Carlisle United, Bradford City, Huddersfield Town (loan), Huddersfield Town, Burnley, Queens Park Rangers (loan) (2009-Still Playing)*
Wells joined Town on an emergency loan in early 2014 from Bradford City and the purpose of the emergency loan was to allow paperwork to be completed. He scored on his debut against Millwall in a 1-0 win and he joined the club permanently after the game and was top scorer for the club in 2014-15 and 2015-16, he also scored 10 goals during the 2016-17 promotion season. After rejecting a new contract prior to the 2016-17 season, Wells was later sold to Burnley in August 2017 for £5 million and he spent the 2018-19 season on loan at Queens Park Rangers.

WERLING, Dominik
Left-back
Town Years: 2009
Born: *1982 Ludwigshafen, Germany*
Playing career: *Huddersfield Town, Darlington, Hereford United, SV Scheibenhardt, FC Homburg, Ånge IF, SV Rulzheim, Karlsruher FV (2003-2017)*

Lee Clark brought Werling to the club in January 2009 on a short term contract and he played just 3 matches at left-back before leaving the club at the end of the 2008-09 season on a free transfer. He later played for Darlington and Hereford United before heading back to Germany to play for SV Scheibenhardt and later FC Homburg. Werling later signed for Ange IF in Sweden in 2014 before leaving to sign for SV Rülzheim in 2016. A year later he signed for Karlsruher FV.

WESTON, Donald 'Don'
Centre-forward
Town Years: 1965-1966
Born: *1936 Mansfield, Nottinghamshire*
Died: *2007 Wrexham, Wales*
Playing career: *Leeds United, Wrexham, Birmingham City, Rotherham United, Huddersfield Town, Wrexham, Chester (1958-1969)*

Arriving from Leeds United in 1965, Weston only spent a year at Leeds Road before heading to Wrexham, where he remained until 1968. He remained in the area, turning out for Chester City and later had a spell at Altrincham. Weston later worked as a senior salesman for Vauxhall in Wrexham before he passed away at the age of 70 in 2007.

WHEELER, William John 'Jack'
Goalkeeper
Town Years: 1948-1956
Born: *1919 North Littleton, near Evesham, Worcestershire*
Died: *2009 Nottingham, Nottinghamshire*
Playing career: *Cheltenham Town, Birmingham City, Huddersfield Town, Kettering Town (1938-1957)*

Wheeler arrived in 1948 from Birmingham City and although he spent some time in the reserves, he eventually broke into the first team. He was part of the 1952-53 promotion winning team and along with five defenders he was ever-present in the 42 league games played. Wheeler remained at Town until 1956 when he signed for Tommy Lawton at Kettering Town.

In 1957, Tommy Lawton became the manager of Notts County and took Wheeler with him as his trainer. Wheeler remained at Meadow Lane until 1983 when arthritis in his hip forced him to retire. During his 26 year spell at Notts County, Wheeler had been the trainer, coach, scout and even caretaker manager. Upon his retirement, he was awarded life membership at Notts County and was even given a permanent seat in the directors' box. He later passed away in 2009 at the ripe old age of 89.

WHELPTON, James Isaac 'Ike'
Goalkeeper
Town Years: 1911-1912
Born: *1887 Sheffield, West Riding of Yorkshire*
Died: *1944 Sheffield, West Riding of Yorkshire*
Playing career: *Mexborough Town, Lincoln City, Birmingham, Castleford Town, Huddersfield Town, Guildford United, Grimsby Town, Bournemouth & Boscombe Athletic (1909-1924)*

After short spells with Lincoln City, Birmingham and Castleford Town, Whelpton signed for Town in 1911. He only played 2 matches before leaving towards the end of the 1911-12 season to join Guildford United. He later played for Grimsby Town and then signed for Bournemouth & Boscombe Athletic after the First World War, which he served in. He is listed on the 1939 Register of England & Wales as a football manager but no more information is known and Whelpton later passed away in 1944 in his mid 50s.

WHITE, Leonard 'Len'
Forward
Town Years: 1962-1965
Born: *1930 Skellow, West Riding of Yorkshire*
Died: *1994 Huddersfield, West Yorkshire*
Playing career: *Upton Colliery, Rotherham United, Newcastle United, Huddersfield Town, Stockport County (1950-1966)*

White arrived at Leeds Road in 1962 from Newcastle United and spent three years at the club, making over 100 appearances and scoring over 40 goals. He left for Stockport County in 1965 and retired from the game just a year later in 1966. After retiring as a player, White worked at David Brown's in Huddersfield for many years, also playing for the work's football team for many years before he later passed away in Huddersfield in 1994 at the age of 64.

WHITEHEAD, Dean
Central midfielder / Right-back
Town Years: 2015-2018
Born: *1982 Abingdon, Oxfordshire*
Playing career: *Oxford United, Sunderland, Stoke City, Middlesbrough, Huddersfield Town (1999-2018)*
After a two year spell at Middlesbrough, Chris Powell brought 'Deano' to the club for the 2015-16 season. He was a regular in the side during Powell's reign and also under Powell's replacement David Wagner. Whitehead signed a year's extension to his contract in 2017 and he retired from professional football at the end of the 2017-18 season. Following his retirement, Whitehead immediately joined David Wagner's coaching staff at Town

WHITINGTON, Craig
Forward
Town Years: 1994-1996
Born: *1970 Brighton, Sussex*
Playing career: *Worthing, Crawley Town, Scarborough, Huddersfield Town, Rochdale (loan), Crawley Town, Rottingdean United, Whitehawk at least, Brighton North End, Three Bridges (1990-2008)*
Neil Warnock brought Whitington to the club in 1994 from Scarborough but he only managed 1 appearance in the first team and was sacked by the club in 1996 for failing two separate drugs tests. He drifted into non-league and played for a number of clubs including Crawley Town. After leaving professional football, Whitington worked in the logistics industry and also worked as a development centre coach after gaining an FA coaching qualification. He is now living in Brighton and works as Chief Operating Officer of the pro-Brexit political party, Time Party UK.

WHITNEY, Jonathan 'Jon'
Full-back
Town Years: 1993-1996
Born: *1970 Nantwich, Cheshire*
Playing career: *Wigan Athletic, Winsford United, Huddersfield Town, Wigan Athletic (loan), Lincoln City, Hull City, King's Lynn (1988-2002)*
After spells at non-league Skelmersdale United and Winsford United, Whitney signed for Town in 1993 and during the three years he spent at Leeds Road he made few appearances before he moved on to Lincoln City in 1996 where he played for three years. He later had a two year spell

at Hull City before spending a year at King's Lynn before his retirement in 2002. Whitney then had a spell digging graves before qualififying as a physiotherapist and becoming Walsall's physio in 2003. In 2011 he was appointed assistant manager, a role he combined with his physio duties. After Sean O'Driscoll was sacked in March 2016, Whitney was appointed as permanent manager, a role held for two years until March 2018. He is currently Company Director at The Fast Zone, based in Stafford, where he also lives.

WHITTAKER, William 'Bill'
Right-half
Town Years: 1948-1950
Born: *1922 Charlton, London*
Died: *1977 Greenwich, Greater London*
Playing career: *Arsenal, Charlton Athletic, Huddersfield Town, Crystal Palace, Cambridge United (player-manager) (1938-1955)*
Whittaker was a wing-half who signed from Charlton Athletic in 1948, he spent two years at Leeds Road, making over 40 appearances for the first team. He became the player-manager of Cambridge United. Whittaker left the role in 1955 and became a coach at Newmarket and between 1956 and 1957, worked as a scout at Doncaster Rovers. He later passed away in August 1977 in Greenwich at the age of just 54.

WHITTAM, Ernest 'Ernie'
Forward
Town Years: 1926-1933
Born: *1911 Wealdstone, Middlesex*
Died: *1951 Huddersfield, West Riding of Yorkshire*
Playing career: *Huddersfield Town, Chester, Mansfield Town, Wolverhampton Wanderers, Bournemouth, Reading, Mossley (1929-1945)*
Whittam made a handful of appearanves during his for seven years at the club and left for Chester in 1933. A one year spell at Mansfield Town followed before playing a single match at Wolves in 1936. Whittam spent three years at Bournemouth before he signed for Reading in 1939, but his career at Elm Park was curtailed after just one match as the Second World War broke out. After the end of the War, Whittam played for Mossley in non-league before retiring as a player and was still living in Huddersfield when he died from cancer in 1951 at the age of just 40.

WHITTINGHAM, Alfred 'Alf'

Forward
Town Years: 1947-1949
Born: *1914 Altofts, West Riding of Yorkshire*
Died: *1993 Altofts, West Yorkshire*
Playing career: *Altofts West Riding Colliery, Bradford City, Huddersfield Town, Halifax Town (1936-1950)*

After playing for Bradford City, Whittingham arrived at Leeds Road in 1947 and he played for George Stephenson's side for two seasons before his departure in 1949, signing for Halifax Town. He spent a year at Halifax Town before retiring from the professional game in 1950, later passing away in 1993.

WHITTINGHAM, Samuel 'Sam'

Left-back
Town Years: 1910-1911
Born: *1884 Stoke-upon-Trent, Staffordshire*
Died: *1958 Agbrigg, West Riding of Yorkshire*
Playing career: *Goldenhill Wanderers, Stoke, Burslem Port Vale, Crewe Alexandra, Blackpool, Huddersfield Town, Mirfield United (1902-1911)*

After a spell at Blackpool, Whittingham signed in 1910 and was a left-back that played one FA Cup game during the 1910-11 season before he was released at the end of that season. He signed for Mirfield United after leaving Leeds Road and later passed away in 1958, having remained in the area since his playing days had ended over 40 years previously.

WIDDOWFIELD, Edward 'Ted'

Outside-right
Town Years: 1935-1936
Born: *1915 Hetton-le-Hole, County Durham*
Died: *1983 Newark, Nottinghamshire*
Playing career: *Birtley Colliery, Huddersfield Town, Halifax Town, Ransome & Marles, Peterborough United, Worthington & Simpsons Committee (1935-1950)*

Widdowfield signed for Town in 1935 from Birtley Colliery but only spent a year at the club before his departure in 1936, after making a handful of appearances. He signed for Halifax Town and during the War, joined the Halifax Police Force and also worked as a carpenter and after the Second World War ended, he signed for Peterborough United in 1949, later leaving the club in 1950. Widdowfield later passed away in 1983 while he was living in Newark.

WIENAND, George 'Tolley'

Outside-right
Town Years: 1937-1938
Born: *1910 East London, Eastern Cape, South Africa*
Died: *1993 East London, South Africa*
Playing career: *Transvaal F.C., Huddersfield Town, Hull City (c1937-1939)*

Wienand signed for Town in 1937 and spent one year at Leeds Road before he left the club in 1938, later playing for Hull City. Wienand was a South African and he later returned to his native country to play cricket until 1954. He died in 1993.

WIGHTMAN, John 'Jock'

Left-half
Town Years: 1935-1937
Born: *1912 Duns, Scotland*
Died: *1964 Blackburn, Lancashire*
Playing career: *Duns Athletic, York City, Bradford Park Avenue, Huddersfield Town, Blackburn Rovers, Carlisle United (1933-1947)*

Wightman arrived at the club in 1935 after previously playing for nearby Bradford Park Avenue. He spent two years at the club, playing as wing-half on over 60 occasions before he left to sign for Blackburn Rovers in 1937. He remained at the club until 1946 but six years of his time at Ewood Park were spoiled by World War Two. he joined Carlisle United in 1946, leaving the following year and retiring from professional football. Wightman later worked as Blackburn Rovers 'A' Team coach and then as the reserve team coach before he died in Blackburn at the age of just 51 in April 1964.

WIGMORE, Joseph 'Joe'

Right-back
Town Years: 1912-1913
Born: *1892 Worksop, Nottinghamshire*
Died: *1949 Worksop, Nottinghamshire*
Playing career: *Glossop, Dinnington Main Colliery, Blackpool, Dinnington Main Colliery, Huddersfield Town, Rotherham Town (1910-1913)*

Wigmore had previously played for Dinnington before he arrived at Leeds Road in 1912, he made one appearance during the 1912-13 season before being released at the end of the season. He later signed for Rotherham Town and at one point, was the landlord of the Saint Ledger Arms in Rotherham before his passing in 1949.

WIJNHARD, Clyde

Forward
Town Years: 1999-2002
Born: *1973 Paramaribo, Suriname*
Playing career: *FC Groningen, RKC Waalwijk, Willem II, Leeds United, Huddersfield Town, Preston North End, Oldham Athletic, Darlington, Macclesfield Town (loan), Macclesfield Town, Brentford (1993-2006)*

Steve Bruce brought Wijnhard to the club at the start of the 1999-2000 season, he was a first team regular until he suffered an injury sustained in a car crash. He later returned to the side in the 2001-02 season but left at the end of the season when Town lost to Brentford in the playoff semi-finals. Wijnhard had a short spell at Preston North End before signing for Oldham Athletic in 2002, spending two years at the club. He went on to play for Darlington, Macclesfield Town and Brentford before retiring from professional football in 2006. Wijnhard went on to run an eco-friendly lighting company and is now running a sports consultancy business from his base in Leeds.

WILCOX, Thomas 'Tom'

Goalkeeper
Town Years: 1911
Born: *1879 Born at sea*
Died: *1963 Blackpool, Lancashire*
Playing career: *Millwall Athletic, Cray Wanderers, Woolwich Arsenal, Norwich City, Blackpool, Manchester United, Carlisle United, Huddersfield Town, Goole Town, Abergavenny (1904-1912)*

Wilcox was a goalkeeper that played a couple of games at Leeds Road in 1911 and he soon left the club and later played for Goole Town and Abergavenny. After he left football, Wilcox worked as a colliery labourer and also owned two tobacconist shops that he later sold before he passed away in 1963 whilst living in Blackpool.

WILKINSON, Joseph 'Joe'

Left-back
Town Years: 2015-2016
Born: *1995 Dewsbury, West Yorkshire*
Playing career: *Huddersfield Town, Hyde United (loan), Bradford Park Avenue (loan), Buxton, Liversedge, Ossett Albion, Ossett United (2015-Still Playing)*

Despite being a left-back, Wilkinson played his one and only game at right-back in the final game of the 2014-15 season.

He never played for the club again and after loans at Hyde United and Bradford Park Avenue, Wilkinson left the club at the conclusion of the 2015-16 season. He is currently playing for Ossett United after previously turning out for Buxton, Liversedge and Ossett Albion.

WILLIAMS, Andrew 'Andy'

Midfielder
Town Years: 1993 (loan)
Born: *1962 Birmingham, Warwickshire*
Playing career: *Dudley Town, Solihull Borough, Coventry City, Rotherham United, Leeds United, Port Vale (loan), Notts County, Huddersfield Town (loan), Rotherham United, Hull City, Scarborough (1985-1996)*

Williams arrived on loan during the 1993-94 season from Notts County and played a handful of games before returning to Meadow Lane before later leaving the club. He then went on to play for Rotherham United, Hull City and Scarborough before retiring from professional football in 1996. Williams worked for Rotherham Metropolitan Borough Council for fifteen years as a performance manager before leaving his job in 2012 and is now working in Sheffield as a government administration professional.

WILLIAMS, John 'Jackie'

Outside-right
Town Years: 1932-1935
Born: *1911 Aberdare, Wales*
Died: *1987 Wrexham, Wales*
Playing career: *Aberaman, Llanelli, Huddersfield Town, Aston Villa, Ipswich Town, Wrexham, Colwyn Bay United, Runcorn (1932-1948)*

Williams arrived in 1932 from Llanelli, he played at Leeds Road until 1935 when he transferred to Aston Villa. He played for just one year at Aston Villa before heading to Ipswich Town. Williams spent two years at Portman Road before heading back to his native Wales for a one year spell at Wrexham. He later had spells at Colwyn Bay United and Runcorn before he ended his career in 1948. After his career ended, Williams worked as a cellarman for a brewery in Wrexham and also as a storekeeper before he later passed away in 1987 at the age of 76.

WILLIAMS, Jordan
Right-back
Town Years: 2017-2018
Born: *1999 Huddersfield, West Yorkshire*
Playing career: *Huddersfield Town, Bury (loan), Barnsley (2017-Still Playing)*
After starting his career at the club as a youngster, Williams was brought into David Wagner's side for the 2017-18 season. Ultimately, he played just 1 cup game at right-back and was sold to Barnsley at the start of the 2018-19 season.

WILLIAMS, Joseph 'Joey'
Winger
Town Years: 1924-1926
Born: *1902 Rotherham, West Riding of Yorkshire*
Died: *1978 Lancaster, Lancashire*
Playing career: *Huddersfield Town, Stoke City, Arsenal, Middlesbrough, Carlisle United, Worksop Town, Burton Town (1920-1937)*
After a spell at Rotherham County, Williams arrived at Leeds Road in 1924, playing for two years and playing his part in two First Division winning sides before leaving for Stoke City in 1926. He also played for Arsenal (with former manager Herbert Chapman), Middlesbrough, Carlisle United, Worksop Town and Burton Town before retiring in the late 1930s. Williams was still living in Cumbria before the Second World War and later worked as a toolmaker and as a publican before he passed away in April 1978 in Lancaster at the age of 75 years old.

WILLIAMS, Michael 'Mike'
Forward
Town Years: 1996 (loan)
Born: *1969 Bradford, West Riding of Yorkshire*
Playing career: *Maltby Main, Sheffield Wednesday, Halifax Town (loan), Huddersfield Town (loan), Peterborough United (loan), Burnley, Oxford United, Halifax Town, Worksop Town (1990-2001)*
Williams arrived on loan from Sheffield Wednesday in 1996 but only managed 2 appearances before he was sent back to his parent club. He is considered one of the club's worst ever players by supporters and he left Wednesday in 1997 to join Burnley for two years before rounding off his career with short spells at Oxford United, Halifax Town and non-league Worksop Town. Williams now works with underprivileged kids that suffer from behavioural difficulties, helping them to learn.

WILLIAMS, Paul
Left-back
Town Years: 1994, 1995 (loan) [two spells]
Born: *1969 Leicester, Leicestershire*
Playing career: *Leicester City, Stockport County, Coventry City, West Bromwich Albion (loan), Huddersfield Town (loan), Plymouth Argyle, Gillingham, Bury (loan), Bury, Leigh RMI (1989-2003)*
Williams was playing for Coventry City when Neil Warnock brought him to the club on loan during the 1994-95 season. He had two spells on loan at the club before returning to Highfield Road at the end of the season. Warnock took him to Plymouth Argyle in 1995 and spent three years at the club, playing over 130 games. He had a short spell at Gillingham in 1998 before spending four years at Bury between 1998 and 2002. Williams had a short spell at Leigh RMI before hanging up his boots. He has since worked as a coach at a number of non-league clubs including Glossop North End and is now living and working in Blackburn.

WILLIAMS, Robbie
Left-back
Town Years: 2007-2010
Born: *1984 Pontefract, West Yorkshire*
Playing career: *Barnsley, Blackpool (loan), Huddersfield Town, Stockport County, Rochdale, Plymouth Argyle, Limerick, Cork City, Galway United (2002-Still Playing)*
Williams arrived at Town in July 2007 but suffered a shin injury in his first training session at the club. He didn't return from injury until December when he made his debut against Leeds United and was a regular under Andy Ritchie and his successor Stan Ternent but lost his place under Lee Clark. Williams left the club in 2010 and joined Stockport County and has since played for Rochdale, Plymouth Argyle, Limerick and Cork City before he signed for Galway United in January 2018.

WILLINGHAM, Kenneth 'Ken'
Right-half
Town Years: 1930-1945
Born: *1912 Ecclesfield, Sheffield, West Riding of Yorkshire*
Died: *1975 Dewsbury, West Yorkshire*
Playing career: *Huddersfield Town, Sunderland, Leeds United (1928-1948)*

After playing local football with Ecclesfield FC and Worksop Town, Willingham joined the club in 1930. He turned professional in 1931 and remained at the club up until the outbreak of the Second World War in 1939. Willingham played 270 matches for the club and during the War he worked as a turner at an aircraft factory. Willingham eventually left the game and became a licensee in Leeds, working as landlord of the Hopewell Inn in Hunslet, before passing away in 1975 at the age of 62. Whilst at the club, Willingham played 12 matches for England between 1937 and 1939, scoring 1 goal.

WILSON, Charles 'Charlie'

Centre-forward
Town Years: 1922-1926
Born: *1895 Atherstone, Warwickshire*
Died: *1971 Atherstone, Warwickshire*
Playing career: *Atherstone Town, Coventry City, Tottenham Hotspur, Huddersfield Town, Stoke City, Stafford Rangers, Wrexham, Shrewsbury Town, Alfreton United (1913-1935)*
After a spell at Tottenham Hotspur, Wilson arrived at Leeds Road in 1922 and played for the club for four years and was part of the 'Thrice Champions' side that won three titles in succession. He left in March 1926 to join Stoke City, two months before the third title was secured, and played 156 league games for Stoke, scoring 112 goals. He later played for Stafford Rangers, Wrexham, Shrewsbury Town and Alfreton United before hanging up his boots in 1935. Wilson later became the landlord of both the Doxey Arms and Noah's Ark public houses in Stafford, later passing away in May 1971 at the age of 76.

WILSON, George

Outside-right
Town Years: 1928-1929
Born: *1905 Kilmarnock, Scotland*
Died: *1984 Huddersfield, West Yorkshire*
Playing career: *Portobello Thistle, Clydebank, Alloa Athletic, Huddersfield Town, Leeds United, Chesterfield (1927-1931)*
Wilson signed from Alloa Athletic in 1928 but only made 1 appearance for the first team, managing to score a goal too. He left in 1929 for local rivals Leeds United and he later played for Chesterfield before he retired in 1931. He later worked as the coach of Chesterfield's 'A' Team between 1953 and 1954 before passing away in 1984.

WILSON, Paul

Left-back
Town Years: 1985-1987
Born: *1968 Bradford, West Riding of Yorkshire*
Playing career: *Huddersfield Town, Norwich City, Northampton Town, Halifax Town, Burnley, York City, Scunthorpe United, Cambridge United (loan), Cambridge United, Rushden & Diamonds (1985-1999)*
Wilson began his career at Leeds Road but was released in 1987 after playing just a few first team matches. He spent five years at Northampton Town between and then appeared for Halifax Town, Burnley, York City, and Scunthorpe United in 1995. He spent two years at the club before rounding off his career with spells at Cambridge United and Rushden & Diamonds before retiring in 1999. He settled in Northampton, where he still lives and works.

DID YOU KNOW?"

"Jermaine Beckford's younger brother, Travis, won the first series of Wayne Rooney's Street Striker on Sky1. "

WILSON, Philip 'Phil'

Midfielder
Town Years: 1981-1987
Born: *1960 Hemsworth, West Riding of Yorkshire*
Playing career: *Bolton Wanderers, Huddersfield Town, York City, Macclesfield Town, Scarborough, Stafford Rangers (1979-1991)*
After a spell at Bolton Wanderers, Mick Buxton brought Wilson to the club in time for the 1981-82 season. He was a regular in the Town first team until his departure at the end of the 1986-87 season, when Steve Smith told Wilson he had no future at Leeds Road. Wilson transferred to York City and played at Bootham Crescent for two years before he had short spells at Macclesfield Town, Scarborough and Stafford Rangers. He worked as an academy coach at Leeds United for 25 years before he was made redundant by Massimo Cellino. He went on to coach at Sheffield Wednesday's academy but is now scouting for the club. Wilson also works at Bradford Goals Soccer Centre coaching and does some freelance coaching as well.

Ray Wilson (right) - statue to commemorate
England's 1966 Wolr Cup victory

WILSON, Ramon 'Ray'

Left-back
Town Years: 1952-1964
Born: *1934 Shirebrook, Derbyshire*
Died: *2018 Huddersfield, West Yorkshire*
Playing career: *Huddersfield Town, Everton, Oldham Athletic, Bradford City (1952-1971)*

Originally from Shirebrook, Ray Wilson has achieved something that no other Huddersfield Town player has done, he won the World Cup in 1966 with England. He signed for Town in 1952 after being spotted playing amateur football whilst working on the railways. Wilson was called up for National Service shortly after this and served in Egypt, returning in 1955. He made his debut against Manchester United and was originally a forward, converting to left-back after he used to cover for Laurie Kelly in training. He won his first of his 63 England caps in 1960. Wilson left Town in 1964 to sign for Everton, where he won the FA Cup in 1966 (it was quite a year, what with also being a member of the England team that lifted the World Cup at Wembley!) and later rounded off his career with spells at Bradford City (also serving as caretaker manager in 1970) and Oldham Athletic. Wilson later became an undertaker in Outlane, Huddersfield before he retired in the late 1990s. He lived for many years in Barkisland, Halifax but later moved to Slaithwaite, Huddersfield. It was revealed in 2016 that Wilson was suffering from Alzhiemer's disease and he sadly passed away in May 2018 in Huddersfield.

WILSON, Robert 'Rob'

Midfielder
Town Years: 1989-1991
Born: *1961 London*
Playing career: *Fulham, Millwall, Luton Town, Fulham, Huddersfield Town, Rotherham United, Farnborough Town (1979-1992)*

After playing in the South for ten years, Wilson arrived in 1989 from Fulham. He played at Leeds Road for two years before he left the club and had a one year spell at Rotherham United before retiring from professional football in 1992. Wilson settled in Yorkshire and is now living in Sheffield and works as a rep for a clothing company and at one point was a season ticket holder at Town.

WILSON, Thomas 'Tom'

Centre-half, Assistant Trainer
Town Years: 1919-1931, 1932-1939 (asst trainer)
Born: *1896 Seaham, County Durham*
Died: *1948 Barnsley, West Riding of Yorkshire*
Playing career: *Seaham Albion, Sunderland, Huddersfield Town, Blackpool (1914-1932)*

Tom Wilson signed for Town in 1919, after League Football had resumed after World War One. He eventually became the club captain at Leeds Road and is one of the most decorated players in the club's history. Wilson was part of the 1919-20 Division Two runners-up side, all three of the First Division winning sides (1924, 25 and 26), the 1922 Charity Shield winning side and also played in four cup finals, winning one. He played a total of 500 games for the club, second on the all-time appearances list. Wilson worked as assistant trainer up until the Second World War broke out in 1939 and had also worked as a factory policeman. He did still help out on the training ground during the War but also worked for British Dyes. After the war ended in 1945, Wilson took the job of trainer at Barnsley and was still working at the club at the time of his death, from a heart attack, in 1948 when he was 51. In May 1948, Town and Barnsley played a benefit match in honour of Tom Wilson and the proceeds were donated to his dependents. Wilson had also played one match for England whilst at Town, playing against Scotland in the British Championships in 1928 where Scotland ran out 5-1 winners.

A Huddersfield factory in WW2

219

Julian Winter

WITHAM, Richard 'Dick'
Left-back
Town Years: 1930-1934
Born: *1913 Bowburn, County Durham*
Died: *1999 Blackpool, Lancashire*
Playing career: *Durham City, Huddersfield Town, Blackpool, Oldham Athletic (1933-1938, 1946)*
Witham spent four years at the club and played 4 league games for Town before leaving for Blackpool in 1934. He retired in 1938 and later worked as timekeeper at Kings Baron Hotel in Dorset and ran a fish and chip shop in Blackpool. Witham had a short spell out of retirement with Oldham Athletic in 1946. Died in 1999.

WITHE, Peter
Forward (player-assistant manager)
Town Years: 1988-1991
Born: *1951 Liverpool, Lancashire*
Playing career: *Wolverhampton Wanderers, Portland Timbers, Birmingham City, Nottingham Forest, Newcastle United, Aston Villa, Sheffield United, Birmingham City (loan), Huddersfield Town, Aston Villa (1971-1991)*
A former European Cup winner with Aston Villa, Withe was coming to the end of his career by the time he joined Town from Sheffield United. He was appointed as player assistant manager to Eoin Hand and played sporadically for the club before leaving in early 1991 to become the Reserve Team Coach at Aston Villa. He had a short spell as Wimbledon manager that same year before being sacked in favour of Joe Kinnear. Withe later took the Thailand national team manager's job in 1998 and remained until 2003. He later worked as Indonesia national team manager from 2004 until 2007 before being sacked and had a very short spell as manager of Woodley Sports (later being renamed Stockport Sports) before working as the manager of PTT Rayong and Nakhon Pathom United. Withe still attends Aston Villa games regularly and to this day he and his son Jason Withe are the only father and son pairing to play in a game for Huddersfield Town (a reserve game in 1990).

WINTER, Julian
Midfielder, Chief Executive Officer
Town Years: 1982-1989, 2016-present (CEO)
Born: *1965 Huddersfield, West Riding of Yorkshire*
Playing career: *Huddersfield Town, Scunthorpe United (loan), Sheffield United (1982-1990)*
Julian Winter is a Huddersfield lad and came through the youth team at Leeds Road before breaking into the first team. He suffered a bad injury at his next club Sheffield United and had to retire in 1990 after having to endure ten operations in four years. He graduated from Sheffield Hallam University and returned to football, working at Grimsby Town and then Watford, serving as community director and then deputy CEO at Vicarage Road. Winter was promoted to Chief Executive Officer at Watford in 2008, remaining until 2011 when he joined his old club Sheffield United in the same role. He left his role in 2012 but returned in 2013 before resigning again at the end of the year. Winter had a short spell at Notts County as CEO before returning to his hometown club in 2016 as CEO and he remains at the club.

DID YOU KNOW?"

"Diego Arismendi was branded a 'noise pest' by neighbours due to hosting late night parties "

WOMERSLEY, Ernest

Outside-right
Town Years: 1949-1957
Born: *1932 Hartshead, West Riding of Yorkshire*
Died: *2018 Huddersfield, West Yorkshire*
Playing career: *Huddersfield Town, Bradford City (1949-1957)*

Originally from Hartshead, Womersley spent eight years at Leeds Road but only made two appearances for the first team. He left the club in 1957, later having a spell at Bradford City. Womersley remained in football running summer schools with Don Revie and was then a coach for Town's school of excellence. He also did match analysis for Liverpool until he was 70 years of age. He later lived in retirement in Fixby, Huddersfield but later passed away in 2018, in Hartshead Manor Care Home.

WOOD, Christopher 'Chris'

Goalkeeper
Town Years: 1971-1975
Born: *1955 Penistone, West Riding of Yorkshire*
Playing career: *Huddersfield Town, Barnsley (loan), Doncaster Rovers (loan) (1971-1975)*

Goalkeeper that began his career at Leeds Road in 1971 but only made a couple of appearances before his departure in 1975. He is currently living in Sheffield.

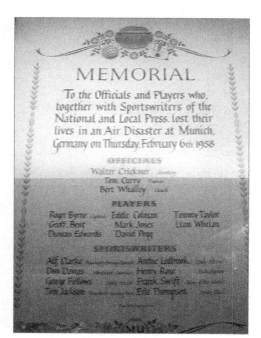

WOOD, James

Right-back
Town Years: 1915-1922
Born: *1893 Sunderland, County Durham*
Died: *unknown*
Playing career: *South Hylton Colliery, Sunderland, South Shields, Huddersfield Town, Blackpool, Fall River Marksmen (c1911-1926)*

Wood arrived at Leeds Road in 1915 after a spell with his local side, South Shields. He played over 100 games for the club during the next seven years and was part of the side that won promotion to the Second Division in 1920 under manager, Ambrose Langley. Wood left the club in 1922 and spent three years at Blackpool before moving to America and playing for Fall River Marksmen.

WOOD, John

Inside-forward
Town Years: 1910-1911
Born: *1880 West Kirkby, Lancashire*
Died: *1916 Somme Battlefields, France (Killed in Action)*
Playing career: *Port Sunlight, Southern United, Derby County, Manchester City, Plymouth Argyle, Huddersfield Town, Aberdeen (c1905-1914)*

John Wood signed from Plymouth Argyle in 1910 but only spent a year at Leeds Road before heading to Scotland to play for Aberdeen. He was called up to fight in the First World War and was enlisted in the 1st Football Battalion of the Middlesex Regiment. Wood sadly died during the Battle of the Somme in 1916.

WOOD, Raymond 'Ray'

Goalkeeper
Town Years: 1958-1965
Born: *1931 Hebburn, County Durham*
Died: *2002 Bexhill, East Sussex*
Playing career: *Newcastle United, Darlington, Manchester United, Huddersfield Town, Bradford City, Barnsley (1948-1967)*

Ray Wood was Manchester United's reserve goalkeeper and also a Munich Air Disaster survivor. He signed for Town soon after the disaster and kept goal for seven years before going on to play for Barnsley and Bradford City. Wood later worked as manager-coach of Los Angeles Wolves and coached in Zambia, Cyprus, Greece, Kuwait, Kenya, Ireland and the United Arab Emirates before he passed away in 2002.

WOODS, Calum
Full-back
Town Years: 2011-2014
Born: *1987 Liverpool, Merseyside*
Playing career: *Dunfermline Athletic, Huddersfield Town, Preston North End (2006-Still Playing)*
Signing from Dunfermline Athletic in 2011, Woods went straight into the first team for the 2011-12 season originally as a right back but was converted to left back following an injury to Gary Naysmith. He was part of the promotion winning side that year, scoring a penalty in the shootout. Woods was released at the end of the 2013-14 season and subsequently joined Preston North End before moving on to Bradford City in January 2019.

WORTHINGTON, Frank
Forward
Town Years: 1966-1972
Born: *1948 Shelf, West Riding of Yorkshire*
Playing career: *Huddersfield Town, Leicester City, Bolton Wanderers, Philadelphia Fury (loan), Birmingham City, Mjällby AIF (loan), Tampa Bay Rowdies (loan), Leeds United, Sunderland, Southampton, Brighton & Hove Albion, Tranmere Rovers, Preston North End, Stockport County, Cape Town Spurs, Chorley, Stalybridge Celtic, Galway United, Weymouth, Radcliffe Borough, Guiseley, Hinckley Town, Cemaes Bay, Halifax Town (player-coach) (1966-1992)*
A legend of the game, 'Frankie' began his career at Town in 1966. Well liked for his performances and cheeky chappie persona, he left the club in 1972 after demanding a bonus as an incentive to stave off relegation. Worthington joined Leicester City and in five years made over 200 appearances, scoring 70 goals. Worthington earned eight England caps and is still revered at his next club, Bolton Wanderers, even though he only played two seasons at Burnden Park. Birmingham, Leeds, Sunderland, Southampton and Brighton & Hove Albion followed, all within three years, before becoming player-manager of Tranmere Rovers in 1985. He later had short spells at Preston North End and Stockport County. He had a spell as player-coach at Halifax Town between 1991 and 1992 before eventually leaving the game at at the age of 44. Worthington has since done punditry work and after dinner speaking. He lives in Outlane, Huddersfield and has been suffering from Alzheimer's disease recently.

WORTHINGTON, Jonathan 'Jon'
Central-midfielder
Town Years: 2002-2009
Born: *1983 Dewsbury, West Yorkshire*
Playing career: *Huddersfield Town, Oldham Athletic, Fleetwood Town (loan), Bradford City, Mansfield Town, FC Halifax Town (2002-2014)*
'Worthy' began his career as a junior at the club and turned professional in 2002. He played a large part in the 2003-04 promotion season and later became captain of the side. He was allowed to leave the club in 2009 after manager Lee Clark informed him that he was no longer required. Worthington joined Oldham Athletic, and later played for Bradford City and Mansfield Town before signing for F.C. Halifax Town in 2012. He later worked as player/physiotherapist at The Shay before leaving the club to work for Town's academy in 2015 as the lead physio. He also runs his own practice from his base in Gomersal, West Yorkshire.

WRIGHT, James
Right-half
Town Years: 1910-1911
Born: *1880 Belfast, Ireland*
Died: *1960 Belfast, Northern Ireland*
Playing career: *Huddersfield Town (1910-1911)*
Wright's Town career didn't last very long and he left after making just 2 appearances. He died in his native Belfast in 1960.

WRIGHT, Mark
Defender
Town Years: 1991 (loan), 1991-1993
Born: *1970 Manchester, Lancashire*
Playing career: *Everton, Blackpool (loan), Huddersfield Town (loan), Huddersfield Town, Wigan Athletic, Chorley (1989-1995)*
Wright originally joined Town on loan in 1991 from Everton and later signed permanently. Since 2001, Wright has run Progress Sports, a large training provider for learners aged 14-19 in Merseyside.

WRIGHT, William
Centre-forward
Town Years: 1920-1921
Born: *1892 Seaforth, Liverpool, Lancashire*
Died: *1945 Liverpool, Lancashire*
Playing career: *Everton, St. Mirren, South Liverpool, Tranmere Rovers, Exeter City, Huddersfield Town, Mid-Rhondda, Yeovil & Petters United (1912-1923)*

Prior scored four goals in his nine appearances before leaving the club in June 1921 to play for Mid-Rhondda and he died in 1945 whilst living in Liverpool.

YATES, Harold 'Harry'

Inside-forward
Town Years: 1943-1950
Born: *1925 Huddersfield, West Riding of Yorkshire*
Died: *1987 Liverpool, Merseyside*
Playing career: *Huddersfield Town, Darlington, Nuneaton Borough (1943-1955)*

Although he spent seven years on the books at Leeds Road, Yates only made a single appearance for the first team. He had had arrived in 1943 as an amateur, turning professional after the end of the Second World War and left the club in 1950 to join Darlington. He spent two years at Feethams before singing for Headington United in 1952. Yates was living in Liverpool when he passed away in 1987.

YATES, Stephen 'Steve'

Centre-half
Town Years: 2003-2005
Born: *1970 Bristol, Gloucestershire*
Playing career: *Bristol Rovers, Queens Park Rangers, Tranmere Rovers, Sheffield United, Huddersfield Town, Scarborough, Halifax Town, Morecambe, Caernarfon Town (1988-2006)*

'Yatesy' signed from Sheffield United in 2003 and was Mr. Consistent during the 2003-04 promotion season with his performances at centre-half. He played most of the following season but towards the end of the season suffered from injury problems and retired from professional football whilst at Town to become a property developer in Crete. However, he turned out for both Halifax Town and Morecambe after that in the Conference. He did later go to Crete, later returning to Bristol Rovers first as Kitman and then becoming First Team Coach. Yates left Bristol in 2017 to return to his base in Crete.

Frank Worthington

YOUDS, Edward 'Eddie'
Defender
Town Years: 2002-2003
Born: *1970 Liverpool, Lancashire*
Playing career: *Everton, Ipswich Town, BBradford City, Charlton A, Huddersfield Town (1988-2005)*
Youds joined from Charlton Athletic in 2002 and was captain of the side at one point before suffering from injury problems. He is now in property development in London.

YOUNG, Alfred 'Alf'
Defender, Coach, Chief Scout
Town Years: 1927-1945, 1948-1952 & 1960-1964 (coach) 1964-1965 (chief scout)
Born: *1905 Sunderland, County Durham*
Died: *1977 Huddersfield, West Yorkshire*
Playing career: *Huddersfield T, York C (1927-1946)*
Alf Young played in the FA Cup Final in 1938 and made over 300 appearances between 1930 and 1939. Young coached in Denmark for two years before returning to Leeds Road in July 1948 as coach. He became the manager of Bradford City in 1957 before coming back for a third spell in 1960 as a coach. Young became chief scout in 1964 before retiring a year later. Died in 1977

YOUNG, Matthew 'Matty'
Midfielder
Town Years: 2006-2008
Born: *1985 Leeds, West Yorkshire*
Playing career: *Huddersfield Town, Worksop Town, Farsley Celtic, Frickley Athletic (2006-2015)*
Young came through the youth system at Town and made a few appearances in the first team. After leaving Town in 2008, Young began working as an Assistant Surveyor for Met Consultancy Group, later studying Civil & Structural Engineering at Bradford University and after graduating with a first class honours degree, he became a Graduate Structural Engineer at Met.

YUILL, John
Midfielder
Town Years: 1935-1936
Born: *1915 Coltness, Scotland*
Playing career: *Huddersfield Town (1935-1938)*
Yuill played just 1 game for Clem Stephenson's side before he left the club in 1936 to join Cheltenham Town and later had a spell at Scottish club Arbroath before seemingly retiring from the game.

THANK YOU

I would like to thank Lorraine and Graham Lynn for information and photos of Billy Lynn. Brian Tickell, Jimmy Nicholson, Paul Walker, Keith Mason, Alex Smith, Terry Curran, Steve Baines and Paul Bielby for for providing me with previously unknown information about themselves.

Lee

Photos